RECYCLED
STARS

CONSOLE-ING PASSIONS

Television and Cultural Power
Edited by Lynn Spigel

RECYCLED
STARS

Female Film Stardom in the
Age of Television and Video

MARY R. DESJARDINS

DUKE UNIVERSITY PRESS

DURHAM AND LONDON   2015

Printed in the United States of America on acid-free paper ∞
Text designed by Heather Hensley
Typeset in Whitman by Tseng Information Systems, Inc.

Library of Congress Cataloging-in-Publication Data
Desjardins, Mary R., 1956–
Recycled stars : female film stardom in the age
of television and video / Mary R. Desjardins.
pages cm — (Console-ing passions)
Includes bibliographical references and index.
ISBN 978-0-8223-5789-6 (hardcover : alk. paper)
ISBN 978-0-8223-5802-2 (pbk. : alk. paper)
ISBN 978-0-8223-7603-3 (e-book)
1. Television actors and actresses — United States.
2. Women in mass media.
3. Motion picture actors and actresses — United States.
I. Title. II. Series: Console-ing passions.
PN1992.8.w65D47 2015
791.45082 — dc23   2014031331

Cover image: *The Gloria Swanson Hour* TV series (1948–49).
Courtesy of Photofest, Inc.

IN LOVING MEMORY OF MY PARENTS,
ROSEMARY MORRISS DESJARDINS (1918–2009) AND
PAUL R. DESJARDINS (1919–2003)

=

CONTENTS

‗

ACKNOWLEDGMENTS

=

In the academic world we get rewarded for scholarship we author. How-ever, behind our individuated authorial signature are those who helped, supported, inspired, and participated in dialogue. Because this particular work of scholarship bearing my name has been long in the making, I have many helpers, supporters, models of inspiration, and interlocutors to ac-knowledge.

I thank my colleagues and students at the University of Texas–Austin and Dartmouth College, the two institutions at which I taught during the researching and writing of this book. Some of the research, as well as the first articles and conference papers related to *Recycled Stars*, were started while I was at UT, where I was lucky to work with many bright graduate students who are now my colleagues in the field. Though I cannot thank them all by name, some were working on smart projects that helped me think more productively about my own: Michael DeAngelis, Diane Negra, Nabeel Zuberi, Susan Murray, Anne Morey, Christina Lane, L. Clare Brat-ten, Jennifer Holt, Cynthia Meyers, Ken Feil, Walter Metz, Jennifer Bean, Joanne Hershfield, Susan McLeland, Megan Mullen, Eric Schaefer, Eithne Johnson, and Rosalie Horton. I was also lucky to engage in lively conver-sations about my work with my UT colleagues Janet Staiger, Horace New-comb, Tom Schatz, Charles Ramirez-Berg, Nikhil Sinha, Bridget Murnane, and Helen De Michel. In particular Janet's early support of many of the ideas that eventually made their way here gave me needed confidence.

Dartmouth gave me generous support, including a Junior Faculty Fellow-ship, at the right moment in researching and writing much of this book. I thank Al LaValley, professor emeritus, for being an early supporter of this work. I always have fun discussing all things star-related with my Film and Media Studies colleague and friend Amy Lawrence, who has written some pretty sharp scholarship in this area herself. Peter Ciardelli helped me, with kindness and humor, to capture the frame grabs that illustrate many of the chapters. My collaborations with Gerd Gemunden on a conference and book collection proved to be inspiring and supportive activities while I was working on this manuscript. I am particularly grateful to my former Dartmouth colleague Marianne Hirsch, who invited me to present some of the ideas in this book at a symposium on "popular memory" that she convened at the college's Minary Center; while there I benefited from commentary on my work from all the participants, especially Dana Polan, Marita Sturken, Nancy K. Miller, and Diana Taylor.

Different versions of several chapters have appeared elsewhere. A small part of chapter 1 appeared in altered form as "'Une élégance . . . presque envahissante': Le glamor et les débats des premièresvedettes féminines de la télévision," in *Télévision: Le moment expérimental*, edited by Gille Delavaud and Denis Marachal (Rennes, France: Editions Apogee, 2011). Parts of chapter 3 appeared in different forms as "Maureen O'Hara's 'Confidential' Life: Recycling Stars through Gossip and Moral Biography," in *Small Screens, Big Ideas: Television in the 1950s*, edited by Janet Thumim (London: I. B. Tauris, 2002), and "Systematizing Scandal: *Confidential* Magazine, Stardom, and the State of California," in *Headline Hollywood: A Century of Film Scandal*, edited by Adrienne McLean and David Cook (New Brunswick, NJ: Rutgers University Press, 2001). A shorter, altered version of chapter 4 appeared as "Lucy and Desi: Sexuality, Ethnicity, and Television's First TV Family," in *Television, History, and American Culture: Feminist Critical Essays*, edited by Mary Beth Haralovich and Lauren Rabinovitz (Durham, NC: Duke University Press, 1999). Parts of chapter 5 appeared in altered forms as "*Meeting Two Queens*: Feminist Filmmaking, Identity Politics, and the Melodramatic Fantasy," *Film Quarterly* (Spring 1995), and "The Incredible Shrinking Star: Todd Haynes and the Case of Karen Carpenter," *Camera Obscura* 57 (December 2004). I am grateful to the editors of these publications for their support of this work. In particular Janet Thumim and Adrienne McLean provided helpful editorial guidance for my arguments about star scandal, and Amelie Hastie's shepherding of my work on *Superstar* on behalf of the *Camera Obscura* collective was sensitively and brilliantly accomplished.

Librarians Ned Comstock at USC's Cinematic Arts Library; Barbara Hall, Val Almendarez, and Jenny Romero at the Margaret Herrick Library in Beverly Hills; Charles Bell at the Harry Ransom Center at UT-Austin; and reference librarians at the New York Public Library for the Performing Arts and at Dartmouth College were consummate professionals in helping me with necessary source materials. At Duke University Press I owe a big thanks to my patient editor, Ken Wissoker, who should know that I wasn't really trying to break records for taking the longest of any author to finish manuscript revisions. Courtney Berger at the start of the manuscript process, and Elizabeth Ault and Liz Smith at the end, have represented the epitome of helpful professionalism. I am also grateful to the thorough and perceptive reading of the manuscript by the two anonymous reviewers for the press. I thank them for their patience and willingness to read more than one draft. Any shortcomings in the final product are my own.

I thank the many friends and relatives who served as hosts when I traveled to do research and presentations related to *Recycled Stars*. Barbara Hall and Val Almendarez, Tara McPherson and Robert Knaack and their son, Dexter, James Williams and Marc Wenderoff, Mimi White and James Schwoch and Travis White-Schwoch, Anna McCarthy, Gus Stadler, Dan Streible, Teri Tynes, Rachel Adams and Jon Connolly, Vincent Desjardins, and Jim Dailey—all opened their homes or lent apartments and provided a warm context for fun during what were often pressured work days for all of us. Our shared laughter was always combined with conversations that challenged me to think about my work differently when I left their homes.

Over the long period of research, writing, and revising, I have shared intellectual dialogue with friends who have enhanced the quality of my life in ways impossible to enumerate: Agnes Lugo-Ortiz, Diane Miliotes, Laura Hess, Amy Hollywood, Reed Lowrie, Janet Lorenz, Brenda Silver, Paul Tobias, Adrian Randolph, the late Angela Rosenthal, Mona Domosh, Frank Magilligan, Irene Kacandes, Philippe Carrard, Brenda Garand, Graziella Parati, Kate Conley, Martin Roberts, Jiwon Ahn, Lynn Higgins, Mary Jean Green, Robert Dance, Anna McCarthy, Michael De Angelis, Kathleen Corrigan, Patricia Corrigan, Kathy Hart, Melissa Zeiger, Jonathan Crewe, Laurie Taylor, Holly Keller, the late Cheri Derby, and Mark Hain. I am sorry that Angela and Cheri are not still here to share my achievement; they were my best interlocutors, as well as cherished friends. Marsha Cassidy, Mary Beth Haralovich, Chuck Wolfe, Edward Branigan, Michael Renov, Pamela Robertson Wojcik, Lisa Parks, Nguyen Tan Hoang, Joy Fuqua, Heather Hendershot, Allison McCracken, James Schwoch, David Crane, Vicky Johnson, Pavitra Sundar, Karen Beavers, Christie Milliken, Stephan Tropiano, Steven Ginsberg, Jane Feuer, Mark Lynn Anderson, Mark Garrett Cooper, Heidi Rae Cooley, Shelley Stamp, Jenny Horne, and Jonathan Kahana have shared ideas and meals that they may not recognize as being a part of this book, but I was listening and absorbing their brilliance. The versatile Amelie Hastie and Mimi White have inspired me through their own work, as well as through their confidence in me. More than once they provided much needed perspective on the manuscript process, and they did so with their characteristic thoughtfulness, kindness, and humor. I am lucky to have them as friends and professional role models. Marsha Kinder was the advisor of my dissertation on a very different topic from *Recycled Stars*, and she has never stopped supporting my work from the day I arrived at USC's then-named School of Cinema-Television in 1984. Thank you, Marsha.

I am fortunate to have had the friendship of Barbara Hall and Val Almendarez for over twenty-five years; their loyalty, humor, and sensitivity have been indispensable to me while this book was in process. My older brothers, Chris and Vincent, got all the creative genes in the family, and I am often in awe of their talent. I thank them for their love and support. Monty and Woodrow were perfect companions but probably wondered why more of this work couldn't have been done at the dog park. My husband, Mark Williams, is a great scholar of film and television, but the way he shares my enthusiasm for the case studies in this book has come from a place both personal and professional. That his enthusiasm has always translated into tangible support speaks to his integrity, love, and understanding. Finally, I owe lasting gratitude to my late parents, Rosemary and Paul, whose love and prayers sustain me, even now.

INTRODUCTION

In an episode of *The Beverly Hillbillies* in 1966 the nouveau riche Clampett clan mistakenly believes the famed Hollywood film star Gloria Swanson is in financial trouble and comes to her rescue. To raise money for her they put their economic capital and acting talent into producing a new film starring Swanson. Central to the episode's comedy are the Clampetts' contradictory and inaccurate beliefs about the star: that she has continued to play starring film roles into the present moment and that she needs to make a comeback in order to hold on to her Hollywood home. The former belief is based on the continued run of Swanson's silent-era films in the Clampetts' hometown of Tughussle (where the psychic reality of the "backward" Clampett family still resides); the latter is based on their misreading of a press account about Swanson's auctioning of her Hollywood home and belongings for charity. As cultural text, *The Beverly Hillbillies* seems to assume that we, like the Clampetts, have absorbed a central lesson of postwar American media (one that explains how the Clampetts can hold contradictory understandings of Swanson's stardom): that the changing symbols of American culture can be tracked through the decline of the Hollywood star system. What's more, the show assumes that it would be funny to reiterate this scenario with Swanson, whose film and television career from the 1910s to the 1960s encompasses both a glamorous stardom from the past and one of the most

FIGURE I.1

Gloria Swanson
recycling her silent film
stardom with Jethro
Bodine (Max Baer Jr.)
on *The Beverly Hillbillies*.
Filmways Television,
1966. Author's
collection.

powerful representations of star loss and return in her portrayal of Norma
Desmond in *Sunset Boulevard* (1950).

But what was in this low-brow television episode for Swanson, who once
was idolized for the way she wore a gown with a four-foot train of pearls
and ermine, respected for her skills as a film producer, recognized as a pio-
neer in early television, and nominated twice for the Academy Award for
Best Actress? The star had innumerable ups and downs in her career, but
she was still more than a little appalled by the effect that playing Norma
Desmond, a delusional has-been, would have on the subsequent jobs she
was offered. Resilient and optimistic, she chose to be the master of the joke
rather than its servant and guest-starred in a number of television programs
in the 1950s and 1960s, including this episode of *The Beverly Hillbillies* and a
famous episode of *The Carol Burnett Show*, that thematize or parody the association of her star persona with the fictional Desmond.

Star studies have typically provided a synchronic explanation of the cultural and social contexts in which stars and their affective relationships with the public are embedded. However, scrutinizing Gloria Swanson as a *transmutable* star sign, one that has endured through various historical moments and in different media incarnations, allows us to see how stars "touch on things that are deep and constant features of human existence" and also how particular star rememberings "translate into the norms and institutions and laws that make some identities more important—and rewardable—than others."[1] *Recycled Stars: Female Film Stardom in the Age of Television and Video* examines change and continuity in star images across different historical periods and different media, with a particular focus on the periods between 1948–60 and the 1980s–90s, in order to expose who is invested in and who profits from the reemergence or sustained popularity of particular stars. A key premise of this study is that the sign of the female star—and the vicissitudes of her identity in a culture in which some identities are more "rewardable" than others—is central to understanding many of the anxieties, as well as pleasures, that recycled stars invoke through their public, multi-mediated emergence, loss, and return. I look at media practices, from mainstream to avant-garde, that explore the contours of the female star's durability. Specific case studies include the stories of female stars who struggled to create new contexts for their past images in emerging new media forms: Gloria Swanson, Loretta Young, Mary Astor, Ida Lupino, and Lucille Ball finding new careers in television, and Maureen O'Hara in court defending her image from the scandal press of the 1950s.

I look at the role of gender in star recyclings practiced through the interlocking relations of the industry-star-fan matrix. Female film stars, and assumptions about femininity and duration that were negotiated through their star personas, have been the subject of a variety of academic studies. For example, in her study of the various "vanishings" of women in modern Western culture, Karen Beckman concludes that the metaphysical terms of the female star body are "anything but stable."[2] In a provocative essay about female stars of silent film serials, Jennifer Bean argues that the technologies of early stardom "flaunt catastrophe, disorder, and disaster rather than continuity and regulation" and that the star remains resilient despite her body's vulnerability to technology.[3] In this book, however, I argue that the loss and resurrection of the gendered star across multiple temporalities and media are related to all kinds of challenges, catastrophes, and cycles. These cycles point to metaphysical states (the emergence into and disappearance out of subjectivity and being that is shared by all subjects) and to the cyclical material practices of the female star in her relation to commodity exchange—

her role in embodying the fashion commodity, her acting labor in the film commodity, and her role as woman in patriarchal culture, in which age, beauty, and fertility sustain her position in the marriage economy. The case studies in this book are focused on the female star because if the film star has served as an anchor point for our affective relations to all kinds of births, deaths, and resurrections, the female star best epitomizes the overdetermined aspects of stardom and most frequently stands in for and withstands the temporal dimensions of how these cycles are played out in modern commodity culture.

I have also chosen to focus on how female stars were recycled between the advent of television in the late 1940s and the peak of television and video as hegemonic technologies, entertainment media, and artistic formats, which took place between the 1950s and 1990s. While recyclings in other media and periods are crucial to the establishment of star recycling practices, the emergence of commercial television in the late 1940s put pressure on existing practices, accelerating, multiplying, intensifying, and normalizing the possibilities for a number of media industries to mine the meaning and labor of older stars, for these stars to exercise new forms of agency in relation to their star images as producers and performers, and for viewers, some of whom were or became fans, to (re)experience the psychic pleasures as well as social and cultural knowledges associated with star images from the prewar period. American commercial television as it was produced and broadcast between the 1950s and 1980s constituted baby boomers' main exposure to Hollywood films and stars from the past.[4] Television broadcasts of studio-era films and of programs with studio-era stars were central to the forging of a shared sense of values and cultural references among baby boomers and their parents (many of whom first saw those old stars in films in the 1920s, 1930s, and 1940s). For that reason, it is not surprising that experimental film- and video-makers have used images of studio-era film stars in their critical and artistic work, examining their personas through the lenses of the politicized social movements and trends of the last thirty years, such as feminism, gay rights, and civil rights, which were agitated for and supported by baby boomers. Shared knowledge about film stars from old Hollywood might have forged a cultural relation between baby boomers and their parents, but this knowledge could be put to use in baby boomers' critiques of the capitalist, patriarchal system they were born into and identified as a creation of institutions—like the studio system—associated with their parents' generation.

Affective Returns

A constituent aspect of the industry-star-fan matrix is that the public's cathexis to the star is worked through the possibility of her loss and return. As Kathryn Fuller has pointed out, an obsession with star death is present in fan discourse going back to the 1910s. For example, in almost every issue of the magazine *Motion Picture Story* in its initial years of publication, beginning in 1915, the Q & A columnist responded to reader requests for verification or repudiation of death rumors about stars.[5] The circumstances of Florence Lawrence, who emerged as a star name in 1910 and is sometimes considered the first film star, bears out this fascination with the possibility of the star's death or loss. At a time when some film companies were not publicizing the names of their acting talent, Lawrence's name (as distinct from her identity as "the girl of a thousand faces" or "the Biograph girl") was initially revealed to a mass audience in a public relations stunt announcing her death and resurrection.[6] Her emergence as a star was, in a sense, already a reemergence, orchestrated by industrial players (her new film company employer, IMP, which stole her away from Biograph) and responded to en masse by fans.

I share the belief held by some scholars that the "death and resurrection" publicity stunt around Lawrence should not be seen as *the* origin of the star system. Richard deCordova and Janet Staiger have provided evidence that the move toward a "star system," or at least a move on the part of film companies to identify their actors under contract by name as a way to publicize films, was under way prior to the IMP stunt with Lawrence.[7] Yet the degree to which this particular narrative worked as a publicity stunt in 1910 (when hundreds showed up to see Lawrence in person after her "safety" was announced) and how it stakes a claim that stars should *matter* to people and will be missed by them when gone suggest it deserves further examination in relation to what most would agree is our longtime affective relation with stars. In other words, it is not only from some privileged view afforded by our point in the present—after *Sunset Boulevard*, after the hundreds of recyclings of Marilyn Monroe, Elvis Presley, Michael Jackson, and others—that we can so obviously see that the possibility that stars disappear (and sometimes come back) is central to the effects they have on us. The cycles of our desires to incorporate their looks or behavior into our identity, to perhaps reject or ridicule them at later moments in our relation to them, to sometimes even deny their death—in short, our experience of the star-fan matrix—is a game of *fort/da*, and a variety of material practices have made it so since at least 1910. The mythology around IMP's stunt is a lesson about the affective relations between film star and fan.

Fort/da is a concept about mastering loss, named for the cries of the child whom Freud witnessed playing a game of throwing and retrieval (or unspooling and respooling) that allowed him to "work through" his mother's disappearances.[8] Such a game may be relevant to the appearing and disappearing of stars, but what I have described in the cases of Swanson and Lawrence as the investments in stars' appearances, disappearances, and reappearances are investments manipulable by industry, labor, and audience. Who is mastering whom, or what, in this game? On the one hand, media industries, including film and television companies and the tabloid press, exploit the assumptions that reiterative, intimate exposures of the star to the public ensure continuity and stability of their technologies and products. Yet these industries profit by ensuring instabilities, and perhaps even temporary or permanent interruptions of the star-fan relationship, through manipulations of the star's disappearances, such as exploiting scandals from a star's past, not renewing a star's contract, refusing to cast older female stars in lead roles, or abandoning genres—and their typical stars—that appeal to female audiences or to a certain generation. They promote new stars when it is believed that further profit from older stars is no longer predictable. Yet in key moments—for example, in the boom-and-bust cycle of film production and distribution in the 1910s, or in the competition and cooperation between the film and television industries in the late 1940s and 1950s, in the work of artist-fans who made experimental videos about old Hollywood stars in the 1980s and 1990s—the reappearance of a star from the past might smooth over or expose disruptive relations with audiences in the transitions to new technologies, modes of delivery, and cultural products.

If this description suggests that the media industries have mastered the game of star appearances and disappearances, then the fan magazines and fan letters of the 1910s and 1920s, the local press and fan interviews regarding Swanson and her promotional tour for Paramount and *Sunset Boulevard* in 1950, the state of California's criminal libel suit in 1957 against a tabloid press that defamed stars from the past, the "national" ritual of mourning after the death of Lucille Ball, the film and video works that recycle and comment on the recycling of old Hollywood stars—all scrutinized in this book—attest that the meanings of stars from the past are actively made by readers and fans in a variety of temporal moments. As we've seen from the episode of *The Beverly Hillbillies* described earlier, the temporal gap between "back then" and "right now" is the fan's lived experience, measured not so much in years as according to *how long it feels* since a star's presence was made known and felt in the circulation of popular culture texts and images. A ghost from the past may be a brief cycle away from making a reappearance and (re)finding old and new followings.

Industrial production and viewer or fan production may not always be in synch, either in the content of what stars mean or in the temporal coordinates of a star's orbit. As for the laborer who embodies the star image, she too is both mastered by the system and an active participant in creating the temporal contours of her reappearances. If Norma Desmond didn't like the word *comeback*, it was probably because it sounds like a command rather than the return that suggests a natural cycle back to those who still love her.

Stars and the Social Imaginary

All of this suggests that film stars have a privileged place in the social imaginary of twentieth-century and perhaps twenty-first-century American culture. I refer to the social imaginary at key moments in this book because it explains what I argue is an inextricably interlocking relation among the industry, stars, and fans. The social imaginary is not reducible to a "social" outside the subject or to the interior fantasies of the subject but facilitates connections between outside and inside. The subject experiences the social imaginary within affective terms and disciplinary frameworks because it is made up of socially mediated practices that function to anchor or contain the fluid movements within subject formation.[9] If the social imaginary is composed of anchoring points for identity formation, then the socially mediated practices around the star-fan matrix is one central anchoring point within a larger chain in which modern American subjects are enmeshed as gendered audiences and consumers. To put it another way, the star-fan bond, as a key feature of commodity culture's social imaginary, is promoted by the industry and experienced affectively by both fan and star. However, the bond holding together the industry-to-star-to-fan relation is not limited to the subject's private fantasies inspired by the emancipatory or disciplinary potentialities of a star persona, nor is it merely an effect of the manipulations of the culture industries that seek to create role models for economic gain. Thus Freud's concept of fort/da, which designates an individual psychodynamic, and which I used as a description for the affective processes in the industry-star-fan matrix, is made more complex if we incorporate it into the idea of the social imaginary. The drive toward mastery implied in the fort/da process of appearance and disappearance can be seen, then, as collective, operating both within and outside of individual subjects. Fans and audiences, star performers, and industries are interanimated through the star figure and the material practices around that figure in which audiences, star performers, and industries engage and change over time.

Recycling Stars through Television and Video

Because the social imaginary can be understood as encompassing both the social and the private self only in their relation to one another, in *Recycled Stars* I employ a variety of theories and methodologies about meaning production around stars, film and television productions, and audiences. Some of the examinations employ theoretical understandings of meaning production that have been most successful in teasing out the operations of one register over the other—the social or the self. Yet no matter the theoretical model I use in various chapters—psychoanalytic theories of narcissism or fantasy, materialist theories of commodity and labor, feminist theories of the body—the goal is always to understand and explore the interrelation and inextricability of both registers of identity and to argue that the social-self dynamic should be a necessary object of study in histories of media stardom that go beyond the goal of merely historicizing media industry practices.

The first two chapters look at the move of established film stars into television from the late 1940s to the start of the 1960s. Unlike studies of television stardom that look at radio and vaudeville celebrities as the inevitable models for the new medium's star figures, I argue that which media background and performing type would constitute the television star was a question in its earliest years as a commercial medium. By tracing debates within the press and production industries, I suggest that film stars from the past were taken seriously as potential stars of television as the medium sorted out the issues of performer presence and expertise, audience and performer relations, and the role that films themselves, as well as memories of them and their stars, would have in broadcasting. In chapter 1 I examine these issues in relation to the glamour that the film stars Gloria Swanson and Faye Emerson brought to their talk shows on early television. I define glamour in relation to the historically specific way women were allowed access to enunciation in mass media of the first half of the twentieth century, and I argue that television production companies were eager to capture the glamour of female former film stars as a way of shaping the fantasies of the female audience. In addition, by using the trope of glamour as one way to look at the various forms of stardom available on television, my argument can also encompass the roles, albeit limited, that African American performers had in television of the late 1940s and early 1950s apart from the stereotypical roles that confined them in previous media and eventually in television as well. Neither this chapter nor this book as a whole takes on the larger task of accounting for the participation of racial or ethnic minorities in all of early television. However, some female African American musical performers—whose images were partially constructed out of film roles fought for or denied them by the film studios—negotiated a glamorous aura for the new medium, attesting to the degree that the category of glamour itself was subjected to in television's massive recyclings of values associated with film stardom.

Chapter 2 continues a focus on film stars who moved into television in its early years, but in relation to anthology series that dramatized the aging or obsolescence of the female performer. I examine not only the narrative, visual, and acting signs apparent in these episodes but also their continuity with myths about and nostalgia for fading stars, promulgated since the 1910s by both fan magazines and films. While all these dramatic television programs raise issues about the power available to the mature, perhaps once glamorous woman, some are constructed around dystopic fantasies reminiscent of the gothic, a genre that establishes the heroine's enunciative or epistemological drive, which leads her to fear for the annihilation of her own subjectivity or to be judged as mad. What is fascinating about the episodes I analyze, however, is that many have as leads female former film stars who are actively involved in producing or directing their own work. These are women who have taken advantage of shifts in industries, media, and audiences, as well as in their own personal and professional lives, to attain powers of enunciation denied them in the studio system that groomed them as stars. I end the chapter with a consideration of *Dreamboat* (1952), a comic film about the emergence of older, studio-era, theatrically released films on broadcast television. This film represents the cultural anxieties cohering around the aging female film star and the feminized male star and also exposes the film industry's anxieties about television's threat to its hegemony as an entertainment medium.

While the aging female stars of television talk and anthology series of the late 1940s and early 1960s rehearsed certain personal and social anxieties about female power in media image-making, the emergence of television "misery" shows, best exemplified by *This Is Your Life*, and the scandal magazine, most notoriously *Confidential*, helped shape the contours of that era's cultural fantasies about the sexually experimenting woman, including fantasies about how to make her submit to normative frameworks. The possibly nonnormative sex lives of white and black female film stars, as well as homosexual male stars, were the particular obsessions of magazines like *Confidential*, which promised to be "uncensored and off the record." Providing access to the stars as they "really are" was also the promise of *This Is Your Life*, but the libidinal effects of catching a star off-guard were managed by the program's unwavering commitment to showing the star's participation in a morally upright family and work life. In chapter 3 I explore scandal magazines and television misery shows as two avenues for the circulation of established film star personas in the 1950s, looking closely at the appearance of Maureen O'Hara in both *This Is Your Life* and *Confidential* in 1957, the same year the magazine came under legal scrutiny by the state of California. In my examination of these cultural productions, which were firmly focused on recycling established film stars in a period of waning film industry power over acting labor, I suggest that shifting ways of producing distinctions between private and public were worked through via film stars who were subjected to the powers of new surveillance technologies, new media industry configurations, new modes of mass production, and changing legal definitions of libel and obscenity.

Lucille Ball was also the subject of the tabloid press in the 1950s. However, the scandal magazines were most interested in Ball's husband, Desi Arnaz, who, they alleged, engaged in drunken trysts with prostitutes. The scandal magazines could sell stories about the couple's marital problems not because they were still active as film stars, as was O'Hara, but because they were among the most famous television stars of the day, performing in the top-rated show *I Love Lucy*, which they also produced and with which they built a television empire, Desilu Productions. Chapter 4 is an examination of how these two stars were reconstructed as a *star couple* through their move into television. Rather than focusing on *I Love Lucy* as the only vehicle for this construction, I first look at the appearances the stars made on other television programs during the first run of their own show. The more adult, more openly promotional aspects of programs like Ed Sullivan's *Toast of the Town* and *The Bob Hope Show*, on which they guest-starred, allowed the performer-producers to display aspects of their off-screen marital reality (both its professional nature and its personal tensions) that could only be referred to in the more family-friendly slapstick humor of *I Love Lucy*. However, the success of *I Love Lucy*, not only in its first run but in reruns, helped construct what many people have described as Ball's "thereness," or constant presence in the social and cultural imaginary. The continuous reruns have also contributed to the ongoing construction of Ball and Arnaz as a couple, despite their divorce in 1960, which came shortly after the scandal magazine reports and the television program's end in first-run broadcasting. I look at how Ball and Arnaz, who emerged as entertainers in the 1930s, were recycled as a star couple in the 1950s and how their status as a couple continued on in news coverage of Ball's death in 1989, then in made-for-television movies, books, and productions by the Arnaz children, including CD-ROM family scrapbooks, for years afterward.

Much of the ongoing cultural production around Ball and Arnaz as a couple reflects ambivalent feelings about the traditional family, sharing with many other discourses both nostalgia for and condemnation of the nuclear family as the master narrative of American culture. The ongoing construction of Ball and Arnaz as a couple is the most successful star recycling, if the criterion is sheer longevity and proliferation of texts and images. But in relation to notions of family there are many film and other media stars from the past who feature in contemporary fantasies and videos, books, and websites. In chapter 5 I examine the experimental film and video work of several media artists who recycle star images from the past to raise issues about contemporary identity politics involving sexuality, gender, and race and reflect on the relation of fan fantasies about stars to individuated psychodynamics of subjectivity. In such experimental films and videos as *Meeting Two Queens*, *Superstar*, *Joan Sees Stars*, and *Rock Hudson's Home Movies*, star images and biographies provide a lingua franca to explore complex issues about the social positioning of the private body, the possibilities of individual agency in our capitalist, patriarchal, and mass-mediated society, and the relations among race, gender, and sexuality as categories of identity. In these works the female star, or the male star in a feminized subject position, functions as the overdetermined surrogate for all subjects in late twentieth-century culture. What is remarkable about these films and videos is that they suggest this contemporary relevance while still conveying the particular powers their star subjects had in their own historical moments. And while the self-consciousness of these works, not to mention their humor, participates in a camp construction of stars from the past, in their use of "found" sounds and images from films and musical recordings they question the temporal boundaries between modes of production, where one might be relegated to the past and another is clearly contemporary.

Looking Forward

Richard Dyer has argued that the star sign is a "structured polysemy," a finite multiplicity of meanings that "are deep and constant features of human existence." All audiences and star signs engage in cultural production in which some of the meanings and affects of the star's structured polysemy are "foregrounded and others masked or displaced."[10] Dyer's description of meaning production around stars seems compatible with my use of the critical term *social imaginary* to identify a process that is not reducible to an outside/inside binary. Because it is a process, it has a temporality that looks backward and forward to moments in which the balance among foregrounding, masking, and displacing might have been or will be different. My examination of the interrelation of industry, star, and fan in star recyclings exposes how the foregrounding, masking, and displacing of stars' polysemic meanings work in a variety of media and historical moments. But recycling, as Pamela Robertson has pointed out, also "signifies transformation, change."[11] From the female film stars who strove for more autonomy and control over their image by moving into early television, to the scandal publications accusing Hollywood of lying about its stars, to the fan-artists who see in stars the dilemmas and challenges of all subjects in capitalist, patriarchal culture, recyclings of star images across historical periods and new media don't just hide or reveal what meanings are already there. They change and question those meanings and the terms by which producers, industries, audiences, and actors profit from the star body reentering our orbit from the past.

CHAPTER ONE

"THE ELEGANCE . . . IS ALMOST OVERWHELMING"

Glamour and Discursive Struggles over
Female Stardom in Early Television

The manner in which Gloria Swanson made food, fashion, and current events grist to her glamorous mill on her 1948 talk show on New York's independent television station WPIX inspired the *New York Times* television critic Jack Gould to remark that the program's almost "overwhelming" elegance might erect road-blocks to the show's longevity. Such elegance, he points out, contrasts sharply with the down-to-earth editorial stance of the station's owner, the *New York Daily News*, one of the very successful press competitors of the *New York Times*.[1] Gould's observations point to an opposition—glamorous versus ordinary—that appears frequently in the discourses of the industry and popular press, and even in film narratives, about television stardom and the behavior of on-camera television "personalities" in the late 1940s to mid-1950s.

The star text of Gloria Swanson, who was one of the first important film stars to have her own television show, provides one of the most complex and telling examples of how film stars negotiated both the transformed terrain of the film industry and the newest broadcast medium in the late 1940s and early 1950s. Her star text and the television genres in which she performed provoked critical discourses that reveal how the television industry and the press were exploring the contours of what television stardom might look and sound like. The television industry and press speculated about female television stardom in relation to an (often unspoken) understanding about the female body and electronic technology and a (usually spoken) understanding of the female viewer as a potential consumer of sponsors' products. They speculated about the entrance of the female film star into television in terms of her relation to the hegemony of a prior medium and its powerful star system, now in a transitional mode. Even as the motion picture, with its spectacle and glamour, still dominated television, its transmissibility on television was through films and stars *from the past*. Would the cultural capital of the past, particularly as embodied by film stars, be passé on television? Or would it accrue greater value as new modes of distribution, such as television, widened the path of its circulation?

In this chapter I look at Swanson's case as she moves from her television talk show in 1948 to her comeback (or, as her character Norma Desmond might say, her "return") in film in 1950's *Sunset Boulevard*. I also examine more broadly the categories of glamour, fashion, personality, age, and comebacks—which Swanson's star text seemed to epitomize or speak to at that time—because they were mobilized by both trade and popular press to discuss more generally the role of stardom and of popular female personalities in television, especially those appearing in nondramatic television genres, in the late 1940s and early 1950s. The primary examples concern the television industry's vested interest in recycling formerly popular stars who had been initially groomed by the film industry, and the female film stars, such as Swanson, whose entrance into television involved a renegotiation of their glamorous personas. I also examine a group of African American female musical entertainers in early television known for their glamorous on-camera personas. Unlike Swanson and other white female film stars who appeared in television at this time and brought a sense of the "extraordinary" they had developed with the studios, these African American performers constructed their glamour out of *reaction to* the vehicles for stardom that Hollywood film studios had designated for them and other African American performers. These performers rejected or modified racially inflected studio casting practices, exemplified by the roles of household maid and exotic musical performer typically offered to nonwhite performers. They did so in their television programs by cultivating personas that projected authority, performing versatility, and glamour—all attributes typically denied them in their work for film studios. While I do not take on the larger task of accounting for all African American performers in early television, many of whom initially performed in films, these case studies of glamorous

African American female television stars broaden the ways media historians and theorists have looked at the phenomenon of stardom in television
and the public visibility of female stars in transitional moments in media
history. That their time on television afforded these stars unprecedented
visibility and yet was also very brief underscores that the questions of who
gets recycled and how are also questions relevant to all the case studies in
this book: Who profits from emerging media forms and transitions across
media, and how?

Film Stars' Move into Television

Changes in postwar Hollywood media industries represented both crisis
and new opportunities for established film stars. The "Paramount decree,"
the Supreme Court ruling in 1948 ordering theater divestment, resulted in
the studios' loss of real estate revenues and guaranteed exhibition of their
films. While this decree was a significant blow to some aspects of the industry's corporate health, its direct effect on film stars is difficult to assess;
for instance, more than a few major stars had been freelancing since the
1930s or 1940s, and the decree itself probably had little direct effect on
their employment. (Barbara Stanwyck, Cary Grant, and Loretta Young were
freelance performers for a decade, give or take a few years, before studio
divestment.) However, studios, no longer guaranteed exhibition of their
films after divestment and faced with rising production costs, produced
fewer films starting in the late 1940s. Even when the number of films rose
in the mid-1950s, this was possible only because the studios had slashed
overhead costs by not renewing star and unit-producer contracts and firing
other employees. Established stars still under long-term contract typically
parted ways with the studios when their contracts expired in the late 1940s
or early 1950s.[2] Since many stars had chafed under the contract system,
this loosened relationship could seem more like liberation than desertion.
For instance, in 1949 Bette Davis refused to do postproduction dubbing on
a film unless Warner Bros. agreed to terminate her contract.[3] Some stars,
more commonly males, started independent production companies to take
advantage of modified capital gains taxes and to have more autonomy in
their careers. In this legal and economic arrangement of incorporation,
stars often joined production partnerships with other established film talent, such as directors, writers, and producers who also wanted or had to
separate from studio employment. They typically carried the patriarchal
"boys club" attitudes and ties from the studio system with them, and very

few female stars were able to benefit from these new arrangements. (The exceptions were those married to producers, such as Joan Bennett and Ida Lupino.)

The images created for stars by the studio system's industrial machinery were now the stars' own "personal monopolies."[4] Press agents working for individual stars, once banned or discouraged by the studios, created and disseminated much of the promotional materials about their clients to keep them in the public view in between pictures and beyond the specific promotional activities the stars were still contracted to perform for studio-produced or -distributed films. Yet however much the studios' crisis meant freedom and autonomy for some stars, the wielding of these monopolies proved difficult for them, as the postwar climate in Hollywood was characterized by a variety of fluxes. The decline in studio production, population shifts to newly constructed suburban tracts away from city theaters, and competition with other leisure industries, such as television, had an impact on the trajectory of some film star personas and careers.[5] Older stars, particularly older female stars subject to gender-inflected age discrimination, were especially challenged by Hollywood's response to the shift of mass audiences from filmgoing to television viewing or other activities—namely, its turn toward a youth market and more action-spectacle genres. Few female stars disappeared completely during this period, but many moved to supporting roles (often playing mothers of teenage or grown children), to self-parody, or to new careers in television.

Although television appearances provided stars with new opportunities to act and promote their films, the complexities of stars' negotiations of their personal image monopolies for this new medium are symptomatic of the ways a diverse media environment challenged the ability of the stars and their employers to sustain the coherency and profitability of star personas. Publicity materials about stars were now originating from diverse sources: studios, press agents, and the actors themselves. Although all these sources could be said to work in and for the media industries, they had individual agendas that could compete as well as overlap with others. Loyalty between studio and star was no longer a given.

In addition television and its explicit commercial ties resulted in new kinds of legal agreements between stars and both past and present employers. A 1952 case concerning the cowboy star Roy Rogers and Republic Studios is relevant here. The star and studio battled in court over the television broadcasting of movies Rogers made for Republic. Rogers, who now had his own company to promote his name as a commodity, did not want to be associated with products that might be pitched by sponsors of the television broadcast of his movies, which were owned by Republic. Jane Gaines argues that this case exemplifies struggles over how to ensure the coherency and profitability of star personas at a time when television and its explicit commercial ties, as well as newly independent stars, threatened the film industry's discursive and economic control over stardom.[6]

Stars and the film and television industries entered into new kinds of relations. For example, Faye Emerson negotiated an early end to her Warner Bros. contract in 1946, which was compatible with the studio's postwar cutbacks in B film production and her desire to enter broadcasting. Ida Lupino was able to start her own production company with her producer-husband, Collier Young; her producing and directing experience, as well as previous acting experience, gave her an eventual edge in television directing and acting. In some ways Swanson was not the typical film star moving into television. When she first came to television in 1948, she had not been under contract to any film studio for many years and had last made a film in 1941. She did not have to renegotiate legal and economic relations with a studio, nor had she been displaced from a contract because of a studio's catering to a youth market. As we shall see, her appearance on television inspired reflection on the past (in particular the silent film era), and after her starring role in *Sunset Boulevard* in 1950 her star text was closely identified with the concept of the aging star. In 1948, however, her recycling from film to television was most frequently conceptualized in terms of the role of glamour in television. Yet despite her somewhat unique legacy of glamour from her association with the silent film era, her move to television put her in the company of many female entertainers — young and old, famous and unknown. All these women were positioned in emerging critical discourses within a tension that pitted glamour against ordinariness.

The Ordinary Personality versus the Glamorous Star

A few decades after Gould's critique of Swanson's show some television histories and theories posited the ordinary personality, as opposed to a glamorous or mysterious star, as the model of television stardom. Cited as evidence for the inevitability of such a model were conceptualizations of the medium's technological characteristics, such as its live transmission; its aesthetic or rhetorical characteristics, such as direct address and continuing narratives; its economic or institutional characteristics, such as dependence on commercial transaction and scheduling practices according to marketable demographics; and its reception characteristics, such as its reception in private, domestic space.

For example, John Ellis argues that what he calls the television "personality" is "qualitatively different" from the star phenomenon found in the cinema. The cinematic star "awakens" the spectator's psychic mechanisms because its construction and appearance in and outside of the cinematic text is based on a presence-absence dialectic. The cinematic star is always "elsewhere": once before the camera but no longer there at the time of viewing. In a sense this dialectic of presence-absence is "repeated" in what Ellis says is the cinematic star's paradoxically ordinary-extraordinary persona, at once like us or close to us but also apart from us, "removed from the life of mere mortals." Ellis points out that "television has used the word 'star' to apply to anybody who appeared on the screen," even weathercasters. But because it does not produce a play between ordinary and extraordinary, does not produce the presence-absence dialectic (television is always there), and always has the promise of liveness, television cannot present the lives of its performers as "anything particularly glamorous."[7] Here glamour is a correlate of film stardom, not descriptive of content (of certain social values and signs, for example) but a position of enunciation inimical to regularized, ongoing presence. Other theorists, such as P. David Marshall, have built on Ellis's points, arguing that the television performer is an ordinary personality, ubiquitous and perhaps powerful, but not a star.[8]

While contemporary television histories rarely pivot on questions of television stardom, it would be inaccurate to say they deny the existence of stardom as a televisual phenomenon.[9] Most historical scholarship of broadcast media implies, even if it does not explicitly adopt, an understanding of stardom as a discursive production that operates by leading the spectator, via questions or enigmas, outside the confines of the enclosed text to speculate on the truth of the identity of the figure on the screen. The truth is defined in the social terms of sexuality, marriage, family, leisure, and consumption.[10] Glamour is a value or sign that can be an effect of certain performances of sexuality, leisure, and consumption. Specifically it is a sign that circulates in the various manifestations of star performativity (in fictional film and television texts, fan magazines, portrait photography, etc.), and it suggests that the star has a surplus of one or more of the following: sexual allure, beauty, taste in fashion, cultural pretensions, disposable income spent on exciting leisure activities or expensive goods. Promotional discourses about female film stars since the 1910s used glamour as a way to distinguish the star's special qualities and consumption capacities. Although the pres-

FIGURE 1.1 Looking glamorous, Gloria Swanson stands before her portrait on the set of
The Gloria Swanson Hour. WPIX, 1948. Author's collection.

ence of glamour can put distance between star and fan, it is also often employed to help fans fantasize about overcoming that distance.[11]

My delineation of stardom and glamour may seem similar to Ellis's; what
I've described suggests that glamorous film stars do seem to have a life above
that of mere mortals. However, I want to reorient Ellis's definitions of stars

and glamour so that they are seen as sign systems indicative of social values, which means that their presence and absence are not necessarily dependent on differences between the apparatuses of film and television. Yet even television histories that might not disagree with my schema often imply an allegiance with the theories of Ellis and Marshall because they tend to focus on the transition of network radio stars to network television or on comedy stars from radio or vaudeville, whose spontaneity, intimacy, and ordinariness supposedly best suited them to television. Their network ties and performance practices made inevitable their elevation as television stars over already established stars from film, legitimate theater, or nightclubs.[12] Stars like Milton Berle and Jack Benny are taken as *the* models of television stardom over Gloria Swanson, Faye Emerson, and Carmel Myers, three former film actresses who had talk shows between 1948 and 1952 that received considerable press and audience interest.[13] Musical performers from the nightclub circuit and fringes of the studio system who moved into television in the postwar era are rarely mentioned as contenders for stardom, much less examination. Many of these were nonwhite performers who had music programs on television before narrative radio programs with nonwhite characters, such as *Beulah* and *Amos 'n' Andy*, had made their transition to television.[14]

However, if we consider that stardom is always a multimedia discursive production and also consider the sheer heterogeneity of genres and rhetorical strategies employed in television, the variance in duration of television programs (from one episode of a television spectacular or series pilot to fifty years of episodes of a soap opera serial), and the convergence between the film and television industries in the past and present, we might conclude that privileging only film as a star medium or only certain broadcast genres as television star genres or even making hard-and-fast distinctions between personalities and stars has problematic implications. In fact television programs from the late 1940s and early 1950s, as well as the discourses found in both the industrial and mainstream press of that period (the period in which U.S. television as a commercial enterprise and as competitor to film and radio was finally possible after years of experimentation), suggest that whatever the predominant model(s) for the successful television entertainer might be—the familiar, ordinary personality or the glamorous star, or both—not all prototypes were agreed on or anticipated in advance of television's arrival. Despite network ties, technological continuities, and overlaps in ad agency investments between radio and television, models for stardom were constructed out of discursive and industrial struggles that were especially contested in the late 1940s and early 1950s. Reporters and critics in fan magazines, the trade press, and the popular press frequently speculated about the viability of various models for stardom, and these were understood to come from preexisting media: stage (vaudeville and legitimate theater), radio, nightclubs, music recording, film, and even the press itself. These discourses prove to be much more open about the shape of media stardom and sometimes less essentialist about television as a medium than much of what has been produced by critics and scholars writing about the topic thirty or forty years later.

While some critics in the late 1940s and early 1950s make implicit or even explicit assumptions about the nature of television that are compatible with those made by later theorists and historians, most demonstrate a marked investment in identifying which models of television stardom or performer might work best for different genres, for different time periods, and for different audiences understood in relation to gender, age, and geographical location. In other words, while some mainstream and trade press critics of that period construct oppositions between the glamorous and the ordinary when considering models for television stardom, attitudes toward the opposition are changeable according to understandings of the variables of genre, schedule, and audience. Even the meanings assigned to the terms *glamour* and *ordinary* are elastic, accommodating varying contexts, so that at times some critics insist that a sophisticated, glamorous star persona is as well suited to project intimate complicity with viewers as the ordinary personality.

My historiographic methodology involves reading widely and closely those mainstream and trade press discourses that explicitly or implicitly sought to identify what kind of star personas or performing styles were successful for audiences, sponsors, and critics interacting with a medium still evolving technically, aesthetically, economically, institutionally, and, in an era before full coaxial hookup, geographically.[15]

Glamour, Film Stars, and Programming on Early Television

Gloria Swanson hosted her own talk show on New York's newest independent station, WPIX. The program, with segments on cooking, fashion, career planning, and interviews with celebrities, was one of the station's debut programs when it went on the air in June 1948. First scheduled for

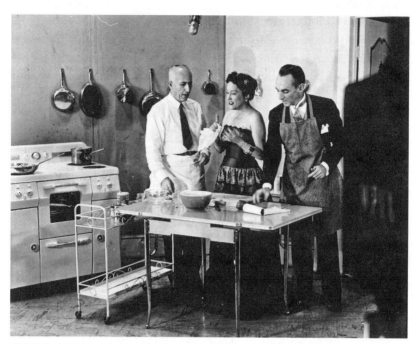

FIGURE 1.2 Cooking segment on *The Gloria Swanson Hour*. WPIX, 1948. Author's collection.

late afternoon, the show earned high ratings, prompting WPIX to move it to the evening when they renewed Swanson's contract in the fall. The show might have run longer than seven months, but according to Swanson in her 1980 autobiography, during a December 1948 hospital stay for an intestinal abscess, she viewed hours of television on a receiver sent to her room by one of the networks and decided she didn't like the medium. Even though she considered her hosting duties (which, she claimed, included her own uncredited participation in producing the show) "fun," she now felt that the medium was "too crude."[16] She would make her triumphal film comeback in *Sunset Boulevard* when that film was released in 1950, and although she would return to television many times as a guest star and even as the host of her own dramatic anthology series, from that point the character of Norma Desmond from *Sunset Boulevard* would mark the terms of her acting career until her retirement.

Faye Emerson, a stage actress and former Warner Bros. Studio contract player in mostly B films and supporting lead in a few A films, had been elevated to high-society status when she married President Franklin D. Roosevelt's son Elliott in 1944.[17] Her status as daughter-in-law to the Roosevelts made her frequent press material, and possibly because of that attention, she hosted a few episodes of the 1948 television program *Paris Cavalcade of Fashions*. Appearing the next year with her husband on the television quiz show *Who Said That?* (in which guests were asked to identify the speaker of quotes about current events), Emerson was so quick-witted and vivacious that the local New York CBS affiliate approached her to star in an evening television talk show that had been slated to star the "bad girl" stage actress Diana Barrymore, who had suddenly backed out of the deal. The 1949 debut of Emerson's show was so successful that it was broadcast nationally a few months later, and she was hired to do a talk show on NBC as well, making her the first performer to have concurrent runs on two different networks and prompting the press to call her "The First Lady of Television" and "Mrs. Television." Much like Swanson's program, the Emerson shows emphasized fashion and talk with artists and entertainers. Emerson set up her own production company (Faye Emerson Enterprises), and the program evolved in format with her input. After she married the bandleader Skitch Henderson in 1950, she had a talk-music series with him as her cohost. (Emerson's excited on-air announcement of her engagement to Henderson was the first time any figure made such an announcement on live television.)

The talk shows hosted by Swanson and Emerson received high ratings and generally positive reviews. The two were considered examples—indeed were exemplary—of one kind of model, at least a feminine model, for television stardom. Swanson's understanding of stardom gained from her experience in show business as both a star and a producer, however, ultimately clashed with the economic, technological, and professional conditions of television production in 1948. For that reason, among others, she took herself out of contention for television stardom for several years. Before discussing in more detail the terms of Swanson's involvement in WPIX's *The Gloria Swanson Hour*, it is important to examine how the critical discourses about these shows evaluated Swanson and Emerson and other female pioneers and competitors as potential television stars. Four contexts are crucial here: (1) the history of television criticism that connected problems of the televisual image with the problems of feminine spectacle; (2) the fashion and shopping show genres popular on both local and national television since the early 1940s; (3) female performers, including African American musical performers, making the transition from film or café society to television; and (4) increasing concern over the decorum of the female image on television in the early 1950s.

World's Fair Beauty Contest was one of the shows broadcast from the New York World's Fair in 1939, where commercial broadcasting in the United States is considered to have begun. One woman from the ranks of female employees at the Fair was selected for her photogenic qualities to be "the Fair's Television Girl." Most of the early discussions about how best to televise human subjects were focused on how to arrange lighting for a natural look and what kind of makeup to apply as support for that goal. Women were often used as subjects for experimentation with lights and makeup for early demonstrations of both mechanical and electronic television. (Most histories of broadcasting include a least one photo of a woman being painted with cosmetics that looked far from natural in traditional filmic media but that registered as natural on television.) The show at the New York World's Fair fits within this context and helped initiate generic television programming in which real women would be used as tests and given rewards for displaying appropriate standards of feminine beauty on the new medium. It also initiated the first critical commentary on audience interest in viewing female beauty on television. A *Variety* television critic claimed that the show provided needed experience for television engineers: "It was more of a filler for the televising eye than most production attempted by picture broadcasters lately," but "after thirty minutes or so of gazing at pulchritude, there was a definite weakening of the eye and interest due to the constant concentrating."[18] Female beauty is naturalized as a pleasurable object for viewers, but ways of photographing, pacing, and commentary on the parade of beauty is what ultimately keeps interest. Between 1939 and the early 1950s critics frequently commented on the physical appearance, specifically the tele- or videogenic qualities, of performers on television, and many reviews after this one follow its lead in adopting a contradictory stance in which female beauty is both naturalized and constructed. A *Variety* review of *Tamara*, a show on the local New York CBS affiliate broadcast in 1941, claimed that the actress-singer is "okay[-looking] for television. Her sexy good looks register clearly via the iconoscope and she avoids mugging." Yet the critic declares *Tamara* aesthetically superior to other shows only when describing how a fuse on a set light blew out, causing the singer's face to be half in shadow, resulting in an "attractively arty quality."[19]

That reviewers' concern with performers' looks in relation to the iconoscope should so often be registered in examples having to do with female performers—their sexiness, their naturalness, their "arty" or theatrical quality—is indicative of how much early television program criticism continues centuries-long stereotypes about nature as a feminine force that must be tamed by a masculine culture or scientific expertise. Cultural and textual criticism, from narratological theories of myth and folklore to psychoanalytic theories of developing subjectivity, have pointed out how mythic texts ally the feminine with nature, the space associated with emergence (birth) and annihilation (castration, loss of bodily integrity, death), which is tamed by, conquered by, or subjugated to the masculine, which in turn is allied with culture, reasoning, and science.[20] Woman's attempts at adorning the body are seen as attempts to hide nature (with both its pleasures and dangers) behind a façade that can lure men. Yet the adorned body also functions as a pleasurable fetish for the very anxieties about what is behind the façade.

A variety of nineteenth-century theories, both popular and scientific, about electricity translated the topological aspects of woman as nature space that must be tamed by man as culture and scientific reasoning into an ethereal mythology in which woman as sensitive medium for the electromagnetic field can be harnessed by man as scientific or spiritual expert. Carolyn Marvin, in her study of the emergence of an electric culture in the nineteenth century, explains that the development of electricity for practical use, in lighting, telephony, and so on, was accompanied by discourses that sought to identify the place and authority of the bodily experience in electronic technology.[21] As Jeffrey Sconce has argued, theories that gendered electromagnetic energy in certain contexts brought together attempts to scientifically speculate about feminine physiology and psychology with those inquiries into the possibilities of electronic communication.[22] Although Marvin is less vested than Sconce in gender discourses, she provides examples of relations between the female body and technology in the nineteenth century that resemble the way women were used in early experimentation of television broadcasting. For instance, for a period in the late nineteenth century there was a vogue for wiring young, working-class women with lights so that they could serve as human lamps to illuminate high-society gatherings. Later, society ladies themselves donned costumes adorned with lights to perform in illuminated tableaux for community and business celebrations. In both cases woman and technology are fused for spectacle and the demonstration of technological power and its effects.[23] Thus experimentation with female models to gauge the perfect televisual image and the criticisms of programs and female entertainers on the basis of how well the female image registers (as natural, sexy, or arty) and keeps audience interest are part of a longer tradition of talking about science's (masculine) conquest of natural (feminine) phenomena. This tradition and its implantation in the practices of the emerging broadcast field suggest that *all* female performers in television were required to live up to certain standards of transmissible beauty. Female *stars* required, perhaps, something more.

The Television Fashion Show and Feminine Performance

What "more" would be required of the successful female television performer or potential star in the late 1940s and early 1950s can be discerned by looking at the fashion show genre and how critics used their discussion of it as a forum for raising issues about feminine competence, charm, grace, and glamour, and to what effect these might be conveyed on television. Fashion show programs, both one-shot presentations and ongoing series (though few lasted long), were popular in both local independent and network broadcasts in the 1940s. They were often sponsored by clothing manufacturers or department stores, at that time closely linked to the identity of specific urban centers. These shows represent one of the first efforts in television to specifically capture the female audience and consumer, efforts that had already paid off in radio broadcasting and would continue to be among the central strategies of the commercial television industry in making the medium profitable.[24] As Anna McCarthy has shown, department stores in the 1940s were often sites for the display of television receivers in an era when many people did not have one in their home. The in-store closed-circuit product demonstration was an attempt to "micromanage both the literal and figurative mobility of subjects in consumer culture." Fashion show programs on local and network television, on the other hand, were part of what McCarthy has identified as department stores' attempts to bring the "sales floor closer to home."[25] Many reviewers of these programs comment on their ability to actually conflate the store and the home by setting the models' parade of clothes, shoes, and jewelry in a stage set resembling a living room.

The reviewers criticized the female hosts of these shows, sometimes fashion critics or editors of magazines such as *Mademoiselle*, *Harper's Bazaar*, and *Glamour*, for being too blatantly commercial. Even though the programs were sponsored by clothing manufacturers or department stores, the female host, or "femcee," was clearly expected to display a charm and friendliness that hid the commercial transaction underlying—and underwriting—the show. The *Variety* critic of DuMont network's *What's New with Mademoiselle*

(1944) complains that while the *Mademoiselle* magazine editors who appear as hosts do a good job of condensing material into a fifteen-minute format, they insert plugs for cosmetic sponsors "not very subtly."[26] This signals that broadcast personalities or stars will have to create a performing style that negotiates the aims of the sponsors with those of the viewer, which might involve something beyond the commercial transaction and perhaps a disavowal of it facilitated by the host's friendliness or glamour.

Critics also judge femcees on how well they maintain what is seen as a necessary flow between shots showcasing details of the fashions, while simultaneously conveying authority and friendliness that will make viewers feel at home and aid them in solving fashion dilemmas. In this context the *Variety* critic writing about *Fashions on Parade* (1949) on the New York station WJZ-TV commends the host, Adelaide Hawley, for her down-to-earth commentary and suggests that it is the director's decision to show clothing in mostly long-shot that derails the success of Hawley's performance strategy.[27] *Fashions of the Times* (1944), a joint venture between the *New York Times* (with its fashion staff) and New York's CBS affiliate, had "lovely" models, according to *Variety*, but its "chatter was confused."[28] *Variety* was harshest toward Estelle Compton, the host of *Glamour's Bazaar* (1949), a Chicago program on WGN sponsored by an eyeglass company. Compton "was no advertisement for her own course in poise as she muffed her prepared script noticeably in several spots."[29] The fashion expert Billie Gould on WABD–New York's *Fashions at the Waldorf* (1949) is criticized because she doesn't have "the necessary vocal authority and is lost without a script."[30] On the other hand, Rose Dunn, the producer, director, and commentator for WBKB's *Telefashions* (1949) in Chicago, is praised for her "caressing comments," which apparently set the right mood for the "eye-catching femme models attired in dresses, hats, furs, jewelry and bridal outfits."[31] The *Variety* critic writing about *Individually Yours* (1949), WGN-TV's fashion show sponsored by Blair Corsets Co., chides the host, Celeste Carlyle, for her gushy and "frou-frou" ad-libs. Yet he also notes with approval that "she knows what she is about."[32] Leona Bender, the fashion coordinator and stylist for the Texas department store Wolff & Marx, has "a pleasant speaking voice" on San Antonio's WOAI program, *Fashions in Your Living Room* (1950), and she is able to describe fashions efficiently, in a "minimum of words," and with clever and subtle references to the store.[33]

Generally, critical commentary on the fashion show programs is invested in how well hosts, models, directors, and technicians do the job for sponsors without being too blatantly commercial. But these reviews also represent an emerging discourse on expectations for the female television performer, who is now more than just a body subject to technical experimentation. She is a figure who communicates with an audience, and if not the subject of intense speculation outside the confines of the televisual text, she does facilitate some kind of audience identification. On occasion critics express some displeasure at what they judge to be evidence of a pretentious taste culture ("frou-frou') that they typically feminize ("gushy"). However, they also state that female television hosts are successful to the extent that they demonstrate authority, expertise ("she knows what she is about"), and even sensual appreciation ("caressing comments") in areas of interest to other women. If the reviews hint at the stumbling blocks a glamorous persona might present for potential viewer identification, they don't dismiss the possibility that glamour can coexist with a femcee's authoritative and intimate rapport with viewers.

Female Film Stars and the Move to Television

Radio and television magazines were also preoccupied with identifying the female television star as both authoritative and friendly, glamorous and down-to-earth, but often in relation to her similarities to and differences from the female star of the fashion runway, the legitimate theater, or the film screen.

Denise Mann has argued that television of the early 1950s displays a marked ambivalence toward the glamorous film star and that variety show hosts, such as Jack Benny and Martha Raye, derive some aspects of their popular television star personas from their careful and witty distancing of themselves from glamorous film stars, who have become "a focal point" for the audience's hostility as well as admiration.[34] While this evidence seems convincing for those shows and the variety genre in general, the television and radio fan and trade publications demonstrate a willingness to arbitrate among different forms of glamour that the female film star might bring to television.

Lana Turner's artificial and overly theatrical glamour won't work on television, predicts the January 1949 article "Is Hollywood Doomed?" in *Modern Television and Radio*, but Ingrid Bergman's "relaxed beauty" will. Bette Davis's "nervousness" and Rita Hayworth's "superglamour" won't work, but the "natural charm, wit, and intelligence" of Eve Arden and Dorothy Lamour will benefit them in the new medium.[35] In "Glamour Is the Bunk" in the same issue, Harry Conover, a model school owner and instructor, states that glamour is important to television but uses the "hollow-cheeked" high-fashion model rather than the film star as the contrast to the kind of wholesome charm and freshness, what he calls the "candy box girl" quality, displayed by the television glamour girl.[36] Both articles recognize that feminine beauty and charm are central to the success of female television performers. Their pronouncements on glamour suggest that the television industry will derive a specific and promotable identity from its on-screen feminine talent by negotiating other aesthetics of beauty and feminine deportment from already established media. Female film stars are placed on a glamour continuum, ranging from an overly studied and too serious investment in star mystique (Lana Turner and Bette Davis) to a superglamour, which is exemplified by the sensuality of a star like Rita Hayworth, and a more natural and relaxed charm and beauty that come from wit and intelligence (Arden, Lamour, Bergman).

In a 1953 article for TV Guide titled "Glamor May Soon Out Dazzle Hollywood," a veteran photographer of film stars, Durward Graybill, is interviewed about the qualities the increasing number of film stars have brought to television. He is much less ambivalent about the role of female film stars in bringing glamour to television than the anonymous author of "Is Hollywood Doomed?," who claims that his remarks are so threatening to the film industry that he dare not sign his name to the article. Graybill, in contrast, believes glamour is needed to make television "complete" entertainment. With glamorous stars, experienced craftspeople who have worked in film, and "romantic" stories (which he says includes "lavish" wardrobes, "painstaking make-up," "glamorous settings," and "mood lighting"), television can compete with film for audiences. When pressed for a definition of glamour, he describes it as a "physical and mental attraction" that has less to do with sex appeal (which might be suggested by revealing gowns) than with "mental poise" and facial "freshness and cleanliness" that indicate the performer has "zip and zoom."[37]

The article's emphasis on the "mental" aspects of glamour is representative, on the one hand, of the multivalent meanings of star allure that go all the way back to Elinor Glynn's attempts in the 1920s to define "It" as something more than a star's sex appeal. On the other hand, the more positive connotations of glamour as a mental faculty facilitated the employment of the term as a weapon in the ongoing competition between the film and television industries. Recent scholarship has eroded the myth that the film industry had no interest in getting in on the television business by showing, for instance, how invested some studios were in acquiring stations for potential networks.[38] In addition, as I have written elsewhere, some of the discourse indicating competition between the two industries was to some extent part of an *intra*television industry competition that pitted East Coast against West Coast as rival centers for television production.[39] From that perspective it is not surprising that film stars would appear to be in competition with New York stage actors for television acting jobs and that the broadcasting trade and fan press would take inconsistent stands on the merits of film stars versus stage actors or new talent for the medium. Articles about the inability of film stars to memorize lines for the long takes in live television are frequently followed by articles in the next issue of the very same or another magazine in which film stars are described as bringing "dramatic polish" to the video screen.[40]

Gloria Swanson and Faye Emerson emerged as potential television stars in the midst of these industrial and discursive negotiations, although their detachment from the film industry by the time of their entrance into television protected them from the sneers of those who saw film stars as a rival's weapon. But they were evaluated in the terms of glamour being contested in the late 1940s and early 1950s. Typically critics express condescending skepticism about their "chi-chi-ness" but are willing to see them in terms of their intended audience and according to how well they balance theatrical glamorousness with authoritative commentary and down-to-earth humor.

When Swanson was enthusiastically signed by WPIX in 1948 she was mainly known as one of the most distinctive stars of the silent film era. Although she actually played among the most varied roles of any film actress of that period (contrasted, for instance, with Mary Pickford or Lillian Gish), from bourgeois wives to prostitutes, she was known as the most glamorous star in Hollywood.[41] Even before her marriage to a French marquis in 1925, Swanson's off-screen persona had been constructed as such and she was often pictured in luxurious surroundings and clothing. Sumiko Higashi has written, "Fan magazines focused on Swanson's persona as a fashion plate rather than on her stature as an actress." She was most frequently discussed and imaged in relation to her roles in films directed by Cecil B. DeMille. These films were lavishly produced romantic comedies and melodramas in which Swanson's character was seen living in wealthy circumstances and dressed in stylish high fashion. DeMille's mise-en-scene for these films, which featured up-to-date fashion ensembles and elaborate bathroom fixtures, functioned as "etiquette manuals for a consumer culture" that was accessible only to the middle and upper classes.[42] Although Swanson made the transition to sound films successfully, the economic complications of her foray into independent production, culminating in the disaster of *Queen Kelly* in 1929 (not released in the United States until the late 1980s), compromised her financially. In her attempts to recoup from that debacle, she had to give up her independent production status and subsequently made pictures for studios in which she had little control and that had little interest in developing her star career. Swanson never left the public eye, although her presence was much lower key in the 1930s and 1940s than it had been in the 1920s. She occasionally played on stage and in films (her appearance in RKO's 1941 film *Father Takes a Wife* was described at the time as a comeback for her) and embarked on a number of rewarding and diverse business ventures, including investing and participating in a patent company employing a number of European émigré scientists and inventors fleeing Nazi Germany.

Articles in the press heralding Swanson's entrance into television in 1948 rarely fail to mention that she is known as a film star of the past and is one of the most glamorous women in America. *Phillips Television World*, a broadcasting trade journal, described her show for WPIX as "one of the most ambitious afternoon shows ever planned for television."[43] The station's hire of Swanson was a strategic move in its construction of a unique identity in an already competitive television environment in New York, which by this time had close to a full complement of VHF stations since their licenses had been accepted by the FCC before the station freeze. One of WPIX's strategies for a distinctive identity involved news programming, which included news on the hour, news specials, and the use of a veteran newspaper staff for reporting and still photographs from the newspaper collection to supplement nonremote telecasts.[44] Another strategy involved an association with motion pictures; the station wanted the public to know, announced *Radio Mirror* magazine in June 1948, that "PIX means pictures."[45] By 1949 the station's owners were bragging in *Radio Best* magazine that they had brought the finest motion pictures to television for showing every Thursday night. At a time when other channels were telecasting only B movies and silent films, WPIX bought the rights to twenty-four British films owned by the Rank Company and a block of independent productions from Hollywood, such as David O. Selznick's 1937 *A Star Is Born*.[46]

The glamorous movie premiere depicted in *A Star Is Born*, which chronicles the rise to stardom of a naïve but ambitious small-town girl, and many other films about Hollywood was mimicked on WPIX's own premiere night. The *New York Daily News* predicted the day before the premiere that the channel would debut in a "star-spangled setting."[47] Jack Gould of the *New*

York Times pointed out that the station lost no opportunity in its opening-night telecast to showcase the "after-dark world" of Broadway's nightclubs, but in the streets and sidewalks outside the WPIX building "all the accouterments of a Hollywood premiere were employed—the presentation of celebrities in the city's political, religious, and entertainment life, the flashing lights of camera men, endless lines of police to hold back the crowds, etc."[48] Imparting an aura of high culture or high seriousness to the Hollywood-like festivities were Virginia Haskins of the New York City Opera Company, who sang the national anthem, and the bishop of the Protestant Episcopal Diocese of New York, who gave the invocation, followed by religious messages from Cardinal Spellman and Rabbi David de Sola Pool.

Swanson's place in motion picture history and her association with its most alluring consumer fantasies might have been considered a strength in WPIX's strategy of associating its channel with the film world, yet she had also been judged by the station manager as "natural" and spontaneous in an experimental broadcast she did with the *Daily News* reporter Jimmy Jemail months before the station's commercial broadcast debut.[49] Since no kinescopes of the experimental telecast or *The Gloria Swanson Hour* exist, analyses of her actual performances are impossible. But in interviews at the time Swanson's own public take on her program and her performance abilities on television seem compatible with WPIX's attempts to mix the glamorous mystique of filmdom with the natural spontaneity already becoming associated with television. In a 1948 interview in *Cue* magazine she claims that working in early television is much like working in film in its early days. Even though she is photographed for the piece in the cocktail fashion she wears on the show, she downplays her reputation as one of the world's best-dressed women as a "distinction without meaning and an honor she has no overwhelming desire to perpetuate." She has no time for women who "have nothing else to do with their time but shop for new clothes." Rather she thinks of herself as a woman with a common touch, about whom one could claim, "Gosh, she's a nice old shoe."[50] Such self-effacement might be an identity Swanson adopted as a way to negotiate television as a domestic medium with middle- and working-class viewers. After all, there she was, on a program that included a segment on high fashion. But the program also had segments on "glamour on a budget" and "beauty makeovers," which blended high-fashion glamour with beauty and clothing standards more attuned to middle- and lower-middle-class viewers. And this blending of the discourses of fashion and work was not out of line with her past persona. Her star text in the silent era connoted glamour but also hard work

and, paradoxically (given that being fashionable assumes a certain conformity), nonconformism. She had success playing upper-middle-class wives
in her films with DeMille, but she played shop girls (*Manhandled*) and prostitutes (*Sadie Thompson*) in films that were also box office hits. In the early
1950s she would again demonstrate this negotiation of gendered class and
taste discourses, when she designed glamorous fashions for the "slightly
large" woman under the label Forever Young for Puritan Fashions, a design
firm marketing to middle-class women. (She designed fashions under this
label for over ten years.)

While the *Variety* critic stops short of calling Swanson a "nice old shoe," he
commends the show for what appears to be a successful appeal to women.
In a part of the review worth quoting at length, he claims:

> In putting the hour together the station perhaps couldn't have made a
> better choice for m.c. than Gloria Swanson. The aura of glamor that's sur-
> rounded the name hasn't diminished much with the years. She still wears
> clothes in a way that can't help but elicit admiration from her sex, and
> the video lens does all the right things by her face and figure. Added to
> all these is the asset of a manner of speech and an overall charm that only
> rubs against the grain when it goes a little too chi-chi. Miss Swanson tees
> off on a new career, to sum up, with all the cards in her favor. Throughout
> the opening installment Miss Swanson maintained a relaxed air and élan
> that, along with a cute chuckle, imparted a sense of knowing what she
> was about and enjoying the job, which is no simple attribute on this type
> of assignment. Her ease and humor was reflected quite conspicuously
> in the minimum of nervousness and awkwardness prevailing among her
> guests and associates on the program.[51]

In this review Swanson's aura of glamour is seen as able to comfortably coexist with a relaxed air and warm humor. In fact the reviewer constructs
an image of Swanson in which self-confidence, or "knowing what she was
about"—which is arguably also an attribute of sophisticated glamour—is
what maintains the flow of the program and makes the performances of
others on the show pleasurable for viewers. In his review of *The Gloria Swanson Hour*, Gould displays more skepticism about Swanson's "glamorous mill"
and her use of "broad a's," at least in the context of the show's ownership by
the "down-to-earth" *Daily News*. But, Gould admits, Swanson is "eminently
videogenic" and is able to provide the gesture "to fit any emergency."[52] Despite the concerns with clashes in taste cultures and his sprinkles of sarcasm, Gould's review of the program is positive. He would very possibly

agree with the *Variety* critic that Swanson "knows what she is about." This becomes more evident when this review is considered in relation to Gould's appraisal of WPIX's opening-night telecast, in which he is concerned with the hosts' poise and presence that keep the flow running smoothly and puts guests at ease. He slams the master of ceremonies Jimmy Jemail for being "in way over his head . . . his brief interviews with visiting celebrities often having comic overtones that bordered on the embarrassing." Gould also criticizes the *Daily News* reporters Ed Sullivan and Danton Walker, who were on camera that night, for lacking "essential tools of the trade of the professional master of ceremonies"—namely "presence and personality."[53] (Such critiques of Sullivan would follow him for the rest of his public life, but he still managed to have a successful thirty-year career in television.)

If television critics and technicians between 1939 and 1948 were mainly preoccupied with how to perfect television's technical prowess and capabilities by experimenting with perfecting feminine beauty, by 1948–49 critics were working through various understandings and valences of feminine glamour as a way to make distinctions between kinds of televisual flow during live broadcasts. These distinctions helped them predict who they thought would be successful on the medium.

The *Variety* review of Faye Emerson's first program, which debuted on CBS in October 1949, even makes explicit reference to issues of flow. While acknowledging that Emerson's last-minute substitution for Diana Barrymore makes the show somewhat "ragged," the critic has nothing but praise for Emerson: "Miss Emerson shows signs she can make out on her own. She has a smooth flow of language, a polished delivery, and a good camera demeanor."[54] Less than a year later, when her NBC talk show debuted, another *Variety* critic describes Emerson as a "glib and glamorous gabber" (using the kind of alliteration *Variety* was famous for in its headlines). Like Gould and his concern with Swanson's use of "broad a's," the *Variety* critic is a bit put off by Emerson's exaggerated display of her taste-culture position; for example, he is dismayed by the "superfluity of superlatives," counting thirteen "wonderfuls" uttered by Emerson in fifteen minutes. But he recognizes her appeal: her glamorousness coexists with an exuberant effervescence.[55] Val Adams, writing in the *New York Times*, reviews Emerson's abilities with both praise and condescension, so that every compliment seems to be backhanded. She is "something less than a great star of stage, screen, and radio," but she has made an impact on television because she can just sit and "ooze personality." She has a "mental alertness," but Adams is grateful that she doesn't express her intelligence in a manner too threatening: "Miss Emer-

FIGURE 1.3 Faye Emerson on one of her television talk shows, ca. 1950. Author's collection.

son realizes that a man can appreciate an intelligent woman so long as she does not suggest that she is as smart as he is."[56] Actually Emerson was well aware that most men did not like to contemplate women being smarter than they were; in 1951 the *Saturday Evening Post* quoted her candid admission that her marriage to Roosevelt failed because "she had outshone him on television": "I was right too often."[57]

In 1950 *Time* magazine defines Emerson's attraction as due to both her glamour, which is referenced in relation to her fancy décolleté gowns, and her "amiable" way with an interview. This article represents one of a number of press discussions on the décolleté of gown-frocked female performers on television in the early 1950s. Cleavage will increasingly be used as a detail in the mounting calls, from inside and outside the industry, for censoring or regulating television content. But in this *Time* article, as well as one in *Life* the same year, Emerson defends her attire with the kind of attitude that again connects glamour with a confident performing style and knowing complicity with her audience. She claims, "I wear on TV just what I'd ordinarily wear at that hour of the night [11 p.m.]," implying that her private life includes late-night fancy-dress parties.[58] She also points out that she asked her viewers to comment on the cut of her gowns. Supposedly 95 percent liked her dressing that way. She continues her defense by saying that she conceives of her role on television as a facilitator for spontaneous but thoughtful talk. "The best thing about the TV camera," she explains, "is when it watches people think."[59] Emerson had left films because she was disappointed by the poor quality of scripts she received. She said that her film work was not allowing her to contribute "anything to cultural America."[60] Her marriage to Roosevelt, during which she was able to socialize with politicians, and later, her appearance on television, in which she was able to socialize on the air with artists and entertainers, gave her the opportunity to do something "cultural." By conceptualizing her television show as an attempt to emulate a café society soirée, with people in fashionable dress and schooled in the art of witty, even intellectual conversation, Emerson manages to respond to critics who problematize the intelligence of the television femcee as well as naturalize her décolleté and cut short the debate on the appropriateness of women's fashion on television.

While some broadcasters and politicians apparently took the issue of cleavage seriously,[61] it seems impossible to find a critic in the trade or mainstream press who thought that décolleté was anything other than a harmless, contemporary standard of glamour that contributed to the construction of the personas of many television performers and stars, giving television what was seen as a much needed sense of spectacle. In other words, they found a way to naturalize décolleté too by participating in what was by now an almost traditional naturalization of the spectacle of "electronic femininity."

In fact by 1951, a year after the *Time* and *Life* articles on Emerson and months after his own columns on the décolleté of the television star Dagmar, the *Los Angeles Times-Mirror* television columnist Hal Humphrey suggests Emerson's show might be better viewed on morning television, for its brand of "Kafeeklatsch intimacy" threatens to make television just "one huge party line with vision."[62] Humphrey sees Emerson, décolleté notwithstanding, as best paired with the folksy Arthur Godfrey, another television host known for successful management of live on-air flow. Glamour has apparently become cozy with folksiness to the extent that both can now be seen as equally facilitating a complicity with viewers. Of all the critical discourses exploring the means by which television hosts might become successful and achieve stardom, Humphrey's column perhaps most explicitly suggests that terms such as *glamour*, *intimacy*, and *ordinariness* were in a state of flux and could not be reduced to teleological definitions of the medium.

Even as they were reviewing the glamorous personas of Swanson and Emerson using sarcasm both class-conscious and sexist, television critics and reporters were acknowledging that their programs benefited from the self-confidence that glamour seemed to have given these film stars turned television hosts. How are we to assess the power of this glamour? From one contemporary feminist perspective, glamour, as understood in the late 1940s and 1950s, might seem at odds with power; that is, by constructing and displaying standards of beauty and modes of behavior that made them sexually desirable to men and idols of consumption for other women, glamorous women participated in their own self-objectification and promoted a class standard impossible for many women. However, feminist historiography has also been open to identifying those spaces and ways in which women have manipulated patriarchal expectations to gain some kind of agency. In regard to the possible connections between fashion and female agency in the late 1940s and 1950s, Karal Ann Marling's discussion of the New Look, the dominant style of high fashion in the postwar period, is relevant:

> In fitting rooms all across America, women twirling before mirrors in their first New Look skirts understood the dynamic [between function and decoration, protection and assertion, concealment and display] perfectly. Pretty clothes not only enhanced the self; the theater of fashion also allowed the *wearer to explore multiple identities and potential starring roles. . . .* The highly successful Maidenform campaign [in which women were pictured half-clothed, wearing only a bra on top, with a caption reading "I dreamed that I went shopping in my Maidenform bra"] drew on suburbanized Surrealism and bowdlerized Freud to glamorize the underpinnings demanded by the new style: the model's "dream" discloses suppressed yearnings of a distinctly genteel sort—to shop, to be an artist, a lady editor, a fashion designer, a grande dame bound for the opera with a neckful of jewels and a mink stole. Nevertheless, her state of semi-nudity establishes the missing costume as a link *between a private, interior life of repressed desires and the public world of action.*[63]

Swanson and Emerson manipulated patriarchal expectations by participating in fashion, which in the context of these talk shows meant not only dressing fashionably but creating discourses about it and instructing other women, even those on a budget, on how to achieve it. As they exemplified glamour in their attire and expression of confidence and poise on their television programs, Swanson and Emerson were demonstrating one way women in postwar American culture could be both visible and audible in the public sphere. When granted visibility as glamorous women, they took the opportunity to explore multiple identities by exchanging ideas with their audiences and guests, including other stars, designers, artists, writers, politicians, and social activists (e.g., Swanson's interview with Dorothy Day). Marling states that despite the "prominence of names like Dior and Balmain," who were male designers, the dress salon of the 1950s "was one of the few places where the professional competence of women was unquestioned in popular culture."[64] Swanson and Emerson were using television as their salons, in both senses of the term: as dress salon and as a place where a fashionable woman presides over the exchange of ideas among a group of wits and thinkers.

While I wouldn't want to exaggerate the feminist claims one could make for these stars' use of glamour, the scant attention to this star value in television histories has resulted in narrow understandings of television stardom and obscured some aspects of the role film culture and film stars played in the social imaginary of an era in which audiences were increasingly urged to look to television for models of social behaviors. We expand the definitional category of early television star even further if we look beyond the glamour of established white, female film stars turned television femcees, for "glamour" was also part of the terminology used by the mainstream black press at this time to account for and optimistically forecast the role of African American performers on television. It is worth briefly looking at this phenomenon because it makes explicit the question Who profited from the translation of Hollywood's cultural capital to television? African American performers, mostly relegated to playing offensive stereotypes in films or performing in musical numbers that were isolated from film story lines (for easy editing out for exhibition in the segregated South), were usually not promoted as glamorous stars by studios and fan magazines at this time. The African American female star had to find the glamour often denied her in the casting and promotion practices of the film industry via her association with live entertainment traditions that could translate to television.

In the early 1950s *Ebony* magazine featured more than a few articles focused on the possibility that "television is free of racial barriers" because "rarely have [African American performers] had to stoop to the Uncle Tom pattern which is usually the Negro thespian's lot on radio shows and in Hollywood movies."[65] With the advent of *Beulah* in late 1950 and *Amos 'n' Andy* in 1951 and the failure of Nat King Cole's program later in the decade, that optimism would be challenged, but the presence of African American musical performers as guest stars on the big variety shows (*Texaco Star Theater, Arthur Godfrey Show,* Ed Sullivan's *Toast of the Town*) or as stars of their own programs on both national and local television between 1948 and 1951 seemed encouraging. The African Americans who starred in their own programs were accomplished concert or jazz pianists who had a background in recording, nightclubs, and guest appearances in film. At least one of these, Hazel Scott, constructed her persona in direct contrast to the kinds of roles offered to the African American female performer in Hollywood films; these were the roles of black domestic or "mammy," played by actresses such as Louise Beavers and Hattie McDaniel. (Lena Horne and, later, Dorothy Dandridge successfully avoided these roles, while Ethel Waters played "dramatically legitimate" versions of them in productions such as *Pinky* and *Member of the Wedding*.)[66]

The television programs hosted by the African American pianists tended to mimic the glamorous settings of café society instead of the movie star penthouse or living room. Yet the black pianist at café society parties had a position in some ways analogous to the glamorous female film star turned television host: granted token acceptance because of talent or beauty but in a world controlled by a white patriarchy. A November 1950 *Ebony* article identifies "society pianist" as one of the most lucrative professions for African Americans, dating all the way back to the 1920s. The article paints a picture of a glamorous profession, stating that while the successful black society pianist playing at the "swankiest and most exclusive affairs" does not initiate friendships with white party guests and discourages the black musicians working under him from doing so, many do enjoy "intimate friendships with European royalty and Washington dignitaries, often being invited to play at their exclusive affairs."[67]

The jazz pianist and singer Bob Howard, the first African American to have his own show on television, was known as the "jive bomber." This title and his fifteen-minute program on New York's CBS affiliate from 1948 to 1950 hardly suggested glamour. But Howard, much like the café society pianist, was hired not only for his musical skills (which were apparently as lively as the title "jive bomber" would suggest) but for his ability to maintain a pleasurable flow of fun. Between songs Howard would talk about other CBS programming to come later that evening.[68]

The musical shows starring Hazel Scott (first on the local New York DuMont affiliate in June 1950, going national on the network in July 1950) and Hadda Brooks (first on the independent Los Angeles station KLAC in

1950 and the San Francisco ABC affiliate, KGO, in 1951) tried to approximate some of the atmosphere of the glamorous café society party. Both stars were classically trained pianists but also played jazz and torch songs (Scott also played spirituals) as they sat, dressed in fancy cocktail dresses, at a grand piano. Brooks, who also sang to her own accompaniment, had not acted in films but had sung in a few major motion pictures, including *In a Lonely Place*. She was frequently described in terms similar to the white female television femcee, as glamorous but relaxed. *Ebony* called her "exotically attractive," projecting her songs "softly and melodiously" and possessing "unbridled confidence."[69] Brooks first gained prominence as a live performer in the integrated clubs of the (mostly white) San Fernando Valley and in clubs on Los Angeles's famed Central Avenue, patronized by white movie stars, producers, and talent scouts. Brooks's opportunity for television stardom was due to these live performances and also to the emergence of African Americans as a potential broadcast market in postwar Los Angeles. Thousands of African Americans had migrated to the area during World War II to find work in defense production; according to Josh Sides, a large number were coming from urban rather than rural areas.[70] We might assume that they would be accustomed to and seek out cosmopolitan musical entertainment, whether in live venues or broadcast media. While housing covenants restricted where African Americans could buy homes, the wages earned in defense work allowed many to become homeowners and consumers of products for the home, such as televisions.

Hazel Scott came from a Trinidadian bourgeois family. Her musical background included the concert stage and café society supper clubs in New York, where an economically viable black-white crossover music scene had existed longer than in Los Angeles. At the time of her film and television career, she was married to the African American politician Adam Clayton Powell. She had performed in several Hollywood films playing versions of herself. Significantly Scott made sure her studio contracts stipulated no maid roles. She was also attentive to the way other black performers were treated on set and visualized for film performance. After she protested the costuming of her costarring African American female performers in "lower-class" outfits in Columbia's *The Heat's On*, she was blacklisted from future studio productions. By the time she came to television in 1950, then, Scott had been recognized as adding café society glamour to a number of musical films as well as being an outspoken critic of film studio practices regarding African American performers. Her own style of televisual presentation would be based on the former achievement, but her critique of film studio attitudes and control over the on-screen images of African Americans is crucial to understanding how the valence of film star glamour that was brought to early television was constructed out of both acceptance and rejection of how white-controlled media institutions used glamour. Scott accepted that film and television could communicate her glamour to a mass audience, but she rejected the politics of exclusion that were endemic to the film industry's power dynamics, in which only white performers, or nonwhites performing under strict constraints, were constructed as glamorous.

Scott's television stage set, as well as her positioning in the mise-en-scene, represented the epitome of café society glamour. As Donald Bogle describes it, "the show opened up with the camera panning across an urban skyline, then revealing a set that was supposedly a room off the terrace of a posh penthouse. There sat the shimmering Scott at her piano, like an empress on her throne, presenting at every turn a vision of a woman of experience and sophistication."[71] Scott's program received positive critical attention from the mainstream press, with *Variety* hailing her as "dignified," "relaxed and versatile."[72] Unlike the programs of other black pianists, hers went national on the network. It might have been a long-running success if she had not been mentioned in the notorious *Red Channels*, a book listing broadcast entertainers associated with communist or leftist organizations. According to the historian Dwayne Mack, her ties to Bernard Josephson, a nightclub owner and former manager whose club Café Society was integrated, unionized, and a known hangout for leftist entertainers (including Paul Robeson), were one of the main reasons for her inclusion in the red-baiting publication.[73] She fought the accusation, but the network did not renew her contract.[74] She spent most of the rest of her career performing in European music venues and films.

The valences of glamour evident in the press promotion and the self-presentational practices of Scott and Brooks have to be contextualized not only within the history of television's promotion of glamorous female stars and the prior denials of this quality to African American female performers in Hollywood film, but also within the history of a politics of appearance in and about the African American community. An emerging black middle class at the turn of the century emphasized "black beauty" discourses as a way to mitigate racist stereotypes that demeaned African Americans on the basis of looks. Several African American women, most famously Madam Walker, became successful entrepreneurs by marketing cosmetics that promised to make African American women beautiful without capitulating to white standards, which demanded bleached skin. In the postwar era

Hear and　　　　　　See The

HAZEL SCOTT SHOW

on Television

EVERY FRIDAY EVENING AT 7:45 E.S.T. • DUMONT CHANNEL 5

1950 Concert Appearances Sunday through Thursday

Miss Scott is now making an airplane Concert Tour of the Northwest
A few open dates in May 1950 in the Midwest and East are still available.

Management: COPPICUS & SCHANG, INC. Div.: Columbia Artists Management, Inc., 113 West 57th Street, New York 19, N. Y.
Steinway Piano　　　　　　　　　　　　　　　　　　　　　　　　　　*Columbia Records*

176

MUSICAL AMERICA

FIGURE 1.4 Ad for *The Hazel Scott Show.* DuMont, 1950. Author's collection.

television programs with glamorous performers and magazines like *Ebony* continued emphasizing a beauty discourse as a necessary accompaniment to class rise and race aspiration. By the time of pan-Africanism and the Black Power movement in the 1960s, the magazine would be charged with promoting white standards.[75] Yet it is evident that even prior to the 1960s the magazine's frequent synonyms for or descriptors of African American

FIGURE 1.5
Hazel Scott in the
glamorous persona
she preferred to
project in concert,
film, and television
appearances, ca.
1948. Author's
collection.

female glamour involved "exoticness," a concept that had been used by
mainstream movie fan magazines (addressing largely a white readership) in
their occasional profiles of African American figures, such as Lena Horne,
or, in concert with the cosmetic industries, as their signifier for transforming white women into figures of sensual mystery through an approximation
of a "dark race" look.[76]

Scott's glamorous self-presentation on television, her "immaculate" appearance that exhibited "sophisticated and fashionable designs in settings
that suggested class, style, and a sense of modern luxury," was an amalgam-
ation of café society urbanity, spectacle production values reminiscent of
her Hollywood musical numbers, and the expression of her desire to inspire racial uplift and high-class aspirations. Like many white female performers, Scott had to prove that her self-presentation functioned in terms
that pleased viewers and advertisers, but she also had to overcome the racist
baggage of reviewers who found her particular vigorous style of mixing

swing, jazz, folk, and classical music "inauthentic," "over-commercialized," or "'niggerly' with 'creative mock-orgasm.'"[77] These remarks suggest that a glamorous persona, which had made her and Lena Horne the first African American female performers in film to project a type that was cultured and educated, might also function as armor against the kinds of critiques she endured even from liberal white music critics. A glamour that suggests "she knows what she is about" projects authority and self-control.

While black performers had a shot at television stardom in the 1950s via a self-presentation that in many ways matched the poise, expertise, and fashionableness of glamorous white female performers, such as Swanson, Emerson, and the hosts of early television fashion shows, they were not playing on a level field when it came to pleasing sponsors. Whether or not these black performers had controversial political views, as Scott did, black advertisers could not afford to sponsor their programs at a national level, and national (white) advertisers did not want their products to be associated with blacks, despite a growing black consumer demographic. Given that these African American musical performers earned their own shows through the iconicity of the café society pianist and because there was an emerging homeowning African American market for broadcast television, the paucity of sponsorship exposes the contradictions in how industry players were understanding their audiences as well as the limitations in how they conceptualized stars as models of social behaviors, particularly consumer behaviors. The ultimate effect was that African American pianists turned television stars were not on the air for long.

In terms of their brevity on television, black performers shared the fate of many early star performers on the medium, including Swanson. Swanson's talk show program was also short-lived, and the reasons why she quit in early 1949, although not as dramatic or politically telling as the reasons for the demise of Scott's program, nevertheless illuminate the complexity of what the glamorous film star was negotiating at this time: television's interest in glamorous film personas as a way to jump-start a new medium, the film industry's renewed interest in the ways this kind of stardom reflected on old Hollywood, and the stars' own perceptions of what this kind of star persona should be able to command in terms of respect and agency.

In her autobiography Swanson says she left the program because when she was finally able to watch television (as she recovered from emergency surgery), she discovered that it was "too crude." But evidence from her correspondence with a WPIX station manager reveals that Swanson had come to that conclusion earlier, as a *participant* in the programs produced on wpix. This suggests that what was important for Swanson was not only the way she looked to others on this new, "crude" medium but also the possibilities its current industrial or economic structures offered for her agency as a performer and (de facto) producer.

In his book *Close-Up on Sunset Boulevard*, Sam Staggs notes that the chronology Swanson offers in her autobiography of when the writer-producer Charles Brackett approached her about the role of Norma Desmond does not match up with evidence from her private papers or from articles written about the film at the time of its release in 1950. Swanson says she received the call from Paramount sometime in late December 1948, not long after her illness and realization that television was not the medium for her, and only an hour and a half later sent her letter of resignation to wpix. She then states that she and her mother were on a train for Los Angeles in January 1949. For Staggs, a September 1948 telegram to Swanson from Brackett about a meeting and a *Saturday Evening Post* article in 1950 in which she is quoted as saying that Paramount first called her in September 1948 are more persuasive evidence of the chronology of her involvement with *Sunset Boulevard*. The writers Billy Wilder and Brackett claimed they first discussed the story with Mae West, Mary Pickford, and Pola Negri, but Staggs concludes that, even though she was still to take a screen test, Swanson was the actress they had in mind when they started writing dialogue and fleshing out story points in the script in late 1948 and early 1949.[78]

I also found evidence that Swanson's memories are not entirely accurate, or at least they don't tell the full story. My interest is in what these mismatched dates tell us about Swanson's reasons for leaving wpix. Although she could have written wpix from her hospital bed (as she says she did in her autobiography), she is still writing letters to the station in early January 1949 complaining about the program's production values and how she is treated. She has not (yet) offered her resignation, nor does she mention her possible involvement with *Sunset Boulevard*, which will start shooting within a few months.

In a letter to wpix's station manager Robert L. Coe dated January 4, 1949, Swanson expresses alarm about the "amateurs" working on her program and that their work will result in damage to her professional reputation. She complains about the lack of professional writers for the program, which "would strike even a layman as being a shocking situation." Her own extensive experience in films—she doesn't explicitly state it, but Coe must have known she meant her experience both as an actress and a producer—has convinced her that nobody working at wpix has had any previous success in the entertainment business. For that reason, they are making a mystery out of what is a "simple medium . . . especially for one who is thoroughly familiar with the motion picture business."[79]

Although this is the harshest letter about WPIX that I found among her papers, it was not the first letter she had written claiming that station management and production budgets and practices were a threat to her ability to work successfully and sustain her reputation in show business. In a letter to WPIX's program manager Harvey Marlow dated July 30, 1948, Swanson complains about the station's poor publicity outlets, cuts in rehearsals, and technical imperfections. She is concerned that the sponsors will think the program looks too cheap and that all of these problems will have an impact on her professional reputation.[80] In a letter to Coe dated November 24, 1948, she complains about having to pay for clothing expenses she thinks should be borne by the station: "I am probably the *only person* in my position being paid such a small salary," while "stars of the stage and moving pictures" are given the services of "personal maids, hairdressers, and the like."[81]

It is possible that by November and December 1948 Swanson had decided to leave WPIX for a return to Hollywood, but her complaints regarding the program and the station's treatment of her date back to the early days of the show. Her concerns are not really so much about television's lack of star treatment as about what she sees as the professional responsibilities entailed in a business presumably based on a hierarchized division of labor and her ability to sustain a professional reputation in a fledgling medium that may not always be capable of living up to those responsibilities. In short, she realizes her own agency as a performer is threatened in an atmosphere of "unprofessionalism" because that agency is partially based on reputation and an image built and mass-produced by collaborative labor.

As her autobiography reveals, Swanson was a relatively reflective Hollywood film star, aware of what her stardom in the silent era was based on. She was a survivor of stardom's vicissitudes because she had developed other economic, intellectual, and emotional resources to sustain her later in life. When interviewed in 1959 by the gossip columnist Hedda Hopper, Swanson offered a cogent analysis of the way the film industry had changed for women, both stars and viewers: "It is women who go to the movies. It is Mary who drags John from his pipe and slippers because she wants to escape in dreams, to escape the worries of the house. So, what do they make movies about now? Men! Men! Men! So the male screen star has remained and the women are all gone. . . . What woman can identify herself with a

FIGURE 1.6 On the set of her television show Swanson greets the silent film star Irene Rich (right) while Swanson's daughter Michelle Farmer (left) drinks tea. WPIX, 1948. Courtesy of the Academy of Motion Picture Arts and Sciences.

twenty-year-old child? Why do we treat maturity and age with such a terrible aversion? It isn't only teens who go to the movies. Adults went to pictures, too. And it was pictures with personal identification for women that made them money, that put this town on the map."[82]

Swanson recognized that her stardom during the silent era had contributed to an emerging public sphere for women, that her visibility on the screen brought women into visibility in the theater and as consumers. Maybe the pictures did get "small," as Norma Desmond would say, but the ways Swanson used her professional expertise about glamour, fashion, and entertainment on television in 1948 suggest she recognized at least implicitly that her visibility in that medium could have meaning for women too, even if it was experienced in the private sphere of the home. What she would recognize in the aftermath of her appearance in *Sunset Boulevard*— by all accounts an entirely rewarding experience and resulting in one of her most acclaimed and memorable performances—turned Swanson again to television.

Sunset Boulevard is probably the most well-known film ever made about Hollywood, inspiring parodies in a variety of media, from television's *The Carol Burnett Show* to film pornography and Broadway musicals, and untold references. (Try, as Sam Staggs did, to count how many times you've read or heard a variation on one of the famous final lines of the film, "All right, Mr. DeMille, I'm ready for my close-up.")[83] It is the story of a former silent film star, Norma Desmond, who seizes the opportunity to attempt a comeback as the infamous biblical siren Salome when a washed-up screenwriter, Joe Gillis (William Holden), accidentally lands at her door. Desmond manipulates Gillis into becoming her writing collaborator and her gigolo. When it is apparent that he not only doesn't return her love but has also been secretly writing a screenplay with another, younger woman, Desmond shoots and kills him. When the police come to arrest her, she has gone mad, becoming the Salome of her script. As the police watch, she descends the staircase of her mansion believing that her former director-husband, now her butler, Max (Erich von Stroheim), is rolling the cameras as Cecil B. DeMille.[84]

While *Sunset Boulevard* was clearly referencing some aspects of Swanson's life, such as her silent film stardom, her work with DeMille and von Stroheim (who was fired from the disastrous *Queen Kelly* by his production partner Joseph Kennedy at Swanson's request), her association with a glamorous lifestyle, and her relatively long absence from film, it was hardly biographical. And despite what was surely a belief on the part of the filmmakers and the studio that people would want to see the film and enjoy it partly because of the resonance between Desmond and Swanson, the film was not promoted to suggest any substantial biographical similarities. Quite the contrary.

Film narratives about "has-been" stars pose something of a challenge for studio promotion departments, for it would be risky to push a slippage between the fallen star in the film and the star of the film. After all, so the studio would reason, if the star *of* the film is a has-been too, who would want to see her? Since the 1960s and the widespread flourishing of a camp aesthetic, this has actually become a marketing strategy, which has only accelerated in the late twentieth century and early twenty-first; for instance, Fox TV's *Celebrity Boxing* and E! Entertainment Channel's *Hollywood True Story* are premised on the spectacle of failed stardom. But in 1950 the studios would not have considered promoting a star on the basis of her failure a workable promotion strategy. (As I discuss in chapter 3, scandal magazines would challenge these promotion strategies later in the decade, by talking about stars in ways that Hollywood wouldn't dare to do.) And Swanson hadn't really "failed" at being a star. One could argue, perhaps somewhat more easily now than in 1950, that she redefined that category by moving on to other, relatively successful endeavors: her patent business received wide press attention during the previous decade, and *The Gloria Swanson Hour*, whatever Swanson's feelings about it, was a rating success for WPIX in a competitive urban television market. Nevertheless her nine-year absence from films and the changes in the film industry, including, most important, a demographics skewed toward a younger audience, were challenging contexts for Paramount and Swanson to negotiate as they promoted *Sunset Boulevard*.

One of Paramount's strategies was to reanimate discourse that had been part of the Swanson star text since the 1920s. For example, one press release was a short biography of Swanson (a relatively typical film promotion and publicity practice was to produce such biographies) that touted the fact that she was the first big Hollywood star to make a film in Europe, to have a baby, to marry royalty—all facts that had circulated in promotion about Swanson during the height of her career.[85] But these were facts that also made her seem quite modern and prescient; after all, this information was released again not too long after Rita Hayworth had married "royalty," and by the late 1940s and early 1950s dozens of stars were going to Europe to make films (including Ingrid Bergman's infamous trek to Italy to make films with Roberto Rossellini). Paramount's biography also highlighted Swanson's many business achievements, such as her investments in a travel agency, a patent development company, a button factory, and a cutting tool business. (These last two businesses were the result of patents developed in the company she had created with European émigré scientists as employees, some of whom were working with metals and plastics.) Her stage and television experience and her past illustrious film career are central aspects of the press release. Her already established belief in health food is mentioned, as is her creation of "natural ingredient" cosmetics. Even her status as the first big star to become a grandmother is given notice, and if this seems like a fact to date Swanson and make her seem as old as Desmond, it is mentioned at a moment when Marlene Dietrich, who was also making a career transition—and quite successfully, in contrast to most female stars her age—was being publicized as a glamorous grandmother on the cover of *Life* magazine.

Newspapers all over the country used material from this press release in stories about Swanson at the time of the film's release. When Paramount sent Swanson to tour the country (twenty-five cities) as a "good will ambassadress" in late spring 1950 to garner publicity for Paramount's 1949 release *The Heiress* and to start promoting *Sunset Boulevard*, which would be released later in the year, local newspapers used much of this press release in reporting on her personal appearances in their towns and cities. But they also combined the biographical material with firsthand observation of Swanson and her interaction with reporters and fans she met while on the studio junket. These news stories are a fascinating glimpse into how Swanson's live performance of her stardom, studio promotional material, and the press's presumptions about Hollywood in the public imaginary interacted to position fans' popular memories of Swanson toward the soon-to-be-released *Sunset Boulevard*.

For example, many papers repeat the studio-prepared list of Swanson's achievements as a silent film star and as an entertainer, businesswoman, fashion leader, and mother and grandmother since her last appearances in film. The headline of the *Des Moines Tribune* story on Swanson's visit was typical in its declaration: "Gloria Noted Actress, Inventor, Too."[86] The story headlined "Swanson Made Many Pictures, Not Only Glamour Gal but Real Actress" in the *Omaha Sunday World-Herald* claimed that "people in their eagerness to class her as a glamour girl have forgotten how she worked in the many pictures in which she starred."[87] This article was among the most elaborate in detailing Swanson's many achievements, enumerating each of the roles the press release listed, including the fact that Swanson was the first major film star to have her own television program, and also patiently quoting Swanson's opinions on fashion and health food.

Press articles also included Swanson's personal spin on her career, in which she emphasized her own agency in countering both changes in public tastes and her failures in independent film producing. To the *St. Louis Star-Times* she admitted to losing $1 million on the production of the unreleased *Queen Kelly*. The article notes that she was successful in "talkies" but that she knew and was prepared for the possibility that stardom was fleeting. She is quoted as claiming, "I know public taste. . . . I wasn't a gal with blinders on, living nothing but pictures, I had other interests."[88] To the *Des Moines Tribune* she phrased that thought more dramatically: "I always defied the laws of Hollywood. . . . Then, when the descent of my career came, I didn't go amuck."[89]

The last remark, made near the end of her junket, seems a response as much to what Swanson might have feared as the public's reaction to her character in *Sunset Boulevard* as to a reporter's query about her own past career trajectory. She collected the press stories about her visits as she traveled across the country, and it can't have escaped her notice that some articles expressed surprise that her new film wasn't based on her own life or that she was still recognized. For example, the *St. Louis Star-Times* article entitled "After Fifty Years, Gloria Still Glitters, Recognized though Years Off Screen" spent a considerable amount of copy describing how good she looks at fifty-one (an age she freely admitted): "She is not seventy-one, but fifty-one, and she is doubtless the most incredible fifty-one the town has ever seen. . . . Only a few wrinkles under the eyes and the slightest hint of a sag under the chin suggest the age of the girl whose movies and marriages lent color to the turbulent twenties. . . . Although her last successful films were made in the thirties, the actress was recognized wherever we went."[90] The *St. Louis Post-Dispatch* of June 4, 1950, claimed that, although Swanson denies it and the "facts of her life bear her out," it had been hinted that the "neurotic former star of silent films [in *Sunset Boulevard*]" is a "thinly disguised fiction of [Swanson's] life."[91] Perhaps in response, Swanson is quoted the next day in the *St. Louis Star-Times* as blaming film producers rather than public taste for the absence of stars from the past on screens today: "A lot of old favorites would be welcomed by the public with open arms if producers would only see it that way."[92]

All the articles were basically positive and in agreement that the actress was a modern, up-to-date woman who still incited interest and perhaps even emulation.[93] In "A 'Parade Roar' Comments on the Star," the *Kansas City Star* reporter wrote that women were still taken with Swanson's stylish taste: "Women in the reviewing stands look down at Miss Swanson in the first row, commenting on the way her white linen cape was buttoned on to the backless sun-dress. She [also] wore long black kid gloves and a black and white beret."[94] Even the *St. Louis Post Dispatch* article that raised the specter of a Desmond-Swanson association is impressed by her appeal to all ages, noting that Paramount, assuming there would be interest in Swanson's appearance from the middle-aged, was surprised at how "youngsters flocked to see her" in Boston. The article concludes, "Despite the fact that Gloria is inseparable from her glamorous past, she lives very much in the present. . . . The twenties are gone and with them all the barbaries of Hollywood's gilded age."[95] A Paramount press agent could not have phrased the studio's preferred reading of Swanson and Hollywood any better.

Either as a way to test teen response to the film or as a way to encourage teen word of mouth, Paramount arranged for a special "teens only" screening of *Sunset Boulevard* in Des Moines in late July 1950. Swanson appeared and talked to the group afterward. The *Des Moines Register* published some responses of the adolescents, who ranged from eleven to seventeen: "'I certainly enjoy seeing old actresses come back,' 'She certainly does excellent acting for a woman her age,' 'She's certainly a glamour girl for being as old as she is,' 'She takes my breath away,' 'You don't think anything about her age, because she can act.'" While all the responses are, at best, backhanded compliments that suggest that older stars were right to be apprehensive about the youth demographic Hollywood was starting to cater to, only one published by the Des Moines paper spoke to what would become Swanson's nightmare. One teen, very possibly conflating Desmond and Swanson, responded simply, "She's nuts."[96]

Swanson's performance received almost universal acclaim after the film opened in August 1950, and she was nominated for an Academy Award. At the time of the ceremonies she was in New York appearing in a Broadway revival of the comedy (about temperamental actors) *Twentieth Century* opposite Jose Ferrer (who did win an Oscar that night, for his performance in *Cyrano de Bergerac*). The Academy Awards were broadcast from both coasts so that nominees in New York could appear live on camera. That night Swanson sat next to another nominee, Judy Holliday, who ended up winning Best Actress for her performance in *Born Yesterday*. (Bette Davis was also nominated, for *All About Eve*, the other big film that year about an aging actress, and people who speculate about such things have suggested that votes were split between Swanson and Davis, allowing Holliday to squeak in as the winner.) In her autobiography Swanson describes how it dawned on her that night that the public expected her to act like Desmond when she lost the award: "They expected scenes from me, wild sarcastic tantrums. They wanted Norma Desmond, as if I had hooked up sympathetically, disastrously, with the role by playing it."[97] Her feelings were confirmed when most of the film offers she received later assumed that Desmond-like roles were all she could play. While she appeared in few films after *Sunset Boulevard* as a consequence of this, Swanson made significant returns to television.

Swanson and WPIX had capitalized on her fame as a glamorous, former silent film star on *The Gloria Swanson Hour*, but the program presented her to the public the way she appeared to herself in 1948–49, as a modern woman living in the present and for the future. Although the adult public at that time remembered Swanson as a silent film star, they had no reason *not* to believe she was that modern woman living in the present. The challenge for Swanson in television after *Sunset Boulevard* was to present herself as the modern woman to a public who could now associate her with a has-been star still stuck in the past, perhaps even morbidly fixated on past glories and achievements.[98] In 1951 Swanson worked on a television series proposal for ABC that seems, from evidence in her collected papers consisting of the descriptions and partial scripts for three episodes, to have been an attempt to work through and even counter various audience perceptions of her star persona at that time.[99] I found no explanation for why the series was never produced, but it is not difficult to guess: it doesn't fit into a particular genre. While it contains segments — on fashion, for instance — that were successful on her 1948 talk show, it seems much more self-referential than that show had been. The segments on fashion would find a way to include Swanson's own designs for Puritan, now in production; the segments on weekly events would be a filmed account of Swanson's activities — eating at Twenty-One and the Colony, going to art galleries and the theater. One segment would reference Swanson's own recent success on Broadway by highlighting the talent of understudies. (An elaborate segment featuring Ethel Merman and her understudy in *Call Me Madame* was planned for the first episode.) Another segment would screen a silent film accompanied by Swanson's commentary; Griffith's *The Painted Lady* with Blanche Sweet was scheduled for the first episode. All of the segments are supposedly held together by a fictionalized self-reflexive story line of Swanson preparing to do a television show.

The second episode incorporates Swanson's expertise in giving a press interview, offering a segment that analyzes how a star gives an interview on growing old gracefully. This episode also planned a takeoff on the assumed ruthless ambition of the star, but instead of Desmond's expression of ambition in self-absorbed delusions of grandeur, the skit has Swanson agreeing to replace an ill actress at the last minute. Swanson would be shown rehearsing the play (Coward's *Hay Fever*) when the actress shows up feeling better; in a scene that one assumes is supposed to be satiric, Swanson gets angry and trips her so that she breaks a leg and can't go on!

The third episode proposed contains perhaps the most obvious working through of Swanson's relation to silent cinema and the 1920s. The character playing her agent represents another fictionalized version of Swanson's life and career; she tended to brag to reporters that she never had an agent, always serving in that capacity herself. He tells her he has negotiated a role for her in a film set in the 1920s and has arranged to bring photographers from *Life* to her home for a photo spread in her "1920s" mansion as a way to publicize the movie. Swanson gets agitated because her interior decoration is entirely modern. Together Swanson and her agent get busy calling antique stores, friends from her days in silent films, and others to furnish her house in furniture and accessories from the 1920s. Apparently Swanson has one trunk left with mementos from that era. She and the agent pull out flapper dresses and beads, raccoon coats, and more and play at the roaring twenties. The clothes and objects provoke Swanson's memories about the past, but the sketch has made it clear that these are memories, usually stored away in trunks, of a woman who lives very much in the present.

Although the proposed series was a pretty obvious attempt to counter the negative associations with Norma Desmond that Swanson now found was part of her public identity, and although this genre hybrid was not quite a talk show, it did extend a trajectory for the star persona she had been constructing for some time, most recently in *The Gloria Swanson Hour*. The core of this star persona was the authoritative woman in the public sphere. In this regard the program's proposed segments on silent film, in which the star was to provide analytical commentary, suggests that Swanson desired to demonstrate that she had been more than a clotheshorse in silent films and that her experience as a silent film actress and producer had given her insights into film and acting techniques she could now use pedagogically. Since the series was never produced, we will never know how that persona might have gone over with the public at a time when silent film was often a subject of parody and the academic study of film, established or emerging in some universities and publishing houses, was probably not familiar to many of television's mass audience.[100] The silent screen star Carmel Myers, whose short-lived television talk show on ABC premiered two years after Swanson's, also experimented with the value of telling stories about the old days of silent filmmaking to television audiences of a new era. To my knowledge, audience response is not documented, but available press commentary seems less interested in this feature of the program than in the way Myers played the ukulele to accompany her stories of the past (a talent she apparently displayed to guests of her New York parties).[101]

The next television genre Swanson became involved in was the anthology drama series *Crown Theater Starring Gloria Swanson*. I have argued that Swanson's initial foray into television enmeshed her in ongoing cultural and industrial discussions about femininity in relation to electronic media's ability to transmit beauty and the relation of star glamour to concepts of intimacy, expertise, and flow. Her participation, along with that of Loretta Young, Ida Lupino, and Mary Astor, in television drama exposes the degree to which the female film star appearing in the new medium after 1950 had to negotiate the impact of her own aging and of Norma Desmond on popular histories of old Hollywood.

≡

CHAPTER TWO

NORMA DESMOND, YOUR SPELL IS EVERYWHERE

The Time and Place of the Female Film
Star in 1950s Television and Film

The status of the aging female film star, as both agent and representation, in television after 1950 was negotiated, in part, within anxieties about feminine survival in the "new Hollywood." These anxieties were related to the material conditions of female labor power in postwar Hollywood as well as long-circulated fantasies about stars, mostly female, who had sadly faded away or come back with diminished status at various moments in or from "old Hollywood." Norma Desmond's character condensed many of these anxieties into a single, pathetic figure who could not make the "return" (as she put it) to public visibility in either film or television, except in the newsreels that document her arrest for murder at the end of the film. In this chapter I examine three film and television genres that work through anxieties and fantasies about the aging female star — domestic melodrama, gothic mystery or horror, and comedy — in the decade following *Sunset Boulevard*.

Melodrama and gothic mysteries were favored genres of the many dramatic anthology series popular on television in the 1950s and 1960s; this format used these genres to explore the time and place available to the aging woman whose self-identity is based on public visibility and continuing adoration. However, there were also film comedy and television-skit renditions of the aging star making a comeback. *Dreamboat* (1952) is a comic film that represents the cultural anxieties cohering around the aging female film star and exposes the film industry's anxieties about the threat of television to its hegemony as an entertainment medium. The film's narrative follows the antics of Bruce Blair (Clifton Webb) and Gloria Marlowe (Ginger Rogers), former costars from the silent era, and renders comic the disruptions in their lives when their past films are broadcast on television. If domestic melodramas and gothic mysteries narrate the vicissitudes of the woman's attempts at specular mastery and control over her labor power and commodity image, and often end in her capitulation or annihilation, comedy often unsettles gender identities and power hierarchies to end with the promise of social integration or romantic union. *Dreamboat*'s comedy offers a more benign fantasy of recovered stardom for both male and female characters via its parodic take on television's commercial foundation and its elevation of film as the truly popular medium. Of the three genres under examination in this chapter, comedy provides the most fluid time and place for the aging female star to make a return. However, all of the texts in the genres I examine expose the degree to which media industries—as well as some of their acting labor—struggle for positions in cultural hierarchies through popular histories and myths of the feminized film star.

Women's Genres

Dramatic anthology series, in which each episode presents a new, discrete story and characters (usually with a completely new or rotating cast), were among the first programs on commercial television. Although live, hour-long dramatic anthology series produced in New York, such as *Studio One* and *Philco Television Playhouse*, are best remembered today because of their high critical profiles,[1] filmed dramatic anthology series produced in Hollywood also proliferated in the 1950s. Many of these included a "hosted by" or even "starring" format, providing a framework of stability in what was otherwise a constantly revolving cast. In the mid- to late 1950s, a number of female former film stars, such as Jane Wyman, Barbara Stanwyck, June Allyson, Gloria Swanson, and, most famously, Loretta Young, became regular hosts or stars of filmed anthology series. In addition many other filmed anthology series, such as *Four Star Theater*, *Thriller*, *Alfred Hitchcock Presents*, and *The Twilight Zone*, often employed both male and female film stars from the past. Although all included comic narratives, because of the discrete nature of each episode these series often took on serious issues that were deemed untenable for an ongoing dramatic story line on other kinds of commercial television programming.

The live dramas so valued by cultural critics of the 1950s have a reputation in standard television histories for tackling serious, even controversial material, such as alcoholism, the legal system, and class struggle. However, some of the less critically favored series—those filmed in Hollywood and casting female former film stars—featured episodes addressing issues of concern to middle-aged women that contemporary critics considered inconsequential and dismissed as the stuff of "soap operas."[2] In retrospect these programs should be seen as, among other things, a rich source of evidence about the contradictions in women's lives in the prefeminist 1950s. The concerns of many female characters in anthology episodes—aging; fading beauty; midlife change; single life in a pro-marriage, heteronormative society; economic struggles—were not unfamiliar to the ordinary female viewer, even if not of concern to all women or even explicitly articulated by those most affected. In a period in which women were expected to marry and have children at a younger age than in previous decades, in which they were increasingly turning to the workforce but in jobs with lower pay and fewer opportunities than during the previous decade, in which dependence on a husband for credit and loans was necessary, personal agency in the face of midlife change was a challenge for the middle-aged woman.[3]

Several episodes from 1950s anthology series that cast female former film stars portray the industrial and generic contexts in which television offered a site for these concerns to publicly emerge. Female former film stars, or the fade-out and comeback narratives most associated with them, were the vehicle for these concerns in television programming. The episodes I discuss work through the social and material realities for female stars and other women in the 1950s in genres that had appealed to female film viewers since the silent era: domestic melodrama, which usually features female characters whose relation to love, work, or family exposes social contradictions under patriarchal capitalism, and the gothic mystery or horror story, which is characterized by the female character's investigation into her own space as she is haunted by a woman of another time.

"It's New, It's Vital and It's Got to Stay!"

Probably more than any other female star persona of the silent era, Gloria Swanson's represented the range of identities possible for the "New Woman," who symbolized the transformative promises of early twentieth-century modernity.[4] While Swanson did not wield as much power in the film industry as did the actress, producer, and studio owner Mary Pickford, nor were her characters usually as sexually free as those played by Clara Bow or Louise Brooks, her persona was a blend of textual and extratextual identities that suggested female self-fulfillment was about taking advantage of the moment and projecting oneself into the future. After a series of very successful films produced by Paramount Studios, Swanson became an independent producer and businesswoman in the 1920s to sustain her labor power and image value. The actress and the characters she played also made the most of the prosthetic potentials of the commodity (e.g., fashion) to control or sustain their place and duration in the marriage economy and to be recognized by their mates and other women for this achievement. Publicity about Swanson during her acting career up to the early 1930s made maintenance of a place in various economies, both traditional and new, an explicit goal, and biographies of Swanson circulated by WPIX in 1948 and then by Paramount in 1949–50 to promote Sunset Boulevard resurrected this narrative. However, audience and press reception of that latter moment suggested a competing narrative enigma: Was Swanson, like Norma Desmond, a "has-been"? Between Sunset Boulevard and the mid-1950s Swanson acted on the Broadway stage, continued with her business projects, and planned a network television variety show. Although she made guest appearances in television programming in the 1960s and 1970s, her last regular involvement with the medium was Crown Theater with Gloria Swanson in 1953–55. The press coverage of the show and the type of character she played in at least one episode attest to her continuing power, but they also suggest she had to contend with the legacy of Norma Desmond.

Crown Theater with Gloria Swanson was produced by Bing Crosby Enterprises Inc., a company that the recording artist and film star Bing Crosby formed in 1946 to improve and market new tape-recording technologies for transcribing radio program performances. (Transcription of radio programs had been frowned on by broadcast regulators, networks, and critics but was becoming more widespread in the late 1940s.) For television the company had produced Fireside Theater in 1950 for the sponsor Proctor and Gamble.[5] Crown Theater was produced for syndication, which meant that it was not produced for a particular sponsor or network but was picked up market by market. CBS Television Film Sales picked it up for the 1953–54 season, advertising in an elaborate brochure that the program was available for market-by-market sponsorship. Although Swanson acted in only four of the twenty-six episodes filmed, she performed as host in all, and her name has prominence in the sales brochure. While there is mention of the quality writers whose work was adapted for episodes, most sections of the brochure consist of press quotes about Swanson—how women emulated her look in the 1920s, her triumphs in television, stage, and screen (including *Sunset Boulevard*), her winning of the Nieman Marcus Fashion Award (both for what she wore and what she designed). In one of the more interesting strategies that must have required cooperation from Swanson, it included a column full of quotes from letters from fans who attest to her continuing popularity and their desire to see her "come back to enchant us again." In prose reminiscent of the press reports of her publicity junket in 1950, the brochure declares that Swanson "at 53 . . . is still lovely, still lively." But it also seems to hearken back to the critical response to Swanson on her first television series, for she is seen to be both ultra glamorous and capable of great intimacy with audiences: "The queen of them all . . . she establishes a close personal relationship with her audiences that is unique."[6]

Although Swanson told TV *Guide*, "Doing a series such as this . . . is harder than anything I've ever done—and that includes trying to top *Sunset Boulevard*," her contract for the series suggests minimal involvement, in contrast to the intensive creative participation required from her first series.[7] The introductory segments in which she performed as host were projected to be shot in succession over a two-week period. The photoplays in which she acted were to be shot in three days each. She was paid a flat fee for hosting, and a fee plus 40 percent net profits for the half-hour photoplays in which she acted. In her collected papers I found no angry letters regarding the series like those she had written about her earlier talk show. But despite what was relatively minimal input from Swanson, TV *Guide* described what power she exercised as excessive, perhaps unwelcome: "Meals were catered from an outside restaurant to please her exacting tastes. Production details were to her liking, or else she stated her views unhesitatingly. Others may forget that once a queen always a queen, but not Gloria Swanson."[8] The article doesn't mention that the production company was selling the series on the basis of Swanson as queen. Apparently television producers and industry press could commodify and profit from the star name, but Swanson had no right to authoritative expression. Even though the article discusses the technical lapses and lack of services for performers that characterized her WPIX program, it makes no connection between her past experience in television and her propensity for stating "her views unhesitatingly" on the set of the new series.

One episode starring Swanson survives in video circulation, "My Last

Duchess," adapted from a short story by Harriett Pratt that appeared in *Good Housekeeping*. Its parallels with *Sunset Boulevard* no doubt have kept it in circulation. Like that film, it concerns a fading female star who longs to make a comeback. But the story's contrasts with *Sunset Boulevard* are telling, and it is not difficult to see why Swanson would be eager to play the part of Eleanor Hallam.[9] Hallam is an aging actress, once a star of stage and screen, now coaching acting students in her modest Beverly Hills apartment to make ends meet and to pay the tuition of her orphaned nephew, studying for his PhD in physics at Stanford. The story tells of her attempts to land a part in a film that she had once triumphed in on stage for 1,664 performances, the role of the duchess of *My Last Duchess*. The film rights to the play have been bought by the "genius" film director Frank Lord (played by Denver Pyle in the teleplay). The problem for Eleanor is that she had Lord fired many years before for badly playing a small part in the Broadway version of *My Last Duchess*. He has shown his vindictiveness over the years, providing entertainment gossip columnists with his hateful opinions of the star, telling one, "The ten most uncooperative actresses I have worked with are Eleanor Hallam."

While the story makes it clear that Lord's remarks have hurt her reputation, and thus her ability to get parts, it is also suggested that her age has made it more difficult for her to get leading roles. Eleanor's responses to age discrimination are honesty and sarcasm. When her young acting student Judy arrives one day for a lesson, excited at her recent discovery that Hallam was once a big star who had acted on stage with John Barrymore and on-screen with Rudolph Valentino, Eleanor does not deny her age. Instead she mugs that she is elderly with no teeth, croaking, "Yes, and I was born in 1899, too." (Swanson had acted opposite Valentino, and she was born in 1899.) Puzzled that Eleanor is now only an acting coach, Judy remarks, "Daddy says you were so wonderful as the Duchess that Hollywood made you come out here and become a big star. Daddy says he just doesn't understand why you haven't made any pictures lately." Eleanor, this time with teeth gritted, answers sarcastically, "Your daddy seems to have an infallible memory."

Both magazine source material and teleplay feature scenes in which her agent reminds her of the vicious Hollywood cycle she is caught in: she could get small roles that would pay less than starring roles, but once producers knew she was willing to accept less money and lesser parts, she would never again be able to command a high salary or get a lead role even if there was one for a woman her age. In addition to fighting age bias, female Hollywood

FIGURE 2.1 Former actress Eleanor Hallam (Gloria Swanson) with her acting pupil in "My Last Duchess." *The Crown Theatre with Gloria Swanson*, Bing Crosby Enterprises, 1954.

stars have to play an image game, pretending they're not desperate for the small parts the system is willing to offer them. This theme is relatively typical of the "star down on her luck" narrative, but it might have resonated beyond the show business context. As becomes clear in many of the dramatic episodes under discussion here, what was deemed successful femininity for most women in the 1950s might just be an act that hides the humiliation and desperation felt by the woman who knows she is judged by how well she can keep up appearances. In other words, women have to hide not only their age and ambition but also their humiliation and desperation.

"My Last Duchess" sympathetically renders Eleanor's plight, but it doesn't dwell on the pathos of the aging actress. It does focus on her pride in her craft; she explains to Judy that doing 1,664 performances of one role was not boring because for a "real" actress, each performance "is just a little bit different, challenging and exciting." Then she tells Judy that she can no longer teach her because Judy is not serious about acting. What supposedly stands in Eleanor's way of being cast in the film role of the Duchess is her honesty about acting: she told Frank Lord the truth about his acting and fired him for it because the greater tragedy would be to let a bad actor think that he is good. Now, when she desperately needs money to live and to support her nephew, she is able to put aside pride and go to Lord to ask for the part. He has turned her agent down and has been hoping that she will come to him, groveling. When she does come to him, he tells her that he will give her the part if she will admit that she fired him all those years ago on a whim because she was a big star. She refuses to do so, responding, "I'm too old to start lying now. You were a rotten actor and I was right to boot you out." Lord suddenly has a change of heart and tells her in words that suggest, if nothing else, he is still a *hammy* actor, "I was an awful actor, wasn't I? I've never admitted it even to myself, but I realize it now. I think if you had lied to me, I'd [have] gone into a monastery." She wins back the part, her pride, and her ability to be the maternal figure she wants to be for her nephew.

The role of Eleanor Hallam gave Swanson the opportunity to revisit the themes of her life and, more significantly, of *Sunset Boulevard* and to counter any public associations those might have with destructive self-grandeur, obsolescence, and madness. Eleanor, unlike Norma Desmond, is not narcissistically fixated on her past image; she cares little for the adulation of others. She too may be an aging star, but she is willing to accept the discrimination that goes with that if she can make a living as an actress and be honest about the importance of craft. However much Swanson must have felt empowered by playing this role, by constructing Eleanor's problem and eventual success around her refusal to be dishonest, the story downplays the social and commercial implications of Hollywood's refusal to employ more middle-aged and older actresses, especially in parts comparable to those that older male stars were typically getting. (The latter fact seemed to bother Swanson very much in her 1959 appearance in *Hedda Hopper's Hollywood*.) Like so much popular culture of the period, including the many television series addressed to women viewers, "My Last Duchess" on *Crown Theater* is able to raise unsettling truths about gender inequity but personalize and ultimately depoliticize them.

The dramatic anthology series *The Loretta Young Show* (called *Letter to Loretta* in its first year) was on the air from 1953 to 1961. The film star Loretta Young served as host, producer, and frequently star. Episodes were often thematically structured around contradictory gender realities experienced by middle-aged women. Young, whose program was on the air longer than any of the others under discussion here—and longer than most dramatic series of any kind from that era—is a study in contradictions. Raised by a single mother who ran a boardinghouse patronized by show business figures, Young had bit roles in silent films while still a child (as did her older sisters, one of whom, Sally Blane, became a B film star in the 1930s and early 1940s). She possessed a mature beauty at a very young age and started playing lead roles opposite male stars when she was a teen; she was fourteen in 1928 when she played opposite Lon Chaney in the silent film *Laugh Clown Laugh*. Her first long-term contract was with Warner Bros., her second with Twentieth Century-Fox, both studios with poor track records in their treatment of female talent.[10] Wanting to escape the control and grind of the studio system, as well as its typecasting, she refused to re-sign with Fox in 1939 and ventured into freelance acting at a time when only a few stars were able to do so successfully. She made it clear to Fox's studio production chief Darryl Zanuck that his prioritizing the careers of male performers over hers was the central reason she was declining a contract renewal; more than once Zanuck had given star billing over her to male actors who had just started in films. At first many studios were slow to hire Young in retaliation for her refusal to renew with Fox, a typical collusive strategy by the major studios at this time. As a result she guest-starred frequently in dramatic radio anthology series, such as the *Lux Radio Theater*. After slowly rebuilding her film career by working mostly for independent producers, such as David O. Selznick and Walter Wanger, and for minor studios, she won an Academy Award in 1947 for *The Farmer's Daughter*.

Known during her film years as a rebel of the studio system but also as the ultimate fashion plate, Young had one of the most complex and hidden private lives of any female star, at least heterosexual female star, of that period. She had given birth to a baby out of wedlock after a brief affair with Clark Gable in the early 1930s. Judging correctly that her career would have been ruined if the public found out, and refusing to have an abortion because of her strongly professed Catholicism, Young was aided by her mother and sisters in keeping the pregnancy a secret. After she gave birth to a daughter, she arranged for a Catholic orphanage to keep the baby for a few months until she could "adopt" her. Rumors circulated about the pregnancy, and although no mainstream publication could have been explicit about the possibility of an illegitimate birth (any fan magazine suggesting her unwed pregnancy would be ruined by the studios as surely as Young would have been), the rumors continued after the "adoption." When Young was terminally ill in 2000, she admitted to her authorized biographer that her "adopted" daughter, Judy Lewis, was really her own child fathered by Gable. She never admitted it to her husband, the advertising executive Tom Lewis, who coproduced her television show. She probably would not have told her daughter if Judy hadn't confronted her when she was an adult and suffering an identity crisis. When Young found out that Judy was writing a memoir revealing the secret, she didn't speak to her for seven years.[11]

Throughout her career Young labored at a public persona in which she was known for her work on behalf of Catholic charities, including St. Anne's Home for Unwed Mothers. (In retrospect this choice seems incredibly transparent.) After she married Lewis and had two sons with him, she made every effort to be seen as the matriarch of an ideal family and positioned her entry into television in that light, as an attempt to counter the "sex and violence" children were exposed to on television.[12] The company she and Lewis established to produce the show was called Lewislor; like Desilu, the production company of Lucille Ball and Desi Arnaz, the name was a blend of the names of husband and wife, emphasizing the family nature of the endeavor. In an article she wrote a year after her show debuted Young claimed that what she loved about working in television was "the intimate, possessive feeling with which television audiences view your visits to the family living rooms."[13] This suggests that she either had an intuitive understanding of the probable viewing contexts of this still new medium or had closely studied the critics who praised the blend of intimate warmth and glamorous beauty of other female hosts. Her desire for television may have emerged from anxiety about threats to "old" values like family togetherness, yet Young remembered later that she had insisted that television would be an answer to the crossroads in her career: "It's new. It's vital and it's got to stay!"[14] A new medium would be exciting for most performers, but television's timely arrival also coincided with an age milestone for the actress, as she turned forty the year her show went on the air.

Young had enjoyed freedom from the studio contract in her work as a freelancer. However, no film company, with the exception of Universal Studios, with its cycle of melodramas starring Jane Wyman and Lana Turner and directed by Douglas Sirk, was particularly invested in making a series of films with older female stars, either under contract or freelance. Consequently the late 1940s and early 1950s was a time when many of her female contemporaries were also moving on, to more stage work (e.g., Rosalind Russell, Jean Arthur), television (Lucille Ball, Ann Sothern, Mary Astor, Ida Lupino, Gloria Swanson), films playing middle-aged mothers (Mary Astor, Claire Trevor, Myrna Loy) or aging, often has-been actresses (Bette Davis, Gloria Swanson), or to retirement from film acting (Irene Dunne, who made her last film the year before Young's program premiered). Her contemporaries Barbara Stanwyck and Jane Wyman would host their own

FIGURE 2.2 Loretta Young often opened her show with a reading from a book of proverbs. *The Loretta Young Show*, Lewislor Productions, ca. 1959. Author's collection.

short-lived television anthology series later in the 1950s, largely because of Young's success in the form.[15]

Besides the biblical and folk proverbs Young quoted every week, the series became best known as a showcase for her acting versatility in hundreds of roles—including housewives, newspaper reporters, nuns, and fashion models—and for her fashion-conscious clothes. Young introduced each episode by stepping through the door of the set wearing a beautiful

FIGURE 2.3
Young knew which gowns would make the most impact for her entrances on *The Loretta Young Show*. Lewislor Productions, ca. 1957. Author's collection.

gown, which she showed to best advantage by whirling around to close the door. While this act was widely parodied at the time, Young valued this part of the program highly, not allowing any guest hosts to copy the move. However, she was also aware that her image as a fashionable woman was time-bound, that she must always be seen as a fashion leader.[16] Consequently she had it written into the contract that these introductory segments were to be removed when the series went into rerun syndication after a certain period of time because the gowns would seem dated. When the network reran the program some years later with the introductions intact, she sued and won, proving her serious commitment to never being out of date.

Young insisted that episodes have an uplifting message, and her reading of proverbs lent a sanctimonious air to many of them. Yet the kinds of characters she played often went against the grain of fiction television, both dramatic and comedic, at that time.[17] Young said she loved playing such diverse women, from every walk of life and nationality; Japanese, East Asian, and Middle Eastern women were among her characters. The variety was a welcome change from the typecasting she and other female stars typically endured while working for the film studios.[18] Most television series represented middle-aged women as middle-class wives and mothers or as spinsters, but the anthology format allowed Young to play both single and married career women; middle-class, wealthy, and working-class women; childless women and mothers. Many of these characters had the kind of midlife crises about aging, beauty, marriage, money, and work that would have been familiar to Swanson's character in "My Last Duchess." In addition these crises were often introduced and resolved within similar narrative, ideological, and gender contradictions characteristic of domestic melodramas.

About half of the approximately two hundred episodes of *The Loretta Young Show* are currently circulating on video or DVD. Of these two are especially relevant in the context of this chapter, "600 Seconds" (aired in 1955) and "The Prettiest Girl in Town" (aired in 1959), both starring Loretta Young. In "600 Seconds" Young plays Katie Wells, a middle-aged, married, childless woman who is the art director for an advertising agency. The episode opens as Katie, dressed in glamorous hostess attire, is entertaining friends in a late-evening supper party in her penthouse apartment. One of her younger female guests expresses her feelings for Katie and her lifestyle, in essence describing all of the essential characteristics the viewer needs to know about her: "I really envy you, in a nice way, of course. You have a beautiful house, perfect servants, an exciting career . . . an adorable boss, a wonderful husband, and you're pretty, too!" Katie responds that she is "just lucky." But as the evening comes to an end, she is disturbed by the bitter remarks directed at her by another guest, Carol, her best friend and contemporary in age. The next day Carol comes to Katie at her office; in tears, she apologizes for her behavior, explaining that her husband had left her for a younger woman. She is sure Katie "has all the answers" and tells her, "I can't face life without Jim. . . . For a woman my age, there is nothing worse than not being married. Nothing!" Katie comforts her and sends her on her way. However, after Katie's boss asks her to go to Detroit on business that weekend, a young woman from her husband's office calls and asks to see her that afternoon. Katie lets what has happened to Carol color her imagination. She fantasizes that her husband Greg's young female coworker is coming to tell her that she and Greg are in love and that Katie must grant him a divorce. The "600 seconds" of the title are the ten minutes of Katie's fantasies, including her reassessment of her own career drive. When the young woman arrives and asks Katie for help in finding her fiancé a commercial art position, Katie realizes her foolishness but decides to cancel the business trip to spend more time with her husband.

The episode follows the narrative pattern of many 1950s television programs in which complex social concerns about gender norms and female power are simultaneously recognized and denied.[19] Women are shown to be vulnerable to male power, potentially abandoned by husbands who find a younger woman more attentive, compliant, or advantageous to their social status. But women are also shown to be capable of challenging and creative work. They are even depicted as admiring other women who have this kind of meaningful work and visibility in the public sphere. But Katie's own fantasies about her age and career as potentially ruining her marriage suggest that she too fears that there is "nothing worse than not being married," and her insecurity prompts her to cancel the business trip. Rather than considering that her attractiveness to her husband might actually be based on her independent attitudes and actions, she capitulates to the fear that, so far, she has been "just lucky."

"600 Seconds" is interesting in regard to Young's own life. She was having marital problems when this episode aired in 1955, partly as a result of disagreements about control of the program. Judy Lewis implies in her book that her stepfather suspected that she was in fact the daughter of Young or one of Young's sisters; one might conclude that there was already a lack of intimacy within the Young-Lewis marriage. In spring 1955, after shooting was finished for the season, Young was hospitalized for peritonitis, requiring emergency transfusions and surgery. In the midst of this, Lewis told the sponsor, Proctor and Gamble, that Young was retiring from the series. When Young found out, she was furious and had her representatives tell Proctor and Gamble that she had no intention of retiring; the program could have guest hosts and stars until she was able to return. Consequently Lewis left the show as producer, and less than a year later he also left the marriage and went back to his old advertising agency in New York. Many, including her husband, interpreted Young's reaction as evidence that she valued career over marriage, a taboo for women at this time.[20] The couple stayed legally married until Lewis's death in the early 1990s, but Young acted for years as if the couple were in a commuting marriage, evidence that she was desperate to preserve the image of the happily married woman. Young's own biographical trajectory, then, suggests that the teleplay was raising relevant themes for women at this time but that it was much harder in reality to solve the kinds of problems caused in part by gender norms in which women were supposed to subordinate all for family.

"The Prettiest Girl in Town," airing several years later, has an even more conservative resolution than "600 Seconds." Young's character, Connie, is a famous fashion model returning from New York to her small hometown for her twentieth high school reunion. She has never married and tells the friend she is staying with, Jackie Krump (who is married and has several children), that she has never regretted staying single. She is part of the New York rat race, in fact "right out in front of the pack." Like Katie's friend, Jackie envies Connie. "You've done exactly what you set out to do. . . . I need a man to lean on," she says. Connie decides to call Earl, a recently widowed boyfriend from the past (who was more taken with her than she was with him), to be her date for the reunion. After the night's events she spends time with Earl and, although clearly attracted to him (he is now a hunky doctor!), is irritated by his constant references to how she has always been catered to, never having to give in return, because she is so beautiful. Connie starts questioning the value of her life as a glamorous clotheshorse. Two nights before she is to return to New York, she confides to Jackie that she has missed out on a "regular" life. What is most disturbing to her is that because she is a model, for whom fashion and a glamorous lifestyle are presumed to be most important, people still think of her as a "girl" rather than a "flesh and blood woman." The next night she confesses to Earl that she wants to stay in town and hopes he wants her to stay. He shows that he does by proposing marriage. Young as host caps the narrative by reading an "old English proverb": "He who gives, gathers."

Like Katie in "600 Seconds," Connie reassesses her nontraditional career life, in which narcissistic pleasure in her own beauty and talent has made other women envious of her. This episode acknowledges that women desire to fantasize about such a life and that public visibility can give women at least the illusion of power. It is suggested that the life of a model—which, like film stardom, offers women a visibility that is coextensive with a commodification of female beauty—infantilizes women, or at least positions them to be infantilized by those who grant women maturity only when they conform to the gender roles of wife and mother. However, the focus of the narrative is less on criticizing those who hold such a view than on Connie's denial of a glamorous life to be a "regular" small-town doctor's wife.

Soon more film stars began appearing on television. In the 1959–60 season Mary Astor (in *Thriller*) and Ida Lupino (in *The Twilight Zone*) played former film stars adjusting badly to their fading beauty and fame. TV *Guide* ran a number of articles on the phenomenon between 1953 and 1955, even reviving questions about whether film stars were actually capable of performing in the single takes necessary on live television or after the short rehearsals allowed for filmed teleplays. One article raises these issues through a sympathetic look at actors who have gained fame by extensive work in television rather than in motion pictures, such as Maria Riva (daughter of Marlene Dietrich) and John Newland (who costarred in and eventually directed many episodes of *The Loretta Young Show*). The article is especially suspicious of television producers who want to cast movie stars because such stars come with an already established "glamour build-up."[21] Other articles, less concerned with the competition film stars might represent for television-trained actors, argue that television has had to *lure* film stars away from their motion picture work.[22]

It is true that many film stars (those who weren't already forbidden by studio contracts to appear on television) were reluctant to try television in guest spots or in their own series; it didn't pay enough, the schedule was too demanding, and they feared overexposure. Oddly enough, however, the TV *Guide* articles never explicitly discuss the changes that the studio system was undergoing or the changes in audience demographics for films, both of which had a profound effect on stars, especially female stars. "Letters to Loretta: 'The Queen' Stakes Her Crown on Television" gives the impression that the motion picture establishment was worried that so many stars were leaving film for television: "Up to now, the movie scions hadn't bothered much with TV's sporadic raiding of the talent rosters. But with Miss Young's defection, the situation is suddenly getting serious. For there, Hollywood sputters, looking back over its shoulder in hurt surprise, goes 'The Queen.'"[23]

Although the studios did not want television programs to compete with their films for audiences, there is little evidence to suggest that the studios were planning to feature Young or many of the other middle-aged female stars who turned to television at this time in leading film roles befitting their talent, experience, and past track record at the box office. Was this reluctance to discuss the studio system's indifference to female stars TV *Guide*'s collusion with a sexist system? Or did the magazine avoid discussing changes in the studio system and public taste because it didn't want television to be seen as a "haven for Hollywood has-beens"? I would argue both reasons, but TV *Guide* admitted to an interest only in the latter question; television as a "haven for has-beens" was an actual focus of one article in late 1954. Of the stars interviewed—Humphrey Bogart, Ann Sothern, Joan Crawford, Red Skelton, Mickey Rooney, Joan Caulfield—only Bogart seemed to think it might function as such a haven for him: "No form of dramatic art is a haven just for has-beens, and television—these days, anyway—very definitely shows signs of being a dramatic art. My own personal feeling, however, is that I won't go into TV until I feel myself slipping."[24] Is it a coincidence that Bogart, the only star interviewed who felt this way, was also the only one among them at this moment with a secure film career (aided tremendously by his own production company distributing with a major studio)? Hal Humphrey, a television columnist for the *Los Angeles Mirror*, displayed less complicity with the film industry, entering the discursive fray by chastising the studios for scrapping actors "whose talents were far from being played out." He declared that film stars entering television were definitely not has-beens; instead television was actually rectifying the film industry's "mistake" of letting such talented performers go.[25]

The Comeback Trail Can Lead to Strange and Sinister Places

Both *Thriller* and *The Twilight Zone*, two anthology series with a focus on uncanny or sinister reality, constructed episodes in 1959–60 with gothic undertones and female stars who were definitively has-beens. Rose French, played by Mary Astor in "Rose's Last Summer," a 1960 episode of *Thriller*, is a woman whose film stardom was ruined by alcoholism and persistent nonconformity. Ida Lupino's Barbara Jean Trenton in the 1959 *Twilight Zone* episode "The Sixteen Millimeter Shrine," is an aging star who longs to be back on the screen as the object of the attention of her fans and her former leading men. She now sits drinking and watching her old movies. Both women have opportunities for comebacks, and their decisions regarding these opportunities lead them into other realities. Like the other anthology series episodes under examination in this chapter, these replay many of the themes set in motion by *Sunset Boulevard* in its treatment of a silent star. How does a female star, whose identity is based on being a desired object, negotiate a new identity when the public (and therefore also the studio) no longer desire her?

The introductory segment of "Rose's Last Summer" immediately suggests an affinity with *Sunset Boulevard*'s gothic or noir contextualization of stardom past. The episode opens with a bartender throwing Rose out of a sleazy cocktail lounge. Obviously drunk, she protests with references to her past status, "What do you think I am? A lousy lush? My credit is good in

FIGURE 2.4 Host Boris Karloff asks the audience if they remember Rose French (Mary Astor). *Thriller*, NBC, 1960.

the best hotels in town!" She picks up a rock, hurls it through the bar window, and stumbles back into the street, where she is hit by a moving truck. As she lies unconscious on the pavement, a crowd gathers. In what by now was a clichéd gesture, someone from the crowd pulls a photo of the young and beautiful Rose French from Rose's pocketbook and exclaims, "You know who she is? Rose French. She used to be a big star." As the camera slowly dollies in to frame the photo in close-up, we hear the voice of Boris Karloff, the program's host and a star of horror films: "Rose French. In the blur of memories the face grows dim. But do you remember the name? Twenty years ago? Rose French." The camera shifts to Rose's room, panning across the wall of her apartment, and focuses on a series of glamour portraits of French that are clearly the studio portraits taken of Astor when she was under contract to Warner Bros., Goldwyn, and MGM in the 1930s and 1940s. "The remarkable Rose French. As a servant girl? Or as a princess? She was a quicksilver star in a celluloid heaven." The panning camera has now reached Rose herself, passed out in a chair, an empty liquor bottle on the table beside her. "If a woman could sell her soul to achieve such fame, what could she do to get it back? That was all she wanted, to relive the past. And those who loved her, Frank Clyde for instance, could do nothing to stop her. But the comeback trail can lead to strange and sinister places . . . to a night of terror. . . . But the comeback trail is a journey without maps as sure as my name is Boris Karloff."

The introduction asks the viewer to embark on a journey in memory, not only "Do you remember Rose French?" but Do you remember Boris Karloff? Although male stars were not abandoned by the studio system to the degree female stars were, Karloff was typecast for most of his career. He considered himself a versatile character actor, but after his appearance as Frankenstein in the early 1930s, he was rarely cast in roles other than monsters or criminals. Like many female film stars of this period, he was vulnerable to the studio system's typecasting practices during its heyday, and now that it was in transition, television and B movies were what sustained his career in the 1950s and 1960s. The presence of both Karloff and Astor in this episode suggests that the question posed about Rose French is really a generic one: Do you remember old stars, stars who were once popular, beautiful, and the object of the fan's adoring gaze? It presents Rose as an alcoholic, patronizing sleazy bars and living in a cheap boardinghouse, and Karloff's introduction raises the possibility that her willingness to get her stardom back will lead to a night of terror. This narrative terrain is recognizable as Norma Desmond country, where comebacks lead to sinister and possibly murderous action.

In the context of the entire episode, however, the introductory segment can be seen as doing most of the work in making the connection to *Sunset Boulevard*, for neither the narrative nor the characterization of Rose sustains the story of a female star who wants to get her past fame back at any cost. Instead the rest of the episode has a convoluted suspense and investigation plot in which Rose is relatively marginalized. After her quick recovery from the accident, which apparently made national newspaper headlines, Rose informs her friend Frank Clyde, who runs a sanitarium where Rose has "dried out" in the past, that she has a new job, as a housekeeper in northern California. Within weeks newspaper headlines are reporting Rose's death, her body apparently found in the garden of a costly estate in the area where she told Frank she would be working. The owners of the estate claim they had no relation to Rose other than discovering her body. Frank can't believe she is dead and sets out to investigate, joined by one of Rose's ex-husbands, the wealthy industrialist Haley Dalloway. Meanwhile we learn that Rose is alive, now playing the part of the rich Mrs. Goodfield, to whom Rose apparently has a resemblance. Mrs. Goodfield is the one who died and was found in the garden. Before her death, which her son and daughter-in-law knew to be imminent, they hired Rose to masquerade as Goodfield because if she died before her sixty-fifth birthday her estate would be turned over to a

FIGURE 2.5 The death of a film star, as depicted in "Rose's Last Summer." *Thriller*, NBC, 1960.

charity trust. By the time Frank and Haley have arrived in town to investigate, the old lady's sixty-fifth birthday has passed, and the Goodfield couple are planning to murder Rose. Frank and Haley piece this together and rush to save Rose at the moment she is fleeing her pursuers. The story ends with the suggestion that Rose has had all the comeback she needs and will go home with her former husband.

Although Rose is initially pleased to get the masquerade job, it hardly represents the kind of star comeback that the program's introduction intimated and that the audience would expect from the comeback narratives that had proliferated in the previous decade. The resemblance between "Rose's Last Summer" and *Sunset Boulevard* is limited to a focus on a faded film star in noirish circumstances. Rose's character, though much less developed, is actually much closer to that of Swanson's Eleanor Hallam of "My Last Duchess." Like Eleanor, she has survived in part through her sarcasm (although, unlike Eleanor, drinking has been a coping mechanism as well). Rose is fairly resigned to her age; what makes her feel alive again is making a living at acting—not dreams of a revived idolization by fans. When she starts to suspect that the Goodfields are trying to kill her, she has a flashback of her arrival at their house. Because the real Mrs. Goodfield is in on the ruse, Rose doesn't think of her job as criminal, and she is shown taking it on with great pleasure. She is excited about studying Mrs. Goodfield so she can learn how to imitate her movements and her voice. We see scenes of her rehearsing and relying less on alcohol to sustain her self-identity. Her acting serves her so well that she is able to successfully flee the Goodfields when they try to kill her. She acts being drunk—what they would expect of her—in order to run away.

What is significant about the episode is that it demonstrates how frequently popular culture was asking viewers to remember the past and how entrenched the trope of the faded female star had become in a variety of genres as a way to remember that past. In 1962 the film *Whatever Happened to Baby Jane* starring Bette Davis and Joan Crawford, arguably the most famous female film stars of the studio period still living at that time who had public struggles with their stardom, would push the horror ramifications of the trope to new levels—a film not just read as camp horror but produced as such. Another interesting level to the *Thriller* episode is its intertextual relation with the star persona of Mary Astor. Like Swanson's and Young's, Astor's career spanned both silent and sound films. She played a variety of roles in major films of the studio era—romantic ingénue (to John Barrymore's Don Juan in the silent film of that name), comical society matron (*Palm Beach Story, Midnight*), dignified society matron (*Dodsworth*), femme fatale (*The Maltese Falcon*), bitchy career woman (*The Great Lie*, for which she won an Oscar for Best Supporting Actress), understanding mother (*Meet Me in St. Louis, Little Women*). By the 1950s, like so many female stars, Astor found it harder to get challenging or important roles. The pressures of work in the studio system (which she loathed) and a troubled private life had contributed to a drinking problem. In 1959, the year before "Rose's Last Summer" was telecast, Astor published the first of her memoirs, *My Story: An Autobiography*, in which she honestly details her alcoholism and her opinions about the lack of roles in film for women her age. She acted in dozens of episodes in live television anthology series, including the part of Norma Desmond in a *Robert Montgomery Presents* remake of *Sunset Boulevard*.[26] (Montgomery was the first Hollywood film star to become a television anthology host.) Astor's comment on her television work voices what many female film stars must have felt about their opportunities in the medium: "I was so very 'lucky' to be wanted for work."[27] The process of acting in live television was exhilarating for Astor; like stage work, it required a kind of energy and spontaneity that film work lacked.

Astor frankly claims that television work also functioned as a diversion from her drinking. The absorption that was needed to concentrate in a

FIGURE 2.6
Publicity still
of Mary Astor
in costume
for her role in
Thriller. NBC,
1960. Author's
collection.

medium that had compressed rehearsal and shooting schedules kept her
from drinking while in production. The increasing trend of autobiographical frankness in star memoirs was distasteful to some literary critics. The *Los
Angeles Times* book critic Robert R. Kirsch negatively reviewed Astor's book,
finding no justification "for scrubbing dirty laundry in front of thousands
of people." He gives the gossip columnist and one-time mistress of F. Scott
Fitzgerald Sheila Graham a pass for writing *Beloved Infidel* because her book
gave details of the last days of an "important literary figure." Kirsch displays
no recognition of the cultural or symbolic power a female star might gain
from exposing the degree to which being a working mother was difficult,
or how lack of privacy, typecasting, and age discrimination were part of her
experience of the studio system and contributed to personal problems. He
makes no mention that his own newspaper published a laudatory interview
with Astor two years earlier in which she recommended self-discipline and
expanding challenges as ways for aging women to make their life meaning-

ful, although the paper was clearly exploiting the "aging angle" in its reporting of older stars.[28] While Astor concludes her book with the statement that her drinking is now under control and "Rose's Last Summer" ends with a potential revival of romance, it is likely that the invitation to remember that the episode extended to viewers the year after Astor's autobiography was published was an invitation to remember not only beautiful stars of long ago like Rose but the troubled afterlife of Astor, no longer young, struggling to survive in a transitional moment for the entertainment industries.

Barbara Jean Trenton in the 1959 *Twilight Zone* episode "The Sixteen Millimeter Shrine" is probably the character most like Norma Desmond in all of the television episodes examined here, and like all of the other characters of the fading female star trope, she is played by a star who had also attempted to circumvent the control of the studio system. Ida Lupino was forty-one when she played Trenton and one of the few female film stars to have formed her own production company in the aftermath of studio divestiture in the late 1940s. Lupino also directed some of the films she and her husband Collier Young produced, making her the first woman to direct feature-length Hollywood films since Dorothy Arzner's retirement in 1942. In the 1950s she became a nonproducing partner and "rotating" star in *Four Star Theater*, a filmed anthology series started by the film stars David Niven, Dick Powell, and Charles Boyer. In the mid- to late 1950s she directed episodes of several television programs, including her own situation comedy, *Mr. Adams and Eve*, in which she costarred with her husband Howard Duff as married film stars.[29]

Although Lupino had already played a comic, vain movie star in her own sitcom, Barbara Jean Trenton's vanity, like Norma Desmond's, is tragic, resulting in retreat and annihilation. The episode opens with Barbara Jean sitting alone in her Hollywood mansion, drinking, watching one of the old films in which she starred. Her agent, Danny (played by Martin Balsam), arrives and confers with Barbara Jean's housekeeper, who is worried about the star's isolation and fixation on watching her old films. Danny is there to tell Barbara Jean that he has lined up a part for her, a "good" one. She is apprehensive because the film is being made by a studio whose chief of production, Marty Sall, is someone she feels is "crude and tasteless." However, she is so eager for a film role that she agrees to meet with him anyway. When she finds out the part is for a "fortyish" mother, she rejects it, angering the producer and ruining her chance to work at that studio, and perhaps in all Hollywood, ever again. Upon returning home, she tells Danny that from now on, the curtains will be drawn and she will never leave the house. Trying to revive her, Danny brings one of her old costars, Jerry Hearndon, to see her. She is horrified that he has aged and sends them both away. True to her promise, she refuses to open the curtains and instead sits in the dark and watches her own movies endlessly. One night she wishes out loud to be that star again and is transported to the world on the screen. Danny, arriving the next day at the housekeeper's summons, turns on the projector and watches Barbara Jean, living now only in the world of the screen.

The similarities between Barbara Jean Trenton and Norma Desmond are immediately apparent. Like Norma, Barbara Jean likes to watch her old movies; she can't get enough of herself. The episode introduction by the host, Rod Serling, is a veritable treatise on the importance of looking to her identity: "Picture of a woman looking at a picture. Movie great of another time. Once brilliant star in a firmament no longer a part of the sky, eclipsed by the movement of earth and time. Barbara Jean Trenton, whose world is a projection room, whose dreams are made of celluloid. Barbara Jean Trenton, struck down by hit-and-run years and lying on the unhappy pavement, trying desperately to get the license plate number of fleeting fame."

The redundant, clichéd introduction forecasts the tragic degree to which Barbara Jean's world will devolve into a singular relation of specularity: Barbara Jean looking at herself. The specular relation she has with herself structures the narrative in almost every way, beginning with her looking at her own image and ending with the power of her look transforming the contours of reality. In between, the judgmental or uncomprehending gazes that others direct at her situate her narcissism as a response to assaults on her self-identity. For instance, while Marty Sall's offer of a "fortyish" mother role does not seem unreasonable or offensive, it does seem contingent on how good she "looks." Before making the offer, he asks her to lift the veil of her hat so that he can see her face more clearly. When Jerry Hearndon comes to visit, he looks at her with kindness, but his kindness is also incomprehension of her plight. He has become a successful businessman upon retiring from films and, like Danny, is "blind" to the fact that women are told that the successful business of femininity is to remain the object of the desiring gaze.

What is a woman identified with such a femininity to do when the only gaze desiring her is her own? In Barbara Jean's case, her past existence as a star, an identity that was constructed out of thousands of mass-produced images, means that she can be both spectator and spectacle. But the gothic overtones of the story (the dark mansion, the strange power of the screen) also suggest the tenuousness of such a dual stance. As Mary Ann Doane has

FIGURE 2.7 Barbara Jean Trenton (Ida Lupino) is enthralled with her own screen image in "The Sixteen-Millimeter Shrine." *The Twilight Zone*, CBS, 1959.

written about the gothic or "paranoid" woman's film, it is a genre structured around an obsession with specularity, a heroine who effects an investigative gaze while she herself is under intense surveillance. The heroine's identity is precarious, haunted by the image of another, prior woman whose fate the heroine seems doomed to repeat. Her role as owner of the investigative gaze is destabilized when she so desires to be desired by the male gaze (as that other woman was) that she is no longer able to differentiate between subject and object, herself and that other woman. For Doane, this structure refers to the primal construction of the feminine subject, castrated and unable to represent her own desire, destined to repeat the place of the mother, with whom fusion is associated with the dread of annihilation.[30]

"The Sixteen Millimeter Shrine" plays with this fearful constitution of feminine subjectivity within the structures of the gaze but also provides a twist on it. While Barbara Jean desires to be desired as the woman on the screen was once desired, the images of the other, prior woman are Barbara Jean herself, twenty years younger. Even as she realizes that she is not that age any longer, she refuses to relinquish the identity that was constructed out of the gaze of others when she was that age. When she is not successful with this strategy in the world outside her projection room, she repudiates anyone (Marty Sall, Jerry) who does not confirm her desirability. Ultimately she refuses to acknowledge the passing of time, represented in her conversation with Danny after the debacle of the meeting with Sall as a refusal to look at any of the new products of the commercial entertainment industries, in fact a refusal to look at anything at all:

> BARBARA JEAN: This is the world now . . . right in here [in my house].
> From now on, I keep the drapes drawn, the doors locked. I don't want any of the outside world coming in. Not the Marty Salls, or the movies without sentiment, actors without undershirts, rock 'n' roll, juke boxes!
>
> DANNY: Barbara, whether you like it or not, that's the way things are. . . . What do you do, Barbara, shut your eyes and say it doesn't exist because you can't see it?
>
> BARBARA JEAN: It doesn't have to exist if I shut my eyes. If I shut my eyes, it all disappears. If I wish hard enough, I can wish it all away. As of this moment . . . these are the thirties again. That was a carefree world, Danny. I'll make it that way again.

Barbara Jean believes that reality is a matter of who controls the gaze. She chooses to control her reality by deciding what she will look at. That she suggests that the 1930s were a carefree time is indicative of what stardom has allowed her to exclude from her gaze; those years could be described as such only by a woman who had wealth and beauty at that time. She chooses now to look only at herself, conflating the control of her gaze with the control she has over the projector she turns on and off when watching her own films. Thus begins her continuous movie marathon, leading to her assumption onto the screen. Her narcissistic look at her own image results in her *becoming* the image. As Doane argues, "Binding identification with desire (the basic strategy of narcissism), the teleological aim of the female look demands a becoming and, hence, a dispossession. She must give up the image in order to become it—the image is *too* present for her." Norma Desmond, after she murders Joe, becomes the image as well. Her narcissism has led to madness; she has given up the desire to *have* stardom again because, in the end, she has *become* the star again. She is the star *playing* Salome for an audience fascinated again with her on- and off-screen personas.[31] In fact she also *is* Salome, having, like that biblical character, killed the man who spurned her love.

In one of those uniquely weird *Twilight Zone* endings, Barbara Jean's wishes are imbued with more utopian potential than those of Norma Desmond. Transported to the screen, she does get to live in the past: Danny turns on the projector and watches her, excited and "alive" again, cavort-

FIGURE 2.8 Barbara Jean's empty chair after she is transported to the reality of the screen. *The Twilight Zone*, CBS, 1959.

ing with her costars from an earlier era. She does not lose the power of the gaze; she looks at him, blows a kiss, and runs into off-screen space. Jeffrey Sconce explains that *The Twilight Zone* typically offers characters and viewers the opportunity to experience a liminal state that can be either an "elsewhere" or a "nowhere."[32] Barbara Jean's afterlife in and on the screen may seem like a "nowhere" from the perspective of the people who deem her a has-been, but Danny knows she now lives in an "elsewhere" in which she is happy. Norma Desmond's exit, on the other hand, is a direct confrontation with the camera, the surrogate for "all those wonderful people out there in the dark" she thinks are still looking at her. She walks right into the camera lens, blurring its focus — rendering it and us incapable of seeing her clearly. Collapsing the clear differentiation between herself and Salome, herself and the camera, Norma Desmond can no longer be seen; she is now "nowhere."

My discussion of the narrative and generic dimensions of the programs starring Swanson, Young, Astor, and Lupino should make clear that I am not just making parallels between star biographies and the characters they played, nor arguing that these television programs offer a simple reflection of social problems of the middle-aged woman in the 1950s. To insist on relations between real life and fictional representation would put my discussion in a thorny, unresolvable theoretical position. The social and personal

FIGURE 2.9 Barbara Jean (Ida Lupino) blows a kiss from the screen world she inhabits at the end of "The Sixteen-Millimeter Shrine." *The Twilight Zone*, CBS, 1959.

problems of women are worked through *fantasy*, specifically through the generic conventions of the domestic melodrama, in which the wife or mother and home are idealized, or through the gothic, in which women's place is rendered as a "nowhere" or an "elsewhere" and the dread of annihilation troubles stable identity. Of course the gothic and domestic melodrama predated 1950s film and television drama, as well as this particular crisis of the female star experiencing the most recent transitions of the film industry. These forms had been popular with female audiences since the previous century, but their success in the 1950s as vehicles for the fading star myth is relevant to the way stars had been configured as part of American culture's social imaginary in continuity with Florence Lawrence's first emergence and comeback in the 1910s.

The material practices of the star-fan-industry dynamic, as exemplified in the trajectories of film stars from the 1910s through the age of television, were among the socially mediated practices that anchored constructions of modern subjectivities for most of the twentieth century. Film industry profit relied in part on manipulation of the cycles of standardization and innovation in personality types identified with particular stars. However, because the social imaginary registers *affectively* as well as through disciplinary frameworks establishing what is normative, it also registers the inevitable loss resulting from cyclical turnovers from old to new. Prior to the emergence of film and television narratives in the 1950s that traced the cultural place of the fading film star, fan magazines and the Hollywood press going back to the 1910s had constructed past film culture within similar affective terms in their frequent ponderings about the temporality of stardom. For example, although some fan magazine articles poke fun at the hairstyles and fashions of past female stars, or gleefully proclaim that the older dynasty must make way for the new, many are ruminations on the impact of rapid turnover in consumption cycles. Especially pertinent to the period are the melancholic essays that imagine stars from early films, such as Florence Lawrence, Mary Fuller, and Marguerite Clark, as either retiring to or attempting to return to films from a rural or secluded space — that is, a space outside of all temporal cycles except those of nature or the domestic sphere. One press account of the career ups and downs of Mae Murray even raises the specter of the gothic in its description of her and her son sequestered behind a "walled garden" or from behind a shuttered window.[33]

The similarities among these fan magazine articles, the industry press discourse of the 1950s and that decade's film and television narratives about fading stars and possible comebacks, suggest that industry, fans, and actors negotiated changes in the modes and meanings of cultural production, as well as women's place, through a consideration of the star's duration. That this duration is not measured so much in years as in cycles of what is considered new or relevant also suggests that stardom and its vicissitudes offer a hyperbolic version of femininity and its vicissitudes in the commodity culture of the twentieth century. The vicissitudes for both women and stars are related to their ups and downs in the commodity cycle. The social and psychic meanings of femininity in patriarchal culture allow the female star on the "out" side of the cycle to be positioned in an idealized space (the pastoral elsewhere or the domestic scene) or a frightening, uncanny space (the gothic mansion). Both spaces are separate from the public sphere, and while the pastoral elsewhere acts as guardian of all that was good and timeless about past film production, the domestic space welcomes the retiring actress to a "nowhere" — truly out of time, in death. The relegation of female stars to these spaces makes it hard for us to imagine them coming back. Eleanor in "My Last Duchess" and Rose in "Rose's Last Summer" can come back into the labor force as actresses, but not as stars who have been rewarded with cultural and economic capital by fans who desire their continuous appearance. Connie and Katie from the episodes of The Loretta Young Show are allowed to live "in time" when they compromise some of their ambition, glamour, and visibility for appreciation of the domestic space. Barbara Jean Trenton of "The Sixteen-Millimeter Shrine" escapes to a time out of time in an uncanny space facilitated by her movement from the gothic mansion to a place that exists only on film.

Some female stars, such as Swanson, Astor, Lupino, and Young, actually did return or endured in the 1950s, yet judging by the films and television programs they frequently appeared in, the examples of their continued real-life successes as working actresses or stars were not likely to be represented in fictional narratives. To put this more theoretically, the social reality of these actresses attested to the way their cultural and economic capital, accumulated after working for years in the industry, gave them a way to publicly and professionally insert a wedge between any easy conflation of femininity with powerlessness, abjection, pathology, subordination, and seclusion. Young in particular became one of the most powerful stars and producers in television, and the moniker "steel butterfly," given to her by her first husband, was resurrected many times in press accounts to characterize her longevity in the media industries as the result of an unyielding strength and a certain coldness packaged within an image of the feminine "weaker sex." At the same time, the female characters she portrayed on television were public sphere successes who were also shaped by the constraints of beauty and family norms for women.

Young and a number of other female stars worked hard for their success in television because the possibility for their continued success as film stars was more tenuous than that of their male counterparts in an industry and society structured according to patriarchal hierarchies. Their success as actresses playing women whose professional power is admired but also questioned, mitigated, or even destroyed exposes a fundamental contradiction for women in twentieth-century capitalist, patriarchal culture: they were necessary as laborers, images, and consumers but representationally (and often legally) relegated to the feminine subject position. This gendered position is a symbol of or even a performance of irrationality and weakness that elevates the masculine subject position in social power hierarchies. The abjectness or difficulties of the feminine subject position so infuse the stereotype of the fallen or faded star that when texts represent a fallen male star, he has to be distanced from pathology or subordination. For example, the melodrama *A Star Is Born*, the 1937 film about a woman's rise to stardom and a male star's descent, which was remade in 1954 to great success, depicts its fallen male star as tragic and ultimately ennobled through action. Much like Norma Desmond and Barbara Jean Trenton, Norman Maine (played by James Mason in the 1954 version) disappears into a kind of no-where when his star has faded; he is first obliterated as a name (someone calls him "Mr. Lester," the surname of his wife, after her phenomenal success), and then, in an act of suicide, he walks into the boundless sea. One possible interpretation of his character is to understand him as feminized; his spectacularization as star and his subsequent vulnerability to the absence of the adoring gaze upon him as his stardom fades put him in the feminine subject position. But the film's wedge to prevent the collapse of Norman Maine into the position of the pathological feminine is to make his choice of suicide strategic, noble, and tragic; he performs this act in order to free his successful wife from the public embarrassment of his alcoholism. (His alcoholism does put him in some kind of pathological category, but his last act nonetheless is meant to be seen as noble and freely chosen rather than compelled by sickness.)[34]

Another way to distance the faded male star from the feminine subject position is to render the situation of stars making comebacks comic. Comedy versions of fallen stars and comeback scenarios, like the melodramas discussed throughout this chapter, manage the anxieties emerging from the industrial transitions from a film culture to a television culture. But this management works within the potential of the genre to disrupt accepted gender identities and their relation to power hierarchies. In *Dreamboat*, a 1952 film comedy, Clifton Webb and Ginger Rogers portray former silent film stars who engage in a number of gendered and economic power reversals when their old films start showing up on television. The film represents a "doubly feminized" male character (a faded male star played by the gay actor Webb) regaining his "virility" as a man and actor, only for his success to be trumped by his female former costar, who literally owns the terms of his return.[35] In addition *Dreamboat* is significant for the subject of this study because it is one of the few films to actually depict the arrival of theatrically released films, including silent films, on the small screen in the late 1940s and early 1950s. This component of the era's intermedial transitions is perhaps as important to the phenomenon of star recycling as is the appearance of film stars on television programs, and its representation in popular culture and industry discourses warrants critical examination.

"Senile Celluloid"? Television Does the Movies and the Movies Do Television

Dreamboat is one of several films of the 1950s that demonstrate a fascination with the silent era in motion picture history. Not surprisingly the narratives of these films were structured around stars of that era, real or fictional: *Sunset Boulevard, Jeanne Eagles, The Buster Keaton Story, Valentino, Man of a Thousand Faces* (a biopic of Lon Chaney), *The Million Dollar Mermaid* (a biopic of Annette Kellerman), *Singin' in the Rain.*[36] Of these films, only *Singin' in the Rain* focuses on the period in which the industry made the transition to sound, but that tumultuous moment seems to have had great relevance for the film industry in the 1950s.[37] During the transition to sound the studios had to reorganize their financial underpinnings, recalibrate their assumptions about audience expectations (including what was assumed morally permissible to be heard), and renegotiate their legal obligations to stars. Stars—those who survived at all—had to relearn the art of screen acting, and many had to accept renegotiated contracts that stipulated cuts in pay.[38] As we've seen, the changes in the film industry and the arrival of television was also a transitional moment for studios and stars, especially female stars. Like *Sunset Boulevard, Dreamboat* references both periods, the 1920s and 1950s, as historic turning points for film stardom. However, like *Whatever Happened to Baby Jane* ten years later, it also imagines specifically what happens to old film stars when their films start showing up on the rival medium of television. If television programs were a crucial avenue for the recycling of film stars, so was television's broadcasting of old theatrical films at this time. This phenomenon proved to be an impetus for the film industry to reimagine its own past once again, as well as find new streams of revenue for its future.

Although the studio system's problems and challenges in the early 1950s consisted of more than its competition with television, the arrival of this new technology held, at least symbolically, a position similar to the one that the arrival of sound technology held in the late 1920s. Just as sound made the industry, stars, and audience rethink the pleasures and commercial viability of practices and forms characterizing the silent film and silent film stardom, so did television's presence make the industry, stars, and audience rethink the kinds of films being made and what kinds of stars to sustain and groom. In addition television's need for product to fill airtime—that is, the need to manage airtime flow—made the option of televising feature films produced by the film industry attractive to some stations. Television's voracious appetite for product and the profitability this could represent for the studios, which were just sitting on libraries of old films, was not lost on the film industry. But the film industry did not consist only of the studios; the property owners—exhibitors—were also part of the industry, and they were worried that if studios were to lease or sell their old films, theater audiences would dwindle to an even lower number than they already had. In an attempt to mollify exhibitors, the studios sold or leased their films to television very slowly. (The studios also had problems selling or leasing their films, not only the potential loss of audience for their current films but also in negotiating contracts with labor unions, such as the Screen Actors Guild and the American Federation of Musicians, for television performance rights and residuals for their members.) Few major studio productions were released to television before the mid- to late 1950s. But by 1957 *Photoplay* would claim that over one-third of viewers' television watching time was devoted to old Hollywood films, in which the stars of yesteryear "live again on your home screen."[39]

The slow release of films to television did not bother the networks. For instance, NBC was building a reputation for providing live programming, and President Pat Weaver was quoted in 1954 as saying that the network didn't have use for "senile celluloid." He believed that "old pictures never die, their audience slowly fades away."[40] However, films on television got very respectable ratings, and as we saw with the strategy WPIX used to build an identity as a non-network-affiliated station, film studio productions from earlier periods were important to many stations and were shown on them as early as the late 1940s. WPIX and other independent stations leased films from the minor studios (very minor: Monogram, PRC, etc.), independent production companies, and those who now owned rights to films once released by the major studios. (This is why schedules often had a mix of British productions with American films produced by David O. Selznick and Walter Wanger.) In addition to some A-quality, independently produced feature films, the leased films included grade B and lower films, western serials, cartoons, and some silent films, including action serials.[41]

The 1952 Twentieth Century-Fox film *Dreamboat* portrays some of the cultural fantasies around the revival of silent films and their stars on television in this period, suggesting ultimately that contrary to Weaver's beliefs, new audiences can emerge for old pictures and their stars.[42] *Dreamboat* is the story of Professor Thornton Sayre (Clifton Webb), a stuffy, snobbish English teacher at Underhill College. The students call him "Old Iron Heart" because he appears to be without sentiment. Widowed, he lives with his daughter, Carol (Ann Francis), who is a student at the college and, because of her uptight, serious demeanor, is also the butt of student jokes. One night a classmate invites Carol to her sorority house to watch television, setting Carol up to see the old silent films that students suspect star Professor Sayre, then known as Bruce Blair. Carol is embarrassed at recognizing her father as

FIGURE 2.10 Gloria Marlowe (Ginger Rogers) tries to convince Professor Thornton Sayre (Clifton Webb) that he should capitalize on his former fame as Bruce Blair. *Dreamboat*, Twentieth Century-Fox, 1952. Author's collection.

the silent-era "dreamboat" performing what she considers to be "shameless behavior." She confronts him later that night, and he admits that before he married her mother he had been discovered by the film actress Gloria Marlowe (Ginger Rogers) while teaching at the University of Southern California and was given a Hollywood contract as Bruce Blair. He is appalled that the films are showing up on television, especially since they are sponsored by the perfume company for which Marlowe now serves as pitch woman. Meanwhile the college board of directors are upset that his former stardom has "sullied" the academic environment, but Sayre promises to travel to New York to stop the films from being shown. In New York both father and daughter experience how Bruce Blair's renewed fame changes their lives. Carol, at first embarrassed at her father's openly romantic and virile displays as Blair, cultivates a more sexually expressive identity as she falls

FIGURE 2.11 Bruce Blair (Webb) and Gloria Marlowe (Rogers) in one of their silent films. *Dreamboat*, Twentieth Century-Fox, 1952. Author's collection.

in love with a young advertising executive (Jeffrey Hunter). Gloria Marlowe so desperately wants to be famous again that she tricks Sayre into thinking she will be without income if he gets an injunction against the owner of the films. In fact she has invested her money from her star years and is quite wealthy. He rebuffs her romantic and business advances, but his own interest in his past star persona starts to be revived. Nevertheless he sues Dependent Artists Agency (the title of which is an insider industry joke suggesting the current dependency of Hollywood actors on talent agencies), the company that owns the rights to the films, and wins the injunction. Meanwhile the college president, Matilda Coffey (Elsa Lanchester), follows him to New York, professes her love for Bruce Blair, and tells Sayre that he will be fired if he doesn't make love to her in the persona of the romantic "dreamboat." Sayre refuses, is fired, and accepts a Hollywood contract to make new films. At the premiere of his first new film—which is represented as a real motion picture starring Clifton Webb, *Sitting Pretty*—he finds out that Marlowe has just bought his contract.

Dreamboat is a satire of both silent film and 1950s television. The silent films starring Blair and Marlowe are the most clichéd melodramas popular in silent films and early talkies—Foreign Legion adventure films, World

War I flying ace and spy films, *Zorro*-like films (e.g., *The Return of El Toro*), and French Revolution action films—with passionate kissing between the two stars at the fade-out. Blair wins every battle with "nauseating regularity." Marlowe's characters are the stereotypical withholding woman or femme fatale who capitulates in the end to the dashing Blair. The telecast uses a projection speed that is too fast (which was the way silent films were often projected after the silent era, when silent film speed projectors were less common), making the films look even more ridiculous. Yet while *Dreamboat* sends up silent films as lacking in contemporary standards of verisimilitude, it doesn't depict them as entirely "senile celluloid." Because of the audience's intense investment in these old films on television, Bruce Blair and Gloria Marlowe become hot properties again.

The film also satirizes television, showing it to be a commercially bankrupt medium with dishonest and manipulative advertising. We see commercials for hair tonics, laxatives, and used cars, in addition to the commercials with Marlowe's exaggerated claims for "Exotic Perfumes." When Sayre takes the television company to court, he first tries to argue that the televising of his films has invaded his privacy. When the defense counters that he knew when he made them that films were meant to be seen and that television is the greatest educational medium ever (meaning it shouldn't embarrass a professor), Sayre puts television literally on the stand and demonstrates by turning on the set that the "educational value" of commercials consists in making products seem the answer to life's problems. To show that the televised films have also been changed to reflect not his original intentions as an actor but the sponsor's intentions, he brings in a kinescope of one of his movies as televised. The sponsor has actually changed some of the film's original intertitle cards to make a pitch for the product. In the new intertitles, Blair's character tells Marlowe's that he loves her because her Exotic Perfume drives him wild with desire—a change that Sayre says makes him look ridiculous. However, though he has rejected his identity as Blair, Sayre actually seems very much invested in keeping his film star persona coherent in the face of television's commercial imperatives. (This was the basis of the Roy Rogers lawsuit against Republic.)

Sayre's initial displeasure in seeing his films on television seems to be because they "satisfied the cravings of middle-aged glandular cases," those female fans who revive or newly discover their adoration for Bruce Blair. Middle-aged women seem to be the film's target, even though their interest in Blair makes them the unwitting catalysts in his own revived interest in the brash masculinity of his former identity. These "female she-wolves," as

Carol calls them, send Sayre flowers at his New York hotel, offering to kill their husbands or take him to a private island if he will love them. Matilda Coffey, played by Elsa Lanchester, an actress specializing in quivering, neurotic mannerisms, changes from a respectable authority figure to a love-sick woman who will stoop to sexual harassment to get Blair to make love to her. She implores Sayre, "[Let] the real you come through." Her character's search for the truth of the person behind the façade enacts what Richard deCordova has identified as the hermeneutic of stardom: a surface or depth logic in which the truth is the most private, which is to say the most sexual.[43] She demands that the private persona (Sayre) reveal the truth of the public persona (Blair) as the "real" truth, rather than vice versa. Since Blair is the sexually expressive persona, she reasons that his sexual magnetism must be the logic behind the mask of the uptight Sayre. No matter how ridiculous or despicable she is made to appear as a female fan, Coffey has correctly identified that Blair has a powerful hold over Sayre. However, her demand also exposes the tenuous distinction between public and private. As Professor Thornton Sayre he is a private individual in the sense that his life as a professor is defined in shunning the mass media, but Sayre is also the identity he claims publicly to be. Bruce Blair is the identity known to all the public, but his relation to Sayre has been kept hidden, that is, kept private. Coffey's demand for the truth resembles not only the hermeneutic of stardom identified by deCordova but some of the logics of the closet.

The closet, of course, is the term most often used to separate private and public by suppressing or hiding a homosexual's sexual orientation in a homophobic society that either denies, devalues, or criminalizes same-sex sexual activity. From the place of the closet, the male homosexual may silence the suspicions of the other with the appearance of asexuality or sexual noncommitment (i.e., remaining a bachelor) or through smokescreens of normative heterosexual masculinity, such as becoming a husband or displaying bravado in a variety of pursuits associated with masculine superiority over women. It is a place of tenuous security, often associated with any number of things meant to be kept secret. In the 1950s closeted individuals were sometimes the particular targets (or agents) of the political witch hunts ostensibly meant to reveal communists in hiding.

The way Carol's college classmates bring Bruce Blair to her attention is depicted as a mean-spirited outing. They take great glee in exposing Sayre as something he pretends not to be. And, like the closeted men fired from the government and military in the 1950s, Sayre's relation to the identity he has kept hidden affects his reputation and ultimately results in his being fired.

This reading is partially supported by some of the extratextual aspects of Clifton Webb's off- and on-screen personas. Although we can identify him as a closeted man since his homosexuality was never publicly declared, there is no evidence that either Webb or his studio ever concocted a heterosexual smokescreen for his behavior, unlike attempts by Universal Studios, the agent Henry Willson, and Rock Hudson to shield Hudson's homosexuality (see chapter 3). The only significant other featured in Webb's promotion was his mother, and his characters, with rare exceptions, were fussy bachelors, widowers, or husbands who didn't express much interest in their wives.[44] The character Sayre performs in his new Hollywood film shown at the end of *Dreamboat* is Mr. Belvedere, an overly fastidious bachelor who uses his nanny job as an opportunity to write a gossipy tell-all book about the town's inhabitants. To great economic success (there were two Mr. Belvedere sequels to *Sitting Pretty*), the studio cast Webb in a series of roles identifying him with the "feminized man," including Professor Sayre in *Dreamboat*.

However, while it might make sense to map some aspects of the closet and outing onto how Sayre positions his hidden and private persona, this mapping could devolve into a reductive binary. The film actually orchestrates a series of convoluted, overlapping, and unexpected identity formations for Webb's character. This mapping also reduces the conflicts of the film to the sexual, when they are also about class and the cultural capital associated with gendered understandings of high and low cultures. Sayre is disturbed by the return of Brue Blair because he associates that part of his life not only with an unsuitable romantic relationship with Marlowe but also with the commercial debasement of his professorial relation with art. The cultural capital he has earned as a Shakespeare scholar is put in peril by his association with the mass-cultural status of the movies. What's worse for him than having appeared in films is that these films are now showing up on television, a medium through which the commercial underpinnings of the mass-culture industries are made explicit and further debased. He despises both movies and television because of their female fan base, which is represented by the adoring women who desire not only Bruce Blair but also the perfume Marlowe peddles in the advertisements that underwrite the appearances of the two stars in the new medium. Although his sexual rejection of Coffey is actually played quite gently, as are his interactions with Carol, these scenes can be read as the text's disavowal of the misogyny supporting its representation of female sexual desire. Coffey and the female television viewers who send Sayre/Blair aggressive mash notes are pictured as pathological in their inability to separate fiction from reality and dangerous in their willingness to inflict harm on their husbands (as in the fan who offers to kill her husband if Blair will marry her) or on other men who reject their sexual advances (as represented by Coffey, who fires Sayre).

Another complicating factor in reading the film solely in terms of the closet is that while Sayre never compliments his female fans or agrees to the screening of his films on television, the effects of the films' reappearance on television ultimately offer a welcome renewal for him in two ways: he begins to enjoy the revival of a favorable critical discourse on his acting, which is compatible with the professorial identity of one who can apply critical standards to the arts, and also entails an appreciation for his past ability to engage in the manly arts of physical prowess and masculine seduction of women. If he has kept aspects of his life in the closet, it is, in comic fashion, a closet that turns upside down the common understandings of the metaphor's relation to sexual orientation. It is the persona of Blair, the one who fulfills (on-screen) heteronormative expectations, that Sayre has been hiding, rather than the effeminate, bachelor-widower he has been presenting openly for the past twenty-five years. The real turning point for Sayre in accepting the heteronormative, masculine persona that television has revealed is his brawl with a male television viewer over his films. While sitting in the hotel bar, he overhears a husband and wife discussing his acting style as they watch one of his films on the bar's television set. The woman finds Blair handsome, romantic, and brave. This reaction arouses her husband's jealousy, as well as his critical approbation, and as a result he makes disparaging remarks about "that drink of water." Sayre reacts, and the two start fighting, with Sayre looking over his shoulder at the television for tips from Blair's acrobatic combat style. Sayre finds a renewed virility, and the Hollywood film industry finds a new star from an old one on television when he agrees to a new film — not television — contract.

Is the comedy drive of *Dreamboat* normative, then, rather than truly disruptive? It does turn Sayre's world upside down only to return him to a more socially acceptable identity for a heterosexual man (even if he rejects amorous overtures from Coffey). However, his performances as Blair may not place him securely within normative masculinity as structured within the binary terms that make femininity its opposite. The dashing bravado displayed in Blair's enactment of movie melodrama heroes is overdone; his stern looks and clenched fists are excessive and appear more so by the cranked-up projection speed used in the broadcast. As Richard Dyer argues about the male pin-up photo (including those of male movie stars), displays that strain "after what can hardly ever be achieved, the embodiment of the phallic mystique," not only objectify the male subject but also destabilize heteronormative masculinity.[45]

Much of the film's camp humor is produced in the tension between what we, the audience, thinks is funny, Sayre/Webb's over-the-top performance of masculinity as Bruce Blair that strains credulity, and what we are supposed to believe the film characters think is both possible and right, that Sayre can now transition from the effeminate male to the manly man. The clip from Sitting Pretty, a real film starring Webb in his most famous "effeminate" role and well known to audiences of the time as one of his central star vehicles, serves as a punchline for Dreamboat and functions like a very sly wink about the charades of masculinity, for it suggests that heteronormative masculinity, of which virility is an assumed attribute, is just an act. The joke also favorably spotlights the power of the film industry to manipulate star images to its economic advantage. The Mr. Belvedere series of films were among Fox studio's most popular films in the 1950s, and the references to them at the end of Dreamboat are meant to remind viewers of the power of film over television in producing successful entertainment.[46]

The film's comic convolutions of Sayre's, Blair's, and Webb's subject positions as heteronormative masculine and feminized masculine, intellectual and mass-cultural idol complicate the viewer's ability to identify a singular masculinity or cultural position for the character. However, the ability of Sayre and Webb to don the mask of virility as the situation merits suggests that the role of movie star is less of a risk for the older man than it is for the older woman. Marlowe's rediscovery brings her product endorsement deals in television and a nightclub singing act, not a new film acting contract. Marlowe, whose first name "Gloria" may be a reference to Gloria Swanson and who never seems to appear anywhere dressed in anything other than full-length fancy dress, has an affinity with some of the female stars under examination in this book. Through television and its exploitation of glamorous female film stars, she finds a way to connect again with female audiences by drawing their attention to products and behaviors that promise to make them too the object of the adoring gaze. Unlike the many female silent stars covered in the fan magazines of the 1910s–20s, she does have a real place in time, albeit behind a television cosmetics counter hawking her products. While the potential for revived film stardom that equals what she had in the past, or what Sayre achieves, is an unlikely scenario for Marlowe, she gets the last laugh in the film because she can afford to buy his contract. Unlike many of the film's characters who have hidden aspects of their personas—Sayre hiding his Bruce Blair identity; Carol hiding the

FIGURE 2.12 Gloria Marlowe (Rogers) becomes wealthy by hosting television screenings of her old films and endorsing commercial products. *Dreamboat*, Twentieth Century-Fox, 1952. Author's collection.

sexually attractive young woman behind her mousy, intellectual demeanor; Coffey hiding her fan fantasies about mass-cultural idols—Marlowe is what she says she is: a woman interested in economic power over everything else. Even when she deceives Sayre to make him believe she needs money, this is so he will agree to the continued television broadcasts of their old films, an arrangement that interests her because it benefits her economically. While her image as star may be subject to the commodity cycles of the 1950s, in which female stars of a certain age are on the outs (it seems significant that she is not offered a renewed contract to act as a romantic lead in films), her ownership of the male star's film contract results in his economic and artistic subordination to her.

The film provides successful closure for Marlowe as a businesswoman and has presented us with a dizzying array of gendered identity changes for Sayre/Blair. In these ways *Dreamboat* would seem to have a sophisticated take on many of the issues addressed by the case studies in this chapter. However, the film's image of the female fan and her relation to the female star suggest that it should also be seen as imposing norms for feminine desire. The television industry of the 1940s and 1950s had an incentive to hire female film stars whose glamour could serve as a lure to attract female consumers it understood in normative gender terms. The stars' connection to the female consumer or fan, however, also put them in association with much that was feared about mass commercial culture, and this was perhaps as responsible for the press's ambivalent attitudes toward them as any glamorous "chi-chi-ness." While Norma Desmond's refusal to fade away, evident in both her over-the-top glamour and her desire to author her own return, is meant as a sign that she is delusional and narcissistic, and suggests wider cultural ambivalence about the aging female star, it also reminds us that female stars were foundational to the power of the Hollywood film industry. Female film stars moving into television, even those working under the specter of characters like Desmond and Marlowe, actually multiplied the valences of glamour and authorship. They made the terms function as signs of their expertise in matters of concern to women and as a vehicle to achieve public visibility. The female film star who invested in television as a producer, director, and actress and who used the public visibility offered by the new medium was able to secure some agency in a place and a time not granted to most women performers in the transformed environment of the Hollywood film studio system of the 1950s.

CHAPTER THREE

≡

MAUREEN O'HARA'S "CONFIDENTIAL" LIFE

Recycling Hollywood Film Stars in the 1950s through
Scandalous Gossip and Moral Biography

A March 1957 *Confidential* magazine article described the established Hollywood film star Maureen O'Hara as having "taken the darndest position to watch a movie in the whole history of the [Grauman's Chinese] theater," spread across three seats with her "happy Latin American" boyfriend in the middle seat. In the playful tone characteristic of its account of the incident the article proclaims that as "far as Maureen was concerned, this was double feature night and she was giving away more than dishes."[1]

Less than a month after this issue was distributed to a claimed circulation of four million readers, the television show *This Is Your Life* broadcast a live episode honoring O'Hara. The host, Ralph Edwards — ever sentimental and presumptuous — lost no opportunity to present O'Hara as a stereotypical "fighting Irish Colleen" whose life revolved around her close-knit family of parents, siblings, and young daughter. A variety of father-mentor figures — including O'Hara's actual father, the actor Charles Laughton, the producer Erich Pommer, the director John Ford, and a famous Irish soccer player — appeared on camera to wish this "very nice girl" well (Laughton's words) and to testify to her loyalty and professionalism. Neither the annulment of her first marriage nor the messy custody battle involved in the divorce of her second husband were mentioned, as Edwards focused on O'Hara's sympathetic mothering abilities. The *Confidential* article, and O'Hara's anger over it, which would result in a multimillion-dollar lawsuit and legal reprisals from the state of California, were also absent from Edwards's account, despite the fact that they could be said to define O'Hara's life at that moment as much as anything revealed by the popular television show.

In this chapter I examine O'Hara's recycling through new media in the late 1950s to explore the conditions under which two seemingly disparate discourses about a film star could circulate simultaneously. Television, one of the new media, created knowledge about film stars at this time by producing moral biography, while the scandal magazines circulated star narratives through outrageous gossip. Scandal magazines wedded aspects of tabloid newspapers from the 1920s and 1930s with those of detective and "girlie" magazines that proliferated in the postwar era. Populist but often cynical in tone, their layout was heavily dependent on composite photos (combining elements from more than one photo or drawing), and their subject matter concerned famous people (politicians and entertainers in particular) allegedly acting in socially, legally, and usually sexually transgressive ways. Although the trial discussed in this chapter temporarily halted some of their practices, these magazines can be seen as the precursors of the tabloid magazines and newspapers that resurfaced in the 1960s and 1970s and still exist today.[2] Both television and the particular scandal magazines under discussion here became available for mass consumption between 1949 and 1959. As discussed in chapter 2, in this period the media industries' production, distribution, and regulation of social knowledge were inflected by economic and legal restructuring of the film industry and its star system, by increased competition among all leisure activities, and by new understandings of audience segmentation and differentiation.

Because audiences experienced television and scandal magazines and their promotional discourses at the same time (a fact sometimes acknowledged, at least implicitly, by contemporary commentators), *contradictions* rather than radical ruptures in the social imaginary could be exposed when multiple players in the new media made exclusive or competing truth claims. The March 1957 recyclings of Maureen O'Hara through moral biography and scandalous gossip complicated the exclusivity of the truths that television and scandal magazines promised to tell about the stars and, in the process, revealed the complex multiplicity of publicly available images of sexuality. But these recyclings also suggest that competing media and their discourses still shared basic epistemological frameworks for knowing, desiring, and identifying with film stars. That is, both television's moral biography and scandal magazines' gossip relied on revelations of the private behind the public face, with the private usually associated with the sexual. These revelations, as well as the *will to reveal*, are part of what Foucault has argued are the technologies of the self in modernity, an era in which "an apparatus for producing an ever greater quantity of discourse about sex" has been installed in, by, and through institutions, collectives, and individuals as a way to administer the body as a subject of knowledge. An "incitement" to discourse about sexuality, while explicitly pursued by scandal magazines in risqué titles, composite photos, and titillating topics, was also operative in *This Is Your Life*'s strategic silence about sexuality that functioned in its own way "alongside the things said" by *Confidential* and other scandal magazines.[3]

The new media of the 1950s competed and converged through their use of stars whose careers and personas had been established by the film industry in the preceding decades. The perspective they offer on the vivid and precarious world they show in the present is stabilized by their claims to offer a privileged, secure view of the past. The star persona of Maureen O'Hara and its various recyclings at this contradictory moment offer a point of contact between the two media.

This Is Your Life and Moral Biography

Since the late 1910s and 1920s film stars have been embodiments of an "ordinary-extraordinary" dialectic regulating the spectator's knowledge of the star.[4] While film stars fascinate and often appear desirable precisely because of that dialectic, some critics argue that television constructs its stars as familiar persons with whom the viewer is more likely to feel a sense of intimacy.[5] As briefly discussed in chapter 2, Denise Mann has examined the way television in the 1950s constructed film stars in relation to concepts of familiarity and ordinariness. In her study of film stars hosting or guest-starring in comedy-variety programs of that period, Mann finds that increased star agency (exemplified by the many male stars who formed their own production companies in the postwar period), the subsequent highly publicized negotiations over image, and the forging of ties with commercial sponsors through television diminished the public's perception of stars as individuals, instead heightening the perception of stars as corporate property. These factors resulted in a "radical transformation in the social imaginary that had . . . bound Hollywood stars to fans." The popular comedy-variety genre contributed to this transformation through the host's direct address to an audience presumed to share his cynical stance about both commercial sponsorship and Hollywood film stardom. The host (often a former radio star) negotiated a distance from the film star guest in skits that capitalized on the star's lingering appeal as an "idol of consumption," while also showing him or her to be an intrusive and threatening force, "the focal point of the public's combined hostility and admiration."[6]

Mann argues that comedy-variety programs assumed a popular memory of past Hollywood stardom as excessive glamour and hedonistic consumption. By ignoring components of star personas that had also constructed them as authentic and ordinary (therefore available for empathetic identification) the programs devised strategies to construct this memory as a hostility that would benefit the less spectacular televisual personality. While textual evidence confirms that comedic genres typically used direct address and parodic strategies that exposed the constructedness of a star's authenticity, I would argue that other genres used a similar direct appeal to feature film stars in ways that did not suggest a radical transformation in the bond between fans and film stars. Some producers and other players within the television industry presumed a residual audience desire to identify with stars within the parameters developed by the film industry and fan cultures since the 1920s. In other words, the social imaginary in the 1950s, as constituted within the terms of the star-fan relationship, is not radically changed so much as accommodating the fluctuating emphases and contradictory messages created under the pressure of new media.

This Is Your Life, a popular television program in the 1950s, combined aspects of talk, game, inspirational, and variety shows to present stars in settings or situations that emphasized their private lives and feelings. It provides an example of one way television in the 1950s negotiated film stardom within terms of familiarity and ordinariness. Like many variety shows of the time, it did trade on the glamour of Hollywood film stardom: Edwards often surprised the program's star subjects at award ceremonies or premieres. Maureen O'Hara was surprised in this way at the press interviews before the 1957 Academy Awards ceremony. However, the primary focus was on the ordinary human being behind the star, the star as authentic individual. Authenticity was displayed on the program in a variety of registers specific to television's particular technological capacities and representational strategies, including episode scheduling, therapeutic confession to in-studio and at-home viewers, and live transmission.

Episodes of *This Is Your Life* focusing on stars and other entertainment personalities during its run in the 1940s (radio) and 1950s (television) were scheduled to alternate with those presenting the life stories of "ordinary" people who contributed in some way to their communities. Stars were thus favorably associated with ordinary people, specifically those with a philanthropist bent. Ordinary people became honored media celebrities, hence extraordinary in the national context rather than unsung do-gooders known only to their local communities. Both kinds of guests were given mementos of their appearance and honored at postshow parties with the people who shared memories and stories on the program. The gifts are exemplary of the way the show attempted to extend its effects into the everyday fabric of the guests' lives: they are quite specifically "memory objects." Bracelets with charms representing milestones in the subject's life (e.g., a baby carriage, a movie camera) were given to female subjects or to the wives of male subjects. Home movie projector systems, including a 16 mm film of the evening's *This Is Your Life*, were another popular gift. These gifts were material and continuous reminders of the way the program was able to shape a meaningful narrative from subjects' lives. They also linked the celebrity guests to ordinary viewers, and both guests and viewers to consumer products, specifically the jewelry maker Marchel Jewelers and the home movie equipment manufacturer Bell and Howell; these were brand-name products that were probably familiar to and possibly owned or coveted by viewers at home.

Edwards's conception of the program provided justification for constructing a schedule that alternated between ordinary people and stars. In trade and fan magazines he downplayed the role that *This Is Your Life* might have in promoting show business, constructing media personalities, or endorsing consumer goods, emphasizing instead the way it revealed the exemplary biography of a moral person: "'In whatever category we pick our principle, we always try,' Edwards explains, 'to make sure it is a person whose deeds and character show a sympathetic nature and whose endeavors in life have been of a constructive nature.'"[7] The program's constitution of the "constructive" life was overdetermined: Edwards not only narrated a moral life story (all the while prodding witness testimony in that direction); he also often surprised guests while they were appearing at charity functions. In many episodes he announced that a check or gift (such as a television) was given to a charitable institution in the honoree's name.

In one interview Edwards explicitly states that the theme of the program is "Love Thy Neighbor."[8] This Christian philosophy was supported by the melodramatic and therapeutic rhetorical strategies in his sentimental

FIGURE 3.1
Ralph Edwards
was dubbed
a "spiritual
prosecutor"
for his probing
dissections of
celebrity guests
like Lillian
Roth in *This Is
Your Life*. NBC,
1954. Author's
collection.

introductions and coaching of both subject and witnesses to related touching stories about the subject's past. Such stories demonstrated the subject
overcoming obstacles, helping others on the way, and ultimately reaching
goals of happiness. In this way stars' lives became emblematic of moral jour-
neys, with surprise guests appearing like cheerleaders on the sidelines or
the weeping women of Jerusalem on the way of the cross, depending on
whether the life depicted was a happy one (O'Hara) or unhappy (Frances
Farmer or Lillian Roth). In the episode featuring the former actress-singer
and notorious alcoholic Lillian Roth, for example, Edwards actually uses the
metaphor of the journey—apparently to hell and back—to describe the subject's life: "Confusion, distress and tragedy walked by your side even as you
rose to the top—and soon all glamour was stripped from you, as drink follows drink, and you sink into a stupor that was to last for 16 years."[9] Roth's
story is indicative of how crucial a narrativizing of the past was to the pro-

gram. Without a past life that could be dramatized—or sensationalized—as full of suffering, and in Roth's case even sordidness, it is less likely that Roth would have been profiled at all, as her few films and recordings were from the 1920s and 1930s and not in circulation.

The melodramatic arc to Edwards's storytelling—the very public and emotional revealing of authentic suffering and virtue in the private life—was central to *This Is Your Life* from its inception as a radio program. In a 1946 episode of Edwards's popular radio game show *Truth or Consequences*, he presented the story of a disabled World War II veteran having a hard time adjusting to postwar life. Edwards's spin on the veteran's situation was in line with the goal of the "inspirational" shows, that the story of someone's life can be an example of hope and courage to others. Edwards and his producers received such enthusiastic feedback from this episode of their usually wacky game show that they created *This Is Your Life* in 1948 to tap into what they perceived as the audience's need for inspiration through moral biography.

This Is Your Life contained elements of the quiz and game show (subjects were asked to guess the identity of speakers behind the stage curtain or in the wings and were rewarded with prizes) and the variety show (the spectacle of surprise, witnesses appearing as guest stars, stories about or photos of subjects providing occasions for entertaining jokes). The format attests to television's long-standing tendency to mediate a relation between consumerism and confessional practices that produce social subjectivity under the rubric of therapy. Mimi White, who has extensively theorized television's engagement of therapeutic and confessional discourses, cautions against claiming that "any individual program is singular" in this practice, but she is interested in how particular programs from the 1980s–90s utilize the therapeutic process.[10] *This Is Your Life* constructs some very specific strategies in the pursuit of the therapeutic goal, many of which were commented on by critics and advertisers at the time, and which made it stand out among other programs.

The Christian philosophy that imbued Edwards's narration of moral biographies is not in and of itself therapeutic; it is its transmission in particular rhetorical strategies that forges the link between therapy and inspiration. The show's reliance on confessions from guests and witnesses to tell the life story is an obvious link to the therapeutic, in that confessions are assumed to lead to a "cure" by releasing the tension caused by keeping the secret and by providing clues to self-identity. (Foucault would argue that confessional speech enacts self-identity.) Edwards's performance as host caused one *Time* magazine writer to dub him a "spiritual prosecutor."[11] Indeed he sometimes prodded both subjects and witnesses to confess by asking them leading or coercive questions. He bluntly asked the former film star Frances Farmer what had landed her in a sanitarium in the midst of what appeared to be a very promising film career: "Was it drugs? Was it alcohol?" Then he brought out guests who testified to the depths to which she had fallen before appearing on *This Is Your Life* as a step in her rehabilitation. Marsha Cassidy, in her discussion of 1950s daytime "confessional quiz shows" (such as *Strike It Rich*, *Queen for a Day*, and *It Could Be You*, the last produced by Edwards), identifies an "I/you" paradigm for such coercive confessions. She argues that these shows exemplify a storytelling mode in which the guest is required to confess aspects of her life, while her ability to tell her story in the first person ("I") is continually undermined by a male host who interrupts her and retells it in his own words and with his own spin ("you"). Such shows validate the silencing or controlling of the female storyteller by offering cash or prizes as compensation.[12]

While *This Is Your Life* did give gifts to its subjects, Edwards continually attested, in both publicity and the show itself, to less tangible rewards, such as helping guests feel appreciated by the community and find happiness and sometimes boosting a stagnant career, as he claimed the show did for Lillian Roth, whose autobiography became a best-seller and a film after her appearance.[13] Such a result was widely circulated and used to validate the host's "prosecution." In other words, Edwards did his best to position the program's affect as sympathetic and touching rather than the product of an authoritarian coercion. Although later in this chapter I will discuss the degree to which *This Is Your Life* participated in strategies of control and silencing, apparently some advertisers were convinced that Edwards's approach was warm and sentimental. Hazel Bishop dropped its sponsorship of *The Martha Raye Show* to sponsor *This Is Your Life* because the company's president Raymond Spector was reportedly in favor of the "sentimental and heavily emotional" in programs. Spector clearly connects the affective aspects of the program's confessionals to consumer confidence: the audience believes *This Is Your Life*, and "if they believe it, then they will believe Hazel Bishop lipstick doesn't smear off."[14]

The program's exploitation of television's capacity for liveness was also a key factor in its success in constructing stars as moral and authentic private individuals. *Liveness* is the technological capacity of the medium to broadcast an event simultaneously with its occurrence. Although not naturally derived from television's electronic technology, liveness has come to signify copresence, immediacy, the capturing of the true or authentic moment as it unfolds.[15] Rhona Berenstein has argued that early commentators on television's possibilities were particularly invested in positing a relation between liveness, immediacy, and proximity to articulate the way the medium could evoke a sense of intimacy for and with viewers and convince them of the actuality of what they were seeing and hearing. A specifically televisual acting style was presumed crucial to television's success with audiences in this regard; consequently coaches emphasized a naturalistic style originating in techniques that matched those qualities of liveness and intimacy.[16]

It was the combination of liveness, immediacy, and surprise that made *This Is Your Life* an especially effective and privileged intimate site for recycling Hollywood film stars. The liveness simulated copresence with the audience, evoking the possibility for the viewer to experience immediacy and intimacy, while the surprising of star guests allowed the program to negotiate key modalities of star identity in relation to the viewing audience (some of whom were perhaps fans or former fans of the stars). Stardom's appeal, constituted in the partially revealed tension between the ordinary, private self behind the glamorous, public persona, was enacted in Edwards's catching the stars off-guard. At these moments of surprise the stars appeared as vulnerable and ordinary as anyone discovering he or she is on national television. (Some, like Nat King Cole, looked more than momentarily horrified.) As their eyes welled with tears when reunited with family, friends, and past mentors, the stars' usually disciplined composure was strained, and viewers sensed they have glimpsed the authentic person. *This Is Your Life* might have offered the acting theorists and coaches the perfect televisual performance according to the terms outlined above: ultranaturalistic because it appeared to not require acting, only spontaneous response to the program's surprise.

Thus the attraction of *This Is Your Life* both for sponsors and for the Hollywood community promoting films and stars was its simultaneous association with the glamour of celebrity, the therapeutic qualities of moral biography, and the intimate authenticity conveyed by television's liveness. Indeed the celebrity's surprise, because indicative of his or her noninvolvement in the planning or production of the show, naturalizes the association between star aura and product. It is therefore hardly surprising that the program became popular with both audiences and sponsors.[17]

The Rise of *Confidential* and Scandalous Gossip

The publisher Robert Harrison claimed that the excitement caused by the 1951 televised hearings of Senator Estes Kefauver's committee on organized crime was the inspiration for creating *Confidential* magazine in 1952. Thomas Doherty argues that television viewers experienced the hearings as "spontaneous, unbidden, intimate, and extended."[18] Harrison learned from them what Ralph Edwards had already established in a different kind of text: that the spectacle of secrets being revealed about powerful people had public appeal that could be commercially exploited if done in a way to promote intimate rapport with readers. Although the hearings may have been the most immediate inspiration for his launching of a scandal publication venture, Harrison was already poised for entry into scandal magazines by the start of the decade. He had vast experience in tabloid newspapers and film industry trade publications since the 1920s, and by the 1940s he was producing "girlie" magazines such as *Whisper* (which he later successfully revamped into a scandal magazine after *Confidential*'s popularity was proven). "Girlie" or "cheesecake" magazines did well in the 1940s, helping to create and sustain the American GI's interest in pin-up art. These and other tabloid publications flooded the market as wartime paper rationing was lifted in 1950. Although many of the titles failed, the theme of female sexual transgression was an already established frame, and *Confidential*'s success in featuring scandal stories about stars and other famous people, as well as exposing racketeering, consumer scams, and political peccadilloes, resulted in dozens of copycat magazines and hundreds of "one-shots" (one-time publications focused on one star or theme) in the 1950s.[19] Those magazines that enjoyed sustained prosperity throughout much of the decade did not owe all their success to the availability of cheap paper and exploitation of name figures. At least three other dynamically related factors secured their popularity with the public and (at least temporary) protection from actions taken by Hollywood and the state: (1) the general legal climate in the 1950s surrounding issues of libel, privacy, and obscenity; (2) the magazines' uses of sources (many who willingly signed affidavits), state-of-the-art surveillance research methods, and what we may call a "tabloid" or "trash" aesthetic for narratives and graphic design; and (3) the ability to sustain plausible fictions about stars at a time when it was no longer clear that the official voices of Hollywood could do so. The magazines realized that the studios' power was declining and that stars, as the symbols of that system, were left vulnerable to attack. *Confidential* and other scandal sheets could even efficiently produce copy about stars by recycling Hollywood's own stories about them.

Cultural commentary and legal cases concerning alleged scandalous behavior or the reporting of it tend to conceptualize libel, privacy, and obscenity as mutually imbricated notions, even though each has a separate legal definition and each can be the cause of a distinct legal action. A variety of historians have pointed to how legal and social institutions have understood—even if only tacitly—all three concepts as concerned with the boundaries and regulation of civility, of what should remain private and what should be public.[20] It is beyond the scope of this chapter to explore all the complex issues surrounding the mutual imbrication of libel, privacy, and obscenity as legal and social concepts throughout history or even in the 1950s, but I will return to their intertwining when I discuss the state's response to *Confidential* in the 1957 trial.

Although the status of defamation laws in the 1950s still made libel "the celebrity's most desirable remedy against scandal magazines," the outcome of civil libel cases was uncertain at this time, at least in the California courts.[21] Not only did testimony at defamation trials require the further recycling of the scandalous stories alleged to be libelous, but if the celebrity had not suffered pecuniary loss, the libelous material had to be defamatory on its face, without the need of innuendo or inducement. Under a special civil code in California law, which exemplified the degree to which the First Amendment was held sacred, if the judge or jury believed that the article was susceptible to an innocent as well as a defamatory interpretation, it was highly likely that the ruling would be in favor of the defendant.[22] Because the scandal magazines anticipated the legal implications of civil libel cases, they followed a number of "research" procedures and made stylistic choices to elude "defamation on its face" interpretations of the law.

Celebrities could bring action against the scandal magazines for invasion of privacy, but as one federal judge put it in 1956, the state of the privacy law was like "a haystack in a hurricane."[23] Originally devised from the famous argument by Samuel Warren and Louis Brandeis in 1890, civil privacy cases concerned the more nebulous area of private feelings, protecting the individual from emotional distress. Warren and Brandeis had argued for privacy law as "a remedy for the threats to personality and feelings posed by 'recent inventions and business methods,' such as sensationalist journalism, advertising practices, and . . . [the] newly invented Kodak, and similar cameras."[24] Warren and Brandeis had thought the technological and media developments of the 1890s made legal protection of privacy especially pressing, so it is not surprising that an increasing number of cases concerning privacy came to state or federal supreme courts in the 1950s as new media, like television and scandal magazines, and new technologies, like sophisticated, often miniature surveillance devices (sound recorders, wiretaps, and cameras), proliferated in use throughout the decade. As with libel cases, bringing action against the scandal magazines for invasion of privacy was tricky; celebrities had to prove that the magazines not only inflicted emotional distress (not too difficult) but were devoid of any educational or entertainment value (much harder). Yet the law could favor the privacy of the star over the press's constitutional privileges if the material published was considered to be of such an intimate nature that its disclosure violated the community's notions of decency.[25]

However, at this time definitions of obscenity—that vague concept having to do with what was considered outside the bounds of decency—were expanding legal, commercial, and social ideas about that issue. The social historians John D'Emilio and Estelle Freedman suggest that the 1946 Supreme Court decision which overturned the U.S. Post Office's denial of mailing privileges to *Esquire* magazine resulted in increased accessibility of erotically explicit material.[26] This ruling paved the way for the appearance of *Playboy* magazine in 1953, which would never be denied mailing privileges, although it did not escape negative commentary. The Kinsey reports on sexuality appeared between 1949 and 1951, and though they sparked debates (both professional ones about methodology and popular ones about sexuality), they attained some respectability. At the same time, publishers of cheaply produced paperback books that were easy for newsstand owners to accommodate in crowded stalls started using sexy graphics on book covers, sparking much public controversy but ultimately little successful legal regulation. The famous *Roth* Supreme Court case of 1957 (which came down the month before the *Confidential* trial started in California), although upholding local censorship efforts, established that sex and obscenity were not synonymous, making it clear that obscenity was intended to arouse prurient interests. In the film industry expansion of what were considered morally appropriate representations of sexuality became possible after the 1952 *Miracle* case, which extended freedom of speech to motion pictures, denied them since the *Mutual v. Ohio* ruling in 1915. While this ruling did not result in immediate changes to the Motion Picture Production Code, it weakened local censorship efforts. In the mid-1950s successful challenges to the Code by Hollywood insiders, such as the director-producer Otto Preminger, preceded Code expansions of admissible representation by the late 1950s.

FIGURE 3.2 *Confidential* magazine, obsessed with nonnormative sexual practices, exploited discussions of obscenity and miscegenation in 1950s American society in its focus on celebrity scandals. Author's collection.

The scandal magazines exploited this changing climate around obscenity, as well as the complexities of current libel and privacy laws, in their efficient mass production of salacious stories about stars. To ensure a constant flow of scandal narratives for bimonthly publication, they evolved a particular philosophy toward hiring and directing personnel and used surveillance research methods and writing techniques that recycled old stories or created "composite" facts as the basis for new ones.[27] Although the magazines usually retained a small permanent writing and editing staff, they employed many writers who were already experienced, legitimate, mainstream or tabloid news reporters. For example, Edythe Farrell, who eventually edited the successful scandal magazine *Suppressed*, had once been a writer and editor for earlier Harrison tabloid publications, and she had also edited the *Police Gazette*, a notorious precursor to scandal publications in its taste for combining sex, crime, and a fascination with the techniques of uncovering secrets to titillate a largely male readership. Harrison's smartest move in relation to personnel was the bankrolling of the organization Hollywood Research Incorporated, run by his niece Marjorie Meade and her husband. This Los Angeles–based business existed as a separate corporate entity from *Confidential* (a shrewd legal protection for Harrison and the magazine in New York), and its main purpose was to recruit writers and hire and pay tipsters and private investigators. Tipsters ranged from call girls and ex-spouses of stars to disgruntled film industry and press employees. Harrison claimed that a star's press agent, or even an important producer, such as Mike Todd, might serve as a story source.[28]

Tipsters provided initial kernels of gossip or leads for information and confirmed rumors. Sometimes the work of tipster call girls dovetailed with that of private detectives, such as when they allowed their phones to be tapped or wore wristwatches equipped with tiny recorders in hope of getting taped confirmation of what was rumored to be true about a star. Next to call girls, private investigators were among *Confidential*'s most infamous research personnel, mostly confirming facts for stories already in progress. These detectives used state-of-the-art surveillance equipment for both audio and visual "proof" of scandalous behavior. The interest in electronically recorded or photographed evidence, like the practice of having tipsters sign affidavits about their stories, was part of *Confidential*'s careful anticipation of legal reprisal.

The magazines recycled, combined, and recombined stories and "facts" that had already appeared in other scandal magazines, as well as in mainstream, respectable newspapers and magazines. Some articles, often grouped around a particular scandal theme, basically just recycled various scandal stories from earlier press accounts, drawing on oft-told narratives about Mary Astor's diary and divorce in the 1930s, Errol Flynn's trial for statutory rape in the 1940s, and Fatty Arbuckle's trial for murder in the 1920s. The composite fact principle permeated almost every scandal story, old or new. The basic core facts of such a story might have occurred or been reported elsewhere as occurring, but the narrative contained important omissions, combined several events that had no causal relationship, and added embellishments, such as salacious titles, colorful graphics, alliteration, and constant reminders that the story was the result of "on-the-scene" reporting. Most articles that did not have photos taken at the scene were accompanied by a composite photo, photos that were taken at another scene and usually when the celebrity was caught off-guard or that were doctored so that material from one photo would be combined with another (a trick of tabloid newspapers for many years). Together these composite forms imputed that the celebrity had engaged in immoral or indecent conduct.

The use of composite fact stories had considerable power because, like many of the magazines' other stories, they involved material recycled from elsewhere. They seemed to offer plausible chronologies for events that had a ring of truth because readers had probably already encountered some aspect of them in newspaper gossip columns, traditional fan magazines, other scandal magazines and tabloids, and even sometimes in feature stories of the mainstream press. They also had power in the legal realm because they provided libel juries and judges with interpretive challenges as to their defamatory or intrusive status. After all, some aspects were true or had been reported before. The magazines' use of surveillance techniques and insider-tipsters gave them tremendous power in their relations with the film studios. For example, if the scandalousness of an act is partly based on the secrecy of its commission, certainly homosexuality or homosexual acts would be among the most scandalous in the 1950s.[29] *Confidential* did "out" Marlene Dietrich and Liberace, but the most significant outing the magazine had at its disposal was of Rock Hudson. At least one participant in an all-male party at the home of Henry Willson (the agent of Hudson, Tab Hunter, Rory Calhoun, Robert Wagner, Natalie Wood, and Guy Madison) had apparently signed an affidavit stating that he saw Hudson engage in group sex with men. In 1955 *Confidential* traded that information about Hudson to Universal Studios for a story about Rory Calhoun (another Universal contract star) as a teenage felon. (He had been incarcerated for stealing cars.)[30] As David Ehrenstein observes, this hardly seems an "even" trade;[31] surely the Hudson story was the better scandal. But if the trade is conceptualized in terms of the magazine's systematizing of scandal, it was better for the future workings of their mass-production system; it forever gave *Confidential* leverage over the studio (and over a major star and his agent) for future stories, as well as exhibited the publication's own mastery over the mass production of star discourse. The Calhoun story also was less likely to create the kind of complaints that often got *Confidential* in legal hot water. In fact because the story included Calhoun's conversion by a prison chaplain, it also gave the magazine an opportunity to claim the moral and legal high ground if challenged in court: how could Calhoun claim that such a story hurt him, when it sympathetically chronicled the transformation of a criminal teen into a spiritual and material success? Wasn't this the kind of story so often published by the fan magazines?[32]

From the point of view of the historian or theorist of scandal, the scandal magazines' research and writing methodologies also demonstrate the publications' own understanding of scandal's definition. In his study of Victorian-era scandals, William A. Cohen does not define scandal as an offensive act *or* the reaction to an offensive act, as dictionaries typically do. He suggests that the event cannot be disarticulated from the public recapitulation of it; they are two moments in the temporal dimension or continuum of scandal.[33] The scandal magazines refused the same disarticulation, as they devised ways, such as surveillance, that made sure the alleged event could move to the stage of recapitulation. Although some of their articles relied on looking to the past, their surveillance strategies look *forward* to the probability of a crime or scandal rather than backward to a committed criminal act, as search-and-seizure tactics do or as their own stories about past scandals did.[34] From a business standpoint, the attitude that scandalous behavior is (and has been) always available to be caught by surveillance technologies constructs and protects the magazines' systematicity, ensuring the continual flow of copy for a regularly scheduled, mass-produced publication. It also links the magazine to a number of alluring practices, such as espionage and forensic science, some of which could be seen as legitimate or objective. Although mock graphics and blaring headlines imparted an air of immediacy to the stories, in some cases the magazines made surveillance strategies and the on-the-scene reporting of the event somewhat irrelevant to the telling, as they rewrote old stories or fabricated new events (such as the O'Hara–Grauman's Chinese Theater narrative).

The recyclings and rewritings of old scandal stories were also important to the power of the magazines to construct a plausible fiction about their motivations. They editorialized constantly about how they would tell readers the *truth* rather than the packaged, formulaic "domestic bliss and patriotic service" narratives created by studios and press agents of the stars, which were fed to legitimate newspapers, general interest magazines, and fan magazines. Using mottoes like "The stories behind the headlines" (*Whisper*), "Stories the newspapers won't print" (*On the QT*), and "Uncensored and

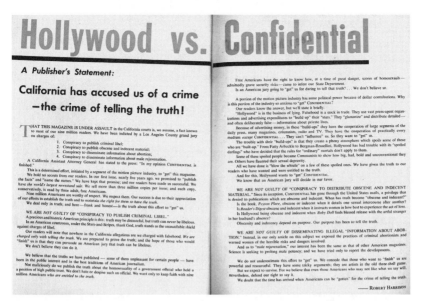

FIGURE 3.3 "Hollywood vs. Confidential." *Confidential*, September 1957. Author's collection.

off the record" and "Tells the facts and names the names" (*Confidential*), the magazines claimed that they would uncover what had been hidden. They attempted to gain their own moral weight in describing their work as historical investigation and heroic journalism.

When fan magazines and the state (through the trial in 1957) started attacking *Confidential*, it defended itself by claiming that it was not the one lying:

> "Hollywood" is the business of lying. Falsehood is a stock in trade. They use vast press-agent organizations and advertising expenditures to "build up" their "stars." They "glamorize" and distribute detailed—and often deliberately false—information about private lives. . . . The trouble with their "build ups" is that they create a phony atmosphere which spoils some of those who are "built up." From Fatty Arbuckle to Bergman-Rossellini, Hollywood has had trouble with its "spoiled darlings." . . . All we have done is "blow the whistle" on a few of these spoiled ones who have decided that the rules for "ordinary" mortals don't apply to them. Some of these spoiled people became Communists. . . . We have given the truth to our readers . . . who . . . were entitled to the truth.[35]

Confidential argues that its credibility resides in its tapping into the popular memory of such well-publicized scandals of the past as the Fatty Arbuckle rape and murder trial and Ingrid Bergman's adultery with Roberto Rossel-lini (including her pregnancy out of wedlock) and the House Un-American Activities Committee calling stars and other Hollywood talent to testify about the prevalence of communism in the film industry. In other words, the magazine posits a secure past, one well-documented and popularly re-membered, as proof that its present and future stories are true and in the public service.

Recycling Maureen O'Hara

How and where did Hollywood lie? Given that most biographical narratives about stars were disseminated through the respectable fan magazines, such as *Photoplay*, *Motion Picture*, and *Modern Screen*, these were most likely *Confidential*'s implied target when the magazine's editorial claimed that "'Hollywood' is in the business of lying" through its vast press-agent organizations and advertising expenditures. For my purposes, it is beside the point if fan magazines lied about Maureen O'Hara. What is significant is that they cre-ated a set of narrative and iconic themes about her that were recycled on television as she attempted to sustain a career in the 1950s.

O'Hara, who had come to Hollywood from Ireland (via England, where she had been chosen for a role in *Jamaica Inn* by Charles Laughton and the producer Eric Pommer in 1939), had a dual contract with RKO and Twentieth Century-Fox from the 1940s to the early 1950s. Throughout the 1940s fan magazines and other kinds of publicity represented O'Hara as the spunky but pure patriotic Irish girl defined by her roles as wife, mother, and professional. Her first marriage, at seventeen, and its subsequent an-nulment in 1941 are rarely mentioned. Her second marriage, to the dialogue director Will Price, the birth of their daughter, Bronwyn, and the continued closeness between O'Hara and her parents and siblings in Ireland are cen-tral to almost all the publicity about her.

Photoplay, *Silver Screen*, and *Modern Screen* titled articles on her "Irish Pixie," "Home Girl at Heart," "Letter to Her Daughter," "Star-Spangled Colleen," and "Pride of the Irish." Newspaper publicity touted her commu-nity service awards, such as "outstanding mother of the year in motion pic-tures" and "outstanding Catholic girl," and published articles containing her pronouncements about marriage and family. In the 1947 piece "Mother-hood Is Women's Real Career," she is reported to be worried about the state of American marriage and motherhood. "She says we're slipping," that we need to "get back to the family—and to religion, too."[36] That year she said that she was "careful to remove every trace of make-up, wear very simple clothes and come home to [her] family without a trace of the studio about [her]." As a proper wife rather than a career woman, O'Hara never discusses her acting or "the day's worries or triumphs": "Unless of course, my husband specifically asks, which he seldom does."[37] A 1942 piece seemed to anticipate the attitudes expressed in the later articles. The newspaper columnist Sidney Skolsky claims that "O'Hara won't pose for leg art and sexy photographs" (which most female stars in the studio system were expected to do). She won't "take a . . . bath for the movies or wear gauzy negligees because 'I come from a very strict family . . . [and] they would think I turned out bad.'"[38]

In her examination of the career of the Irish American silent star Colleen Moore, Diane Negra argues that 1920s discourses about femininity positioned the "Irish girl" as a corrective to the "vamp" and other modern women. While the vamp foregrounded her own self-manufacture in ways that "foreclosed the shaping influence of patriarchy," the Irish girl presented herself as "a resource to be acted upon by patriarchal and capitalist influences."[39] O'Hara's image in publicity and promotion as the definitive example of "Irish femininity" seems similarly positioned in the 1950s. While many articles on female stars at this time are insistent on constructing them as mothers and wives, O'Hara's status as such is maintained via her Irish ethnicity. In a 1947 *Los Angeles Times* article, she acknowledges a home economics class she took in a Dublin convent school as one source for the belief that motherhood and marriage are women's "real" careers.[40] In *Modern Screen*'s 1949 article "Pride of the Irish," O'Hara's heritage is credited for her dislike of modernity and her ability to create a traditional home life for her husband and daughter.[41]

The 1957 episode of *This Is Your Life* replays many of these themes. Edwards surprises O'Hara outside the Pantages Theater, where the 1957 Academy Awards are being held and where O'Hara is giving a radio interview about her upcoming film, *Wings of Eagles*, costarring John Wayne and directed by John Ford. Noticeably breathless after running from the Pantages during the commercial break, the two enter the NBC studios' "homey" stage set approximating an Irish pastoral scene with a wrought-iron garden bench and fake trees.

Edwards frequently teases O'Hara about her childhood and, although positioning her spirited responses as proof of an "Irish temper," associates her Irish ethnicity most significantly with her identity as a daughter, sister, and mother. Most of the guest witnesses to her life are her family—parents, siblings, daughter—and consequently most of the biographical stories told about her are of her past private life as a child and young woman in Ireland. With obvious affection, O'Hara's siblings describe her as a tomboy, with anecdotes about pranks, songs, and sports providing evidence. In a discussion with her parents, it becomes evident that any rebellion signified by her desire to become an actress was tempered by a willingness to be shaped by her father's influences: she agreed to study stenography as a "backup" profession in case she failed as an actress.

Patriarchal influences are also apparent in anecdotes about O'Hara's career. After Edwards points to John Ford (who directed her in five films) sitting in the studio audience, O'Hara beams with pride and announces that her stenography training extended her work for the director; she took his notes about the script for *The Quiet Man* in shorthand and subsequently typed them. Eric Pommer, the producer of two of O'Hara's films (as well as some of the most important German films of the Weimar era), is elderly and recovering from an illness at the time of the episode. In the kind of emotional moment typical of the series, he comes out in a wheelchair and recounts how he orchestrated her name change from FitzSimmons to O'Hara.

The actor-producer Charles Laughton, with whom O'Hara acted in three films, appears in a live broadcast relay from New York to talk about their first meeting. As the camera captures O'Hara alternating between laughter and tears, Laughton recounts how she looked in her first screen test: "On the screen was a girl—she looked at least 35, she was over done-up in some night-time evening dress, very made-up face, and her hair in an over grand style. Just for a split part of a second, in the close-up, the light was off this face and you could see, as the girl turned around, this absolutely beautiful profile of yours, which you couldn't see under all the make-up." Laughton was able to see the less mature, child-like woman he needed for *Jamaica Inn* under the makeup O'Hara had intended to make her look more grown-up and, undoubtedly, more sexual. Laughton further desexualizes her image when he discusses her reply to his query at the screen test of why she wanted to be an actress: "'When I was a child,' you said, 'I used to go down to the garden and talk to the flowers . . . and I would pretend I was the flowers talking back to myself.' It had to be a pretty nice girl and a pretty good actress too [to do that]. Heaven knows you're both."

This Is Your Life thus recirculated discourses that had been successful in constructing a wholesome image of O'Hara for some time. But some might also have seen it as a partial recycling of aspects of her persona. At least

FIGURE 3.4 "It was the Hottest Show in Town When Maureen O'Hara Cuddled in Row 35." *Confidential*, March 1957. Author's collection.

since 1950 O'Hara's "pure Irish lass" persona had existed in tension with a persona more befitting a "sand-and-bosom opera queen." Because of her frequent casting in costume dramas emphasizing sex and adventure, the columnist Erskine Johnson had declared, "Maureen . . . is a movie queen whose endowments sell tickets at the box office the way a lass bursting out of her bodice on a dust jacket sells historical novels by Kathleen Windsor." Seeming to ignore her earlier concerns with revealing negligees, she told Johnson that she wasn't ashamed of costumes accentuating décolletage: "I feel that if God gave you something beautiful, you should use it."[42] Perhaps under the pressure of Hollywood's construction of the "bombshell," in 1955 O'Hara starred as the notorious Lady Godiva. While a number of articles make great copy from descriptions of her costume (some sort of concoction of a bikini, tights, and a long wig) for the Lady's infamous nude ride, she gives interviews stressing her talent at playing a screen lover and argues for "biological casting." For O'Hara, this is casting opposite male stars with whom she shares a "chemical" and "psychiatric" affinity, male stars whose casting will create "sparks" and make them appear to be convincing lovers.[43]

Despite these attempts to construct a sexier O'Hara persona, signifiers to her Irish ethnicity reappear at this time in traditional fan magazines, functioning as reassuring proof of her wholesomeness and decency. So a beautiful bosom is "God-given," and although she has "a Pre-Raphaelite beauty with an Amazonian body," she is "unselfconscious," a homebody, and not "prompted by the vogue of Marilyn Monroe" to fake glamour.[44]

The *Confidential* article "It Was the Hottest Show in Town When Maureen O'Hara Cuddled in Row 35" does not recycle any specific piece of "sand-and-bosom opera queen" publicity, but surely the memory of the tensions between that kind of narrative and the wholesome family girl narratives that both fan magazines and *This Is Your Life* replayed could have worked to give the scandal magazine's article credibility for some readers. The *Confidential* piece was a composite-fact story. In it a theater usher alleges that he caught O'Hara having sex with an unnamed Latin American "lothario" in the back row of Grauman's Chinese Theater. *Confidential*'s attorney Daniel G. Ross claimed at the trial that the magazine had an affidavit from the former usher that the story was true, but he also admitted that he and the editor Harrison were influenced by a number of legitimate newspaper headlines about O'Hara when they were considering the publication of the story.[45] These headlines, such as "Ex-Husband Says Star Lives in Sin," concerned allegations made by Will Price in 1955 that O'Hara was openly "consorting" with a married Mexican businessman, Enrique Parra, "at all hours of the day and night" in both her Los Angeles home and his in Mexico.[46] Price was attempting to get custody of their eleven-year-old daughter, Bronwyn, and the matter was eventually settled out of court, with Price withdrawing the allegations, the lawyers renegotiating the terms of Price's visitation with his daughter, and O'Hara agreeing to stay silent about the agreement.

The scandal magazine *On the QT* had already used the newspaper reports as composite facts in its 1956 story "The Strange Case of Maureen O'Hara."[47] They rehashed the custody battle but also took the opportunity to construct rumors of a conspiracy. Why had Price withdrawn his allegations so quickly, the article asked. Was it industry pressure? Although *Confidential* would often claim that the film industry was behind many a hush-up of scandal, its story about O'Hara drops all aspects of the star's involvement with Parra that were linked to the child custody battle as well as suggestions about industry attempts to silence Price. It reimagines what "consorting" with a Latin American boyfriend "at all hours of the day and night" might include. The article describes the behavior of O'Hara and her escort as "torrid," as so uncontrollable that the usher has to ask them three times to break up their "petting." The unnamed Parra supposedly sits with his coat off, "his collar hanging limply at half mast," while O'Hara's white silk blouse is apparently no longer "neatly buttoned." To add to the story's spice, the magazine illustrates the article with a photo of O'Hara taken elsewhere in which she seems to be adjusting the top button of her dress or blouse. The caption of the photo states, "Redheaded Maureen's blouse needed plenty of fixing after bouncing and bundling with that Latin lad in Grauman's Chinese Theater."[48] The article displays an obvious relish in exploiting the disparity between the earthy, animalistic scene that was allegedly taking place inside the theater and the glamorous aura attached to Grauman's, the site of some of Hollywood's most elaborate premieres. In that way the article attacks Hollywood in general as well as O'Hara specifically.

As these examples demonstrate, "It Was the Hottest Show in Town" was vivid in detail and sensational in its implications. Whether readers believed the narrative is a question; such lively sensationalism could be read as credible because of its detail or seen as too theatrical to be the truth. (Besides, what star with a nice, private home in Beverly Hills would choose a public and uncomfortable movie theater as a site for lovemaking?) If the scandal magazines' fiction about their strategies was relatively sustainable in the late 1950s, it was more likely because Hollywood's own ability to sustain a fiction about stars was waning.

Fan Magazines Respond to Scandal Magazines

Since the studio breakup following the Paramount divestment decree of 1948, many stars were no longer under long-term contract. Some stars had independent production companies; others were under contract to studios only on a per-picture basis. (However, Rock Hudson, Rory Calhoun, and Tab Hunter—all stars who had articles about them published or threatened by *Confidential*—were under long-term contracts to studios.) As discussed in chapter 2, the studios still managed promotion and publicity for single films, but much of the star-oriented publicity was coming from the press agents stars could hire on their own in the wake of the studio breakup and from the stars themselves, such as in their television appearances. While all could be said to work on behalf of the industry, the difficulties of sustaining the power of studio contract morality clauses and the coherencies of star personas, as well as a unified discourse about Hollywood, were becoming more apparent as the decade wore on.

The traditional fan magazines exemplify these difficulties. After the Ingrid Bergman–Roberto Rossellini adultery and pregnancy scandal and the Robert Mitchum marijuana bust in the late 1940s, the fan magazines went into overdrive to protect readers' beliefs in Hollywood morality. Yet their response to scandal under the cloak of moral uplift was contradictory. In some articles published between the Bergman and Mitchum scandals in the late 1940s and the *Confidential* trial in 1957, the fan magazines rather paradoxically supported traditional morals through a marked investment in specific details of stars' possibly indecent behavior. In other instances they assumed a strategic silence that discretely spoke about scandal through a self-conscious avoidance of its name.

In the late 1940s and early 1950s—before the scandal magazines' arrival—some stories were surprisingly explicit in particularizing the Bergman and Mitchum situations. For example, *Photoplay*'s 1948 article "The Truth about Dope" not only gives details of the actual drug bust involving Mitchum; it speculates that Mitchum might have smoked marijuana in order to feel more confident. The article's attempt to clarify "the truth about dope" and not completely condemn Mitchum before his trial puts it into the interesting—and, by contemporary standards, sensible—position of suggesting that what Mitchum did wasn't very bad because marijuana is not as harmful and addictive as heroin.[49] In February 1949 *Modern Screen*'s "An Open Letter to Robert Mitchum: The Case for the People," also explicitly states why Mitchum is in trouble with the law, but it takes the scandal as an occasion to flatter its readers by extolling their sense of fair play toward the unconvicted and their charity toward those who, found guilty, pay their debt to society.[50] *Photoplay*'s April 1949 "What Now for Mitchum?" praises the actor for pleading guilty and sparing Hollywood and the nation—especially the teenagers who idolize him—the scandal of a long trial and the subsequent sensational press coverage.[51]

Generally sympathetic to Mitchum in this specific scandal—in fact they served as one important venue for his public rehabilitation, as they did for Bergman—the fan magazines at this time also published many articles that replaced understanding with condescension for stars whose lives included rebellious, unhappy, or generally scandalous behavior in the past.[52] In *Photoplay*'s June 1950 article "I Call It Scandalous!," what is scandalous, according to the author, Elsa Maxwell, is that Bergman thought Hollywood was wrong for her and left for Italy, Mitchum was not properly schooled by his studio in his responsibilities as a star, and Shirley Temple was not taught that testifying against her husband, John Agar, at their divorce trial would have been more seemly if done in another state.[53] In *Modern Screen*'s June 1952 "Hollywood's Most Tragic People," the author, Louella Parsons, engages in recycling scandal to argue that most stars who have been involved in scandals, from Wallace Reid and Mabel Normand in the 1920s to Judy Garland,

Robert Walker, Franchot Tone, and Carole Landis in the late 1940s and early 1950s, are to be pitied rather than condemned. One of the photo captions even describes these figures as pathetic.[54]

Another fan magazine response to more openly known star scandals was to publish articles that dealt with issues of star morality while avoiding re-hashing previous scandals. These provided more general, simultaneously obscure and heavy-handed responses to charges that Hollywood was an environment for scandalous behavior. Some of these, such as *Modern Screen*'s February 1950 "Hollywood's Ten Best Citizens" and *Photoplay*'s August 1950 "The Other Side of the Hollywood Story," are inspired to report stars' charitable activities from a desire to rectify what is vaguely described as misplaced emphasis in newspapers and magazines on the less positive contributions of Hollywood citizens. Both pieces pompously exaggerate their mission, with *Modern Screen* declaring its article as one of the most important it has ever published.[55] *Photoplay* offers, with "editorial pride," a chart that "took months of concentrated effort" to put together. The chart exhaustively details statistics for about 150 stars that apparently prove their worthiness as model citizens: statistics of their marital, parental, and home-ownership status, as well as of community service and honors.[56] *Modern Screen*'s issue includes a "special report" on Hollywood morals, grouping together articles on Mitchum, Judy Garland (who had attempted suicide), and Hedda Hopper's attempts to keep stars out of trouble. (If only they had taken her advice, claims Hopper.) While this report dares to actually speak the terminology of scandal ("How Sinful Are Movie Stars?" is the title of one article), like the stories in *Modern Screen* and *Photoplay* earlier that year it works to prove with statistics its argument that contemporary Hollywood is very moral indeed. A chart accompanying the report proclaims that, in Hollywood during the previous fifteen years, only ten of fifteen thousand actors were in major scandals; there were only two murders and six prostitution cases; and there were eighty-four times more sex offenses in New York City. (Should any historian of Los Angeles or even a casual reader of Raymond Chandler or James Ellroy question those statistics about murder and prostitution cases in Hollywood during this period, the text accompanying the chart clarifies that those figures are really for Beverly Hills, an upscale, largely residential town where many stars at the time lived.)[57]

After the scandal magazines arrived on the scene and started to make an impact, signaled by the national attention that articles in *Time* and *Newsweek* and a series of civil libel suits gave them in the mid-1950s, the fan magazines became even more reticent to specify scandalous allegations made about stars.[58] Because the Bergman and Mitchum scandals had made headline news in legitimate national newspapers and magazines, the fan magazines could be explicit in their details. As noted, in the case of Mitchum they could even turn these into recuperative copy. But the scandal magazines were considered illegitimate and read by a smaller audience than the legitimate press (though the circulation figures claimed for *Confidential* ranged from 250,000 to 4 million, which put them in good competition with fan magazines). It was believed that repeating information from them could provide further means for circulation and amplification of alleged scandalous behavior.

The fan magazines resorted to a strategic silence about specific details of the scandals broken by *Confidential* and its imitators. This resulted in titillation and incoherencies. For example, an editorial entitled "Scandal in Hollywood" in the July 1955 issue of *Photoplay* claims that stars have been recently subjected to vicious attacks but never specifies the allegations. It states that the "scandal-mongering" implied not only marital infidelity but "the worst in human behavior."[59] The reader is left to wonder which kind of scandal applies to which of the stars listed in the editorial (Rory Calhoun, June Allyson and Dick Powell, Alan Ladd and Sue Carol, Burt Lancaster, Van Johnson, Lana Turner) and what exactly constitutes the "worst" in human behavior. *Photoplay*'s February 1956 story "Kim Novak: Stabbed by Scandal" never mentions the article but was written in response to *Confidential*'s January 1956 "What They 'Forgot' to Say about Kim Novak." *Confidential*'s story claimed that Novak was "kept" by a New York businessman. *Photoplay* argues that Novak had been scandalously depicted as "ambition-driven" and discovered by an agent while riding her bicycle in town. With these vague and seemingly inoffensive details, the reader might wonder why stories about her discovery on a bike or her ambition would be so upsetting or scandalous and imagine a worse emplotment of Novak's "ambition" than *Confidential* had declared.[60]

The fan magazines' strategic silence about scandal was characteristic of their balancing of secrecy and revelation since the 1920s, a tension that fascinated readers even as it allowed the publications to maintain the boundaries of social propriety. Gaylyn Studlar argues that the fan magazines of the 1920s resorted to "a strategy of indirection that relied heavily upon the reader's preexistent knowledge of events gleaned from other sources, not the magazines themselves."[61] This method was a voluntary response to the social pressures and economic risks stemming from a series of Hollywood scandals in that decade (those involving Fatty Arbuckle, Wallace Reid, and William Desmond Taylor, all in 1922). In the 1930s the fan magazines had more or less capitulated to the demands of the studios to publish positive articles written by studio-approved writers.[62] However, manifestation of a similar reticence in fan magazines of the 1950s might have been puzzling to readers who remembered the publications' obvious investment in other scandals (such as the Mitchum and Bergman scandals) in the more relaxed years of the late 1940s. Because of the studio breakup, competition with the scandal magazines for readers, and changing societal beliefs about obscenity, fan magazines in the mid- to late 1950s seemed uncertain about what the readers wanted, what they might already know, and what the implications of too explicitly acknowledging reader desires and knowledge might be.[63]

While their control over the coherency of publicity and promotional discourses was clearly weakened in the 1950s, the film industry still had the production of motion pictures as a potential weapon against the scandal magazines. In 1956 MGM produced *Slander*. Starring Van Johnson as Scott Martin, Ann Blyth as his wife Anne, and Steve Cochran as H. R. Manly, *Slander* tells the story of how the fictional scandal magazine *Real Truth* ruins the life of a newly popular television puppeteer (Martin) when it runs an article about his arrest for robbery as a teen. The magazine publisher and editor Manly really wants to run a story on Mary Sawyer (never seen in the film but described in a way to suggest an Ingrid Bergman–like star who has played Joan of Arc and other saintly characters). His "researchers" have found that Sawyer knew Martin's mother. The film implies that Mrs. Martin once arranged for Sawyer to either get an abortion or give up an illegitimate child for adoption.[64] Manly attempts to use the story about Martin's juvenile delinquent past to blackmail him for details and verification of the information about this more important star. When Martin refuses to act as a scandal magazine "tipster," his wife leaves him, the story about him is published, he temporarily loses his job, and his son is killed when he runs in front of a car to escape the children taunting him about his "jailbird" father. Manly is then shot and killed by his mother (Marjorie Rambeau), who hates the way her son's magazine has ruined lives.

Anticipating the kind of interest the state would take in the scandal magazines' operating strategies, the film focuses on the way the magazine orders its researchers to find damaging information about famous people, uses blackmail to pressure tipsters, engages in trade-offs of stories, and revels in its cynical attitude. (Manly declares, "There's something dirty in everyone's past. . . . The cleaner they are on the surface, the dirtier they are underneath.") The tipster system of research and fact validation is portrayed as almost as dangerous as the publication of scandal. Martin's wife leaves him because he doesn't choose that option in the face of his own sordid past being revealed. Even though his son is killed as a result, Martin gains self-respect and confidence (and eventually wins back his job) by the way he stands up to the magazine. Clearly drawing on *Confidential*'s story on Rory Calhoun (of course, the trade behind that story could hardly be revealed in 1956), *Slander* reiterates a typical fan magazine discourse about the digging up of old scandals about stars. That is, no story from the past reflects what the star has become in the present, which is hard-working, home-owning, and family-loving. Hollywood was willing to concede that times had changed to the extent that the public was beginning to expect some scandal in a star's past, but it was still hoping to shape public discourse into accepting that whatever their past, stars were now ideal citizens of 1950s America.

The State of California versus *Confidential* Magazine

The film industry probably wished that the scandal magazines could be as easily dispatched as the fictional H. R. Manly was by his mother's gunshot. Certainly reports of how studio bosses pressured California politicians into quashing the scandal magazines are not uncommon in histories of the *Confidential* trial.[65] However, evidence suggests a much more complicated picture of the film industry's relationship to the political and law enforcement activities directed at *Confidential* in 1957. In February of that year two hearings by California state senate committees, the Interim Committee on Collection Agencies, Private Detectives, and Debt Liquidators and the Judiciary Committee, investigating the use of surveillance equipment in the state, had used in their evidence the "research tactics" of the scandal magazines as examples of abusive intrusions of privacy. The former committee had even subpoenaed the famed baseball hero Joe DiMaggio and Frank Sinatra to testify about the role of private investigators in the famed "wrong door raid," in which DiMaggio, Sinatra, and others had allegedly broken down the door of an apartment expecting to find DiMaggio's ex-wife Marilyn Monroe in flagrante delicto. *Confidential* had reported this incident using the files of one of the private investigators hired by DiMaggio to follow Monroe. Sinatra's very reluctant testimony and its aftermath (the state considered filing perjury charges against Sinatra because his story differed from the private investigator's), as well as the testimony of the private investigator, Fred Otash, on how he spied on Hollywood figures to confirm stories for *Confidential*, resulted in high-profile coverage of the committee's work in national media.[66]

Given the news media's almost exclusive, and rather embarrassing, focus on only one aspect of the hearings' evidence-gathering—the connection between Hollywood, the private eye, and the scandal magazine—it is probable that the film industry would have supported the legislation to curb the scandal magazines' operations that both the senate committee chairman Fred Kraft and Governor Goodwin Knight proposed to the media as the hearings concluded in March.[67] The legislation did not materialize, but State Attorney General Pat Brown worked with the Los Angeles district attorney to bring charges against *Confidential* of criminal conspiracy to commit criminal libel and to publish obscenity. Because of failure to extradite Harrison from New York, the only individuals they could bring to trial were the Meades, who ran Hollywood Research Inc. as a front for the magazine. Conspiracy to commit criminal libel meant that the magazines had malicious intent in publishing the scandalous stories. Yoking that charge to the charge of conspiracy to publish obscene material worked as a contaminating factor in two ways. It put the case into a social arena in which the magazine might be judged as a moral contaminant in society (as moral crusade discourses usually described obscenity), and it contaminated the libel charge, potentially predisposing jurors to find the magazine's whole operation sleazy, and therefore to find its stories malicious in intent and its reporting of private acts outrageous and of no social value.[68]

Film industry support of legislation was one thing; it meant the dirty work of fighting the scandal magazine would be in the hands of legislators in Sacramento. But support of a criminal trial to take place in Los Angeles was surely another. Stars would be subpoenaed for testimony and the scandal stories would be read aloud in court, become part of the public record, and reported on by national media. In short, the scandals would be recycled and potentially amplified in the process. And the outcome was unpredictable. Reports early on in the July–October 1957 trial indicated the stars would like to settle out of court, and sure enough, once subpoenas were prepared, many managed to be out of town.[69] When the Motion Picture Industry Council made statements to the media through its president, the actor (and future senator) George Murphy, it focused on the way the trial provoked "disgust and anger" in Hollywood and how it was trying to make sure that such a trial would never again take place.[70] Murphy ostensibly meant that the Council wanted to attack the magazine's libelous activities, but an underlying meaning was that the Council wished there had not been a trial to reveal so many negative stories. A *New York Times* article appearing the same day Murphy's remarks were made public quoted an unnamed source saying that the industry had considered doing something to stop the magazines but dropped the project "when the studio heads became apprehensive of becoming involved with the magazines and feared a boomerang."[71]

The famed Hollywood attorney Jerry Giesler (he represented Mitchum and Lizabeth Scott in their civil libel cases against *Confidential* and had been Mitchum's attorney in the 1948 trial) publicly stated on numerous occasions at the time of the hearings and trial that Hollywood "never gives help on the battlefield, but is always glad to provide a pat on the back after the fight is over. . . . It's strange how all their organizations run to cover."[72] Kenneth Anger claims that the film industry sent a public relations man to Pat Brown, threatening withdrawal of campaign funds to the Republican Party in the next election if his office filed criminal charges that would involve a trial. This seems dubious, since Brown was a Democrat, but the general picture Anger paints of the industry being reluctant to have the case go to trial seems to be compatible with evidence found elsewhere.[73]

News reports indicate that Hollywood was nervously anticipating the recirculation and amplification the trial would give the scandal stories. Contemporary accounts don't point out that the film industry might have been justifiably apprehensive about other revelations the trial might provoke, such as how Hollywood's systematizing of star discourse also involved fabrication, invasion of privacy, and intimations of sexual misbehavior (even if in the service of recuperating that sin with stories of reconciliation and domestic reunion). The state was interested in raising issues about the magazine's surveillance tactics to demonstrate that it was not just reporting old scandals but actively (maliciously) creating situations to construct scandals, that it was "a smut factory."[74]

However, neither the state nor the industry might have anticipated that *Confidential*'s attorneys (their libel attorneys used in consultation, not the defense attorneys for Hollywood Research Inc.) would justify these activities in testimony as being a response to Hollywood's successful mass production of star discourse and the breakdown in its once systematized regulatory functions. For example, *Confidential*'s attorney Daniel G. Ross claimed that press agents and fan magazines were the ones lying about the stars, and their success had resulted in the stars being worshiped as "false idols" by the public. *Confidential*, said Ross, was providing a public service in telling "the truth about these personalities."[75] At another point defense witnesses changed strategies and claimed that some "true" material about sexual behavior had come from Hollywood itself, from press agents, studio employees, and even fan magazines. *Confidential's* legal advisor Albert DeStefano stated that the magazine had taken material from a fan magazine in writing "How Long Can Dick Powell Take It?," an article describing trouble in Powell's marriage with June Allyson because of Allyson's relationship with Alan Ladd.[76] Fred Meade, one of the principal defendants in the case, argued that it was the film industry's refusal or inability to act on one of its main regulatory procedures, the exercise of morality clauses in star contracts, that was responsible for the success of magazines like *Confidential.*[77]

Meade's defense of blaming breakdown in Hollywood's regulation of morality, like Ross's claim that *Confidential* performed a public service by revealing the sins of "false idols," was a defense not only against libel (and invasion of privacy, which the magazine was not officially on trial for) but also against the obscenity charge. These claims took the moral high ground in justifying the publication of sexual material as educational, but the defense witnesses also had to argue that the articles were not obscene because they did not arouse "a sexually itchy reaction, an uncontrolled desire to commit depraved acts."[78] In fact, said DeStefano, many of the articles were humorous, and a story "cannot be obscene if it makes the reader chuckle."[79] Furthermore, went the argument, if obscenity is determined by the standards of the community, then *Confidential's* repetition of material accepted previously by the public—that is, already in the public record—such as the accusations about O'Hara's relationship with Parra first mentioned at the O'Hara-Price custody dispute, could hardly be obscene.[80] The sensational trial involved high drama and humor: the assistant district attorney, an avowed churchgoer, reading racy *Confidential* magazine articles aloud to the court; *Confidential* attorneys pulling out novels like *Peyton Place* to suggest the magazine was no more obscene than many best-selling books; Maureen O'Hara angrily declaring that she could prove that she was out of the country at the time *Confidential* alleged she was having sex with Parra in Grauman's Chinese Theater; and Dorothy Dandridge calmly testifying that she could never and would never have had sex in the Lake Tahoe woods with a white musician, as *Confidential* claimed. She would not even have taken a walk with a white man because "Lake Tahoe . . . was very prejudiced. Negroes were not permitted that freedom."[81] Despite the powerful and convincing testimony provided by O'Hara and Dandridge, the jury deadlocked over the verdict in early October 1957. When the state declared a willingness to start with a new trial, *Confidential* agreed to cooperate and change its policies in order to avoid mounting another expensive defense.

While the strategies Hollywood and *Confidential* devised in 1957 to defend their own systematization of star discourse in the face of a public trial seem understandable, the state's motivations in attacking *Confidential* and not bowing to the film industry's wish to avoid a trial are not entirely explainable, or at least not verifiable. One significant possibility is to be found in relation to the state senate committee hearings several months before the trial. Both hearings examined the role of institutions (collection agencies, debt liquidators) or individuals (private investigators, criminals) using tactics that invaded citizen privacy and sometimes challenged constitutional rights concerning protection from search and seizure (Fourth Amendment) and self-incrimination (Fifth Amendment). Examples from scandal magazine surveillance practices were used by both committees in their hearings and garnered them much publicity during the actual proceedings. However, the reports published at the hearings' end, which were certainly not read by very many in the public, suggest that these examples were only a small part of the committees' concerns.[82] Did the highlighting of the scandal magazines by the committees and the press during the hearings function as a public display of the state's concern for protecting citizens' right to privacy?

Why would this be necessary? Possibly because both the state of California and the federal government were massively undercutting those very rights in the 1950s and had been doing so since at least the beginning of the cold war at the end of the 1940s. Loyalty oaths and surveillance through FBI wiretapping and U.S. Post Office monitoring of publications had been used in both Washington and California as a means to expel communist or other "subversives" (such as homosexuals) from civil service and other forms of public life.[83] The House Un-American Activities Committee had targeted the film industry in two large "show trial" hearings in less than a decade, and the University of California's firings of professors suspected of leftist sympathies had been much publicized. Both California senate committee reports demonstrate concern with the way uses of surveillance outside of law enforcement were increasing at this time. The reports conclude that recent Supreme Court restrictions on law enforcement surveillance tactics and rapid developments in sophisticated surveillance devices provide opportunities for ruthlessly and criminally intrusive individuals and institutions to undermine law enforcement.[84]

These reports suggest that the state could be constructing an "other" to take the blame for what it perceived as its diminishing surveillance powers, or what the historian might perceive as its abuse of surveillance power. The trial could be seen as an extension of the state's "othering" of the scandal magazines to mask its own power. However, libel laws and their enforcement also raise broader issues about community that are central to another important facet of this case. Robert C. Post argues that defamation laws, when understood as protection of reputation as dignity, are concerned with not only the individual's interest in dignity but "the enforcement of society's interest in its rules of civility, which is to say its interest in defining and maintaining the contours of its own social constitution."[85] This notion of defamation entails an understanding of how societies exercise power to designate who is a member of society (who deserves respect) and who is not (who is a deviant because of unacceptable behavior). Protection of dignity is a "confirmation of membership" in a community. Defamation threatens this confirmation, and libel trials are "an arena in which the parties [the defamed and the defaming] are free to present 'competing interpretations of behavior.'"[86] The *Confidential* trial was not just about the state proving its power over scandal magazines but was also a ready forum to raise, and perhaps settle, "competing interpretations" of a number of behaviors, most involving sexuality, that troubled and fascinated society.

Stars and the Performance of Societal Norms

For most of the twentieth century stars had been constituted by the very terms — the private self behind the public image — that suggest the "processes through which our society constitutes sexuality as an object of knowledge and fascination."[87] In this understanding knowledge of the stars is knowledge of sexuality is knowledge of the self. Knowledge of the stars was regulated by Hollywood to create desire and maintain certain boundaries of sexuality — monogamous heterosexuality practiced by people of the same race — which presumably were internalized by the public through acts of self-policing. The public gained knowledge of the stars by looking at their images or reading about their lives in gossip columns, fan magazines, general readership magazines, and, by the 1950s, scandal magazines, listening to their radio appearances, and watching them as characters or as themselves in films and television programs. In many of these media audiences weren't just exposed to discourses about stars but were witnesses to stars' *enactments* of certain social roles as characters in fictional narratives and as "real" people who attended nightclubs, premieres, and award ceremonies and who were guests on radio and television variety programs, game shows, and even *This Is Your Life*. *This Is Your Life*, *Confidential* magazine, and the *Confidential* trial raised questions about the sustainability of stars as the performers of and models for sexual self-policing, while demonstrating for today's historian past social struggles over normative definitions of sexual and gender behavior. *Confidential* magazine obviously raises these questions through its revelations, true or not, about stars' "deviant" or "immoral" sexual behaviors. But how can *This Is Your Life* and the *Confidential* trial be seen from such a perspective? Didn't the trial demonstrate the force of the state's disciplinary power over institutions or media that dare impugn stars' morality? Didn't *This Is Your Life* create moral biographies to inspire rather than raise questions about morality?

Again the simultaneous recyclings of Maureen O'Hara in 1957 are illuminating. While the scandal magazines overtly exploited discourses of the sexual, *This Is Your Life* participated in discourses that positioned O'Hara's private life within the "feminine mystique" of the 1950s rather than with that decade's growing fascination with the sexually experimenting woman. However, Foucault argues that "silence . . . the things one declines to say, or is forbidden to name, the discretion that is required between different speakers . . . functions alongside the things said. . . . There is not one but many silences and they are an integral part of the strategies that underlie and penetrate discourses."[88] *This Is Your Life*'s construction of O'Hara as loyal daughter, sister, mother, and protégée of elderly male Hollywood figures works, in part, because of who is *not* on the program, what is *not* said. Absent guests include not only the infamous Parra but all the young male costars of her films, such as John Wayne, Jeff Chandler, John Payne, and Anthony Quinn. Her first husband is never mentioned, and mention of her second, Will Price, whose 1941 marriage was "dissolved some years later," seems necessary only as an explanation for her daughter's existence. Although *This Is Your Life* gives us no reason to disbelieve O'Hara's basic decency and her patriarchally shaped femininity, other discourses circulating about her and female sexuality in the 1950s might, at the very least, reveal contradictions in Hollywood's discourses as represented by this television series. The program's success in making the viewer believe he or she was seeing the "real" O'Hara might have been powerful enough to mitigate the force of those other discourses, but for the historian—and maybe some 1950s viewers—what Edwards chooses to say about O'Hara and who was invited to appear on camera function as a strategic silencing of as well as a will to silence discourses about her sexuality.

Foucault's argument suggests that discourses are constructed out of en-actments, and even keeping silent is an enactment. What made *This Is Your Life* such a powerful and memorable part of recycling stars in the 1950s are its strategies, many discussed earlier, that seemingly allow the star to enact the "private self." Despite perhaps some initial embarrassment, O'Hara must have found the program's timing in covering her life fortuitous, as she was trying to control the proliferating negative (socially disapproved) discourses about her private self. The O'Hara episode is perhaps the most obvious example of how *This Is Your Life* could function to shore up tradi-tional discourses about stars and confirm contemporary patriarchal sexual and gender norms. Yet the program's focus on enactment — of surprise; of reunion with family, friends, and colleagues; of silence — made its ability to control events on stage or reactions of the audience (in the studio or at home) insecure.

Sociologists and historians studying 1950s American society frequently point to concerns with keeping up appearances as a central motivation for its behavioral norms and representational strategies. Historians have sug-gested that the obsession with creating or imparting to others a favorable impression, which necessitates a constant surveillance of others to find a demeanor pleasing to them, characterizes a progressive decline of "charac-ter" and subsequent rise of the "personality" since the late nineteenth cen-tury. Yet 1950s American culture had its own specific manifestations of "im-pression management."[89] The television historian Lynn Spigel argues that examples of this can be seen in the propensity of early television and ad-vertisements for television sets to theatricalize domesticity as a site for con-sumer display and a showcase for middle-class tastes and mores.[90] Sociolo-gists writing during the period, such as David Riesman and Erving Goffman, stress the theatrical or performative nature of social behavior — behavior that includes watching others as well as oneself — which was geared toward success in corporate environments (the "outer-directed man" of Riesman) or toward a socially "competent" performance that would result in the be-stowal of esteem and full participation in society (Goffman).[91] Of course, these behavioral performances — what constituted competence and re-sulted in esteem from the community — differed in part on the basis of the performer's gender. Although Riesman wrote of the negative aspects of the outer-directed man, women were assumed to be outer-directed, that is, constituted to please others. Feminist scholars have argued that women in patriarchal society internalize the gaze of others and conform their body and social behavior to gain men's approval. In the 1950s white, middle-class standards for female beauty and behavior resulted in women having to constantly calibrate a "womanliness" that was both sexual and maternal, gracious and "lady-like."[92] For both men and women of the period, certain sexual performances were considered nonexistent, or not to be engaged, or enacted only in privacy.

The degree to which *This Is Your Life* facilitated an enactment of such norms was exposed by delicious spoofing in a 1954 episode of the comedy-variety program *Your Show of Shows* in a segment entitled "This Is Your Story."[93] Carl Reiner, a program regular, appears as a Ralph Edwards–like emcee, announcing to the audience, "Each week we give you the intimate and inside story of someone's life." As he walks off the stage and into the audience (as Edwards sometimes did in early episodes), he suggests the power behind the surveillance and the surveillance power of the show: "You don't know who it is, your neighbor doesn't know who it is. . . . The only people who know who it is are we people backstage." Reiner asks a number of men in the audience if they could be the focus of the show, finally settling on the row in which Al Duncie (played by Sid Caesar) is sitting. As Reiner looks in Al's direction and asks "Could it be you?," Al smiles gleefully at his neighbor, as if to suggest that it is "some other fool" who is the show's focus. When the emcee insists that it is Al who is the focus, Al promptly faints. When he awakes, he stands and pushes Reiner away and tries to slap him, and when the emcee succeeds in getting him to the stage, he runs back into the audience, heading for the rear door. Theater ushers have to *carry* Al back on stage, while Reiner explains, "He is a little overwhelmed."

Once on stage Al is subjected to the usual *This Is Your Life* treatment. He is expected to listen to the host's heavy-handed, sentimental retelling of his life, which is rendered with lots of allusions to the "kindness and encouragement" Al received when he was discouraged in the past. He is also expected to guess the identity of the guests speaking about him and to him from behind the curtain. He is often unable to guess, and once asks the speaker to repeat himself. A series of relatives and mentors—including a fireman, Mr. Torch (played by Louis Nye), who once saved Al's life—come out to greet him. Al's "Uncle Goopie" (played by the series regular Howard Morris) is especially enthusiastic, and he and Al repeatedly engage in hugging, kissing, and crying. At one point the sobbing Uncle Goopie stoops down and clings to Al's leg, not letting go even when Al walks back to the couch on the stage. All of these hysterics stop the emcee's biographical narrative dead in its tracks and force him to separate the uncle and nephew. The last guest, a beautiful woman whose voice Al is unable to place, comes out and the two look at each other with eager anticipation. Al yells to her, "Oh honey . . . baby!" and starts to kiss her with gusto, repeatedly ignoring Reiner's plea for him to identify her to the audience. Finally, Al says he doesn't know who she is, but adds, "She is all right with me!" When he starts to kiss her again, Reiner separates them and, realizing the mistake, claims that she is a guest meant for the next week's show.

A number of socially acceptable behaviors of the 1950s are breached here, and in demonstrating their breaching with an exaggerated hilarity (confirmed by the raucous laughter from the studio audience), the spoof exposes the degree to which *This Is Your Life* depends on a certain socially sanctioned performance of those behaviors. As Goffman observes, the competent social actor performs with a "dramaturgical discipline." He is able to receive the approval of his audience (i.e., society) by respecting certain boundaries between on-stage and off-stage behavior and by performing his part with discretion. "He is someone with 'presence of mind' who can cover up on the spur of the moment for inappropriate behavior on the part of his teammates. . . . And if a disruption of the performance cannot be avoided or concealed, the disciplined performer will be prepared to offer a plausible reason for discounting the disruptive event. . . . The disciplined performer is also someone with 'self-control.'" Furthermore he can "suppress his emotional response to his private problems" in order to prevent improper disclosures and "offense to the working consensus."[94]

Clearly Al and Uncle Goopie are incompetent performers in these terms and care little about the show's or society's "working consensus." They exercise no self-control, exhibiting inappropriate displays of emotion toward one another. Instead of what the viewer sees in episodes of *This Is Your Life*—the simple embrace that Maureen O'Hara gives her parents, or the respectful, albeit tearful, "Hello" Pat O'Brien whispers directly in the camera to his mother, who is watching the program on television from her hospital bed—Al and Uncle Goopie sob, kiss, beat their breasts, cling to one another. Howard Morris later said that playing the role of Uncle Goopie in this sketch was a "milestone" in his theatrical career: "For the first time I was allowed to take over and do whatever the hell I wanted in a sketch." He also told colleagues that his idea for clinging to Caesar's leg came to him from watching Cheeta, the chimpanzee who was Tarzan's pet and helpmate in the popular films.[95] Behavioral cues from animals would hardly result in socially approved behavior in the 1950s.

Perhaps Al's biggest behavioral breach is his inappropriately long kiss with the mystery guest. The breach widens when the emcee and audience

learn that Al doesn't even know who she is and that he can't control expressing himself in such a sexual manner with a stranger. One is reminded here
of Edwards's strategic silence about O'Hara's teenage marriage and annulment, of the absence of her young, *sexually attractive*, male costars. While
This Is Your Life traded on catching stars off-guard so the audience could
sense the "real" star behind the public face (or, in Goffman's terms, get a
peek at off-stage behavior), the program obviously manipulated situations
to maximize the possibility of the star giving a "disciplined," morally acceptable performance. (This is not to say that O'Hara might have given a morally
unacceptable performance in other circumstances.)

Although many players in the hierarchy of the 1950s American social
scene would not have advocated television's showcasing of stars in a way
that would allow them to appear "socially incompetent" or immoral — as
Confidential obviously did — *This Is Your Life* and Edwards's performance on
the show did provoke some negative commentary, even generating controversy about invasion of privacy that evokes comparison with the scandal magazines. Two of the most critical articles about the program came
from prominent television critics writing for national publications in 1954
and 1958, during *Confidential*'s heyday. Jack Gould, writing for the *New York
Times* in 1954, excoriates *This Is Your Life*, putting it in the same category as
other "misery shows," like *Strike It Rich*, which exemplify television's debasement to "the extent of exploiting raw emotions of the unfortunate or catering to the craven curiosity of the mob."[96] In a 1958 TV *Guide* article Gilbert
Seldes argues that *This Is Your Life* forces people to be emotional — they are
"compelled to expose themselves" — comparing this to the English nobility's
practice of gawking at inmates in Bedlam in the eighteenth century. He describes Edwards's face as "lit not with sympathy but with glee over the tricks
he has pulled."[97] Even largely positive articles on the program tended to
use phrases like "trapped guests," "sensational," and "spiritual prosecutor."[98]
While no articles comment on the eroticization of the spectators' curiosity,
the vociferousness of their tone indicates the charged atmosphere of the
program's reception. TV *Scandals*, for example, seems to have intuited the
potentially sexualized nature of Edwards's "exposures": "Week after week,
people tune in to the show hoping that one of these days his fancy 'element
of surprise' will blow up right in Ralph Edwards' face. What then? What
if the victim simply refuses to go through with the noisome spectacle, re-
living his life in the glare of the lights and before the TV camera? . . . Some of
the stars . . . have passed the word around that they'll walk off at the psychological moment and leave Edwards holding his impotent mike."[99]

While Edwards's performance was geared toward presenting the star's past in terms of moral biography—which could sustain or revive public approval of the star—these quotes indicate that stars might resent the intrusion on their privacy and having to maintain socially competent performances before millions of people in a surprise situation (although the last quote also suggests that the public's judgment is possibly directed at Edwards and not the stars). Dredging up events and people from the past always ran the risk of improper disclosures, even if inadvertent. What Edwards assumed to be a secure, moral past life surely contained contradictions of which the program's honoree might be all too aware. On occasion guests seem to share some of the anxiety expressed by Al Duncie: when Nat King Cole is surprised by Edwards, he looks fearful and embarrassed and makes as if to walk off stage. The journalist Lowell Thomas expresses obvious anger at the surprise "honor." Even when a guest such as the former film star Frances Farmer knew of the show in advance, there was the potential for embarrassing intrusions into the past. Recalling Marsha Cassidy's point that sob quiz show hosts appropriated the stories of female guests, Edwards makes Farmer submit to intense grilling about her path to an insane asylum and back. She stands, with what appears to be rigid composure, and answers with "no" a series of questions about drugs, alcohol, and atheism. (Farmer had won an essay contest in high school writing about the death of God.) He mentions that he has contacted over 125 producers to watch this show and call her with offers, setting her up to public failure should audiences not see her in movies and television in the near future. Years later she wrote that it was one of the "most distasteful episodes" in her life (and there were plenty!). "Nothing ever cheapened me in my own sight as did my appearance on This is Your Life." As to her appearance being prearranged, Farmer sarcastically noted, "It seems they could not risk taking the tempestuous id of Frances Farmer unaware."[100]

Obviously many stars called to testify at the Confidential grand jury or trial also feared the intrusion of privacy and the retelling of past events in their lives. Many managed to be out of town when subpoenas arrived. Yet an examination of the state's use of Dorothy Dandridge, Liberace, and Maureen O'Hara as grand jury witnesses undercuts simple assumptions about the meaning of the trial, both in terms of the trial's participation in the state's "othering" of Confidential to mask its own surveillance powers and of the goals and effects of certain stars' performances on the witness stand. In other words, a "repressive" thesis is not a model for understanding what transpired in the trial. Specifically the way the state became invested in particular *Confidential* stories through the willingness of those star subjects to participate in the state's case, suggests that the trial was not a mask for the state's totalitarian tendencies, that the state had complicated, even ambivalent notions about who should be included in the membership of society, and that the public might not have understood the state's motivations in the way the state hoped it would, or accepted all of the state's interpretations.

For instance, Pat Brown claimed many years after the trial that his office filed criminal charges against *Confidential* not because of industry pressure but because he felt it maliciously defamed Dorothy Dandridge.[101] In his version of the state's motivation, Brown, a devout liberal who wanted his legacy to include defending civil rights for black Americans, remembers it in terms of Dandridge's dignity and right to be accepted as a full member in American society. Fabricating, hinting at, or documenting instances of interracial sex was a prime tactic of the FBI and right-wing groups to smear civil rights activists at this time. *Confidential* had a similar smear ethic, especially regarding female African American entertainers. The magazine used defamation in an attempt to exclude African American entertainers from membership in society by appealing to racial bigotry that abhorred miscegenation, and it described African American women as animalistic, always primed for sex. *Confidential*'s story portrayed Dandridge in this way, so Brown's use of the article as generator of the charges was an attack on this system of defaming African Americans and on negative stereotypes of black femininity.[102] From another perspective, no matter what Brown's motivation was, the state's defense of Dandridge confirmed intolerance for interracial sexual relationships and confirmed that the only African American woman whose privacy was worth protecting was the "proper"—that is, asexual—lady.

Liberace's willingness to give testimony to the grand jury was a major part of the publicity surrounding the state's case (though to my knowledge, he never testified at the trial). The *Confidential* story "Why Liberace's Song Should Be 'Mad about the Boy!'" suggested he aggressively demanded kisses and other attention from a male press agent.[103] A star's homosexual identity at this time was a more explosive secret than interracial heterosexual romance, but Liberace's case is complicated by the degree to which his sexuality might be considered an "open secret" to at least portions of the American public (in a way that Hudson's was not, although it was an open secret in Hollywood). By accusing the magazine of libel, Liberace is suggesting their story has threatened his membership in the community, in essence asking the court to affirm that the community's identity excludes homo-

FIGURE 3.5 Maureen O'Hara and Liberace testify before the grand jury convened in 1957 to investigate criminal charges against *Confidential* magazine. Author's collection.

sexuals. By doing so, Liberace assents to a homophobic idea of community, and the court also assents and rewards him by taking his accusations seriously enough to serve as testimony in indicting *Confidential*. However, if we agree that some people knew or wondered about his sexuality, even if only the writer and several million readers of the *Confidential* article,[104] they also knew that the story was not entirely libelous. This means that defamation law as a tool for some part of the community to maintain its power might be seen by some or participated in by some as itself an "open secret." In other words, in supporting Liberace, the state not only maintains a homophobic community but also risks exposing the libel law as adjudicating *not truth* but who shall have power to stay a member of the community and under what conditions.

The *Confidential* story about Maureen O'Hara plays with the growing fascination with the sexually experimenting woman, eagerly read about in the Kinsey report and *Playboy* but usually counterposed to the wife and mother ideal prevalent in so many other representations in this period. In press interviews after her grand jury testimony, O'Hara defended her accusation of *Confidential* as libelous by appealing to how it hurt her as a professional, and it concerned her as a mother that such material would be available to children.[105] The latter defense allied her stance with both the maternal ideal of the 1950s and the moral crusades of the era that decried a number of popular culture representations and media (e.g., comic books) as bad influences on children. Her concern for her standing as a professional was both a plea for recognition that one's believability or attractiveness as a public figure can depend on the dignity accorded by the community and for recognition that she was a worker and an image with a value in the market. Unlike many of the witnesses, O'Hara displayed obvious anger on the stand. Although this was frequently read as displays of "Irish temper," it was not a trait encouraged by the feminine mystique of the time, nor was her constant reminder that she was a professional as well as a mother. The state (through the trial), rather than functioning as a monolithic machine of repression, provided contexts for O'Hara performances that represented nontraditional feminine images, even as it was attempting to silence *Confidential's* nontraditional feminine portrait of the actress.

The jury's inability to come to a decision about the charges against *Confidential* might have been because the complexity of the legal issues or of star personas as they were revealed by the case involved too many contradictions that were salient but not solvable, fully understood, or perhaps speakable at the time.[106] For that reason, either convicting or clearing *Confidential* would send a message about the stars as members of the community that was impossibly definitive. *Confidential* and the other scandal magazines became tamer in the years immediately following the trial. (Harrison sold off *Confidential* a few months later.) They would eventually be replaced by the tabloid papers popular today, most of which have adopted *Confidential's* aggressive surveillance tactics.

Although they may differ in their moral contextualization of sexuality, the ways *This Is Your Life* and the scandal magazines speak or keep silent about it exemplify the fluid discursivity around that issue in the 1950s. Their strategies, which include intrusions of privacy and forced confessions, open their subjects to multiple interpretations, ultimately assuming a similar reading or viewing subject who is in position to judge, condemn, or empathize with the star performing under scrutiny. In this way they question whether the past and present lives of the stars can serve as models for public emulation. Both *This Is Your Life* and *Confidential* also trade on candid reactions to constructed surprises through the various strategies, such as liveness and composite fact stories, available through their specific media technologies and histories. Surprise performances or revelations draw the reader or viewer in by promising immediacy and a look at the backstage, keeping alive the public's interest in past and present stars. Ultimately the star system is reanimated by the media's display of fresh markers of authenticity.

CHAPTER FOUR

≞

AFTER THE LAUGHTER

Recycling Lucille Ball and Desi Arnaz as a Star Couple

I Love Lucy is widely considered to be the single most successful and best-recognized program in television history. In its thirty-minute format it ran on CBS from 1951 to 1957; the sixty-minute *Lucille Ball–Desi Arnaz Show* ran monthly from 1957 to 1960. In its first run the program placed number 1 in the Nielson ratings for four years and was never lower than number 3. It was rerun on CBS in prime time before first-run episodes left the air, and it has never since then been out of syndication in some television market in the United States. It has also seen wide international distribution. At the time of Lucille Ball's death in 1989 the program was translated into twenty-three languages and seen in fifty countries. Ball starred in three other series for CBS between the early 1960s and the mid-1980s, but the continuous, global presence of *I Love Lucy* reruns for almost fifty years alone could account for why commentators have argued with some credibility that Ball's face is the face seen by more people more often than that of any other human — ever.[1]

Not surprisingly given this evidence for the continuous mediation of her image, Lucille Ball's death on April 26, 1989, was the occasion for network television, particularly CBS, to reassess the star's place in television history and American cultural life. CBS stations broke into regularly scheduled television shows in the midmorning of April 26 to announce Ball's death; by noon news programs broadcast reports from Cedars-Sinai Hospital, where she died, and from the home of the comedian George Burns, himself a veteran of a popular CBS television program and, like Ball, one half of a successful husband-and-wife comedy team. The evening national news shows had long segments honoring Ball, including an interview with former president Ronald Reagan. The syndicated entertainment news series *Entertainment Tonight* devoted its entire show to summarizing Ball's career, interviewing Hollywood stars as well as fans on the street for their reactions to the news of her death. Scooping the national edition of CBS news, it reported that President George Bush had delayed a public appearance that day to make a twenty-minute phone call to Gary Morton, Ball's husband of twenty-seven years. ABC's *Nightline*, a late-night news program covering serious topics, devoted its episode to remembering Ball, and CBS canceled its regularly scheduled programming at 10 p.m. to air a one-hour tribute to Ball hosted by its nightly news anchor, Dan Rather.

Lucille Ball joins this book's cast of characters who made the transition from film stardom to television stardom between the late 1940s and early 1960s. The particular parameters of her moves from film to radio to television (and occasionally back to film again) with and without her husband Desi Arnaz, and how aspects of her film stardom resurface in the fictional persona and industrial promotion of "Lucy Ricardo," have been taken up by other authors. In this chapter I take on the daunting task of analyzing much of the postmortem television broadcasting and publications focused on Ball, Arnaz, and *I Love Lucy*, and in doing so, shift not only the terms of scholarship on Ball but also the focus of this book to the last decade of the twentieth century, when television was no longer a new media form.

It would perhaps take an entire book to explain all the reasons why Ball and *I Love Lucy* received so much attention and inspired such an unprecedented amount of television coverage at the time of and since her death. Certain themes about Ball's comedic genius and her marriage and business partnership with Arnaz pervade the television and print texts immediately following her death and in the decades since. I argue that despite the obvious focus on Ball as an individual, which frequently defines her not in terms of her film career but as the epitome of television's "thereness," the postmortem coverage participates in a recycling of Ball that conjoins her with ex-husband and costar Arnaz as a *star couple* who were central to the development of the situation comedy as a television genre and to understanding the meaning of family in postwar America. This is a recycling that was first put in place in some of the promotions for the *I Love Lucy* program and has only become more characteristic of Ball's recycling in the years since her death, as television institutions and texts, as well as critics and commentators, have become more self-conscious about the medium's history and its place in American cultural and family life. Although this recycling of Ball as part of a star couple is anticipated in past promotions of *I Love Lucy* and is the most common way she is recycled in the present, it is by no means the inevitable (or only) means of recycling this star. But television's operating logics about its own history and relation to viewing families, the Arnaz children's control over their parents' images, and the currency of anxieties about gender and family in contemporary American culture overdetermine the recycling of Lucille Ball and Desi Arnaz as star couple and as the premiere television family.

Fantasy, the 1950s, and *I Love Lucy*

The degree to which many of the same themes, images, lines of dialogue, comedy routines, histories of television, and star narratives are repeated in the various and numerous recyclings of Lucille Ball and Desi Arnaz— whether in books, magazine articles, CDs, documentaries, anniversary shows on television, computer advertising campaigns, fan "collectibles," or U.S. postage stamps—suggests that the recycling phenomenon associated with Ball and Arnaz be examined from the perspective of theory that explains what is so appealing or necessary about repetition.[2] Histories of television and *I Love Lucy*, as well as biographies of Ball, explain the continued popularity of the star and her first television situation comedy in part by pointing to an industrial context: the decision of her husband costar (and eventually executive producer) Arnaz to film *I Love Lucy* rather than broadcast it live, which has made possible fifty years of continuous reruns and exposure to Ball's and Arnaz's faces and performances. While the reruns of *I Love Lucy*, and the industrial conditions that make reruns possible and profitable, are crucial factors in the Ball-Arnaz recyclings, economic and industrial contexts don't fully explain the degree and length to which Ball has been recycled in a variety of media and genres, nor why her persona should be so closely linked in these recyclings to her character Lucy Ricardo and to the persona of her ex-husband so long after they divorced and decades after their deaths. These contexts do not explain the *appeal* of such repetition to viewers.

Psychoanalysis does theorize the appeal of repetition in its examination of repetition's role in the structures of obsession and fantasy, which emerge in this theory as key elements in the construction and maintenance of human subjectivity. A number of literary and film critics have identified fantasies of origins, which in Freudian terms are part of an enigma-solving process the self engages in to explain its origins, as central to the pleasures and politics of popular narrative. As Jean Laplanche and Jean-Bertrand Pontalis argue in their explication and elaboration of Freud's model, fantasies are *settings* for desire where the borders between conscious and unconscious are fluid: "Like myths, they claim to provide a representation of, and a solution to, the major enigmas which confront the child. Whatever appears to the subject as something needing an explanation or theory, is dramatized as a moment of emergence, the beginning of a history."[3] The emergence of sexuality is dramatized in fantasies of seduction, and the origins of the differences between the sexes is represented or dramatized in fantasies of castration, the origination and formation of the self in fantasies of the family romance. Significantly Laplanche and Pontalis situate fantasies as *claiming* to provide a solution to the major enigmas, for they are not really solvable, at least not once and for all. Hence the need for the subject to repeat the fantasies.

While a number of critics have credibly proposed fantasy theory as applicable to popular film narratives, it would seem to be even more pertinent to an understanding of series television, which, like the fantasy scenario, is marked by a prolongation of desire.[4] Serial television narratives, in which character growth and plot lines develop over time in a progression of episodes that forestall a definitive closure, are more obviously tied to the sustenance of scenarios of desire. But series television such as *I Love Lucy*, in which episodes are discrete scenarios of disequilibrium and resolution, can also be seen as prolonging desire; their resolutions don't fully effect a mastery of the narrative's problems because week after week the initial premise of the series keeps motoring disequilibrium. For example, Lucy never learns her lesson; every week she struggles for attention, trying to get into the act or subverting Ricky's dictums about money, clothes, furniture, or gossip, alone or with the help of Ethel and sometimes Fred. Even when she and Ricky are on the same side, her feelings of lack and her schemes propel the narrative forward. David Marc has argued that *I Love Lucy* works according to the production and narrative economies of four characters: the housewife Lucy and the bandleader Ricky and their best friends and landlords, Fred and Ethel Mertz.[5] In Marc's terms, this is an efficient economy since it uses the basic relationships among the four to generate a variety of plots based on shifting power alliances: Lucy and Ethel can gang up against the men; the Ricardos can fight with the Mertzes; Lucy and the Mertzes can work together to subvert Ricky's attempts to keep them out of his show; all can turn against Lucy. Marc stops short of identifying the status of character alliances in the program as a libidinal economy, but the mobile positionings of these characters within a highly charged atmosphere of romance, marriage, family, work, and performance link the program's narratives to the originary fantasy scenarios that work out enigmas of the self in relation to sexuality and power. The flexibility among the characters' relations to power suggests what Laplanche and Pontalis emphasize as the subject's lack of fixed position in regard to the objects and events fantasized and his or her identification with or desire for them.

What is central to this study, however, is the historically and socially specific working out of these psychic processes, how they are part of the process of constructing a social imaginary in relation to stars. The historically specific correspondences between the scenarios of *I Love Lucy* and originary fantasy scenarios continue, or become transformed, through history and relate to the ongoing recyclings of the program's star couple. In her examination of the relationship between originary fantasies and what she terms film "body" genres (pornography, horror, maternal melodrama), Linda Williams suggests that the most difficult work for critics is "to relate original fantasies to historical context and specific generic history."[6] Yet Williams herself proposes a relation when she argues that these film genres, which in their own specific reworkings of originary fantasies function as "cultural problem solving," sustain their popularity to the extent they continue to address persistent cultural problems while recasting the nature of these problems through time.

Given that a number of critics argue that *I Love Lucy* elicits viewer pleasure and recognition from Lucy's infantilization (meaning both the childishness of her behavior and her positioning by Ricky's punishments, including spankings), the program's narrative logics would seem to be linked to the fantasy of castration. From this perspective Lucy's failure to alter her subordination to Ricky constitutes the problematic of sexual difference within a patriarchal culture in which woman is symbolically castrated. For example, Lori Landay points out that Lucy's ineptness mitigates her subversion of Ricky's rules.[7] Alexander Doty argues that the program conflates "the infantile and the female through its characterization of Lucy through her various lacks" (lack of control over language, music, and her own body).[8] Patricia Mellencamp sees Lucy as a "rebellious child whom the husband/ father Ricky endured, understood, loved, and even punished, as for example, when he spanked her for her continual disobedience."[9] All of these critics historicize the series' repetitious infantilization or castration of Lucy as representative (however comic or improbable her behavior or Ricky's punishments) of the gendered containment characteristic of 1950s American culture. Polarized and contained gender roles and spheres of action (male/public vs. female/private realms) in the 1950s are seen as supports of larger geopolitical stances of the U.S. government at that time: containing the threat of alien, other ways of life inimitable to white, capitalist, patriarchal, and heterosexist American society.

Mellencamp explicitly frames her discussion of *I Love Lucy* within Freudian terms but uses his theories of the comic and humor rather than his fantasy theories to examine Lucy's gendered containment. She argues that Lucy's antics must be seen as both comic, in which vulnerable human beings are pitted against a powerful external world, and humorous, in which pleasure through joking is substituted for hurt or anger over victimization. *I Love Lucy* provides historically specific versions of both, as each offers pleasures and strategies of survival not only for Lucy in the face of patriarchal law but also for the 1950s female spectator at home, who is able to avoid the displeasure of Lucy's situation through laughter at her antics (which include failing). Mellencamp's theory is relevant for my purposes because it acknowledges the flexible power dynamics pertinent to the comic and humor: whether the spectator experiences distanced but empathetic comic pleasure or gallows humor pleasure (pleasure in spite of the distressing affects that interfere with it) from Lucy's antics depends "on one's view of who the victim is," Lucy or Ricky (or, for that matter, Ethel or Fred). Ricky can often be seen as the victim, not only because Lucy ruins his show but because the program, following 1950s geopolitics and ethnic discrimination, positions his Latin heritage as lack, as not giving him control over language or the symbolic. Mellencamp is able to come to a similar conclusion about the relation between pleasure or identification and humor as Williams is about the relation of body genres to cultural problem solving through fantasy; the fluidity of spectatorial and character positions "suggests a complexity of shifting identifications amidst gendered, historical audiences."[10]

Mellencamp identifies *I Love Lucy* and Ball's comic persona developed (in part) through her role as Lucy as symptomatic of the 1950s as much because of Lucy's resistance to containment as its achievement. Lori Landay ultimately argues something similar when she writes that Lucy is a "liminal" character who "enacted survival strategies that call attention to the possibilities *and* the limitations of the social relations of the sexes within domestic ideology" (my emphasis).[11] Gustavo Perez-Firmat, in his study of Arnaz as representative of a certain generation of Cuban Americans (those born in Cuba but spending their life from childhood or adolescence onward in America), frames the issue of liminality and *I Love Lucy* with much less ambivalence than Landay or Mellencamp.[12] He downplays the consequences of the characters' victimizations of one another. Ultimately he describes the program as a fantasy about sexual and cultural difference magically overlaid by a fantasy of seduction. Lucy and Ricky love one another *not in spite of* but *because of* cultural difference; cultural difference is what fuels their pleasurable, mutual seduction. In this perspective *I Love Lucy* shows, to borrow Landay's terms, the "limitations and possibilities" for an ethnically mixed marriage and for Cuban Americans in the 1950s. Perez-Firmat, commenting on the fact that the "I" in *I Love Lucy* refers first of all to Ricky/Arnaz loving Ball/Lucy, suggests that the program is about sexual intimacy; it is a lover's discourse on heterosexual love and love for Americanness.

For Perez-Firmat, the program's treatment of the Ricardos' bedroom is exemplary of the dangers a lover's discourse might pose for a situation comedy in the 1950s that supported polarized and hierarchized gender roles. He rightly points to the uniqueness for 1950s situation comedies of the Ricardos' pushed-together twin beds in the first season. He suggests that the beds were pulled apart sometime in the second season, during Lucy Ricardo/Lucille Ball's pregnancy, because their evidence of a "lover's discourse" provoked tensions in the 1950s discourse about marriage, sexuality, and gender roles: "It could be that the combination of Lucy's pregnancy and joined beds was too visible a reference to the couple's sex life."[13] Ricky's nightclub suggests the more appropriate separation of gendered spaces for the 1950s; it is the secure professional space for Ricky, in which he rules. The Ricardos' living room, on the other hand, is a "carnivalesque" or "liminal" space of "shifting identities and fluid boundaries." It might be the space where Lucy rules, just as the nightclub is Ricky's space, but it is also the place for the couple's "intercultural encounters," where the outcomes are not necessarily what's expected. Perez-Firmat foregrounds the functions of the living room and the "I" in the series title, which I argue link the spectator's experience of the program to the fluid points of view available in the fantasy scenario. The "I" in the title may on one level refer to Ricky or Desi, but just as the fantasizer can project himself or herself into the scene from multiple points of entry, the viewer can project his or her own identity onto the anonymous pronoun, identifying with Ricky/Desi as well as with Lucy. And many viewers and critics in the 1950s (and later) did.

Crossing Wavelengths with Lucy and Ricky and Fred and Ethel: Promoting the Star Couple in the 1950s

As I have suggested, media historians and theorists have provided a number of reasons for *I Love Lucy*'s popularity in the 1950s, and their readings of the program's negotiations of the "possibilities and limitations" of 1950s expectations about gender roles through humor and liminal characters or space can be linked to a historically specific understanding of how originary fantasies become mobilized and publicly shared at a particular moment.[14] But questions still remain: How to account for the *continuing* popularity of not just *I Love Lucy* but also its stars? How did *I Love Lucy* and its promotions set up current recyclings of Ball and Arnaz? The former question was basically the one posed in many of the broadcasts immediately following Ball's death, at which point *I Love Lucy* had already been airing for over thirty-five years. In the *Nightline* show devoted to Ball's passing, which, like all the news reports at this time, was focused on Ball the television star rather than Ball the film star, the news correspondent Aaron Brown asked the former television comedians Sid Caesar and Jerry Lewis why the character of Lucy Ricardo, a character that is "really a throwback" because she has to fight to work outside the home, still "works for a generation of women for whom there are women on the Supreme Court . . . [and] running for vice-president." Brown also asks if they think *I Love Lucy* could be made today (in the late 1980s). Caesar replies that the show still works because there is enough commonality between the 1950s and the 1980s for people to recognize Lucy's predicaments: "Because women still take care of our houses, still care for children, they still take care of it. I think it's imbued in the public that they know what she's doing . . . what she was doing." Lewis takes umbrage at the historical and pseudo-feminist perspectives implied by Caesar's point (and, unlike Caesar, conflates Lucy Ricardo with Lucille Ball): "Lucille Ball's work had nothing to do with feminism, had nothing to do with politics, the question that you [Aaron Brown] had asked Sid. It had to do with a simple premise, and we must not miss this premise — this was a funny broad, she was a funny lady, she did funny things. . . . She was magic. And she was magic because she made the people in Bangladesh forget they were hungry. That's what comedy is."

Humor arising out of a fictional housewife's subversion of gender roles seemingly transcendent of historical context? *Nightline* was one of many television news shows covering Ball's death that offered both these reasons for the longevity of *I Love Lucy* and Ball's star persona. With the exception of Lewis, none of the commentators or interviewees seems to feel there is a contradiction in the suggestion that the program or Ball could be capable of producing more than one kind of humor (though, to my knowledge, only Lewis overstates the "transcendent" power of Ball's comedy to the point where it alleviates famine). But there is a noticeable linkage—not confined to the Lewis interview—of Lucy Ricardo to Lucille Ball and the latter to Desi Arnaz in most of the commentaries and interviews, with little attention given to Ball's many (over eighty) roles in films since the 1930s or to her television programs after *I Love Lucy* (two long-running shows and one short-lived).[15] Lucy Ricardo's subversion of her 1950s gender role through scheming and humor is often placed as either an ironic counterpart to Lucille Ball's validated and celebrated work outside the home or as an apt comparison to Ball's own act of subversion—which, in her case, was subversion of separate-sphere culture by having both career and family. (As recounted over and over in the news broadcasts, Ball had desperately wanted Arnaz to costar with her on television because he would have to take his band off the road and stay home to start a family with her.) In other words, Ball's relation to career, marriage, and family is seen as inextricably intertwined with what made television's Lucy Ricardo (rather than the many film characters Ball played) possible in the first place and what makes her comedy still so appealing many years later.

The linkage of the career-driven Ball/Ricardo to marriage and family is often assumed by both popular media commentaries and scholars. Journalists and scholars take note of the parallels and ironic contrasts between the Ricardo and Arnaz marriages, of the origins of the program in Ball's desire to find a project that Arnaz could be involved in so that they could be together and start a family, and of the kinds of publicity generated for the show that highlighted the fact that Lucy and Ricky were played by a real-life married couple. But no one has analyzed how extratextual and textual discourses produced Ball and Arnaz as a star couple and also might have encouraged multiple, sometimes contradictory readings of the programs and the stars in the 1950s and fueled the recyclings of these stars in the years since.

Of all the scholars writing on *I Love Lucy*, Lori Landay has provided the most thoroughly detailed contextualization of the show and the Ball-Arnaz marriage in the historical moment of the 1950s. She rightly points out that the tendency of mainstream, general readership magazine articles (such as those in *Life*) to focus on Ball as a "housewife at heart" was contradictory considering Ball was not a housewife, nor did she play a character who wanted to be a housewife. Nonetheless Landay suggests that such an emphasis on happy housewifery in secondary texts of the time reinforced the program's re-creation of the real-life marriage as a happy one and helped blur the lines between public and private. Landay argues that it was only in 1960, when the couple divorced, that "the layer of fiction that *I Love Lucy* and Desilu provided was stripped away, ironically revealing married life to be a 'nightmare.'"[16]

Actually the layer of fiction about the Ball-Arnaz marriage was continually, if slowly, being stripped away already during the course of the first run of *I Love Lucy*, making available multiple and perhaps ideological contestatory readings of the program and the series. Mainstream magazines were not the only publicity sites for Desilu and its promotion of the star couple and the program; certain media forms and their conventions recycled the star couple and the fantasies of sexual difference and seduction available from *I Love Lucy* in contexts in which containment is more visibly unstable. For example, the many appearances Ball and Arnaz made in comedy-variety shows at the time of *I Love Lucy* demonstrate how other genres participated in some aspects of that program's historically specific versions of originary fantasies; they also expose what other fantasy variations about marriage and sexuality were available at this time. The contradictions and negotiations of norms of gender, marriage, work, and ethnicity rehearsed by *I Love Lucy* were more explicitly, variably, and, even more complexly, rendered at that time in the appearances Ball and Arnaz made on other television programs in the 1950s, such as Ed Sullivan's *Toast of the Town* (CBS, 1948–71, renamed *The Ed Sullivan Show* in 1955) and *The Bob Hope Show* (NBC special, airing periodically since 1948). An examination of these programs suggests that the more adult, more loosely narrativized genre of the comedy-variety show, with its sexually risqué jokes, open promotional function, and generally parodic stance, did not blur the lines between private and public as much as reveal the tensions between the "reel" and the "real" of this show business couple; that is, they revealed the difference between the Ricardos and the Arnazes, situating Ball and Arnaz as stars negotiating the burden of acting out the antics of the Ricardos.

Analysis of these guest appearances on comedy-variety programs reminds us that viewers in the 1950s simultaneously enjoyed the representations of marriage and family life in the situation comedy *I Love Lucy* and representations that parodically destabilized some of its conclusions about love, sexuality, and race and gender hierarchies through play with the Ball and Arnaz personas. If Ball and Arnaz are most frequently recycled since their deaths in relation to *I Love Lucy*, it must be understood that those re-cyclings are informed by dystopic narratives of marriage and family life that are first evident in some of the television and print texts that supposedly promoted the successful 1950s situation comedy.

In order to promote Desilu productions, the appearances of Ball and Arnaz on comedy-variety programs, sometimes playing the Ricardos and sometimes playing themselves, function by making comparisons between the reel-life marriage and careers of Lucy and Ricky Ricardo and the real-life marriage and careers of Lucille Ball and Desi Arnaz, a working, cross-cultural couple, parents, business partners in a media empire made possible by the success of the Ricardo family. Mimi White has theorized the role of interprogram referentiality and diegetic mixing (varied practices, which include characters or stars of one program appearing on another program, story lines begun in one program continuing on another, the practice of spinoffs) as a way American broadcast television has attempted to construct and keep the potential audience for any individual program by creating a "broadly conceived generic television audience." This audience recognizes and presumably negotiates fantasy relationships with these stars or characters "across temporal, spatial, and narrative diversity."[17] As the lines blur between programs once considered separate fictional constructs, a self-totalizing televisual world is created in which the ideal spectator is one reassured and unified by the sameness of all television. White makes these claims to explain the prevalence of interprogram referentiality in 1980s network programming, when the rise of cable threatened the exclusive relationship between audience and broadcast television that had been operative since the days of *I Love Lucy*. Her insights nevertheless help explain the promotional logics behind the 1950s practice of stars from one show guest-starring on another network program. However, the appearances of the sitcom stars Ball and Arnaz on comedy-variety programs in the 1950s suggests a gap between an ideal spectator reassured and unified by the sameness of all television and an audience that recognizes the differences between the narrative and visual strategies and the moral status of the two genres. This is an audience constructed out of all the texts and intertexts — including the mainstream press, scandal magazines, and television and film appearances — circulating about and around *I Love Lucy*, many of which contradict or conflict with one another. What is supposed to promote *I Love Lucy* may in fact do so only by revealing its omissions and constructions.

In 1954 the cast of *I Love Lucy* appeared on Ed Sullivan's *Toast of the Town* in a skit built around Sullivan's attempt to get them on his show. By the time of this appearance Ball and Arnaz were enjoying great success from *I Love Lucy*: the show was the top-rated program on television, Arnaz had assumed the title of executive producer of *I Love Lucy* in 1952, the birth of Desi Jr. in January 1953 had stolen the headlines away from Eisenhower's presidential inauguration, Desilu was expanding television production, and Ball and Arnaz had starred in the box-office hit *The Long, Long Trailer* (MGM, 1954). *I Love Lucy* ancillary products, from dolls and comic books to cookbooks and sheet music, were enjoying great popularity, and stories about the Arnazes' off-screen family and work life appeared in magazines like TV *Guide* and *Life*.[18] The Sullivan skit does little to suggest rifts in this successful image, but the fiction it creates of the real-life family underscores the constructed nature of the reel Ricardo family as it plays with a tension endemic to star discourses, what Richard Dyer has identified as between "extraordinary" and "ordinary" poles of identity.[19] This dialectic presumably works to make fans both idolize the extraordinary aspects of the persona and identify with the ordinary aspects of the star. Many star personas are successful to the extent that they resolve the contradictions of this dialectic. As I have argued in previous chapters, this tension had to be negotiated by various television personalities and genres to fit perceived audience desires in the late 1940s to early 1950s. Many variety shows favored representation of the extraordinary star persona, but by the mid-1950s, due in part to the success of situation comedies like *I Love Lucy*, the ordinariness of the star was emphasized, but not without gaps and tensions.

The *Toast of the Town* skit opens with Lucy and Desi in a simply furnished living room presumed to be part of their Beverly Hills home. The couple is dressed casually, Desi in his stockinged-feet and Lucy in robe and curlers. Desi is reading the Sunday paper, and Lucy is knitting baby clothes, which she holds up for Desi's admiration:

DESI: Lucy . . . again? We've already done that bit!
LUCY: Don't be silly! This is for Eve Arden's baby.

Desi's characterization of a potential pregnancy as a "bit" reminds us of the historic *I Love Lucy* episode featuring Little Ricky's birth and of how the Arnazes' own lives have provided material for the television program.[20] In Desi's remark we see the Ricardos as fictional characters and the Arnazes as performers who have to negotiate the demands of real life with work, as they did when Ball became pregnant during the show's second season.

The *I Love Lucy* episode "Lucy Is Enceinte," which announced Lucy Ricardo's pregnancy, gave viewers apparent access to the real married

FIGURE 4.1 Lucille Ball and Desi Arnaz as "just folks." *Toast of the Town*, CBS, 1954.

couple when Ball and Arnaz break down in what appears to be a genuinely spontaneous flow of tears as Ricky sings to Lucy "We're Having a Baby, My Baby and Me." But journalists commenting on the place of Ball's pregnancy in the show's plot lines often reinforce or even extend the *Toast of the Town* sketch's satiric look at the constructed relation between the reel and real couples. For example, *Life* calls the birth of Desi Jr. and "Little Ricky" "one of the niftiest mixtures of science and showmanship."[21] *Newsweek* suggests that Lucy's pregnancy has functioned as a publicity gimmick, claiming that upon finding out she was expecting a child, "Lucille and Desi immediately saw what the real-life baby could do for their careers as Lucy Ricardo and her husband Ricky."[22] Several articles, including this one, link the pregnancies of the two Lucys to the show's mode of production; they produce new variations in the established narrative patterns for the program, providing a "limitless supply of comedy material in bringing up the child."[23] It seems that the efficient production and narrative economy of four characters that Marc describes can profitably enlarge to an economy of five when Ball becomes pregnant. In this view the Arnazes' involvement in commodity production exploits Ball's pregnancy as it encompasses the supplying of both babies and programming for the pleasure of millions who love Lucy, as well as their own material profit.

A number of articles focus on what might be the more typical commodity production associated with television programming, such as the ancillary products and commercial endorsements coinciding in 1952–53 with the show's success and the birth of Desi Jr. While some articles share either the promotional motivations or the cynical positionings of the articles covering other aspects of profitable Arnaz-Ricardo doublings, others exhibit a register of anxiety about the effects of the reel baby on the real baby. These tend to reassure the reader that the Arnazes are not exploiting the labor or image of Desi Jr., even though many of the products exploit Lucy's pregnancy and Little Ricky. For instance, Eleanor Harris writes in *The Reader's Digest* that although *I Love Lucy* has "mushroomed [through commercial enterprises] into 'I Love an Octopus,'" the Arnazes have turned down commercial endorsements featuring Desi Jr.'s name or likeness. The image of *I Love Lucy* as octopus suggests with some ambivalence the ability of the program, Desilu, and the Arnazes to grab and capitalize on anything to make the show or themselves a success, whether it is events in the couple's real life or ancillary products. Perhaps to alleviate any anxiety raised by such comparisons, Harris then quotes Ball as saying, "The real symbols of success are a happy and healthy family."[24] Similarly, after describing the many products inspired by *I Love Lucy* and the Arnazes' record $8 million contract with CBS, TV *Guide* reports that the couple expect little Desi to succeed in life "on his own two feet."[25]

The *Life* cover story shortly after Desi Jr.'s birth perhaps most subtly displays anxiety and ambivalence about the exploitiveness, constructedness, and ordinariness of the Arnazes. The family is featured in the cover photo, in which Desi Sr. and Lucie (born three months before the first episode of *I Love Lucy* aired) are huddled around Lucille and the infant son she cradles in her lap. The three are smiling, and all eyes are focused on the baby. The photo seems to capture the typical 1950s family; only the caption defines them as special, as "TV's First Family." "Lucy's Boys," the article inside the magazine, is more about the Ricardo family and the labor behind it than the Arnaz family. There are photos of Ball preparing to return to the program after maternity leave as well as of the twin infant sons who will portray Little Ricky. Several features of the article and photo spread suggest that representing families on television is an act or business operation. For example, a series of photos has Ball holding one of the twin infants who play Little Ricky, with a lengthy caption emphasizing her ability *to act* as if the child were her own son. Another photo features the twins' mother and grandmother, the on-set nurse, and the female social worker supervising the filming. The article discusses how labor laws necessitate the use of twins, since each baby can work only two hours per day. Mention is also made of the Arnazes' $8 million CBS contract, and photo captions claim that the couple will profit from products associated with Little Ricky and that the twin babies playing the character will make $25 per show. Readers are left to their own conclusions about the disparity between the two families' salaries and the ordinariness of the Arnaz family.[26]

These images and texts about the Arnazes and *I Love Lucy* at the time of Desi Jr.'s birth suggest that the couple's guest appearance on *Toast of the Town* might be read with greater skepticism than textual evidence from the program alone reveals. Although it makes clear that the couple have movie star friends (Lucy mentions Eve Arden, who had costarred with Ball in films and was at this time starring in a Desilu production), the skit downplays the extraordinary qualities of the Ball and Arnaz personas. It smoothes over the difficulties of the real couple having to negotiate real events (like pregnancy) for the sake of the reel family and its audience by a focus on the ordinariness of this star couple.

For instance, after they receive a phone call from Sullivan requesting their appearance and announcing an imminent visit to their home, they madly dash around the room cleaning. Lucy is afraid of being seen as a slob:

LUCY: What's the matter with you? We don't want him to see the house looking like this!

DESI: What's the matter with it? It looks fine to me.

LUCY: For Heaven's sake!

DESI: Honey, why don't you let him see you the way we really are? You know . . . natural, with no pretensions?

LUCY: The show's called *Toast of the Town*, not *Crumbs of the Town*!

They change into evening clothes and rehearse responses to Sullivan's request that emphasize their modesty and surprise. In contrast to the usual configuration of Ricky and Lucy, Lucy and Desi are *equally* foolish as they both claim no interest in their fame. Although their quick transformation into elegant attire and narcissistic preening links them to glamorous stardom, their nervousness about meeting Sullivan and appearing on his show makes them seem as vulnerably ordinary as those surprised on *This Is Your Life*.

Vivian Vance and William Frawley (Ethel and Fred Mertz) appear one at a time after Sullivan's arrival, each offering the explanation that he or she was just strolling through the neighborhood. Vance and Frawley (who ap-

FIGURE 4.2 Lucy and Desi awaiting Ed Sullivan. *Toast of the Town*, CBS, 1954.

parently hated one another in real life)[27] are depicted as having a friendly relationship with the Arnazes outside the confines of the show, which works to naturalize their relationship on the show and represent them all as "just plain folks." Their performances also make the skit resemble *I Love Lucy*, in which the Mertzes' past as vaudeville entertainers is often central to the plot. Here they bring out music and vaudeville costumes that they just happen to have with them in order to audition for Sullivan.

Much of the work in drawing parallels between the off-screen lives of the *I Love Lucy* cast and the sitcom itself is displaced onto the performances of Vance and Frawley. They behave as they do on *I Love Lucy*, whereas Ball and Arnaz do not. Although Ball and Arnaz do perform comedically, the *Toast of the Town* skit suggests parity between the couple. This conforms to the image they liked to project to the public: press releases and captions for photos of the couple emphasize their roles as president and vice president of Desilu Productions (Ball was second in command, although legally she had creative control over Arnaz on *I Love Lucy*), Ball as comedic genius and Arnaz as business genius. At this time infantile Lucy and volatile Ricky were not to be confused with Ball and Arnaz.

That tidy assigning of Lucy and Ricky to fictional constructs and the Ball and Arnaz of this skit to the more realistic status of business partners and

FIGURE 4.3 William Frawley and Vivian Vance just happen to drop by to see Ed Sullivan. *Toast of the Town*, CBS, 1954.

ordinary folks is complicated by the second half of the *Toast of the Town*. Here Ball and Arnaz are roasted by celebrities (an odd group, consisting of the actor John Hodiak and the baseball star Dusty Rhodes) and business executives (Harry Chesley, an executive at Philip Morris, one of the sponsors of *I Love Lucy*, and the MGM executive Howard Dietz). At the end of the roast Ball thanks Desi, who stands and tearfully says, "You know . . . we came to this country and we didn't have a cent in our pockets. . . . From cleaning canary cages to this night in New York is a long ways, and I don't think that any other country in the world would give you that opportunity. I want to say thank you, thank you, America!" While Arnaz is speaking, Ball, sitting on the other side of Sullivan, is clearly moved, and she too seems to be holding back tears. She leans forward a number of times to better see Arnaz on the other side of their host and perhaps to better participate in the moving moment. Clearly Arnaz's story is not ordinary, even though it might conform to certain stereotypical rise-to-success narratives in the American cultural mythology. Arnaz's emotion is not the expression of an angry patriarch, which is the usual emotion excessively expressed by Ricky Ricardo, but of a sentimental and grateful immigrant toward whom his wife shows empathetic solicitation. More significant, Ball and Arnaz appear to be spontaneously reacting to events of the moment rather than acting. Like the responses from the surprised guests on *This Is Your Life*, the couple's reactions appear to give the audience a glimpse of the real people behind the star construction. Yet roasts are ritualistic functions honoring people of renown, and Arnaz's patriotic speech comes a year after the infamous accusations that Ball was a "Red" because she had registered to vote communist in the 1930s to please her grandfather. After that event Arnaz was ready and even used to proclaiming his (sincere) patriotism. This episode of *Toast of the Town* presents multiple views of Ball and Arnaz and reveals the variety of components—from scripted linkings to and denials of the television characters associated with the couple to revelations of alleged unguarded behavior—that go into the construction of their star personas, denying the possibility of a single grounding for identity.

A later appearance by the couple on *The Ed Sullivan Show* suggests a less complex view of the couple, even as it suggests more serious cracks or tensions in the construction of the personas of Arnaz and Ball as happily married star couple that the first appearance had worked hard to secure. Arnaz and Ball made this 1956 appearance to promote their newly released film, *Forever Darling* (MGM, 1956), which the couple produced through their Zanra (Arnaz spelled backward) Production Company. In their third and last film together Ball and Arnaz play Susan and Lorenzo Vega. Susan, a spoiled woman from a rich family, feels neglected by her workaholic chemist husband. Her guardian angel (James Mason) intervenes by advising her to pay more attention to Lorenzo's work. After she takes his advice, the squabbling couple rekindles the romance in their marriage.

Lucy introduces a film clip from *Forever Darling* by comparing the marriage of Susan and Lorenzo with her blissful marriage to Desi: "I'll just say *Forever Darling* was a joy to make because it depicts complete married bliss . . . the happy, serene everyday home life of two people just like Desi and me. They have such complete understanding of each other." But the film clip is a scene in which the characters are fighting. Susan, who has accompanied Lorenzo on a research trip to a swamp, has upset the couple's raft and ruined Lorenzo's samples. He shouts, she wails, and they both flail in the murky water. When the clip is over and Sullivan points out that the scene hardly depicts a blissful couple, Lucy and Desi desperately search among their cans of film for a happy moment from the movie but are unable to find such a scene before the commercial break. In this way the Arnazes appear more like the Ricardos than the equal partners promoted earlier by Desilu.

While these comic moments of marital discord are reminiscent of *I Love*

FIGURE 4.4 Lucille Ball, with Desi Arnaz and Ed Sullivan, tries to find a scene of "marital bliss" from *Forever Darling. The Ed Sullivan Show*, CBS, 1955.

Lucy and therefore suggest a promotable slippage among the Arnazes, the Ricardos, and the characters in *Forever Darling*, the film is much more convincing than *I Love Lucy* in its depiction of Ball's character as miserable being a housewife. Although Susan doesn't want to break into show business or get a job, as Lucy Ricardo does, she is deeply alienated by her husband's prioritizing of career over marriage. She and Lorenzo have unfunny, bitter arguments about whether they still love one another. She goes to a movie starring James Mason and projects herself into the film as a passionate romantic interest for Mason's character, whose treatment of her suggests a sadomasochistic relationship. Susan even seeks a psychiatrist after the angel who looks like Mason has appeared to her. These aspects of the film, although superficially similar in emphasizing the discontents of married life, are far removed from the universe of *I Love Lucy*. In that universe the love between Lucy and Ricky triumphs over temporary (albeit perennial) dissatisfaction, and on more than one occasion Lucy skillfully manipulates psychiatrists who try to pathologize her desires rather than seeking them out.

Forever Darling and the *Ed Sullivan Show* sketch promoting the film might

FIGURE 4.5 "Does Desi Really Love Lucy?" *Confidential*, January 1955. Author's collection.

have also resonated (as they most certainly do now) with the increasingly prevalent rumors of discord between Ball and Arnaz. By the mid-1950s scandal magazines like *Whisper* and *Confidential* were publishing stories about the Arnazes' marriage. In 1955 *Confidential* alleged that the union was stormy. It recycled gossip from the early period of their marriage, when Ball filed for divorce in 1944. It claimed that Arnaz now had a drinking problem and frequent liaisons with call girls. Readers were asked to imagine a hot-tempered Ball with a "flat-iron in her hand," ready to strike Arnaz when he returned home after a night of carousing.[28] The *Confidential* article relishes in revealing the problems in the marriage, never losing an opportunity to use exclamation points, alliteration (e.g., "duck-out daddy"), or ethnic stereotypes ("Latin Lothario"). Robert Harrison, the magazine's publisher, claimed that his four million readers liked reading about the "truth" behind Hollywood stars' public images.[29]

The Arnazes' next variety show appearance, on *The Bob Hope Show* in 1956, is pertinent to this scandalous context, as they parody *I Love Lucy* through sexually risqué jokes and situations. Hope introduces the skit in a playfully indulgent monologue: "You know, I've known Lucy long before Desi, and I've often wondered what would have happened if she married me instead of Desi—if I were the husband in *I Love Lucy*." Hope here mixes Lucille Ball with Lucy Ricardo and Desi with Ricky. In addition he intro-

FIGURE 4.6 Lucille Ball as Lucy Ricardo and Bob Hope as Ricky Ricardo in a skit on *The Bob Hope Show*. NBC, 1956.

duces a rivalry with Arnaz/Ricky: "I know one thing, she wouldn't be doing those crazy things if I were her husband." The curtain then opens on a re-creation of the Ricardos' home — not the Arnazes' home.

In the skit that follows, Ball and Vance play Lucy and Ethel, but Hope plays Ricky, Arnaz plays Fred, and Frawley plays Captain Blighstone, the owner of the trained seal that Lucy is using in an audition. This repeats a plot device of *I Love Lucy* since, once again, she is trying to crack the world of showbiz.

Like the fantasizer of originary fantasies, Hope projects himself and his aggressive comic persona onto a scene of desire. In this case it is a scenario with the Ricardos, assuming a place in the scene — that liminal space, their living room — of marital discord and desire presented weekly in the sitcom but dislocating the matches between characters and actors. This calls attention not only to the romantic movie partnering of Hope and Ball in their film career pasts, but also to the fictional constructions and the functions of coupling itself in *I Love Lucy*.[30]

Hope continues to dominate Arnaz's character through ethnic jokes and making fun of his accent:

ARNAZ (as Fred) expresses surprise when the trained seal throws a hoop over his neck.

FIGURE 4.7 Desi Arnaz as Fred Mertz and Bob Hope as Ricky Ricardo. *The Bob Hope Show*, NBC, 1956.

HOPE (looking at Arnaz): What happened? Did you just come back from a wetback luau?

Hope plays Ricky without any signs of Cuban ethnicity. This gives him power over both the reel and real personas of Arnaz and raises the specter of the stereotypes in *I Love Lucy*, which Mellencamp argues are evident in the way Ricky is never given complete symbolic mastery because of his accent.[31] But it also trumps that show's stereotypes in its explicit aggression. At one point Arnaz-as-Fred says that Hope-as-Ricky lent him his golf clubs but did not give him any "balls," surely a sexually charged joke. In 1946 Ball apparently appealed to Hope to give Arnaz and his band a job on Hope's radio program so that she and Arnaz could be together (i.e., so he would stop philandering on the road), and it has been suggested that Arnaz wondered if Ball and Hope had ever had an affair.[32]

The risqué antics may recall the rumors of adultery in the *Confidential* article, but Arnaz is potentially the cuckold this time. The sexual joke also connects Hope's ethnic stereotyping to masculinist, heterosexual competition, potentially exposing links between patriarchal control of gender and ethnic definitions at this time. This linkage remains hidden in the textual dynamics of the *I Love Lucy* program, which stages its understandings of gender and ethnicity in struggles between a husband and wife.

Hope's film star persona was based on the feminized man. He frequently acted the coward who had trouble getting the girl, such as in *The Princess and the Pirate* (Golden, 1944), *Monsieur Beaucaire* (Paramount, 1946), and the Road movies with Bing Crosby: *Road to Singapore* (Paramount, 1940), *Road to Zanzibar* (Paramount, 1941), *Road to Morocco* (Paramount, 1942), *Road to Utopia* (Paramount, 1945), *Road to Rio* (Paramount, 1947), *Road to Bali* (Paramount, 1952), and *Road to Hong Kong* (United Artists, 1962). As a variety show host, not unlike his USO show persona, Hope is transformed into a sophisticated wielder of sexual and ethnic jokes. Lynn Spigel points out that the variety genre came under increasing scrutiny and critical disapproval throughout the early 1950s. Much of the comedy in *The Milton Berle Show*, the most popular program before *I Love Lucy* bumped it down in the Nielsons, was inflected by Yiddish-vaudevillian humor, which was not presumed to play well to the rural midwesterners who were able to receive the show live when coaxial cable was laid in the early 1950s. In addition "critics found the outlandish behavior, risqué jokes, and abrasive personalities of numerous variety clowns unsuitable for a family medium." Spigel argues that situation comedies that incorporated the liveness and spontaneity of variety comedy, such as *I Love Lucy*, were able to include some of the qualities (rowdy outlandishness) that made the variety genre so appealing by packaging it in "middle-class codes of respectability."[33] Because of this, situation comedies became more and more popular for networks and sponsors trying to court a nationwide, middle-class audience.

Hope's 1956 special, then, is a kind of "return of the repressed." This specific skit, which exemplifies the variety show's parodic stance, suggests that what is repressed in the family sitcom is sexual desire. The narrative line, which has Hope-as-Ricky trying to discover Lucy's scheme, is interrupted repeatedly by bedroom farce. Lucy puts Captain Blighstone (played by Frawley, the oldest and least sexualized of the foursome) in the Mertzes' apartment and suggests that the Mertzes sleep in her apartment. But Lucy Ricardo keeps slipping into Lucille Ball every time Ethel/Vance seems to be enjoying Arnaz-as-Fred too much. Ethel/Vance repeatedly leans on and kisses Arnaz-as-Fred, which contrasts with her behavior to Frawley-as-Fred on the *I Love Lucy* show. In one scene Arnaz-as-Fred enters the dark closet where the seal is hidden. After the seal has apparently bitten him, he comes out with a smile on his face and asks Vance if she had followed him and given his neck a "lovebite." This scene initiates the possibility of Ethel/Vance's sexual desire, an issue rarely broached in *I Love Lucy*, in which the Mertzes have a decidedly nonsexual marriage.[34] Lucy's behavior reminds us

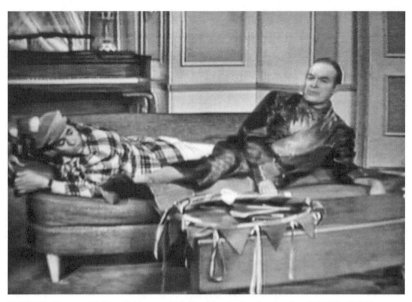

FIGURE 4.8 Hope-as-Ricky and Arnaz-as-Fred bed down together for the night. *The Bob Hope Show*, NBC, 1956.

that Lucy Ricardo is a fictional construct and that Lucille Ball has real-life relationships with Arnaz and Vance that include expectations about appropriate roles for husbands, wives, and friends of the opposite sex.

In its emphasis on a mobile sexual desire, this fantasy of seduction subverts the 1950s domestic sitcom, which insists on monogamous heterosexual coupling. Homoerotic possibilities between characters are made accessible to the fantasizer and viewer of this scene, as Lucy's plans necessitate that she and Ethel share a bedroom. This fantasy might not be totally removed from the parodied sitcom; Alexander Doty argues that a lesbian reading of *I Love Lucy* is possible because the two women often scheme to in some way dispense with the men and much of the pleasure of the program revolves around the women's relations to one another.[35] However, to my knowledge no one has claimed a homoerotic reading for Ricky/Desi's character, but one surfaces here between Hope-as-Ricky and Arnaz-as-Fred as they end up sharing a bed and jokes together (just like Hope and Crosby in their series of films together).[36] Yet despite this skit's foregrounding of sexuality and the way it permits the characters to try out alternative conceptions of their sitcom identities, it does not effect a complete reversal of engendered power. Hope-as-Ricky evidences desire for Lucy, Ethel and Lucy are rivals for Arnaz-as-Fred, while he and Hope-as-Ricky enact a rivalry over masculinity. In other words, heterosexual patriarchal prerogatives are stabilized through the centering of the women's desiring of the men and the men's competition through "exchange" of the women. When the men do bond, it is not homosexual but homosocial; they joke about what they perceive to be their sorry lot as husbands tied to manipulative and silly women. Arnaz-as-Fred listens to Lucy's scheming, then turns to Hope-as-Ricky and says, "I feel sorry for you." He looks at Ethel nodding at Lucy's series of lies and adds, "I feel sorry for me too." This homosocial bonding not only stabilizes patriarchal heterosexual prerogatives but could also mitigate the ethnic power Hope has over Arnaz in its display of men united against women.

The television guest appearances of the *I Love Lucy* cast in the 1950s were made to promote the show and the expanding Desilu empire of media productions. The tensions between the Arnazes' on- and off-screen personas and between 1950s gender norms and the demands of work surface in the need to promote Lucy and Desi as married stars, business people, and fictional characters, the Ricardos, who *do* ultimately support contemporary familial ideology. By the 1990s, however, stardom and 1950s families had become objects of scrutiny. Behind the public façade of success and happiness lies the truth of stardom as well as of the 1950s family. Both recent studies of stars and social histories have revised our notions of the 1950s through their exposure of the myths about gender and success that had previously sustained familial ideology and public institutions of that period. Social historians, many of whom counter recent calls to return to the "family values" of the past, have pointed to the oppressive roles that men and especially women had to perform—often at the cost of their own psychological well-being—in order to create the domestic version of the state's containment policy toward alien, other ways of life.[37] Similarly both academic studies of stars and best-selling star biographies since the 1950s have emphasized the repressive nature of the Hollywood studio system and its promotional operations. In these revisions "Hollywood stardom helps produce an abnormal personal life."[38] In light of these rewritings, growing up in either a "regular" or a star family of the 1950s was a matter of "preventing the outside world from learning the harsh realities of family life."[39]

This is the context for many of the recyclings of Ball and Arnaz in the years since Ball's death, and it is crucial to understanding many of the recyclings in the 1990s. But in addition to the context of the dysfunctional family, there is another context in which the star couple—and in some ways Ball in particular—is associated with family at this time: the context of network television's nostalgia for the past at a moment when it had a diminished ability to secure the family audience. Between 1979 and 1989 network television experienced a 26.5 percent ratings drop and 25.5 percent share loss. This was largely because households receiving cable television rose from 17.1 percent in the late 1970s to 57.1 percent in 1989. During this same period the three networks (NBC, CBS, and ABC) had, for the first time since the demise of DuMont in the 1950s, competition from a new national network, the Fox network. By 1988 60 percent of households had a VCR, which allowed them to time-shift (tape programs and watch them at another time) and to "zap" through commercials in the programs they recorded.[40] This is not a reality that the network news specials after Ball's death explicitly addressed, for to do so would be to publicly admit that the networks' function and history (being formed to bring the national audience together for advertisers) was increasingly irrelevant as cable and satellite alternatives, remote-control viewing, and VCR time shifting became more and more prevalent. Instead, utilizing film and video clips from past broadcasts, the networks produced programs celebrating anniversaries of past series and personalities that were once popular with the family audience whose viewership the networks successfully captured in the 1950s to 1970s. These kinds of specials are what we might loosely term the network's own "fantasies of origin." So, while the specials aired after Ball's death exhibit a multilayered sense of nostalgia, in a fundamental way they are as much (disavowed) obituaries of the networks' importance in American family life as they are obituaries of Lucille Ball.

At stake in these fantasies of origins for the broadcast networks is perhaps most immediately apparent in *Lucy: A CBS News Special*, which was televised the night of Ball's death in April 1989. Recycling Ball/Lucy (and to a lesser extent Arnaz/Ricky) in this video obituary benefits the institutional discourses of the networks in relation to their self-positioning as controllers of the television supertext, as curators of TV history, and as providers of viewer access to the real through their mediation of crisis moments (like death) at a time of their diminishing power in the wake of cable's ascendancy. (In clever postmodern promos and scheduling cable networks like Nick at Nite and TV Land claimed to preserve "our television heritage" by recycling old network TV shows, including *I Love Lucy*).[41]

Ball's death provides the impetus for the CBS network to demonstrate its performance of all of these services. The broadcasting of special news reports, whether in live transmission or prerecorded tape, creates an opportunity for networks to control the television supertext by interrupting or preempting the regular flow of programming. The television supertext is not really a text so much as a way of conceptualizing the flow of texts — a specific program and all the introductory and interstitial material around or during it — in relation to their place in the schedule. While this control of segmentation and flow has many effects and implications for the function of television and our study of it, the network's control of the supertext is significant primarily to the extent that it has a relation to television's providing access to the real. This ability or illusory effect is often discussed in terms of television's place in the everyday livedness of its viewers, its literal place in the home, and the technological possibility of transmitting image and sound live. Since the advent of telefilm and videotape production, live programming is actually employed only for some news broadcasts, for special entertainment events (certain awards or sport shows), and for special reports of crises and catastrophes, when death and destruction — the real — erupt into the sameness of everyday life and regularly scheduled programming. The schedule of television programming according to the model developed by the networks, which Nick Browne argues has a relation to the structure and economics of the work week of the general population, is an important component of our understanding of everyday life.[42]

Ball's death functions as an occasion for the networks' performance of this liveness and provision of the access to the real. On CBS regularly scheduled programming was interrupted for both live news stories about Ball's death and for the prime-time special (with a mixture of both live and taped segments), and some regularly scheduled programs that were broadcast on other networks changed their content to include a focus on Ball (such as ABC's *Nightline* and the syndicated *Entertainment Tonight* devoting whole programs to her). The CBS news special is something between a special entertainment event and a crisis, an indeterminacy perhaps increasingly significant to television, as seen in the carnivalesque television news reporting of riots and murder trials. Dan Rather, the network's news anchor who hosts the special, introduces the broadcast with an announcement of Ball's death, but the crisis factor is ameliorated by his suggestion that what is to follow is a celebration.

The coupling of crisis and entertainment is extended by the coupling of interviews featuring entertainers, among them Dick Van Dyke and Dinah Shore, with interviews of former president Reagan and the CBS CEO William S. Paley. The interviews and commentary by Rather construct a series of homologies between different levels of family, from which Ball emerges as a kind of mother of all of them. Rather first addresses the audience by announcing, "We lost one of the family today." This is evidence not just that television stars are just like us but that the audience is a family unit and that this family is an extension of the "family" at CBS. The presence of Dick Van Dyke, who at that time was a former CBS TV star, the CBS news reporters Rather, Charles Osgood, and Mike Wallace, and CBS president Paley overdetermines the televisual mourning as the activity of a linked unit, with Paley referring to Ball as the "first lady" of CBS. Of course, this designation simultaneously elevates her as network mother and CBS as the first family of broadcast television. (Although the network's existence preceded *I Love Lucy*, it is implied that the success of Ball's show helped confirm CBS's prominence. Certainly the fact that it knocked NBC's *Milton Berle Show* out of first place in the ratings would lead one to this conclusion.)

The presence and performance of Reagan anchors the links between the different registers of family and power. As a former entertainer and a former president, the head of the nation's "first family," he speaks to Ball's significance as a television performer and maternal presence and unwittingly suggests how the two subject positions can and will be collapsed in the contemporary recyclings of her persona. He discusses his personal relationship with Ball in terms of her maternal concern for his wife Nancy after her cancer surgery, but it is his explanation of Ball's place in TV history that most suggests the fantasy of origins that the television as an apparatus can provide and how Ball's persona and success exemplify this function. Reagan says that Ball will have a permanent place in television history because of the medium's continual "recapping" of her shows and films. Although "recapping" suggests summation, it is also close to the concepts of rerunning and recycling, descriptions of television signifying practices that reaffirm the curatorship assumed by this CBS family special, while also suggesting that the historical significance of a star's persona resides in his or her ability to sustain a continual presence on television. It is this continual presence, the always already thereness of Ball—"there" mostly being her presence as Lucy Ricardo on reruns of *I Love Lucy*, which in some cable or satellite television packages is viewable five or six times a day—that associates her most clearly with the maternal of primal fantasies of origins and with the conceptualization of television as a maternal tube of plenty. Turn it on, and out flows images and sounds that continue whether it is watched and listened to with rapt attention, in distraction, or not at all. In Beverle Houston's terms, this is television as "sourceless, natural, inexhaustible, and coextensive with psychological reality itself."[43] The most perfect promise of television and Ball are that they are always there for us, at the flip of a switch and a click of the remote.[44]

The episode of ABC's *Nightline* broadcast the same night constructs a video obituary that confirms the already thereness of Ball/Lucy. The host, Aaron Brown (substituting for the regular anchor, Ted Koppel), opens the broadcast with an appraisal of the star that testifies to the public's comfortable but libidinally charged familiarity with Ball/Lucy: "There are performers we respect, performers we admire, performers we take to for a season or two of passionate obsession and then cast aside to ask a few years later, 'Whatever happened to what's-her-name?' And then once in a long while there is a public figure that we come to love—permanently, ineradicably, utterly. If someone told you earlier today 'Lucy died,' you didn't have to ask, 'Lucy who?' You knew who. You knew she had made you laugh even if she had done it on a TV film made a quarter of a century before you were born. Her gifts were enormous, they were timeless, they were universal." The reporter Judd Rose, speaking over a montage of clips from *I Love Lucy*, suggests that familiarity with Ball's antics as Lucy Ricardo had, through repetition, become a part of the public's memories of themselves: "Lucy makes candy. Lucy makes wine. Lucy makes a commercial. . . . We've seen these moments so often it's as if we've lived them ourselves. We smile because they're familiar. . . . We have loved Lucy since we—and television—were young." The last line almost echoes Houston's argument that the logic behind television's apparatus (which includes its technological base and also the particular material practices in which media institutions and audiences situate it and themselves) is to appear "coextensive with psychological reality itself."

Although network television's commentary on its own history tends to make inflated and self-interested claims, the thereness of Ball/Lucy is a trope in the public's response to her death as well. In Hollywood Peggy Robinson, the manager of a shoe store along the "Walk of Fame" (the sidewalks along Hollywood Boulevard in which names of film, television, and recording stars are embedded), left a few cards on the day of Ball's death for passersby to write their thoughts. Several days later there were 127 poster-size cards filled with messages, including one signed, "The homeboys of East L.A. love and miss Lucy." When Robinson presented the cards to Ball's husband Gary Morton, she told the press she knew why people loved Lucy: "She raised us. She raised our children. I mean, she's just there for us and she always will be."[45] Within days of her death the *Los Angeles Times* published letters from readers who had similar thoughts about Ball's thereness in their lives and as part of a process of intergenerational transmission of family values: "I have loved Lucy since I can remember and so have my children"; "I love Lucy because I grew up watching her. And thanks to reruns, my 16-month old son, Steven, can grow up loving her, too"; "I realized I had always thought of her not as an inaccessible icon of stardom so much as a lifelong friend. Whenever I needed to get away from my own troubles . . . Lucy was there." One woman writes that reruns of *I Love Lucy* helped a friend get through therapy for and ultimately survive a rare form of cancer.[46] The Santa Monica priest who celebrated one of the three memorial masses for Ball held in three cities on Monday, May 8, 1989, told the press that one parishioner came to the mass because watching reruns of *I Love Lucy* was "the only joy her mother had in the days before she died of cancer." (Monday was the night CBS broadcast *I Love Lucy* in first run; Ball's family said a Monday night was chosen for the mass because it was the night "most of the nation was used to being with Lucy.")[47] By 1989, twelve years after his death, fans of Elvis Presley were making hagiographic claims for their dead star, but unlike Presley, Ball had never fallen in the public's estimation, so she was available for immediate hagiographic consideration.

Perhaps one of the weirdest obituary tributes to Ball in this regard was written by Thomas Cottle, a lecturer in psychology at Harvard Medical School. In *Television Quarterly* he wrote a tribute to Ball that consisted mostly of long quotes from an elderly African American woman, Hattie Dinsmore, who shared her fandom of Ball with several generations and who died two years before Ball. Apparently she gave up all prescribed medication (except for her blood pressure) because she was "better off with Lucy any day." Her commentary stresses the immediate thereness of Ball as Lucy and what she means to the American public:

> [Lucy] comes into my room, you understand what I'm saying. Woman isn't just on the television, she comes into this room here with me, with those long legs of hers, and all that red hair jumping about. . . . Has to make you laugh, no matter how sick you are. I got a great granddaughter lies down next to me, she's laughing, and eighty years down the road, here I am, laughing right with her. . . . Here I am hugging my great grandchild, don't you see, because of what that lady's doing on television. . . . You know when you have the power to make a person laugh, you got some special power. But when everybody in this country's doing the exact same thing, sitting in front of some silly old machine, laughing their fool heads off because of this lady, then I say you just got some of the power of the Lord. . . . That woman going to die, this country going to cry one whole lot of tears. Folks don't know that yet. . . . This country is going to miss her plenty.[48]

Cottle doesn't seem particularly interested in analyzing Dinsmore's relation to television and one of its stars or her grandiose claims about Ball, television, and the American public. He goes for dramatics, ending his article with the punchline that Hattie Dinsmore was born blind. Cottle never considers that perhaps because Ball's comic training was honed on her 1940s radio program, *My Favorite Husband*—which served as a template for *I Love Lucy*—she might have seemed so present to Dinsmore, a woman who could only hear Ball's antics. Instead the implication is that Ball/Lucy is apparently even there for those who can't see her, which feeds into the miraculousness that hovers about the star in this postmortem period.

I find interesting the discourse about the almost spiritual nature of Ball/Lucy and of the fan interaction with her, but I don't want to suggest that her fans are constructing a true hagiography of Ball. While alleviation of suffering and bringing together families is claimed as part of Ball/Lucy's power, every interviewee comments or implies that there is an everyday, almost mundane quality to her presence, her iteration on the domestic medium of television. In other words, because of her continuous presence in reruns of *I Love Lucy*, the claim that she has "always been there" for "us" while whole generations were growing up is to claim not a miracle but the everyday functioning of television in the context of American broadcast industry practices and the social evolution of its reception.[49]

The CBS news special, like the public response to Ball's death, focuses on the actress's singular place in television history, but it does ultimately anticipate the more recent interest in Ball and Arnaz as a star couple. It includes an interview with Arnaz from several years earlier in which he attests to Ball's willingness to do anything to make Lucy funny and, with some wistful sentiment in his voice, claims that *I Love Lucy* was a once-in-a-lifetime experience "if you are lucky to have something like it in your life at all." In his interview Paley tells Rather that Arnaz was a great producer, a talent that would never have been tapped by the television industry if not for Ball's insistence on doing a show with him. However, it is the final images and sounds of the special, which consist of a montage of scenes from various Lucy shows (with a heavy concentration on kissing scenes from *I Love Lucy*) and a soundtrack on which Arnaz sings the words to *I Love Lucy*'s theme song ("I love Lucy and she loves me / We're as happy as two can be"), that most suggests the two as television's first couple. Although Ball's twenty-seven-year marriage to Gary Morton (a marriage seven years longer than her union with Arnaz) is mentioned in Rather's reporting, Morton is not interviewed and is only fleetingly glimpsed in archival film footage that lasts about two seconds. With its concentration on *I Love Lucy* and the achievement of closure through an audiovisual coupling of Ball's persona with Arnaz's, the special effectively elides the significance of her life or career after the simultaneous demise of *I Love Lucy* and the Ball-Arnaz marriage in 1960. (She filed for divorce the day after the taping of the last *Lucy-Desi Comedy Hour*, the hour-long version of *I Love Lucy*.)[50]

Twelve years later, in November 2001, CBS broadcast a special honoring the fiftieth anniversary of *I Love Lucy*. While it focuses on the history and qualities of the series rather than on its stars, the special takes for granted the construction of Ball and Arnaz as a star couple, and Arnaz shares equal billing with Ball as subject. It begins with an image from the "Sentimental Anniversary" episode of *I Love Lucy*, in which Lucy and Ricky celebrate their wedding anniversary and look at a photo album with *pictures of Ball and Arnaz* as young marrieds fifteen years earlier. The special closes with a montage sequence that starts with images from the same anniversary episode, eventually ending with a clip from the episode "Lucy's Last Birthday," in which Ricky sings "I Love Lucy" to a very emotional Lucy in his nightclub. In the two hours in between these clips, the special gives Arnaz equal credit with Ball as a force behind the series' incredible popularity. Various Latino, including Cuban, entertainers are interviewed in relation to Arnaz's significance as a Latino icon and musician. The film actor Andy Garcia and the trumpeter Arturo Sandoval, both Cuban exiles, identify Arnaz's talent in terms of the way he brought not only Cuban music but also the exile experience to the American public at large. They speak of their own experience of exile to address what they assume was his experience of homesickness.

The Arnaz children, now middle-aged and executive producers of the special, pay tribute to both parents in segments about their hometowns. After Lucie Arnaz, in direct address to the audience, says that her mother never lost her small-town, middle-class values, a film clip shows her and Desi Jr. and his family traveling to Jamestown, New York, to visit the houses in which Ball was born and raised. Desi Jr., who has never seen these homes, is visibly touched as his sister recounts episodes in Ball's life as experienced in these rooms. However, the spectacular segment honoring their father suggests that they claim his legacy over Ball's; they sing a bilingual song together in his honor about longing for Cuba, followed by their accompaniment (on drums, including Desi Sr.'s signature conga drums) of the contemporary Cuban American singer Jorge Morena in "Babalu," his homage to Desi Sr. If the way to talk about Ball is in terms of small-town family values and a belief in her already thereness, perhaps the way to talk—or sing—

FIGURE 4.9 Title credit over a photo of Lucille Ball in Hollywood shortly after her arrival in the early 1930s. *Lucy and Desi: A Home Movie*, NBC, 1991.

about Arnaz is in terms of exile from home, a not-thereness. This could be read as another anxiety about origins: Where do you come from when a parent is in exile? It could also be read as a displacement or strategic avoidance of talking about Arnaz in relation to a different kind of not-thereness, his highly publicized philandering and drinking that characterize most of the media constructions of his persona since the simultaneous end of his marriage with Ball and *I Love Lucy*. But it is also a rehabilitation enabled by a much more self-conscious appreciation of multiculturalism—at least in terms of its manifestation in an entertainment market—than existed either in the 1950s or at the time of the deaths of Arnaz and Ball in the 1980s.

The Arnaz children's involvement in the *I Love Lucy* fiftieth anniversary special is a culmination of their involvement in rewriting the ways the American public sees their parents' marriage and their parents as individuals with unique histories. But it is also a kind of rehabilitation of their relationship with CBS. In 1991, after CBS okayed production on and aired *Before the Laughter: The Lucy and Desi Story*, a television movie biography of Ball and Arnaz, Lucie Arnaz had a very public falling out with *I Love Lucy*'s home network. In 1993, when she and her actor-husband, Laurence Luckinbill, coproduced *Lucy and Desi: A Home Movie*, a biographical documentary about her parents using home movie footage, she deliberately brought it to NBC for airing. The production history of these two specials suggests, again, the degree to which the recycling of these stars functions for the networks' institutional power, as much as for the social or psychic engagement of the audience (or of the Arnaz children).

According to Lucie Arnaz in a *TV Guide* interview published the week *Before the Laughter* was broadcast, she and her writing partners, Luckinbill and Larry Thompson, first presented CBS with a script for a TV movie about Desi Arnaz's life. CBS rejected it because they wanted a story about Lucy *and* Desi (perhaps repeating the discrimination motivating their original rejection of Arnaz when he and Ball presented an idea about a show to CBS forty years earlier). Lucie softened toward the idea for a joint biography after her mother's death but withdrew her involvement when told she could not have final script approval. She claims that CBS led her to believe that they would not produce the film without her cooperation. When she found out that Thompson and the network were producing *Before the Laughter*, a film that she claims sensationalizes her parents' problems, she "felt raped" by CBS, the network her parents believed was "family to them."[51]

The extreme terms in which Lucie Arnaz frames her reactions to CBS's move suggests the degree to which CBS's self-promotion as a TV family had combined with and collapsed into the Arnazes' personal family history. *I Love Lucy* was originally pitched to CBS so that Ball and Arnaz could stay together and start a family, a fact CBS had not neglected to exploit in the special airing after Ball's death. The ultimate result was a situation in which the Arnazes' conception of themselves and their roles could now be identified as victims of a kind of institutional incest. This struggle over the production of a television narrative about Lucille Ball and Desi Arnaz is evidence of a struggle over points of view on the couple as they relate to (different kinds of) fantasies of origins. CBS's *Before the Laughter* traces the stormy relationship between the stars within a narrative framework that uses the production of the first episode of the *I Love Lucy* series on CBS as a structuring device. The couple's relationship is told in flashbacks as memories each character recalls as they prepare for the filming of the premiere episode of the television series produced as a way for Ball to keep Arnaz at home as a husband and father. While this TV movie produces Ball, Arnaz, and CBS as the origins of this historical TV series that consolidated the network's dominance, *Lucy and Desi: A Home Movie* produces Ball and Arnaz from the point of view of their children, as origins of not only public myths about marriage and family but also of the children Lucie and Desi Jr. and their own problems with marriage, career, drug and alcohol abuse, and recovery. Despite their differences, however, both programs produce a notion of origins of the self as a self within some concept of family as a dysfunctional unit that has an institutional and personal legacy.

That *Before the Laughter* should construct its notion of family in sensational (lots of details about Arnaz's affairs) and self-serving terms should not have come as a surprise to Lucie Arnaz, given the generic conventions and institutional pressures the commercial networks claim in the production of made-for-television movies. These movies, as one-shot attempts to capture an audience, have what the industry considers promotional challenges. Since they do not have returning characters or narratives like a television series, for which each weekly episode serves as a kind of promotion for the next, TV movies have to secure audience attention before the one-time airing. Some critics have suggested that TV movies are for this reason produced and promoted according to a philosophy in which sameness and difference (figured as the sensational) are held in balance. According to Laurie Schulze, the TV movie must "provide curiosity by the promise of the unusual or the scandalous and immediately mark itself off as different. Yet it must be familiar at the same time, and reassure by its reference to the instantly recognizable. If the concept proposed to the network by the independent producer cannot be condensed into this brief sensational/familiar narrative image, the project stands little chance of being developed."[52]

The story of Ball and Arnaz provides familiarity and recognizability; after all, *I Love Lucy* is the longest continuously rerun show in the history of television, and the couple's marriage and divorce have been the object of intense attention in fan histories of the show, Arnaz's own autobiography, and the many televised and print interviews with Ball and Arnaz before their deaths. The inclusion of the tumultuous relationship of the couple, which included extramarital affairs, ethnic prejudice against Arnaz, Ball's miscarriages and final successful pregnancies after her fortieth year, makes *Before the Laughter* conform to what Schulze has identified as the more sensational nature of the TV movie. Those plot points conform as well to the kinds of obstacles to success that George Custen argues appear in most film and TV biographies of famous people (with the sensational, "victimizing" obstacles more pronounced in the TV versions of biographies of the "famous").[53] But, as Schulze suggests, the production pressures of framing TV movie narratives within the different or the sensational allow them to be open as "the site of an immense and intense ideological negotiation, limning, as it does, the more salient and disturbing phenomena on the social agenda."[54] In the

1980s one of the most disturbing phenomena of the social agenda for many was the "decline" of the American family. Social scientists and politicians were successful in getting media attention by citing statistics about marriage and family, such as that the divorce rate had tripled between 1960 and 1982, that by 1986 the rate of unmarried teenage mothers was at 61 percent compared to 15 percent in 1960, and that 25 percent of all children now lived in a single-parent (mostly single-mother) home.[55] Jane Feuer argues that 1980s made-for-television movies can be considered at core "trauma dramas," which represent real social frustrations of the time, specifically the "entire New Right agenda of terrors posed to the nuclear family of the 1980s—everything from child abduction and murder to teenage cocaine abuse." Although she argues that the films are "not unambiguously right wing in sentiment," Feuer establishes that most have narratives beginning with the premise that the family is the ideal and norm of happy American life and that many can be read in relation to the New Right's anxiety over the moral and cultural tone of liberalism fostered since the 1960s, which is considered to be the cause of statistics such as those above.[56]

Before the Laughter's focus on Ball and Arnaz's struggle to have and be a "normal" family suggests a certain affinity with the "trauma dramas" Feuer describes. But *Before the Laughter*'s centering on the difficult courtship and marriage of Ball and Arnaz in relation to their careers suggests a negotiation with another contemporary social agenda of the 1980s–90s, the social agenda of feminism, or at least a popularized, middle-class feminism, which is largely preoccupied with women's attempts to balance career and family. It fits more comfortably in the framework Elayne Rapping has suggested for the made-for-television movie of the 1970s–80s, in which there is a focus on concerns most closely associated with female gender roles in a time of flux. Rapping identifies the women's movement of the 1960s–70s, which questioned the logic of separate-sphere culture, as a major contributor to the flux experienced in American culture—especially by women—in the 1970s–80s. Of course the New Right's anxiety over "liberal permissiveness" included a critique of the women's movement, and according to Feuer's model, one would expect it to be evident in many of the made-for-television movies of the time. But Rapping sees women-centered made-for-television films of this period as sympathetic to the changes wrought by feminism, even though they tend to show characters negotiating social change within simplistic, didactic frameworks that result in rationalized, "curative" solutions.[57]

The characters' negotiation of career and family is not given a "curative" solution in *Before the Laughter*, although it emphasizes the importance of *I Love Lucy* and the network's agreement to Ball and Arnaz working together to the couple's ability to stay married at this time. The complexity of the problem of combining work and family, however, is not dealt with in *Before the Laughter*. On the one hand, the narrative insists on a "she said, he said" structure, with flashbacks supposedly alternating to show the varying perspectives of Ball and Arnaz, which suggests that the problems in the marriage are the result of personal differences. On the other hand, despite an equal number of flashbacks for each character, scenes tend to focus on how all action has implications specifically for Ball's happiness. Arnaz's negative behavior does not contribute to the representation of a complex character or social context, but instead results in Ball expressing fear of not being attractive enough to keep Arnaz, or her desire to get pregnant and carry a baby successfully to term. Lucie Arnaz is not completely wrong when she suggests in the TV *Guide* interview about *Before the Laughter* that the tele-film makes Ball the hero and Arnaz the villain. For Lucie Arnaz, this personalization does not work because of her intimate knowledge of and love for the real people involved. But the personalization does not work—or at least not entirely—on the politically progressive level advanced by feminism. The telefilm shows Ball's struggle to succeed in marriage and career derailed mainly by Arnaz's infidelity. While the media industry's discrimination against Arnaz is represented, there is no indication that there are other obstacles to balancing career and family for women than just this couple's idiosyncratic ones. In other words, as is common in made-for-TV movies, systemic problems in the institutionalization of discrimination and of family and work in a capitalist, patriarchal culture are not examined, yet those very problems may in fact draw women to therapeutic solutions or to TV movies like this one.

Lucy and Desi: A Home Movie claims to provide access to the authentic Ball and Arnaz because it is not merely a representation of the behind-the-scenes life, with actors portraying the star couple as in *Before the Laughter*. Instead it consists of home movies that bear an indexical relationship to the actual Ball and Arnaz. It supplements this veneer of realism with interviews of friends and family. These people, Lucie Arnaz suggests, have never been interviewed about the couple and are now glad to express what they had kept "bottled up" all those years.[58] This strategy might support the 1950s discourses (such as their appearance on *Toast of the Town*, which defined

FIGURE 4.10 *Lucy and Desi: A Home Movie* represents the Arnaz children's attempts to reevaluate the musical career of their father, Desi Arnaz. NBC, 1991.

the couple as ordinary folks rather than stars), but it also complicates this picture, at least insofar as it tries to particularize Ball and Arnaz in terms of class and ethnicity.

For example, Arnaz's Cuban heritage is described by friends and musicians who either share or understand that heritage. Their emphasis on the importance and popularity of his Latin music contributes to the documentary's strategy of portraying him sympathetically and reevaluates his place as an entertainer alongside Ball. An extended discussion of both stars' mothers attempts to portray them in terms of differing class and cultural and ethnic backgrounds. Interviewees explain Ball's desire to have her mother and other family members participate in Desilu business and the Arnaz family life in California as her reaction to the devastating effects that working-class and Depression hardships had on her family's survival. It is revealed that Ball's own mother could not always live with her children because she needed to find work, and at one point, young Lucille was sent to step-grandparents to live. Arnaz's lifelong economic protection of his mother is explained in terms of his upper-class background, Cuban exile, and the Latin tradition of extended families. As an adolescent exile in Miami after the Cuban Revolution in 1933, the once financially secure Arnaz cleaned

FIGURE 4.11 Lucie Arnaz Luckinbill and Desi Arnaz Jr. discuss their parents. *Lucy and Desi: A Home Movie*, NBC, 1991.

birdcages to help support his family.[59] The historian Stephanie Coontz has argued that what we now think of as the nuclear family of the 1950s was not the last appearance of a long-established norm or reality of family life; it was a relatively *new* form enabled by particular material circumstances and ideologies.[60] After diasporic childhoods and adolescences, the family life Ball and Arnaz wanted and to some extent achieved was new to them.

Yet *Lucy and Desi: A Home Movie* suggests the illusory nature of the equation between domestic togetherness and happiness. The interviewees emphasize that there was always trouble between the couple and the threat of dissolution. Their testimonies are affectionate but provide honest assessments of the problems and contradictions faced by the couple. Their words are sometimes used in support of visuals that illustrate the couple's love and happiness; at other times they work in counterpoint to these images, indicating tensions not visible in promotional photos or home or promotional movie footage.

In this way the documentary uses home movies to provide a critique rather than a celebration of 1950s familialism. Lucie Arnaz Luckinbill suggests that the image we have of the 1950s family from TV programs like *Father Knows Best* (1954–63) and *The Donna Reed Show* (1958–66) gives a

FIGURE 4.12 Desi Arnaz kisses Lucille Ball. *Lucy and Desi: A Home Movie*, NBC, 1991.

false impression of family perfection and security. As Patricia Zimmermann has argued in her study of home movies of the 1950s, these amateur productions, usually made by the family patriarch, elevated and worshipped the family in its most "secluded interactions."[61] In contrast to what is depicted in these home movies—Lucy and Desi cavorting at parties at their ranch home, cuddling with the children, acting as the patriarch and matriarch at Desilu's company picnics—interviewees comment on the negative impact on the marriage of work pressures and even of aspects of family togetherness (including having children and supporting aging mothers). They name these as contributing factors to a difficult marriage because the family was supposed to compensate for the harsh realities of modern life in which both parents desired recognition and self-fulfillment.

The failure of Arnaz and Ball as patriarch and matriarch of the Arnaz family parallels the loss of the nuclear family as a master discourse of contemporary life.[62] *Lucy and Desi: A Home Movie* reveals this loss in sometimes obvious ways. Looped images of the couple showing each other affection punctuate commercial breaks. A sentimental song (in both English and Spanish) describes melancholy, irrational love affairs likened to the off-kilter movement of the stars in the universe. Ball and Arnaz are figured in this stylistic rearrangement of the home movies as a besotted couple unable to ever separate or truly be together.

More complex is the way the film signals loss through deployment of a "therapeutic ethos." Leslie Irvine, in a study of the discursive strategies of codependency, defines the therapeutic ethos as a collection of discourses characterized by a belief that everyone is "entitled to happiness, high self-esteem, and personal satisfaction."[63] The discourse of codependency, which Irvine says emerged in the 1980s as one response to the rising divorce rate and increasing (perception of the) fragility of relationships, sees the "dysfunctional" family as the source of the individual's inability to gain self-esteem and personal satisfaction. In other words, loss of family function results in loss of self.

In his interview in the documentary, Desi Jr., who in the 1970s and 1980s had much publicized affairs with older women (the actresses Patty Duke and Liza Minnelli) and drug problems, describes his attempts to get his father into alcohol and drug abuse recovery programs after he himself had become sober.[64] The father's addictions are offered up as one of the reasons the children are now mourning the loss of the family, the loss of their parents to each other, and even the loss of their family to us, the "viewing family." Yet the son states that the film program is about "recovery, a spiritual recovery" from various "addictive behaviors." The father's Latin heritage again resurfaces in a positive, albeit more stereotypical manner as Desi Jr. recalls how much his father had an appreciation for the joy and sensuousness of everyday living. Like her brother, Lucie Arnaz identifies a sense of both loss and empathy when speaking of their parents' difficulties in making both work and family "functional." She tries to articulate the lesson her parents' "workaholism" taught her as a "working mom" of the 1990s (and unwittingly suggests what Ball's celebrated thereness meant to her as daughter): "When my mother came home, she would still be working—she would still be working. I have to fight every day of my life not to go home to my kids and be there physically but not be there. . . . It was really hard for her to be there. . . . I just think that these two people had enough problems of their own . . . that they needed that work."

The home movies shore up this loss because they combine with confessional strategies that elicit truths about this couple and, in doing so, act as therapy for the interviewees and, presumably, for us. Mimi White describes the apparent paradox of the contemporary therapeutic discourse as signifying both loss and recovery: "[The therapeutic discourse] can be seen as one manifestation of post-modern logic, perpetuating confessional discourses among an array of positions with no master position to which to refer them or give them a final, determinate meaning. And yet the contemporary thera-

FIGURE 4.13 Desi Arnaz teaches his children the joy of everyday living. *Lucy and Desi: A Home Movie*, NBC, 1991.

peutic ethos proposes itself as a response to the loss of logic, coherence, stability, and order."[65] The home movies, which appear in the documentary amid interviews that underscore the ephemerality of the Arnazes' happiness, represent loss, but also the possibility of recovery. They preserve an image of the family of the past for the family of the present, making that prior family and its private interactions available for explaining the origins of present problems and dysfunctions.

Lucie Arnaz, through the corporation Desilu, Too, has used her control over her parents' estates (she had control over Ball's estate from the time Ball died, even though Gary Morton was still living) to manage the licensing of their images and to make popular productions that are in effect publicly visible inquiries into her own family history. *Lucy and Desi: A Home Movie* evidences one way that her inquiries have endeavored to represent her famous parents empathetically while trying to put their mythic status as television's first family into specific personal and social contexts. After that production her next big project related to the large amounts of personal memorabilia she inherited from both Ball and Arnaz and provides an interesting comparison and contrast to the 1993 television documentary. In 1997 Lucie Arnaz produced a CD-ROM Lucy and Desi "scrapbook," using photos, birth certificates, family crests, and other items from her parents' collections, supplementing the visual material with interviews with family and friends (some of whom appear in the earlier documentary as well), even including audio material from her father's appearances on *The Tonight Show* in the 1970s–80s and the audio cassette recordings her mother had taped while preparing a biography with a professional writer in the 1960s. (It was finally published, to great fanfare, in 1996 as *Love, Lucy*.)[66] The CD-ROM, *Lucy and Desi: The Scrapbooks, Volume 1*, distributed through Luckinbill's company, Education Through Entertainment, is available singly or as a package that includes an instruction booklet and a second CD that demonstrates how consumers can put together a CD scrapbook of their own family history.[67]

Pam Wilson explains that the impulse that motivates people to trace their genealogy was once practiced mainly to establish one's genetic trace to royalty, and that this has often facilitated belief in the tracer's entitlement to social privileges (especially in regard to how it might encode and celebrate white heritage). She also examines the curious history of the genealogy in CD-ROM form. This practice was pioneered by members of the Church of the Latter-Day Saints, who have changed genealogy from a localized, amateur cottage industry (using pen and paper) to an industrialized form, a professional participant in the market economy of major software companies. In the Mormon religion tracing family has a special importance because it helps current members of the church identify their ancestors and, in a virtual going back in time, baptize them in the Mormon faith. Wilson says this connection between family genealogy and the Mormons is one reason why the practice is still seen as racially and politically conservative. But she also describes other groups, such as ethnic minorities, who have found genealogy an empowering tool and can now practice it with greater ease because of the availability of services on the Internet and in CD-ROM form. Like White's positioning of therapeutic discourses on television, Wilson ultimately positions current genealogy practice as a manifestation of the anxieties over the loss of the patriarchal family as a master discourse in (post)modern life.[68]

Lucy and Desi: The Scrapbooks fits within Wilson's context for the form and practice. It is at once an empowering tool for Lucie Arnaz to further explore her ethnic minority background and, like the documentary she produced earlier, evidence of a desire to both acknowledge and restore the loss of her family. But it is also a more conservative situating of Arnaz's family history than the documentary, which additionally attempted to shatter the power of family (and show business) mythology.

FIGURE 4.14 Lucie Arnaz Luckinbill produced *Lucy and Desi: The Scrapbooks, Volume 1* as a CD-ROM. Education through Entertainment, 1996. Author's collection.

The CD has twenty chapters, ten for the history of each parent. But the first thing the viewer sees is a brief clip from an episode of *I Love Lucy* in which Lucy and Ricky are looking at an album of childhood photos. This fades to black, and an intro card comes up featuring animated stick figures of Ball/Lucy and Arnaz/Ricky that resemble those used on *I Love Lucy* to introduce the show's credits and the commercial breaks of the first-run series. (The syndicated reruns replaced these with the title of the program written against rumpled satin sheets, which is the most familiar opening for viewers today.) Each figure holds an album, and upon clicking on one of these albums, the viewer is given the chapter titles for the life of that figure. Even though the intro card encourages a by now familiar blurring of Ball and Arnaz with Lucy and Ricky, these virtual scrapbooks are resolutely the lives of Ball and Arnaz, not the Ricardos. The chapters can be looked at in any order, but each chapter is first seen as a card that resembles the page of an old photo album; photos are arranged on the page, appearing to be fastened with paper corners. There is minimal labeling, but upon clicking on a photo, the viewer gets either sound clips, image and sound clips, written text, more photos, or enlarged versions of the photos on the intro page. Icons on the side of the page can be clicked; the one that looks like a television provides quick-time videos of people interviewed for the CD, talking about events, people, and places related to the time period represented on that page. Another icon, which looks like a radio, has audio-only interviews, including actual recordings of Ball or Arnaz (Desi Jr. also reads from Desi Sr.'s book in some of the chapters of his story).

Much of the same biographical ground is covered as in the documentary, although, because of the audio recording clips, Ball and Arnaz seem to have more control over telling their own stories than in the former production, and the viewer learns much more detail about their careers prior to their marriage and *I Love Lucy*. Although *Lucy and Desi: A Home Movie* was Lucie Arnaz's much-publicized response to CBS's rejecting a biography of her father and producing a made-for-television movie in which he featured as the bad guy, the CD scrapbook is probably the more effective corrective. Photos from Arnaz's life in Cuba, including Cuban newspaper photos that reported on the importance of the Arnaz family to the civic life of Santiago, and archival newspaper and magazine footage that document the popularity of his band and musical performances in Miami and New York attest to his importance as an entertainment figure whose work helped transform American popular music and transform exile into an American success story. The inclusion of contextual material from the contemporary press also distinguishes the CD from a family photo album.

Other kinds of documents authenticate the family to itself and to us and, combined with stereotypical family portrait photos, formal and informal, evidence a conservative restoration. The use of so many family documents, such as family trees, birth certificates, death certificates, marriage certificates, what appears to be pages from the family Bible of ancestors of the Hunt (maternal) side, and the Arnaz family crest, defensively overdetermines the authenticity of the family, rejects its fragility, and suggests a certain fetishization of origins. Written texts and interviews seem to caption or anchor images so that the kinds of contrapuntal, ironic juxtapositions of image and voice in the documentary are absent. The result is that instead of questioning the nature and power of the fantasies of origins, as the documentary often did, the fantasies of origins are confirmed. Paradoxically although this is a family album made public of one of the most public families, "conventions of family photography [and family documents] are designed to keep the family secrets and to protect it from public scrutiny."[69] At least that is the effect here, in contrast to the earlier documentary.

Other qualities of the CD-ROM support this conservative positioning of the family. The innovative promise of the CD-ROM form has, in part, been presumed to reside in its allowing the spectator or reader control of some aspects of the narrative or visual experience: how long to dwell on a part of the text (in contrast to viewing a film), how to make connections to other parts of the text and in what order. Although the viewer is allowed these possibilities in this CD scrapbook, the "romance and marriage" plot determines much of our experience of the individual parts of the text. First, the subtitle of the CD is *Made for Each Other*. The opening film clip from *I Love Lucy*, which appears on the screen unbidden, forecasts that the CD is about coupling, and the fact that Ricky and Lucy are looking at a photo album is telling: part of what constitutes them as a family is looking at the family album. A variety of scholars of family photography theorize this mutual imbrication of family and family album. Annette Kuhn writes, "In the process of using—producing, selecting, ordering, displaying—photographs, the family is actually in the process of making itself."[70] Marianne Hirsch, in her study of family photography, notes, "The family is an affiliative group, and the affiliations that create it are constructed through various relational, cultural, and institutional processes—such as 'looking' and photography, for example."[71] The sequence of chapters for each life story (if read in order) lead to the meeting and marriage of Arnaz and Ball, to the constitution of the family. Finally, since the scrapbooks include only material through the first year of the Arnaz-Ball marriage, the issues of its eventual dissolution and how its problems were part of a social context that television of the 1950s denied or simplified are not used to question the power of the romance and marriage mythology in patriarchal, capitalist culture.

Lucy and Desi: The Scrapbooks, Volume 1: Made for Each Other is an entertaining and often moving series of texts. The dense, layered texture of each of the albums and attempts to resurrect the earlier historical milieux of various Cuban and American locales (upstate New York, New York City, Montana, Miami, Hollywood) suggest that the Arnaz children have a grasp of their parents' autonomy as products of a different historical moment. But the conventionality of the scrapbook album and its contrast with *Lucy and Desi: A Home Movie* is linked to the differing motivations and commercial imperatives of the two productions. The CD-ROM is pitched to fans of Ball and Arnaz, of course, but it is also linked to a larger commercial project of selling families a "how-to" on constructing family histories. The melancholic and myth-shattering attitudes evidenced in the documentary wouldn't motivate most people, who have little to prove to the public about their families, to buy a CD such as this one and produce a family history.

Summary

Life goes on as if they were still here; simply off somewhere, on location perhaps, and unable to get to a phone. . . . I'm sure, that they are *almost* busier now than when they were alive!

LUCIE ARNAZ, FOREWORD TO *LOVE, LUCY* BY LUCILLE BALL
AND BETTY HANNAH HOFFMAN

The proliferation of scholarly studies,[72] fan books, print, video, and CD-ROM biographies and autobiographies, continuing reruns of *I Love Lucy*, and *I Love Lucy* collectible merchandise (approximately nine hundred products are currently authorized) attests to the sustained interest in the Arnaz-Ball star couple and their television series. As texts they suggest varying relations to originary fantasies about the couple or television and its institutions.

Lucy and Desi: A Home Movie in 1991 and the television appearances of Ball and Arnaz in the 1950s expose the work that goes into being a star couple negotiating personal and social pressures associated with family and career, while television news specials and anniversary programs reveal a vested interest in exploiting them to construct a fantasy of (network) television as family. As these television portrayals suggest, the Arnazes' desires for family happiness and business success as well as their problems in attaining those were key components in their stardom. The 1950s skits promote these aspects of their stardom as a way to promote *I Love Lucy* and its Ricardo family. As this promotion centers and validates family as a key site for audience identification, it also constructs and holds it as a market for the developing television industry of that time. Network television specials in the 1990s hoped to shore up the loss of that family. Although *Lucy and Desi: A Home Movie* centralizes family in its subject matter and audience address, it makes an intervention in the familial ideology that sustained the earlier portrayals of the Ricardos and the Arnazes. This ideology works only at great cost to its subjects and is materialized in certain media fictions, such as the sitcom and the home movie. Yet the looping of certain home movie images of Ball and Arnaz and the sometimes emotional testimony from loved ones of the couple also suggest the difficulties in rewriting mythologies of the family. In that way it is compatible with both the recent social histories and star studies that have interrogated the oppressiveness of familialism in patriarchal culture and the tenacity of our desire for family and its place in our fantasy life.

≡

CHAPTER FIVE

STAR BODIES, STAR BIOS

Stardom, Gender, and Identity Politics

As we have seen, media that recycle stars — or are about the recycling of stars — are often anchored in notions of the biographical or depend on spectators' extracinematic knowledge of biographical anecdotes. If, as critics have argued, the production of "meaning in biographical form is a powerful force in shaping and reshaping cultural memory," biographies can provide crucial sites of contestation or material for contemporary identity politicking.[1] And because the body is the "material embodiment for ethnic, racial, and gender identities, as well as a staged performance of identity," it is central to those contestations of identity politics.[2] Much of the machinery of star making at the industrial level as well as audience and spectator reception has affirmed the role of the body in constructing the star as a cultural ideal. It is not surprising, then, that star recyclings in film and television or video biographies foreground how stars literally and figuratively embody cultural contestation over identity and even reveal the similarities between stardom and the construction or performance of the body.

Stars perform identity through corporeal signs that are idealized embodiments of cultural values and norms. Traditional star biographies tend to naturalize this process of identity production so that the manufacturing of the identity is seen not as a "stylized repetition of acts" but as the "discovery" of "raw" talent or beauty, which is brought to the attention of an (eventually) accepting public.[3] In these narratives obstacles to or interruptions of the subject's stardom are presented as accidental or self-inflicted or as the culture's temporary misrecognition of the subject's talent rather than as the star's failure to obey culture's injunction to be a particular kind of subject. Many print biographies of stars follow the genre conventions that efface such a process, as do most television and Hollywood film star biographies. However, there is an increasing number of experimental films and videos relying on stars' biographical narratives that interrupt the success story trajectory by exposing the way the star's body engages in a staging of identity in response to culture's requirements for certain kinds of subjectivity. These biographies focus on stars whose ailing, aging, or transgressive bodies fail, exceed, or "defy the injunction by which . . . [their identities] are generated."[4] If, as William H. Epstein, following Foucault, suggests, the biographical "life-text" has been "appropriated by the nation-state of industrial capitalism as an articulation of its knowledge-power," these star bodies trouble the process by which biography has traditionally plotted the trajectory of the body in cultural discourse. Consequently the focus on the failed body undermines biography's typical support for patriarchal, capitalist culture's "administering the body and controlling its insertion into the machinery of production."[5]

In this chapter I examine two biographical texts about the 1970s singing star Karen Carpenter, *The Karen Carpenter Story* (a made-for-TV movie, 1989) and *Superstar* (an experimental film, 1987), and the videos *Meeting Two Queens* (1991), *Rock Hudson's Home Movies* (1992), and *Joan Sees Stars* (1993). They are examples of star recyclings that use the biographical form or what is assumed to be audience knowledge of stars' life stories to explore the relationship between stars as idealized embodiments of cultural ideals and the body as enacting the staged performance of identity in contemporary capitalist, patriarchal culture. These explorations demonstrate the extent to which the star's body has become a crucial site to focus anxieties about cultural and identity politics and to rehearse anxieties about how the biographical genre does the work of history. Biography as history is both big business (e.g., A&E's series *Biography*, the Biography Channel, PBS's *American Experience* and *American Masters*, the E! Entertainment Channel's many biography series, the many biographical books on the best-seller lists, etc.) and part of a self-conscious and often heated discussion about multiculturalism and the value of "great men narratives" in public education. Since biography is a media genre that is invested in both history and storytelling in narrating the self within a specific social milieu, the films and videos discussed in this chapter demonstrate, perhaps most explicitly of any of the texts examined in this book, how stars can function as part of a culture's social imaginary.

The works under consideration specifically explore the tensions under which the star's body in biographical representation performs its work in capitalist patriarchal culture and becomes visible in history. These tensions are evident in the variety of thematic and formal concerns raised by the films and videos examined here: the necessary substitution of another performing body for the body of the biographical subject in the dramatized or staged biographical text (*Superstar, The Karen Carpenter Story, Rock Hudson's Home Movies*), the conflicted terms of ownership of the biographical narrative or star image (*Superstar, The Karen Carpenter Story, Rock Hudson's Home Movies, Meeting Two Queens*), and the linkage of star body norms (health and beauty) to the ideological and metapsychological implications of the classical Hollywood film image and the narratives in which it is typically embedded (*Superstar, Rock Hudson's Home Movies, Meeting Two Queens, Joan Sees Stars*).

As Epstein argues, the traditional biography's collection of facts introduces the "natural event" into the cultural text, turns the nonnarratable, unlimited semiosis of the body (birth, growth, reproduction, illness, death) into a narratable text. In other words, the "thing of nature" becomes a "thing of culture." But "textualizing the 'natural' inevitably involves a loss, a falling away from some posited 'ontological state of wholeness and order.'"[6] Although Epstein is writing about the development of the English literary biography of the eighteenth and nineteenth centuries, his argument seems to address inherent representational problems for traditional film biographies of well-known media stars. They must represent, rather than present, the aura or uniqueness of their star subjects; they must convince us of the star's worthiness for narrativization while another star or performer portrays the subject of the biography. Biopics have their ways of compensating for this lack, this falling away from wholeness: having a major star with his or her own aura play the subject (Barbra Streisand playing Fanny Brice, James Cagney playing George M. Cohan); having the star subject dub the singing voice of the actor playing him or her (e.g., film or television biographies of Al Jolson, Judy Garland, and Tina Turner); casting an actor who bears a close physical resemblance to the subject (James Franco playing James Dean); and in rare cases having the star play himself or herself in the movie (as Sophia Loren did in the second half of the made-for-TV movie about her). *The Karen Carpenter Story, Superstar, Rock Hudson's Home Movies,* and *Joan Sees Stars* share these representational challenges and expose their problematics by attending to the ailing, dying, or corruptible star body.

Although of the texts I examine here, only the television movie *The Karen Carpenter Story* is the product of mainstream, mass media practices and institutions, the other four poach or directly quote images and sounds produced by certain stars for those mass media institutions by reproducing or copying them onto 16 mm film or low-end, home-consumer electronic devices, embedding them in new contexts, and circulating them in new venues. These are practices that have gained them attention from the popular press and, for *Superstar*, even legal action and public notoriety. This suggests that the relations are porous among media practices, media institutions, and their audiences in contemporary capitalist culture and that the star's orbit in culture is *potentially* without limits when put into circulation by technologies available to the home spectator or the financially challenged video artist or experimental filmmaker. I emphasize that this kind of star recycling is potentially unlimited because, in fact, legal claims of ownership and copyright do constrain to what extent the technologies available to many—VCRs and DVD players, video cameras, tape recorders, computers—enable the spectator or consumer to become public (oftentimes even non-profit) producers of or commentators on star images and sounds from the past and present.

The right to revive or represent the star presence through evidentiary material, such as the traces of recorded voice and photographed image, is central to the production of many biographies. It is well-documented that many biographers working in the literary mode or in traditional Hollywood film and television have legal problems with estates that refuse to grant access to letters, manuscripts, and photos, but those estates are rarely able to prevent biographies from being written or filmed at all. These conflicts have become so heated that books and articles have been written about them. In her book examining biographies of the poets Sylvia Plath and Ted Hughes, Janet Malcolm has compared the negotiations between biographers and the subject's relatives (often the owners of the estate) to the tensions and skirmishes between an imperialist explorer and hostile tribes guarding territorial resources.[7] If Malcolm's metaphors are overstated and perhaps self-serving (she is clearly on the side of those guarding territorial resources and thus absolves herself as imperialist explorer), her centralization of family dynamics, including the family's tendency to claim ownership of the famous figures, to the exercise of estate and copyright power is significant. Extensions in copyright ownership have been spearheaded by the widows of Fred

Astaire and Sonny Bono. Their efforts have contributed to the increasing inaccessibility of some media images and sounds to cultural reworkings.

Most of the texts examined here, however, are products of media practices and biographers possessing unequal access to the images and sounds of public figures because these practices and their ideological underpinnings have unequal access to capital, both economic and symbolic. For that reason, who is the imperialist exploiter and who is the victim guarding the resources of meaning is left open, or is the reverse of Malcolm's frame of reference. For example, Mark Rappaport, the writer-director of *Rock Hudson's Home Movies*, would see Hollywood institutions as the imperialists: "My excuse in a court of law [for using clips from Hollywood films] would be that these images have corrupted us and it's our turn at bat."[8] Joan Braderman, who wrote, directed, and acted in *Joan Sees Stars*, subscribes to theories of cultural production in which spectators produce by ascribing meaning to cultural signs. She asks in the voice-over, "How can MGM own what is a part of me?" *The Karen Carpenter Story* was produced in alliance with members of the Carpenter family and a television network, uniting rights to the image and the voice with economic and cultural capital. But the other four are products of marginalized media practices allied with performance art, critical theory and academic institutions, and traditions and economic supports associated with alternative or even subversive cultural production. This kind of economic marginalization made it impossible for Todd Haynes to fight back when A&M Records and the Carpenter family prevented him from distributing *Superstar*, which used audio clips from Karen Carpenter's performances.[9] Although of the videos and films under examination here only Braderman's directly addresses this issue in the text itself, all foreground the issue of representation of the star's body or likeness and all elicit understanding partly by assuming the spectator's extratextual knowledge about the star and production contexts of biography, supporting a reception context in which questions about ownership of film images and star bodies—which are among the most visible bodies in our culture—are raised.

Star Bodies, Star Bios, and Sexuality
Meeting Two Queens

Meeting Two Queens, identified as central to what was considered the New Queer Cinema of the 1990s,[10] belongs in a tradition within the avant-garde known as the "found footage" film, a tradition including such films as

A Movie and *A Report* by Bruce Conner, *Rose Hobart* by Joseph Cornell, and *Standard Gauge* by Morgan Fisher. Film scholars have placed these works in the avant-garde because their appropriation and juxtaposition of fragments from a variety of films supposedly offers a commentary on the meaning process of all films—a self-reflexive exposé of how meaning is read not only from each shot of a film but from the juxtaposition of shots within narrative units such as the scene and the sequence. While *Meeting Two Queens*, a video constructed of fragments from films starring Greta Garbo and Marlene Dietrich, shares this metafilmic strategy, it is different from these other texts in ways that are significant for readings produced by, for, and within a politics of identity. I argue that the significance of *Meeting Two Queens* vis-à-vis identity politics lies less in its self-conscious exposure of how cinematic meaning is read than in its interpellation of a spectator who identifies with the images as a fan and responds to their strategies of affect. The video's use of close-ups of the star's face, that part of the body most crucial to the signifying systems of melodrama, is central to this production of affect. The responsive fan spectator is conceptualized in both historical and metapsychological terms; the video acknowledges the existence of a historical lesbian or bisexual audience and a spectatorial position—which presumably can be taken up by anyone—that is defined in terms of a fluid sexuality.

Since *Meeting Two Queens* has been mainly seen on the film and video festival circuit and is indescribable by conventional plot recitations of two or three sentences, an explicit recounting is helpful. Cecilia Barriga uses footage from Hollywood films starring Garbo and Dietrich, organizing the images into thirteen sections. Each section is titled according to a theme, setting, prop, or narrative gesture shared by the shots it lifts from the films. "The Lake," the video's opening sequence, cross-cuts shots of Garbo and Dietrich enjoying idyllic interludes with male companions. The video cross-cuts on eyeline matches of each star so they seem to be as interested in each other's approval as that of their male lovers. "The Suitcase" is much less self-contained; instead of a mini-narrative preserving the classical unity of place (as in the previous part), it presents us with a series of images of Garbo and Dietrich as world-weary characters arriving and departing from various exotic destinations, which so often provided the settings in their films. "The Hospital" depicts a search for an injured or ill loved one. "The Library" juxtaposes images of Garbo and Dietrich to suggest a playful seduction, and "The Job" constructs them as housewives.

With "The Persecution" the video shifts tone, from sexy playfulness to cliff-hanging suspense reminiscent of a Griffith last-minute rescue, as it

FIGURES 5.1 AND 5.2 A sleeping Marlene Dietrich is the object of Greta Garbo's gaze.
Meeting Two Queens, Cecilia Barriga, 1991.

cross-cuts between Garbo's frantic driving of a team of horses and Dietrich's attempts to elude a pursuer—who appears to us to be Garbo—by automobile. "The Telephone" and "The Hat" orient their images of the stars around the props that perhaps most characterize the mise-en-scène of the classical Hollywood romantic comedy or woman's film, the two genres with which Garbo and Dietrich are most associated. These sections use only close-ups of the two stars, as if they are suggesting the appeal of these genres through the production convention that most created and revealed star power in classical Hollywood. Garbo and Dietrich were never cast in the same film, but through cross-cutting and the optical effects of "The Dialogue" they appear next to each other in the frame. The soundtrack's somber music and the stars' overwrought gesticulations and mouthing of dialogue construct this fantasy as an unhappy love story. "The Gesture" extends this mood, using images from films in which Garbo and Dietrich seemingly fulfill unhappy destinies. A hand brought to the mouth, the blowing of cigarette smoke, a slow turning of the head are recognizable as the gestures of defiance or resignation that enact the melodramatic mode and seem to condense all our understandings of these two stars and the bittersweet pleasures of the unhappy ending in classical Hollywood films. In "The Meeting" and "The Alcove," the stars reemerge triumphant. In the former section, Garbo is seen as Queen Christina, Dietrich as Catherine the Great. As each parades in full regalia down rows of courtiers and soldiers, the screen direction is manipulated by shot juxtaposition to suggest that the two will meet in their full glory. In "The Alcove" that meeting is suggested through cross-cutting between images of the stars disrobing as an opportunity for lovemaking between the two "queens." Finally, in "The End," Garbo and Dietrich are caught in the fade-out kiss; the male lovers have returned but again compete with women for the stars' attention. We last see the faces of Garbo and Dietrich in a series of superimpositions. In close-up (from *Blonde Venus*) Dietrich sheds a tear, which quickly dissolves into an image of Garbo's face. As Garbo's countenance fills the screen, a superimposition of Dietrich's face gradually overwhelms hers, until it seems to ripen into Garbo's once again—and for the last time—as the image fades to black.

Identity Politics and the Lesbian Fan

Contemporary theories of identity politics tend to explore the tension between postmodernist or poststructuralist ideas of subjectivity—which posit identity as split between fictional agency and unconscious desires but fragmented in terms of class, gender, race, and sexual orientation—and the historical reality and lived experience of groups or subjects marginalized by these same terms of class, gender, race, and sexual orientation, in which each category is constructed as "other." The tension is between an unfixed, plural identity and a (provisionally) fixed one, wherein the individual is disempowered by some mark of "otherness." Marginalized groups trying to theorize or practice an identity politics typically find themselves having to acknowledge differences within and among groups, while providing a provisional unity to struggle against common oppressors (e.g., alliances between straight and gay feminists against patriarchy).[11]

Meeting Two Queens fits into this context in the way it makes available readings that suggest a provisional straight-gay feminist alliance or, more accurately, an overlap in terms of how straight women and lesbians might negotiate pleasures and self-identity in patriarchal culture and its ideological apparatus, such as the classical cinema, even as it gestures toward the impossibility of fitting into just one of those identities—or perhaps any. *Meeting Two Queens* accomplishes this in part because it is a fan text, made by a fan of Greta Garbo and Marlene Dietrich for fans or potential fans of these two stars, who are significant in film history, in feminist criticism, and especially in lesbian subculture.[12] While it could be said that all found footage films participate in what Michel de Certeau calls "textual poaching," in that they take material from other texts and recontextualize it or put it to new use (through new juxtapositions), *Meeting Two Queens* manifests a poaching particular to fan activity.[13] It creates a sense that the material poached—specifically images of Garbo and Dietrich—matters as what Larry Grossberg calls "investment portfolios" or "billboards" of investment, which secure or advertise the place within which fans locate self-identity.[14] The film prompts the spectator's self-recognition through its production of affect, the sense that these stars and the scenarios they are enacting matter to the filmmaker and to us.

One way *Meeting Two Queens* produces affect is by activating our investment in the extratextual discourses about Garbo and Dietrich so that we get even more pleasure from the text if we read star images and performances not solely from within how the stars play a character in a specific diegetic context. We get more pleasure from the fictionalized meetings between Garbo and Dietrich if we read them against gossip, a form of "biographical" narrative that promises to tell something hidden but "true" about another. Gossip is the most prevalent form for the circulation of extracinematic knowledge about stars. (The amount of gossip about a star always exceeds the quantity of legitimate biographical tellings.) It is also an enunciative activity, which Patricia Meyer Sparks says "embodies an alternative discourse to that of public life, and a discourse potentially challenging to public assumptions; it provides language for an alternative culture."[15] In her essay "'I Get a Queer Feeling When I Look at You': Hollywood Stars and Lesbian Spectatorship of the 1930s," Andrea Weiss uses this definition of gossip to describe the creation of a lesbian subculture. According to Weiss, gossip helped foster (especially pre-Stonewall) lesbian subculture because it offered a discourse alternative to that of public life at a time when public life offered no visibility to gay culture and experience. She argues that rumors about film stars' possible lesbian or bisexual affiliations were empowering to an emerging lesbian subculture between the 1930s and 1950s because they helped members reread in lesbian terms what was ostensibly a straight narrative or straight scene.

As an example of this interpretive strategy, Weiss discusses a scene from *Morocco* (which is poached by Barriga), Dietrich's first American film, in which she costarred with Gary Cooper (an actor often coded feminine in many films and publicity stills and who is the object of some speculation and desire within the gay male subculture). In this scene Dietrich, dressed in top hat and tails, kisses a woman and takes her flower, but gives it to Cooper. Some critics have suggested that Dietrich's intent is heterosexually motivated and that the scene's hint of lesbianism is to make her exotic or to titillate a masculinized spectator assumed to be heterosexual. Weiss counters, "If we bring to the scene the privileged rumor of Dietrich's sexuality, we may read it differently: as Dietrich momentarily stepping out of her role as femme fatale and acting out that rumored [bi- or homo-] sexuality on the screen."[16]

This rereading of classical Hollywood film images is potentially empowering in part because it allowed pre-Stonewall lesbian-identified spectators to have role models who were stars of a popular medium—a medium that captured the imagination of the whole moviegoing world, not just that of a gay subculture. As Weiss argues, "Unlike racial and ethnic minorities, [gays] grew up in households where their parents not only did not share their lifestyle but actively fought it with the help of the law, psychology, religion and sometimes violence. For a people who were striving toward self knowledge, Hollywood stars became important models in the formation of gay identity."[17]

But Barriga is not only relying on extratextual knowledge of Dietrich and Garbo to enhance the possibility of a specifically lesbian pleasure or self-recognition in her video. She also counts on the spectator operating and identifying within *intra*textual knowledge of both the stars' Hollywood films and her own video. In her reappropriation of images, shots from different films are juxtaposed so that Garbo and Dietrich appear to gaze at one another. This reminds us that many of these stars' films depicted lesbian behavior, as the scene from *Morocco* or the image of Garbo from *Queen Christina* in male garb kissing her young lady-in-waiting might imply. It also suggests that through poaching Barriga creates a lesbian text (instead of a subtext) and licenses an explicit lesbian identification rather than relegating such a desire for being and having the other to a closeted activity, which was most likely the case for the identifying lesbian spectator going to the movies in the 1930s and 1940s. For example, in the parts titled "The Library" and "The Alcove," the video uses footage of Dietrich from *Song of Songs*, one of her more conventional films (and one in which she was cast by Paramount in part to counter audience impressions that she was too mysterious and unnaturally under the power of von Sternberg), to subvert a straight reading of Dietrich and the characters she portrays. In the original film, Dietrich plays a sheltered young woman who becomes a model for a sculptor who sees her as the ideal of feminine beauty. For "The Alcove," Barriga selects shots from this film in which Dietrich is dressed in conservative nineteenth-century garb, has her hair in a braided bun, and acts insecure and apprehensive. In *Song of Songs* Dietrich's character is shy and submissive toward the male character, who fetishizes her beauty. In Barriga's film Dietrich appears to act this way for the masculine-garbed Garbo; that is, she is a femme lesbian acting out coy sex and the masquerade of womanliness for the butch lesbian played by Garbo, dressed here in men's clothing (from a scene in *Queen Christina* in which she is masquerading as a man).

Sue-Ellen Case has argued that the role-playing of the butch-femme lesbian couple confounds the phallic economy and received psychoanalytic wisdom that women can't claim possession of the phallus openly but only through reaction formations in which they must masquerade femininity to hide the illicit possession of the penis. The butch and femme couple role-playing, which consists of the butch openly displaying her possession of the penis and the femme compensating for her "lack" through exaggerated femininity, reorients the masquerade of gender as one between women. Case suggests that the butch-femme couple underscores that the two roles are "two optional functions in phallocracy," which can be assumed in a politically progressive way because they demonstrate that "penis-related posturings" are roles, "not biological birthrights, nor any essentialist poses."[18]

While I agree that this argument provides one way of reading the scene between Dietrich and Garbo in "The Alcove," the section titled "The Library" suggests that the fantasies in the butch-femme role-playing are not confined to such a male-identified interpretation of butch, in which women must don the appearance and gestures of men to play with masculine and feminine, passive and submissive categories. While the shots of Dietrich in this section are similar in content to the ones used in "The Alcove," this time Garbo expresses her forthright desire to the shy Dietrich while dressed in the ultra-feminine costumes of the character Camille.

Queer theory holds that feminist film theory has repeated patriarchy's binary notions of masculine/feminine in its designation of transvestism (a woman dressing in men's clothing) as the only activity for the female spectator as desiring subject. Lucretia Knapp suggests that a queer voice is audible in the interaction between spectator and classical Hollywood text, refuting the theoretical account of the female spectator only imagining "active agency with men's clothing": "Desire [in Mary Ann Doane's analysis] is thought in heterosexual terms and thus contained by a dichotomous structure of male and female, masculine and feminine. However, pumps and loafers are not adequate assessments or reasonable representations of desire. . . . Such an account of spectatorship seems similar to Freud's analysis of the lesbian: if a woman desires a woman, she takes up the position of the man. The concept of transvestism is not as threatening to patriarchy as the image of the lesbian is, for transvestism still implies masculine privilege. However difficult she is to imagine, when a woman desires a woman, she is not a man."[19] Barriga's selection of images of Garbo and Dietrich, attesting to the diversity and multiplicity of their role playing, seems to imagine that woman Knapp describes and confirms queer theory's rejection of either/or gender choices and sexual performances.

The Rhetoric and Fantasies of Melodrama

It is no surprise that Meeting Two Queens has been hailed as part of a New Queer Cinema and has already achieved cult status. Ranging in tone from parodic humor to heartfelt homage, Meeting Two Queens seems at once to confirm the queerness of so many moments in classical Hollywood films and to address a historically defined lesbian spectator who will knowingly nod at the poaching of images from specific Hollywood films, those starring Garbo and Dietrich, who, enthroned as queens in gay folklore, mark the growth of gay subculture in the twentieth century.[20]

FIGURE 5.3 Garbo and Dietrich have an "impossible" conversation. *Meeting Two Queens*, Cecilia Barriga, 1991.

Yet I don't think the controlling agenda of *Meeting Two Queens* is to out Garbo and Dietrich. This could have been accomplished with another kind of poaching. Barriga could have used images and text from media sources more conclusive about the stars' sexual orientations than their films. *Confidential* magazine had outed Dietrich in the 1950s; Mercedes de Acosta, the female lover of both stars, had published an autobiography in the 1960s that, although not explicit in sexual details, makes clear the nature of the author's relationships.[21] Even promotion and publicity disseminated by the studios and the complicitous fan magazine industry play (however unconsciously) with the notion that these stars elicit an erotic cathexis with the female as well as male audience.[22]

While that kind of poaching would yield its own pleasures, insights, and potential empowerments, it is significant that Barriga did not choose a more empirically historical content and style for this celebration of Garbo and Dietrich. Such a documentary approach would have made it easier for a straight audience to distance themselves from the queerness of these stars and their films. I want to suggest that the video is pleasurable to an audience of diverse sexual and fan orientations in its use of the rhetoric and fantasy scenarios recognizable from melodrama, which do not limit the production of pleasure to a straight/gay polarization. Melodrama is the genre and mode that film and literary scholars have distinguished from others by its excessive generation of affect. The video deploys this rhetoric through the musical score, which follows most film melodrama's scores in its miming and signaling of excess or moments of great significance, through the use of mostly close-up shots of Garbo and Dietrich in which they express intense emotion (joy, desperation, melancholia, sexual desire, etc.), and through an ordering of narrative sequences that builds to a climax of sexual seduction and ends in scenes of a fall or triumph. I will focus on the latter two strategies in relation to how they facilitate the fantasy scenarios of melodrama that have special appeal to women and gays (male and female), those spectators Peter Matthews suggests have the most difficulty in bringing their "subjective desire into conformity with the rule of the [patriarchy's] reality principle."[23]

A number of critics have accounted for Hollywood film as a "pleasure machine" in terms of its production of fantasy scenarios or narratives.[24] As discussed in chapter 4, Linda Williams has explored the excessive pleasures of such Hollywood genres as the horror film and the maternal melodrama (as well as the non-Hollywood genre of pornography) by using the definition of fantasy provided by Laplanche and Pontalis: "Fantasies are not . . . wish-fulfilling linear narratives of mastery and control leading to closure and the attainment of desire. They are marked, rather, by the prolongation of desire, and by the lack of fixed position with respect to the objects and events fantasized. . . . Fantasy is not so much a narrative that enacts the quest for an object of desire as it is a setting for desire, a place where conscious and unconscious, self and other, part and whole meet."[25]

Meeting Two Queens is structured like a fantasy as Williams and Laplanche and Pontalis describe it. The video consists of a number of sequences in which shots and scenes are edited to suggest a certain theme, which in turn suggests a prop or setting or activities to facilitate the staging of desire: the lake, the alcove, the hospital, the hat, the telephone, the suitcase, the job, the meeting. All of the sequences, except perhaps "The Alcove" and "The End," have beginnings or endings that are arbitrary in that they are not dictated by classical goals or closure. They seem to exist, as do Garbo and Dietrich, in and for themselves.

The facial close-ups of Garbo and Dietrich serve as crucial props or settings in the staging of desire. They are cues for accessing one kind of fantasy scenario melodrama evokes: the fantasy of origins and their loss. This fantasy, which is most frequently appropriated by the maternal melodrama in its stories of mothers sacrificing of and for their children, is a replaying of the imagined union and loss of the mother's body, site of all humans' origins and later, in the mirror phase of identity, the facilitator of the split within subjectivity (the split between self and other, the signifier and the signified) and its fantasy of wholeness. Some critics claim that the photographic or cinematic images of the female face recall this multiple and ambivalent notion of the mother: "At moments it almost seems as though all the fetishism of the cinema were condensed onto the image of the face, the female in particular. . . . The face is that bodily part not accessible to the subject's own gaze (or accessible only as a virtual image in a mirror) — hence its over-representation as *the* instance of subjectivity."[26]

Diana Fuss writes that the spectatorial pleasure taken from the close-up of the female face might have a special intensity for the female viewer, who, no what matter her sexual orientation, (re-)experiences a homosexually inflected relation with the mother: "The female subject, whose hold on subjectivity is always a precarious one [because of identification with the mother], may derive a special pleasure from this 'face-to-face' encounter with a shimmering, luminous, reconstituted image of the mythic 'Mother'; the photograph's structure of visualization stages a homosexual-maternal encounter by symbolically imagining for the spectator a fantasized pre-oedipal relation with the face of the maternal."[27]

Film theorists have analyzed the films and performances of Garbo and Dietrich in similar terms. Gaylyn Studlar writes that Dietrich's characters, performance, and appearance (costuming, makeup, quality of photographing her close-ups) in her films directed by von Sternberg suggest an enactment of the pre-Oedipal child's fantasy of the powerful phallic mother.[28] Matthews has posited that Garbo's mysterious "Mona Lisa smile" reveals her phallic maternity, the woman without lack. That gazing face of Garbo is "the hieroglyph that memorializes a prehistoric perversity anterior to the formation of the codified 'symbolic' gender positions of masculine-active and feminine-passive." Matthews argues that its fetishization in Garbo's woman's films invites the female spectator to enjoy a "'utopian' space of feminine rapport" and the gay male spectator to "take his own person as a model in whose likeness he chooses the new objects of his love."[29]

Meeting Two Queens accentuates the relation between the close-up of the female face and the lost, phallic maternal. The video offers its images of the stars by fragmenting narratives, poaching individual shots from a variety of films. The close-ups, then, are torn from their original narrative context, affording the spectator the opportunity to focus sole attention on the stars' faces, which the gorgeous soft-lit and soft-focus photography of some of Hollywood's greatest cinematographers have rendered as icons of ideal feminine beauty. On the one hand, this potentially facilitates the spectator's meditation on the meanings of such filmic conventions, a consideration for any argument on the video's place within the avant-garde. On the other, this potentially facilitates the spectator's entrance into the imaginary through the illusion of direct rapport with the star, something Laura Mulvey claimed Dietrich was able to effect even in the context of a classical narrative.[30]

Perhaps the most significant use of facial close-ups in *Meeting Two Queens* is in the last sequence, "The End." It is this sequence, which ends by alternating superimpositions of the two stars' faces, that most suggests to me the video's play with melodramatic narrative blockages and resolutions and its envisioning of a utopian relation between women.

To understand this final part of the video, it is important to examine its relation to the other sequences. It shares with many of them images of the two stars that encode them as fallen women. We know they are fallen women even if we did not know that they often starred in the "fallen woman" subgenre of melodrama, for they evidence a recognizable semiotics of what in patriarchy equals a sexually knowing (and therefore fallen) woman. Overly made-up, with the excessively frilled, cheap garments traditionally associated with prostitutes (as the images from Garbo's *Anna Christie* and Dietrich's *Blonde Venus* exemplify) or in the stylish costumes of the demimonde or café society (as the images from Garbo's *Camille* and *Susan Lennox: Her Rise and Fall* and Dietrich's *Morocco* represent), Garbo and Dietrich are coded as transgressive women. In the Hollywood film narratives that trace the trajectory of such women, their first, moral "fall" necessitates a second "fall" that demands (sometimes) economic punishment and submission to patriarchal authority. Although *Meeting Two Queens* plays on our recognition of Garbo and Dietrich as stars of this kind of melodrama, and therefore playing characters subjected to a punitive patriarchy, its reappropriation of images and narrative contexts from the original films tends to leave out all those moments when the characters were subjected to or punished by men. Here they are subjected to a mutual gazing by and for women, as—with a couple of exceptions—men are elided out of the images altogether. This is true even when the video does use a punishment scene. "The Gesture" poaches shots of Garbo going to the firing squad in *Mata Hari*, but since here we see only the punishment and not the crime, Garbo's dramatic walk to her execution (dressed in simple black, denied all her sexually alluring clothes) comes off as a supreme example of a star turn. This contributes to the video's

FIGURE 5.4 Dietrich produces a tear of Garbo's face. *Meeting Two Queens*, Cecilia Barriga, 1991.

overall strategy: presenting us with a series of images of women. Garbo and Dietrich are shown playing different women, which makes us aware of them as images or as playing roles of femininity, so that they, and maybe we too, are all of these women or perhaps none at all. Identity is problematized even as Garbo and Dietrich, the great stars with so much style and feeling, are being celebrated by a fan filmmaker and fan spectators.

"The End" in a sense condenses into one sequence the strategies of multiplying identities and of turning any punishment or unhappy ending into triumph for the female stars. The series of images of Garbo and Dietrich in the sequence evoke fallen women, butch lesbians, heterosexual lovers, and pensive, perhaps even tragic women. But instead of an unabashed celebration of multiple identities, the sequence is melancholy. The music is somber; the final images figure the stars' faces as transformations of a tear. Is this a registering of the loss of these two stars (although Dietrich was not yet dead when the video was made)? Of sadness that they couldn't come out in their lifetime?

I would suggest that this is a perversely happy ending to the video, one that is complicit with the fantasy scenarios evoked by melodramatic structures of blockage and resolution. The pleasure of the fantasy scenario is in the expression of the wish, the setting out of desire, not necessarily in its fulfillment. This is why melodramas are so pleasurable: they set up so many roadblocks to the fulfillment of desire in the form of missed meetings, misunderstandings, and illness. In melodramas with unhappy or unresolved endings, the fantasy can be prolonged. *Meeting Two Queens* suggests such a prolongation in several of its sequences—in a kind of playful, teasing way in "The Meeting," in which Garbo and Dietrich are the queens who will never meet in the same frame; in "The Alcove," in which they are disrobing lovers who we will never see embrace. These sequences are satisfying because they operate by teasing us with what we know can't happen (and for that reason are more successful than "The Dialogue," where the two share the frame through optical effects).

The final images of "The End" are complex in this regard. A tear produces the last glimpse we have of Garbo and Dietrich. In the terms of melodramatic resolutions described earlier, this unhappy ending could suggest the continuance of *our* desire to see them together. On the other hand, the way the faces are superimposed onto one another could convey their union and perhaps a transcendence of fate. It does seem significant that one woman gives birth to another, comparable to Barriga's (re-)creation of their images by textual poaching. This is as much constitutive of the video's utopian vision of the relation between women as the way it prolongs our desire for the two stars. It suggests the opening of a feminist space for reading. *Meeting Two Queens* causes us to reflect on how meaning and identities are constructed and why we get so much pleasure and pain out of that ultimately elusive process.

Rock Hudson's Home Movies

While some of the pleasurable effects of *Meeting Two Queens* relies on audience knowledge of biographical truths about Garbo and Dietrich, the video is not in the spirit of an outing. Debates about the ethics and political effectivity of outing gay public figures were ongoing at the time of *Meeting Two Queens'* production in the early 1990s, but one effect of its celebratory cinephilia is to suggest the fluidity of sexual identification and desire, not insist on an "in or out" dichotomy.[31] Mark Rappaport's *Rock Hudson's Home Movies*, which uses found footage from films starring Rock Hudson and was released not long after *Meeting Two Queens*, is also not an outing. Like *Meeting Two Queens*, one of its prime goals is to use found footage from classical Hollywood cinema to strategically shake up what is presumably that regime's ideological positioning of the spectator. But this action is not necessarily synonymous with *revealing* secrets about Hudson's life. For one thing, by the time the video was released in the mid-1990s Hudson had been dead for almost ten years and his secret had been revealed publicly a few months before his death; for another, Rappaport is more interested in what one does with the secrets.

Yet to claim that *Rock Hudson's Home Movies* is not an outing or does not explicitly refer to the contemporary debates about outing is not to say that it doesn't reflect some of the same urgent issues of the 1980s and 1990s with which the debates over outing were dealing. Rappaport has written that he had been interested in the idea of working with found footage from Hollywood film in a relatively unfocused way for several years prior to production of this video, but it was the urgency of "dealing with gender issues, role-playing, homosexuality, and AIDS" that made him choose Hudson and his movies as the specific topics for his work.[32] *Rock Hudson's Home Movies* is in part a response to anxiety over how Hudson will circulate in popular memory since his death was preceded by the highly publicized revelation that his body was ravaged by AIDS. As Richard Meyer explains, at the announcement of Hudson's treatment for AIDS, the popular media configured AIDS not just as a sign of the star's physical illness but as "the evidence and horrific opening of Rock Hudson's closet."[33] Rappaport's video is, in part, an attempt to change the valence of that closet's opening, to compete with the popular media's designation of Hudson's sick body as the final image we are supposed to remember of him. Quite specifically the video is an attempt to replace the image of Hudson's body that conflates homosexuality and death (and thus perpetuates homophobia) with an image of Hudson as an active agent in his own performance of homosexuality and stardom.

Although it mentions his death from AIDS and its last long montage sequence includes scenes in which Hudson dies or is ill, *Rock Hudson's Home Movies* never gives us the image of the ill Hudson that was featured in newspapers and tabloids across the world, as well as on ABC's *Nightline* and the cover of *People* magazine. The video is not about Hudson as victim, but about the Hudson who survived for so long in a system supposedly intent on making his gay identity invisible. *Rock Hudson's Home Movies* not only makes Hudson's homosexuality visible but multiplies the sites at which we allegedly can read signs of a gay identity from the corporeal signs through which his stardom was constituted. The sites for such a reading include the performance of the actor Eric Farr as Hudson and providing the voice-over, as well as filmic images of Hudson himself portraying various characters in the adventure films, melodramas, and romantic comedies in which he acted in his thirty-five years in Hollywood.

Through the caustic remarks and sly smirks of Farr and the repetition, slowing down, stopping, and juxtaposing of various images of Hudson from his films, the video suggests that it is possible to read, or perhaps reread, what were once thought to be the signs of heterosexual masculinity as Hudson's signature of a gay authorial position. The first half of the video features clips from Hudson's films that serve as a veritable compendium of the trope of the reluctant male (Hudson's characters) pursued by zealous women (characters played by Doris Day, Dorothy Malone, Gena Rowlands, and Jane Wyman, among others). The second half of the video mostly consists of clips from the romantic comedies Hudson starred in with Doris Day and Tony Randall. In two of these films, *Pillow Talk* and *Lover Come Back*, Hudson's characters play-act as effeminate in a complicated maneuver to seduce Day's characters, who, although career women, are typically naïve and unlikely to engage in subversive masquerade. However, the video poaching involves repeating, and literally stopping, scenes between Hudson and Randall from the same films to suggest that while the former scenes with Day were queer performances within heterosexual encounters, those with the two male actors are barely disguised performances of the signs of gay identity. The characters played by Hudson and Randall bicker like two married people and direct gazes at each other's bodies that subvert the typical strategies of performance, mise-en-scène, and editing for scenes between two male characters in Hollywood films. In a clip from *Send Me No Flowers* the characters undress before each other and share the same bed. Although the actor playing Hudson admits, "Tony and I didn't write these scenes," he implies that his credibility as an actor in these films is based on the way they allowed him to express some aspect of his own experiences.

This is a particularly interesting strategy in relation to the history of Hudson's constructed biography for fan magazines and other forms of movie promotion and publicity in the 1950s and early 1960s. Richard Meyer and Richard Dyer have both pointed to how Hudson was depicted in these media as not only a "safe" and wholesome body but as a somewhat impossible one in its purity and naturalness. They argue that this image was in contrast to the body images constructed for and enacted by Montgomery Clift, James Dean, and Marlon Brando, actors whose on- and off-screen personas seemed deliberately intent on questioning (hetero)normative modes of masculine appearance and behavior. Dyer points out that these stars—rather than Hudson—served as pin-ups for gay men of that period,[34] while

Meyer presents evidence that Hudson was specifically constructed in opposition to the overly sensitive, unruly, even decay-symbolizing bodies of stars like Dean. In other words, Hudson was constructed, in part, as an antidote to the feminization of the American male film star. What these critics don't mention is how these same stars were also respected for their acting abilities, authorized in part by their association with the stage or method acting, an acting style that (at least as it is popularly understood) encourages the performer to connect character with personal biography. Hudson had to constantly fight the impression that he was less worthy as an actor because he was so much a product of the studio system; as Farr says over images of Hudson beating up Dean in *Giant*, "I enjoyed decking James Dean. I didn't like that son of a bitch. He thought he was acting while I was standing around not wanting to get my hair mussed. I got an Oscar nomination for my role in *Giant*—my only one." By giving Hudson an authorial position based on his personal biography, which was subversive of the system that produced him, *Rock Hudson's Home Movies* opens up a reading space for Hudson to be elevated as an actor and as an agent of his own career rather than a studio puppet.

Rappaport has said that *Rock Hudson's Home Movies* is a "child of 15 or 20 years of critical theory," a fact that contextualizes all of the experimental films or videos under discussion in this chapter.[35] Presumably he is referring to critical theory's attention to the construction of sexuality and gender in film and other cultural texts, to the place of "the look" or "gaze" in classical Hollywood cinema, to textual instabilities, and to the ideological underpinnings of cultural production. These concerns are central to deconstruction and to psychoanalytic and materialist (Marxist) interventions in critical theory that started to permeate both film criticism and experimental production in the late 1970s.

Yet the video's insistence on reading Hudson's performances for the truth of his identity as a gay man as a way of giving Hudson authority as an actor and, in the "fictitious autobiography" spoken through Farr's reading of Rappaport's script, an authority in his role as witness to film history, opens theoretical and historical questions not fully considered by the text. These questions also potentially mitigate the video's politically progressive ideas about AIDS and homophobia that Rappaport claims elsewhere are signs of *his* authorial agency.[36] One unanswered question that immediately springs to mind: What is the granting of authorial agency to Hudson saving the star *from*? As discussed earlier, granting Hudson authorial agency does recuperate the star from the homophobic image of him dying of AIDS. It does save him from being seen only in terms of the commodity image and therefore as less of an actor than Dean. In other words, Hudson is saved from the vulnerability of being defined only in terms of spectacle, a position historically held by women. One question that must be asked of *Rock Hudson's Home Movies*: Is granting him an authorial position saving Hudson from being in the feminine position? (This is *not* to ask whether or not the film promotes a "macho" image for Hudson. It does not; it is as cynical about the macho Hudson as about the "homo" Hudson.) Given the oppression of both women (straight and gay) and gay men in patriarchal culture in general, we might conclude that this position as historically defined and held is something to be saved from. Yet the video often takes note of the way signs of masculinity slide, how often the signs ostensibly defining straight masculinity—the collusive looks between men, their talk of "scoring," the mentoring of younger men by older men—can also be read to define gay masculinity. But it never considers that this sliding signification could work for men, no matter what their sexual orientation is, at the expense of women and definitions of femininity. The video doesn't complicate Hudson's agency by suggesting that Wyman and Day had any comparable subversive agency in the kinds of roles they played. Are they the "straight men" to Hudson's gay authorship? And if so, what are the implications for a queer reading that is sexist? (Can it be a queer reading if it is sexist?)

Matthew Tinkcom argues that the reality of "queer labor [in the studio system] is not simply the effort of queers expended on a particular commodity but the particular effort to ensure the commodity's multivalence, in that it can be consumed by queer and nonqueer consumers alike for retaining camp features or not."[37] Steven Cohan constructs an argument compatible with Tinkcom's point in his examination of the sliding signification among definitions of masculinity at the time the Hudson films were made.[38] One of the major images of masculinity in the 1950s was embodied in the figure of the playboy, a heterosexual male refusing the responsibilities and ties that the role of husband and breadwinner of domestic ideology deemed appropriate masculine behavior. As Cohan argues, because the hedonism enjoyed by the playboy bachelor is focused on consumerism and predatory behavior toward women, it is supposed to be evidence of his virile heterosexuality. But the very way that the playboy image is constructed in discourse, which includes elaborate descriptions of the bachelor pads inhabited by the kinds of character Hudson plays in his sex comedies with Day and Randall in the late 1950s and early 1960s, suggests a necessary "theatricalization" of masculinity. It is the bachelor pad's assumed function of theatricalizing (i.e., the playboy's display of his seduction prowess at parties) and yet containing masculinity in one place (i.e., the playboy's private bedroom) that makes it evoke the closet.

What is significant about Cohan's analysis is that he defines this discourse on masculinity in terms of its historical legibility in the 1950s and early 1960s and, most important, of its enabling a representation of women in which their own rebellion at this time — their own marks of agency — was masked so they could serve as the screen on which men could project their own problems and desires. He also suggests, as does Rappaport's video, that Hudson's biography is included in these sex comedies. Cohan, however, sees this partly as a function of how much the extratextual discourse about the star was invested in the same discursive terms about masculinity circulating elsewhere in culture, terms that were unstable regardless of any association with Hudson. Cohan comments on how much Hudson's character in *Pillow Talk*, in order to bed Day's character, employs stereotypes about masculinity that were not only similar but direct references to the types of men he portrayed in earlier films, such as *Giant*. While Cohan is able to see the playboy discourse as subversive of traditional forms of heterosexuality, especially as it circulates in the Hudson films in a self-reflexive way about the star's own masquerades on-screen and off, he does not impute this subversiveness to an authorial agency Hudson possessed via truths about his sexuality. Cohan's argument decenters authorial agency in the face of larger historical forces, of which Hudson's performance is only one manifestation.

Although I don't believe that the video conveys the same complexity toward Hollywood film or queer film history as the queer historiographic analyses of Tinkcom and Cohan, it does have a powerful take on history. The force and pleasure of the video's humor seems more related to the kinds of quick, visceral remarks one throws at the screen when a film's outdated assumptions, definitions, or conventions are too transparent. The video re-creates the kind of agency (with all its strengths and limitations) viewers have when performing camp readings on films from the past. By juxtaposing parts from many films to demonstrate consistency and continuity in the assumptions and conventions of Hollywood films that used gay actors to play straight characters, it also makes a point about the continuities in and obsessions of Hollywood film production over time, a point that might be lost, or at least not clearly articulated, in camp readings of a single film.

Rock Hudson's Home Movies, however, does not reflect on the social history of the period in which Hudson's star text circulated in Hollywood films and affiliated media. Rappaport's analysis of Hudson's "queer labor" is not in synch with Tinkcom's important point about the "multivalence" of the Hollywood product; the video restricts as much as it expands the multivalence of the commodity (Hudson's star image) even if the actor playing Hudson insists that the star was producing another way of looking at texts via his performing straight characters as queer. In the actor playing Hudson, one voice designates what is historically relevant about the film footage. For that reason camp is never considered to potentially have its own (sexist) blind spots, or (nonsexist) multivalency, in its reading or positioning of femininity. In contrast to *Meeting Two Queens*, which both acknowledges the historical queer spectator and star and offers viewers fantasy scenarios that have no clearly unified authorship and in which sexuality is fluid, *Rock Hudson's Home Movies* asks for a reading of these films as primarily signatures of Hudson's gay authorship under the conscious control of the star and at the expense of any subversive authorial positions of Hudson's female costars.[39]

However, in addition to its poignant reinscription of the last image the public had of Hudson (dying of AIDS), the video does demonstrate quite powerfully how questions of stardom and biographical truth are important to historical understandings of identity politics. For example, at what point is the truth about Hudson (or the films he starred in) settled by recourse to his sexual orientation in real life? What does it mean to find the truth of stars' identities by recourse to their real life or to their body, especially outside of an understanding of the body's intelligibility as a sexually performing body at a specific historical moment? And whose moment is it, the biographer's or the star's? These are questions that can be asked about Karen Carpenter as well, another star whose untimely death inspired conventional ideas about biographical truth to clash with critical theory's interrogation of such a category.

Star Sick: Stardom and the Failing Body
The Incredible Shrinking Star: *The Karen Carpenter Story* and *Superstar*

In a TV *Guide* article published the week *The Karen Carpenter Story* was broadcast on CBS (January 1, 1989), producer Hal Galli is quoted as saying, "We're not really making a movie about anorexia. It's a story of Karen Carpenter and her career of 20 years."[40] But if Karen Carpenter, the more critically acclaimed half of the brother-sister singing group The Carpenters, had not died of anorexia nervosa, it is unlikely Galli would have produced this TV movie biography. Stardom and anorexia, as both disease and social scandal, overdetermine Carpenter's story. The processes and achievement of stardom and anorexia involve discipline, surveillance, and hyper-visualization of the body, conceptualization of perfection, and attainment of ideals. It is the intersection of these two modes of identity, star and an-orexic, in Carpenter's story that makes it the subject of two very different film biographies and biographical practices, *The Karen Carpenter Story*, with its made-for-television movie framework of "disease of the week," and Todd Haynes's controversial *Superstar*, which uses dollhouses and doll furniture as sets and casts Barbie dolls to portray Karen, her family, and the recording producers and stars around her.[41] This intersection allows the films to reso-nate with contemporary struggles over and contradictions in the meaning of the female body and female agency, discursive categories and lived reali-ties for women after the women's movement. The films' willingness to enter this particular contradiction-ridden topical arena is perhaps obvious. After all, modern women are supposed to have and do it all (exercise agency), yet they are constantly encouraged to idealize what they don't have: the body of the female star. The female star seemingly has cultural power, but she is constantly exposed as pressured, manipulated, disciplined by others. The filmmakers must have known that Carpenter's story would generate viewer interest because of the ubiquity of these messages in contemporary culture. But given the biopic's difficulties in representing the star subject, how can it represent the anorexic star body? And what are the implications for how the two films do this?

The representational problems that plague film and video biographies of stars in relation to the substitution of or for the star body, what Jean Luc Comolli calls the "body too much,"[42] would seem to be especially pertinent to a biography of an anorexic star, whose defining physical characteristic is a lethally thin physique. When a star subject has a visible physical affliction or a body changing radically over time, at the very least a convincing makeup job is needed. In a method acting approach, Robert DeNiro in *Raging Bull* can gain seventy pounds to play Jake La Motta in his later years, but to por-tray an anorexic in a parallel understanding of authenticity in performance would require an actress to lose weight to the point of jeopardizing her life. (While a large segment of the public believes many actresses in Hollywood are anorexic and are pressured to be so by movie producers, a production company could hardly publicize this.) There are precedents in actresses risking death for filmic authenticity, such as Lillian Gish under D. W. Grif-fith's direction in the ice-floe sequence in *Way Down East*, yet threats to life and limb usually exist as the outmost limits of truth in performance.

The producers of *The Karen Carpenter Story* widely publicized their cast-

FIGURE 5.5 Richard and Karen Carpenter (left) are played by Mitchell Anderson and Cynthia Gibb in *The Karen Carpenter Story*. Weintraub Entertainment, CBS, 1989. Publicity still. Author's collection.

ing of a thin, small-boned actress (Cynthia Gibb) as Karen, claiming she wore padding during the scenes depicting Carpenter's years before the onset of anorexia. Although there are a couple of shots of Gibb's naked back (in which she hunches forward slightly to make her spine and ribcage more prominent), Carpenter's emaciated body is mostly suggested through dialogue and reaction shots of characters looking horrified when they hold or touch her. In *Superstar* Karen and the other characters are played by Barbie dolls, which first appear in the film after a subtitle announcing that what is to follow is a "simulation." To represent the passing of time and the progression of the disease in the course of Karen's self-starvation, Haynes carved into the doll's plastic face to suggest emaciation (the doll playing Mrs. Carpenter was partially burned to suggest age and horror). Later I will discuss some important implications of the director's choice to cast dolls in the film in relation to the biopic genre's epistemological and fantasy status. But a crucial point about the choice should be made here, in this context of female agency and stardom: the female child is encouraged to play with dolls as a way to narrativize adult identities for her future self. Although this play is suffused with potential resistance to patriarchal roles, girls are usually encouraged to play with dolls as a rehearsal for them (i.e., playing mommy). In ironic contrast Haynes's use of dolls rather than human beings allowed him unlimited power over the bodies of his female "performers." This particular and unusual directorial power seems to simultaneously call attention to and critique how little power female stars have at the same time that it authorizes Haynes to somewhat aggressively (cutting, burning) and fantastically assert his director status over them.

The inability to use an actual anorexic body is not evidence that the films have forsaken a politics of authenticity or presence or biographical truth. The use of Carpenter's singing voice to structure the narratives of both films and assert an authorial or authorizing voice for their producers indicates that they are very invested in presenting traces of the singer's presence. Both films have an investment in another register of authenticity in relation to stardom: authenticity in relation to scandal. This register is crucial to the films' ability to draw audience interest, and it demonstrates, again, the interrelatedness of stardom and anorexia in terms that offer constructions of femininity on which the films rely or comment. The frameworks of scandal and sensationalism also provide opportunities for cultural players (such as film directors, producers, and the star's family) to claim ownership of the definitions of femininity, anorexia, and stardom.

George Custen has written that the star biopic of classical Hollywood presented stardom as a ritual of democracy. A person with talent is given a "fair hearing on a popular stage" and, after the ups and downs of a career, is taken into the hearts of the diegetic audience that represents the historical audience of that entertainer's time.[43] Authenticity or the truth of stardom is found in the link between the diegetic audience that has accepted the star and the real audience whose presence at the film suggests an implicit recognition of the star's worthiness. Knowledge of the star's career validates or authenticates the popular judgment of both audiences. Contemporary biopics associate authenticity with knowledge of scandal. The possibility of scandal has existed as an underside of star discourse since it began in the 1910s to focus on the star as a private individual.[44] Scandal erupts when the constructed discourse is unable to contain the visibility of the private within socially acceptable parameters. Of course what is judged as acceptable or not are the private concerns of (gendered) sexual behavior, or other kinds of behavior indicating sensual desires: excessive consumption of drugs, alcohol, or food. Scandal, in its assumption of giving the audience a glimpse behind the image, gives the sense that what one is seeing is real biographical truth.

Changes in moral standards and in obscenity and libel laws, the decentralization of the origins of star discourse, and the rise of new media as sites for star discourse have all contributed to revelations of star scandal. The increasing and repeated revelations of star scandal changes what can be considered scandalous; for example, heterosexual activity outside of marriage, except when involving murder, abuse, or incest, is rarely scandalous now. (The triangle involving Woody Allen, Mia Farrow, and Soon Yi Previn in the 1990s involved the possibility of molestation and incest.) Revelations about a star's homosexual behavior or diagnosis of AIDS is still scandalous (most of the time). Drug addiction and eating disorders, especially when they end in death or near death, are also still scandalous. The latter behaviors suggest deviance from what is considered to be natural or healthy behavior in regard to recreational consumption of mood-altering chemicals or of eating. To the nonanorexic, anorexia as self-starvation is a taboo death wish. From this perspective, the motoring force behind the narrativization of Carpenter's stardom cannot be disarticulated from the scandal of her anorexia, and Galli's remarks appear naïve or disingenuous or (transparently) political vis-à-vis his dependence on the cooperation of the Carpenter family in making the telefilm.

The narratives of stardom and self-starvation have similarities; they are about the construction of an image as a fantasy ideal; they involve struggles over agency and control; and they involve the subject's discipline, especially discipline of the body to achieve the ideal image. Since the women's movement both stardom and anorexia narratives have gained currency as speaking to and about political and symbolic gains (greater numbers of women entering college, laws against sexual discrimination in the workplace, women's greater reproductive control) and losses (the continuing legacies of unequal pay and defining female success in terms of achievement of certain idealized body images). Some of the contemporary interest in such stars as Marilyn Monroe, Judy Garland, Rita Hayworth, and Frances Farmer, for example, revolves around their putative lack of agency, their victimization by the studio system and its repression of their rebellious feminine desires. Feminists, whether writing for mainstream or academic presses, routinely use female stars or images from music videos, films, television, or magazines as examples of how all women are constructed by the patriarchal imaginary. Feminist cultural critics, as well as clinical researchers, psychiatrists, and psychologists, emphasize the statistical evidence of anorexia as a "female disease," for at least 90 percent of its sufferers are women. Despite disagreement about the significance of various determinants, they tend to concur that anorexic women experience feelings of powerlessness and impose a regime of discipline on their body in which the choice between eating and not eating is a way to control one essential thing about their lives.

Karen Carpenter's story becomes, then, an overdetermined story of femininity in contemporary culture after the women's movement, as it combines narratives of stardom and self-starvation. The particular ways CBS's *The Karen Carpenter Story* and Haynes's *Superstar* express an interest in femininity are analyzable, in part, in relation to their production contexts. Critics and industry insiders generally agree that the typical made-for-television movie is addressed to a female audience, defined by the industry as a valuable consumer market of women between the ages of eighteen and forty-nine. If women like to watch stories about other women, as television executives claim, *The Karen Carpenter Story*, with its focus on a young woman's life, career, suffering, and death, fits that bill.[45] The film's depiction of anorexia reflects the industry's use of topical issues and real people to continually resecure audience interest in a genre that offers women a chance to watch the stories, usually traumatic (and often triumphant), of other women. Critics' interpretations of this status of the made-for-television movie have ranged from claiming that it taps into the political right's fears about the collapse of the family to designating it as one television form that has consistently provided a sympathetic look at female gender roles in flux.[46]

Superstar uses the made-for-television movie as a template for its own narrative. It follows the form's focus on individual trauma and the crisis to the family, as it shows all of Carpenter's achievements and problems as a star impacting and related to her parents and brother. It seems to share with *The Karen Carpenter Story* what Elayne Rapping has identified as the television movie's assumption that the "relational" self defines femininity.[47] On the other hand, the film evidences a relation to experimental, independent cinema. Employing an artisanal mode of production, with found and hand-crafted objects as props, the film plays with the conventions of the documentary, biopic, and women's film and combines live action featuring real people with what appears to be doll animation. (Actually the dolls are moved by people off-screen; they are not animated in the traditional sense.) Like many experimental films since the intervention of feminism in media studies, *Superstar* cites past films and genres to expose the strategies of narrative cinema as they depend on the representation of the female body. These production contexts suggest that the struggles over the meanings of the female body take place across modes of filmmaking and reading communities even when the relationship between authorial sources and feminist discourse varies.

Balancing the promotional advantages of sensationalism with a desire to avoid lawsuits, television movies based on the lives of real people are usually made in cooperation with the subject or the family. For *The Karen Carpenter Story*, cooperation with the Carpenter family was essential to secure music rights and to have access to aspects of Carpenter's life not in the public record. Consequently the television movie has to negotiate the meanings of her life not only across the various registers of signifying activity operating around any television movie—the industry's production and marketing practices, the textual practices deriving from genre conventions of the woman's film and biopic, and the reception context of an assumed female, middle-class audience—but also across the authorial prerogatives of family and copyright. From this perspective, Galli's contention that the film is a story of Carpenter's career rather than her anorexia is a fictive construct that recognizes the version of her life authorized by the Carpenter family, especially Richard Carpenter, the executive producer and Karen's brother and former music partner. In interviews immediately following Karen's death and right before the airing of the film, Richard expressed skepticism about the social and cultural analyses of anorexia, claiming it was genetically determined, having little to do with family dynamics or show business. While made-for-TV movies tend to manage unruly social and cultural problems through an emphasis on individual afflictions, cures, and recoveries, they typically assume a pedagogical or even therapeutic role by having diegetic characters as well as recognizable authorities in promotional contexts (network affiliate news segments, public service announcements following the film, etc.) spell out the causes, symptoms, and cures of the disease or disaster of the week.

The influence of Richard's beliefs about Karen's anorexia—that it is "genetic in the same way talent is"—would seem to mitigate this overtly prosocial function of the made-for-television movie.[48] (If it is genetic, it may be unchangeable. Even if it was changeable, Richard's linkage of anorexia to the talent contributing to stardom subverts the curative drive.) In the *TV Guide* article that ran the same week the movie first aired, the actress Cynthia Gibb is reported to be so afraid "the family won't accept [her]" if she concedes a typical psychiatric conclusion that anorexics tend to come from families in which "honest, direct communication about feelings" is avoided or controlled by authoritative parents, that she leans over and shuts off the writer's tape recorder when this issue is broached.[49] The actress's complicity with or fear of the family prevents her from performing one of the typical roles of television movie performers playing ill characters: spokesperson for the public service announcement touting curative solutions that invite audience participation. In the film itself, the term *anorexia nervosa* is mentioned only in the last twenty minutes, in the scene depicting Carpenter's psychiatric treatment, while scenes of her early life are careful to show her once healthy relationship to eating. (A scene near the beginning of the film, for instance, has her yelling "Yippee!" when a pizza dinner is announced.) There is also a noticeable lack of emphasis on the industrial, promotional, and fan community configurations of the recording business and the pressures of stardom. The producer Herb Albert and other A&M Records executives are portrayed as benevolent businessmen and connoisseurs of Carpenter's vocal abilities. While a construction of the culture industries as conspirators in her starvation for an ideal image would be problematic, they are depicted here only as the perfect conduit for her voice to reach listeners around the world.

Despite its experimental status, *Superstar* is invested in clearly defined explanations of anorexia that we typically expect of educational documentaries. For example, a voice-over narration breaks into the narrative story world to historically contextualize women's relation to food and body ideals in postwar America. Such hybridization of the documentary and narrative functions in a prosocial pedagogical role missing in *The Karen Carpenter Story*, even as such displays remind us of the film's relation to the anti-illusionist, nonclassical mode of alternative cinema. The nonnarrative discursive modes of explanation employed in these segments contrast sharply with the narrative segments depicting the music executives as causal agents. Their banal commentary about Carpenter's voice is rendered menacing by slowing down the soundtrack so that the actors' voices are deep and their speech slurred. Despite *Superstar*'s multiple hybrid strategies for causal explanations, and despite Richard Carpenter's stated beliefs about the origins of anorexia, the two films do share a primary target of blame for Karen Carpenter's disease: the family, especially the mother. The two films most powerfully overlap in bringing together the underlying fantasies of the biopic and the family (particularly maternal) melodrama.

Maternal Origins, Recovering Bodies, Vocal Presence

The reluctance of *The Karen Carpenter Story* and Richard Carpenter to concede any agency to the media in the construction of a feminine body ideal for Karen is arguably matched by the television industry's need to avoid controversy over the workings of the culture industries. But the film's adherence to mainstream narrative and genre conventions positions dramatization of conflict as a necessary representational strategy in the depictions of Carpenter's life and eventual demise. Conflict has origins, and since contemporary concepts of verisimilitude, as well as contemporary sociological categories such as the dysfunctional family, name the family and romantic love as credible sites of conflict, it is not surprising that *The Karen Carpenter Story* traces Carpenter's search for an ideal in the need for demonstrations of love from family and the "right" romantic partner. While the emphasis on family also honors the Carpenters' own understanding of the familial context for events in their lives, it contradicts Richard's belief that family relationships had nothing to do with Karen's anorexia.

In other words, the film's need to have topical, dramatic, and, as we shall see, fantasy origins for Karen's anorexia wins out over Richard's belief about the lack of connection between the disease and family dynamics. This need ultimately displaces all of the cultural determinants of anorexia onto the mother of Karen and Richard. This struggle over the authorization of Karen's starvation is crucial to understanding how the film participates in contemporary notions of the female body and in the biopic's depiction of the female star body. *The Karen Carpenter Story* and *Superstar* construct Karen's stardom and anorexia as related to struggles to separate from the mother (and the mother's body), use the conventions of the family melodrama to dramatize this, and conceptualize the biopic and its use of the star's voice as a way to resurrect the female star body.

The Karen Carpenter Story, like so many melodramatic narratives in patriarchal Western culture, conceptualizes feminine identity in terms of its closeness with the maternal. In this theorization women are assumed to be too much body, doubled as they are with the body of their mother that they did not have to completely relinquish in the movement out of the Oedipal moment. Melodramas often focus on the conflicts between mothers and daughters.[50] While the threat this closeness poses to heterosexual attachments can be viewed as subversive, the patriarchal contextualization often figures the mother as possessive and suffocating. Until a social constructionist, historiographic feminist perspective became influential, such

Oedipalizations were also common in sociological and medical literature on anorexia. Joan Jacobs Brumberg's survey of anorexia literature found that when a parent is implicated in the causes of a young woman's anorexia, "it is almost always the mother . . . [who] is unable to see and reflect her daughter as an independent being."[51] Not surprisingly Mrs. Carpenter is depicted as loving but controlling every aspect of Karen's identity. She sews her clothes, resists Karen's move to her own place (she finally consents when Richard suggests she live with him in a house not far away from the parents), and disapproves of Karen playing the drums because it is not ladylike. When Karen finally seeks psychiatric help, her mother refuses the psychiatrist's pleas that she tell Karen that she loves her, saying, "Karen knows we love her." Mrs. Carpenter's assumption that mother-daughter closeness can take love for granted thus enables her to wield a powerful psychic hold over Karen. She is even shown making decisions for Richard; in one of the campiest scenes, she pushes her son into taking Quaaludes because "they're not drugs, they're prescription medicine."[52] The casting of Louise Fletcher as Mrs. Carpenter accentuates the phallic associations of this maternal construction. An actress whose lips seem to be always cast into a downward position, Fletcher's most famous role was as Nurse Ratched in *One Flew Over the Cuckoo's Nest*, who tyrannizes a group of male mental patients with sadistic psychological disciplinary practices.

Placing all of the origins of anorexia in the suffocating closeness between Karen and her mother has implications for how the film depicts stardom. On the one hand, the film makes stardom a narrative catalyst for Karen's literal starvation. (She reacts to a newspaper review that describes her as "pudgy" by dieting.) Her constant public visibility, which results in such commentary on her weight and derision of her clothes, underscores her inability to experience a sense of self and get love from others, which is ironic since stardom supposedly promises that love. On the other hand, in its combination of the biopic and the maternal melodrama, the film depicts stardom as the ultimate space for Karen to have a body. Music and the stardom that goes with her musical talent are shown as avenues for Karen to express her separation from her mother. The slender body becomes a self-imposed ideal to make others (such as critics) love her more as a star and to separate from her mother's smothering body. In one of those quick diagnoses in movies that is even more exaggerated in this telefilm since it occurs in the last twenty minutes, the psychiatrist explains that the disease is simply symptomatic of Karen's need for love and attention. Mrs. Carpenter finally tells Karen she loves her at the family's last Thanksgiving together before

Karen's death. Karen hears the message, fulfilling melodrama's fantasy of a possible utopian relation of closeness between mother and daughter and the biopic's fantasy that the subject will be recognized and approved of for the unique star she is. But a defining element of the melodrama is the mistiming of realization and expression. The anorexia has already damaged her heart, and she dies, intertitles tell us, a few months after this touching moment.

Are the melodramatic tensions and poignancy between mother and daughter, in which bodies are too close, another substitute for the film's inability to actually show us an anorexic body? Or perhaps they displace the problem of both anorexia and the film's inability to really show us evidence of the disease onto the problem of a daughter having a separate, visible identity from the mother. But, significantly, the film also substitutes Carpenter's voice for her body. All of the biographical materials circulated after her death designate her voice as the defining element of her stardom; to remember it or hear it again, claim record promoters, critics, biographers, and family, is to understand why she was a great star. Such comments suggest the extent to which the recorded voice can act as a fetish object for signifying presence in the absence of the loved one.[53] Carpenter's special phrasing, which is claimed to simultaneously express irony and vulnerability, constitutes the "grain" of her voice, what Roland Barthes calls "the body in the voice as it sings."[54] *The Karen Carpenter Story*, with authorized connections to the legal and familial ownership of Carpenter's voice — which it uses constantly over the images of Gibb — claims to recover the fullness of Carpenter's body, which is not only now gone but was shrinking or fading in the last years of her own lifetime, just as the public memory of her may have been shrinking prior to the production of this film (and *Superstar*).

Despite its maverick status as an unauthorized film, *Superstar* shares with *The Karen Carpenter Story* the challenges in representing the anorexic body and its attempted resurrection through the star's voice. Its citation of the family melodrama could also be read as a citation of the simultaneously utopian and dystopian fantasy of plentitude and serve as explanation for its similarly negative portrayal of the mother. We see here too Mrs. Carpenter sewing Karen's clothes, making comments about the anti-family values of show business life, resisting Karen's move into autonomy. The parents' home, just as in the television movie (both use the actual Carpenter house in several shots), is a crucial setting to portray Karen's life as enmeshed in a claustrophobic relation to her family.

But Haynes and his cowriter, Cynthia Schneider, trouble claims to both realism and melodramatic sincerity by using dolls to play the characters and

FIGURE 5.6 Karen Carpenter's claustrophobic relationship to her family is represented in this image from *Superstar*. Todd Haynes, 1987.

mixing live-action doll performance with dramatizations and documentary sequences analyzing anorexia using human actors. *Superstar* is deliberately campy in its self-conscious exposure of filmic representational practices and the conventionality of genres and narrative verisimilitude.[55] Haynes is quoted many times as saying that he wanted to use dolls for actors so that viewers would be conscious of how conventional narratives coax us into identification with characters and their ideologies.[56] The portrayal of Mrs. Carpenter as tyrannical phallic mother is not based on the film's assumption that mothers and daughters are psychically or essentially close. *The Karen Carpenter Story* expresses this assumption by representing the mother as both controlling and desirous (however late) of a loving, accepting relationship with her daughter. The bad mother is centralized in *Superstar*, however, because it is a genre convention of the melodrama and the female star biopic (*Mommie Dearest, Frances, Gypsy*) to have a controlling maternal figure as the prime impetus for the star daughter's rebellion. There is no depth to the portrayal, no dramatic change to fulfill the melodramatic fantasy. This potentially makes the figure open to analysis as an obvious stereotype. Yet ultimately *Superstar*'s investment in an analytical stance toward genres and character types does not circumvent its conveyance of the sexist notion that mothers are often the worst, albeit unwitting, purveyors of patriarchal ideology. This is most evident in how the doll representing Mrs. Carpenter appears monstrous; the plastic face has been burned, and she is often shot in low-angle close-up, as if she is looming over Karen. She is prone to pivoting quickly, so that her body—matched to an actress whose voice-over is performed in condescending or whining tones—turns to look at Karen in disbelief at her daughter's meager attempts at asserting agency over her own life. She continually spouts clichéd, conservative laments about the immorality of contemporary culture, especially show business culture, as a way to prevent Karen from emerging as a sexual being.

The problematic aspects of this contradictory imaging of the mother's role in the daughter's anorexia—as both patriarchal mouthpiece and stylized element in the film's strategic self-reflexivity about the ideological underpinnings of narrative conventions and spectatorial identification—is offset by other strategies the film uses to depict and explain the twin narratives of stardom and starvation that overdetermine Carpenter's life. Although problematic, these strategies align the film more closely with some of the explanations of anorexia offered by feminist theorists that refute simplistic condemnation of the maternal figure. Susan Bordo, working with feminist theory and the diaries of anorexics, positions the condition in terms of its individualized psychodynamics and its cultural determinants. She describes eating disorders as negotiated responses to "the general rule governing the construction of femininity [in patriarchal culture]: that female hunger—for public power, for independence, for sexual gratification—be contained, and the public space that women be allowed to take up be circumscribed, limited."[57] Women must fulfill an emotional economy, says Bordo, that is other-directed yet also exhibit the mastery and emotional discipline required to be accepted into once male-only spaces of public visibility. Self-imposed discipline on the body (including self-starvation) is one kind of negotiation of this double bind.

If the contradictions surrounding these expectations for femininity in contemporary culture are constructed around power through possibility of visibility, certainly the female star—as a figure constituted through mediated instances of visibility to a mass public—would seem to particularly emblematize the vicissitudes of femininity in contemporary capitalist, patriarchal culture. *Superstar* is interested in Carpenter's biography in these terms and in the irony of using a "shrinking" star to take on the burden of embodying feminine visibility. The use of Barbie dolls or Barbie clones to portray the characters is the most obvious—and infamous—strategy of the film to contextualize Carpenter's dilemma within an immediately recognizable and widely accessible representation of femininity in postwar American culture. Barbie brings her own intertextual baggage to the film, a history that includes one of the great success stories of any product of postwar corporate America, the most significant achievement of which was to wed the notion of an ideal, sexualized female body centered around commodity purchases of clothing, accessories, and dream houses to little girls' fantasy narratives of successful maturation.

Barbie, modeled after a very sexualized German doll named Lili (a sort of Lili Marlene or Lola, cabaret singer and prostitute figure), has qualities of the star. Jacqueline Urda and Alan Swedlund write that her "resilience, appeal, and profitability stems from the fact that her identity is constructed primarily through fantasy and is consequently open to change and re-interpretation."[58] In the years after the women's movement, the sexual revolution, and counterculture, Barbie—like Carpenter, who was derided for representing reactionary values—became a "bad object" for educated, middle-class adults who reject aspects of patriarchal and corporate ideology. Lynn Spigel argues that Barbie "has been a primary vehicle through which strained relations between different points of views of feminism surface in our culture."[59] Spigel reveals that adult female collectors of Barbie dolls, some of whom are self-identified feminists, find her image—that resilience, that openness to change and to multiple fantasies of female possibility—empowering. In contrast, other groups of self-identified feminists define the ideals, especially body image ideals, that Barbie seems to represent as highly problematic. Spigel notes that the mainstream press usually pits these groups against one another in sexist, predictable debates between mass culture and high culture. In interviews Haynes never articulates a wholesale condemnation of Barbie, but it is clear that his film speaks to the ways Barbie is a bad commodity fetish or part of the culture's "false consciousness."[60]

To underscore the point that stardom and Carpenter's self-starvation are to be associated with the false consciousness of contemporary mass culture via their connection to Barbie, televisual images from other examples of 1960s and 1970s pop culture are juxtaposed with the dolls, whose stiff limbs and movements render them zombie-like. In a rapid montage sequence near the end of *Superstar*, images from *The Brady Bunch* and *The Partridge Family*—television shows contemporaneous with the rise of the Carpenters in the 1970s and, like them, presumed to be a return to more wholesome family values after the 1960s—are a visual backdrop to Carpenter's purging

FIGURE 5.7 Karen Carpenter sings at the White House in *Superstar*. Todd Haynes, 1987.

routine. As the film lets us glimpse what is real about Carpenter behind the constructed image of a happy, sweet femininity, video clips show how popular culture products of this time formed a web of constructed images of ideal youth, a web in which Carpenter was hopelessly caught.

In this montage sequence television images of Nixon, the Vietnam War, and student protests, accompanied by voice-overs describing The Carpenters' music, embed the history of popular culture into a larger history that sees the 1960s and 1970s as periods of massive resistance to capitalism and military imperialism. In this context The Carpenters are depicted as a singing group whose function was to cover up the subversiveness of contemporary youth rebellion. The group's invitation to sing at Nixon's White House is a highlight of the film, and Karen's song there implores the audience to also sing, but of "good things, not bad." As the images of spankings inserted throughout the film suggest the personal psychodynamics of Karen's acts of punishment and repression, The Carpenters' music is depicted as a sociocultural fantasy mechanism of repression that keeps more troubling realities from surfacing to consciousness. Similarly the film's use of documentary found footage of the abundance of mass-marketed food products in American chain grocery stores in the postwar period puts Karen's relation to food and self-starvation into a larger history of consumption in a nation of abundance as well as within the cultural prescriptives for women to consume, but not too much.

The most problematic use of documentary conventions in the film is its use of found footage images of dead, emaciated bodies from Nazi concentration camps. Earlier in the film intertitles explain the psychodynamics of anorexia as making victim and punisher one; anorexic as fascist is the comparison explicitly made. While the metaphorical construction of anorexic with fascist may have some explanatory power vis-à-vis an individualized psychodynamic, comparing self-imposed starvation with the forced starvation of victims of genocide raises more questions than it answers. But the use of the images of emaciated concentration camp victims for their shock or comparative value exposes again the difficulties in presenting and representing the anorexic body within traditional narrative, or even untraditional biographical narrative conventions. Another body must substitute for Carpenter's anorexic body, whether it is the concentration camp victim or the Barbie doll in its shiny plastic carapace.

Superstar doesn't really need to show us concentration camp victims to point out that Carpenter's anorexia was leading to death, because the very use of dolls and miniature props already does part of that work. Susan Stewart, in her study of the gigantic and the miniature as cultural forms, argues that the miniature evokes a removal from lived experience, a perfection "protected from contamination" because absolute boundaries are maintained. It mimes a perfection known only in death. Anorexics' self-imposed ideal of the perfect body, uncontaminated by food or unacceptable feminine desires, is uncontaminated by the material processes of living. Stewart also describes the function of the miniature, such as the dollhouse, in terms of the way spectators experience it as a tableau representing the tension between inside and outside. *Superstar* evokes such a tension in its juxtaposition of scenes using dolls with the repeated live-action tracking shots taken on the streets of the Carpenters' neighborhood. The "frozen in life" quality of ideal femininity that is epitomized in the rigid, unchanging miniature doll is contrasted with the movement of the camera as an endless searching in suburban America. This is a contrast that suggests — as Stewart does about the miniature — the house as simultaneously prison and haven, as representing an interior self that is always unrecoverable.[61]

Like *The Karen Carpenter Story*, *Superstar* employs recordings of Carpenter's voice as a way to recall her presence in the melancholy void that characterizes these representations of her life and body. At times both films actually use the same songs as voice-over in representing particular moments in her life. For example, both depict her short courtship and marriage in a couple of brief scenes in which "Masquerade," a song about the masquerades of identity we assume in relationships, serves as vocal backdrop. Despite the television movie's inscription of a sincere melodrama, like *Superstar* it lets Carpenter's voice take on the burden of authorial irony. In Haynes's film, he and other actors portray music critics in a mock talking-heads documentary sequence in which three of the four claim that Carpenter's genius—the basis of her stardom—was in the way she could control or create ironic inflections in otherwise uninteresting kinds of mass-produced music.

In the need to produce a star body and an acting agent for filmic biography, each film recovers Carpenter through her voice. In working out these representational challenges and determining what agency might mean in a political context that also sees women as afflicted by the images and constraints produced by patriarchal ideology, Haynes's film affirms some of the norms that its ironic citations seek to undermine. But *Superstar* and, to a lesser degree, *The Karen Carpenter Story* thematize issues of control and agency that also inform their own production contexts and the legal fights between Haynes's author status and the ownership claims of Richard Carpenter, A&M Records, and Mattel Toys. My discussion has been able to make claims about agency only in relation to these particular production and textual contexts. But a study that would go further in terms of possible reception contexts would be involved in those same dilemmas, for fans and readers surely claim to possess the star in their own ways, while patriarchal culture continually raises its stakes on the female body. These two film biographies ask, and only sometimes answer, a few of the questions of stardom and the female body: Who owns the star's voice and image? Who owns the female body? These are questions that Joan Braderman, a media producer who is both a critic and a fan, addresses.

Joan Sees Stars: Feminist Autopathography and Hollywood Stardom

Joan Sees Stars is an experimental video using found footage of star images and Hollywood films to construct a feminist autopathography. Through special effects, Braderman inserts or superimposes her own body onto the images she appropriates, so that she shares the screen with the stars who most fascinate her: Elizabeth Taylor, Judy Garland, Vivien Leigh, and Ava Gardner. On the soundtrack Braderman provides a running commentary on the Hollywood-produced star and narratives. In part 1 of the video, titled "Star-Sick," Braderman recounts parallel illness and pain narratives, the story of her own ulcerative colitis (a degenerative autoimmune disease) and the story of the AIDS that is slowly killing her friend Leland, with whom she has communicated via telephone about their mutual television viewing and star worship. In part 2, "Movie-Goddess Machines," she appropriates and examines images of the technologies of pain and suffering, from sadism and masochism in film noirs, melodramas, and teen films of her youth to the tattooing of her own body and her meditation on the aging Ava Gardner.

Maureen Turim explains that experimental videos using found footage or imitating classical narrative strategies risk not reaching a successful level of metacriticism or irony because they imitate or incorporate the very forms on which they are commenting.[62] But some film and video artists use this tension of metacriticism versus imitation (or what some theorists of post-modernism might call the tension between parody and pastiche) as one of the focal points of their work. For Braderman, to be political is to use "the most public language," which she designates as video or TV, even if this means the video artist is "caught between Van Gogh and MGM, real art and a factory." Video artists like Braderman, who work within a feminist or queer context, are increasingly situating themselves and their work between Van Gogh and MGM as they turn to found footage or parody to investigate how popular culture informs constructions of self-identity, especially embodied, gendered, and sexed self-identities. Turning away from the formal rigors of the structuralist, feminist filmmaking practices of the young Chantal Aker-mann or Laura Mulvey and Peter Wollen, which sought to destroy the spec-tatorial pleasures afforded by classical cinema, these video artists celebrate their power to manipulate mass-mediated images to involve the spectator in their own liminal status — to experience popular culture's utopian prom-ise while putting "utopia" in quotes, as a construction not divorced from institutional or historical origins, and therefore not divorced from political implications about the workings of power in contemporary capitalist, patri-archal culture. In many videos star images are the focus of poaching or ap-propriation from other works. Stars, who perform identity through corpo-real signs that are idealized embodiments of cultural values and norms, are produced in narratives and images by a capitalist, patriarchal institutional media machinery; however, in circulation these narratives and images be-come appropriable by audiences for their own ends — as objects and sites of pleasure, resistance, complicity, or prosthesis — even as they continue to profit their producers.

While *Joan Sees Stars* shares the project of exploring star images and narratives with many current experimental videos using found footage, it also uses "the most public language" of television in the first person, in an autobiographical mode. Many literary and film critics have argued that traditional autobiography is a self-represented life story that tends to cover up the discontinuities that characterize identity in master narratives of conflict resolution and development.[63] In this way the traditional autobiography, like the traditional biography, discussed at the start of this chapter, turns the natural event into a cultural text, a nonnarratable, unlimited semiosis of the body (birth, growth, reproduction, illness, death) into a narratable text, making life texts appropriable for the nation-state of industrial capitalism to articulate its knowledge and power. Braderman's employment of an autobiographical voice in *Joan Sees Stars*, however, participates in two subgenres of autobiography that can problematize this trajectory by focusing on the vicissitudes of the body: the feminist autobiography and the autopathography, or illness autobiography. Both these subgenres foreground the act of enunciation and its relation to an embodied self, denaturalizing the movement from bodily semiosis to narratable text. The female autobiography appropriable for feminism explores how women can enunciate and defy "the inherited frame of an essentialized embodiment" through which patriarchal culture insists on defining femininity,[64] while the autopathography, an autobiographical narrative of illness or disability, narrates how illness and pain change the subject's relation to her body. The attempt to communicate this change foregrounds the somatic experience of the body as a fundamental constituent of identity.

Braderman had worked as a feminist video artist for many years before the onset of her illness, but her experience of illness changed the form, focus, and timetable of this video. At one point her illness was life-threatening; her subsequent sense of mortality and then the chronic pain and other disabling symptoms that emerged as her disease was "under control" changed her relationship to television viewing and star fandom and the direction of her video. Her television and video watching and the reading of star biographies become the catalysts for reflections on the production of identity in patriarchal, capitalist culture, on the relation between identity and the healthy body, and on the significant role that images of film stars have in shaping female self-identity and a sense of the embodied self. Ann Hunsaker Hawkins argues that autopathographies can emphasize "the pragmatic reality and experiential unity of the autobiographical self" that is in the crisis of disease, yet illness can also threaten the autobiographical subject with dissolution of a sense of a unified identity.[65] The subject may react to illness with attempts at control that are narratable — often dramatically so — but the pain that is experienced can also momentarily disrupt meaning and social connection. Even when endurance of intermittent or ongoing pain is possible, the ill subject often recognizes herself as a being that is as much *subjected to* as a subject.

The most obvious things that ill people are subjected to are medical discourses and treatments that delimit the boundaries between health and pathology. Curiously, given the trend of most autopathography narratives, which obsess about medical treatments and discourses, Braderman is less interested in medical discourses per se than a variety of discourses that act in complicity to facilitate the insertion of the body into the machinery of capitalist production and consumption. For that reason the star image and its availability to us through television and home video delivery systems become central to her examination of her own identity formation as a woman and as a sufferer of chronic illness. The star, whose highly valued status in our culture is evidenced by high salaries and massive public exposure, is offered to the female subject for identification through her incorporation of the star's physical appearance in acts of self-policing the body. For both male and female subjects, the star biography is offered for consumption as a success story to be imitated with a celebration of capitalist culture.

Although no one can be fully interpolated through the hailing of dominant ideology or achieve the subjecthood that the star image, star biography, and star film vehicle invite us to realize, perhaps the chronically or mortally ill subject can best understand such failure. Braderman and her friend Leland become fixated on Elizabeth Taylor and their own television viewing activities as a way to work through precisely this relation of their identities to the idealized embodiments of healthy and productive subjectivity offered by the media. Through Braderman's spoken discourses and through surreal image juxtaposition provided by television channel surfing, this part of the video attempts to establish who the productive subject constructed by American commercial media actually is and how she and Leland fit that identity. Images of Taylor in *Butterfield 8*, a film in which the star plays a high-class call girl, predominate the image track in this section. At one point Braderman uses a purple digital image of her eyes and nose to mask over parts of the film image so Taylor can been seen only through Braderman's orifices, through Braderman's incorporation of her. Her voice-over asks, "Were vcrs designed for the age of AIDS, chronic fatigue syndrome, environmental illnesses, Republicans who don't care and don't want

FIGURE 5.8 The video artist Joan Braderman shares the screen with Elizabeth Taylor. *Joan Sees Stars*, 1993.

you to either, for people with long-term illnesses locked up in post-nuclear families where everybody has to work outside the house to pay the bills?"

Braderman identifies specifically postmodern conditions for the body, its supposed productivity, and its socialization and marginalization in the home. We might add the following to this list of conditions: environmental and job safety deregulations, job de-skilling, job down-sizing, multiple jobs, part-time jobs, all of which dominate the global economy and postindustrial flow of capital and which demand flexible workers. In other words, productive subjects are expected to be as flexible about working or not working as they are about changing products or changing lifestyles in their roles as consumers in capitalist culture, which they should continue doing, by the way, even if they are sick or unemployed. Television, predicated as it is on fragmentation and seeming choice while actually opening up desire, reflects this situation, and perhaps trains us to be better at it or endure it. As a kind of textualization of this theoretical understanding of postmodern identities and commercial television, the video juxtaposes images of Taylor with Abraham Lincoln, Oscar Wilde with Kenneth Anger, scenes from *Love Connection* with *Butterfield 8*, and news programs with the film *Cleopatra*, representing in more compressed form the kind of surreal encounters of consumable personal identities and juxtapositions that television can offer us sequentially over the temporal dimensions of the supertext or through viewer controls, surfing channels for something to put an end to the desire that television repeatedly encourages.

But if some critics, like Beverle Houston, characterize the nature of that surfing not as a sport but a form of panic, TV watching does provide other compensations for the postmodern or ill self. As Houston argues, it is always there for us at the click of a button, as "co-extensive as psychological reality" itself. One historian calls television the tube of plenty.[66]

This understanding of television suggests that it functions as a possible extension or support of psychological reality for the fragmented subject, that is, as a prosthesis. Braderman explores the compensatory aspects of television as a prosthesis for those chronically ill locked up in postnuclear families. The sufferers of autoimmune illnesses, such as she and her friend Leland, are included in this circle of postmodern hell with the flexible workers. Here the chronically unemployed and the chronically ill are linked by discourses that define the corporeal body in terms of business, an "engineered communications systems" and economic or bodily failure (stress-induced or autoimmune illnesses) as system breakdowns, in which parts of the body no longer successfully interface with one another. In other words, for both workers and the ill, if the body is too present in its limitations, it is a liability in competition with machines that not only have a greater capacity for interfacing but do so with greater speed, ability to repeat, and endurance. The ill especially exist within a peculiar tension, paradoxically too much and too little body. Those in pain are hyperaware of their embodiment. When you are in pain, it is hard to not think about the biological, bodily foundation of your consciousness; it's like being all body. At the same time they are also compelled to disappear, either literally wasting away or absenting themselves from the visible public sphere as vehicle of contagion or because pain's demands interfere with coherent or sustained communication. For these subjects, investment in star images, specifically idealized star bodies, makes television and video watching function as prostheses for their imperfect, sick bodies. While the image of her prone body seems to float over the image of a satin-slipped Elizabeth Taylor, Braderman says, "Leland and I plied ourselves with movies. The illnesses sucked at our physical lives, at different paces. But our life with the stars was like being set free in a zone where there's no gravity. A world without our sick bodies—only their perfect ones. Cable TV and video stores had reached into our houses, with movie history, stories, and stars—permanently wedding the domestic to the fantastic."

There is a slippage here between television and video technologies serving as prostheses and the star image itself, internalized or incorporated through spectatorial activities, functioning as a prosthesis. Taylor's image is a psychic prosthesis for Leland not only because of her perfect beauty that is still available in repeated video watching of *A Place in the Sun* but because she is a kind of goddess of resurrected hopes. She has undergone multiple changes in the kinds of character she played, the number of marriage partners she had, in her state of health and her weight, yet at some core level she stays Elizabeth Taylor. Her image suggests the paradoxical possibility of a unified self sustained through fragmentation. It can serve as prosthetic support for the postmodern subject in pain to the extent that it offers a replay of both identity's dispersal and the illusion of its ability to maintain a unified core identity.

Braderman shares with Leland the desire for stars as prosthesis through television and video viewing, as well as the spectatorial participation required for internalizing stars as psychic prostheses, but she remains skeptical about how these desires and processes might be complicit with patriarchal, capitalist culture's conflation of productivity with consumption and regulated gendered behavior. The second part of the video, "Movie-Goddess Machines," moves away from an overt referencing of her illness to a more focused examination of how images, biographies, and film vehicles of female stars become incorporated by the female fan. These incorporations are technologies of the gendered self. In patriarchal culture some of these technologies of gender are also technologies of pain, and Braderman wants to distinguish between those that provide opportunities of agency and resistance and those that seem to offer ready-made scenarios of a female masochism complicit with patriarchal positionings of femininity as submissive, pathological, or hysterical. Braderman's ambivalence about stars as prostheses for the fragmented or failed subject is most clearly evident in her discussion of Gardner, which frames part 2.

We first see a photograph of Ava Gardner taken at the peak of her youth and beauty, exhibiting the codes of the publicity still, that industrially produced image of the Hollywood star meant to initiate spectatorial desires that will presumably be fulfilled at the movie theater while watching one of her films. Within a few seconds a hand flips a series of photos over the glamour still of Gardner, partially obscuring her body. These are pictures of a teenage girl walking on a beach. Braderman's voice-over, speaking for the first time in the second person—implying that this narrative is applicable to the female spectator of the video as well as to Braderman herself—wistfully recalls the activities that preoccupy the preadolescent girl, who, in the limi-

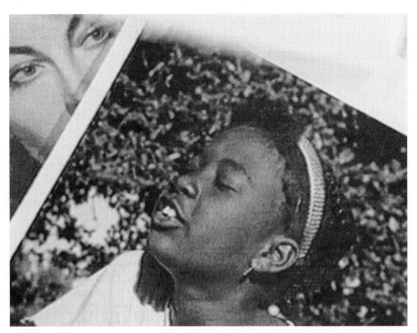

FIGURE 5.9 Braderman contrasts the image of Ava Gardner with a Carrie Mae Weems photo of a young African American girl. *Joan Sees Stars*, 1993.

nal state before girlhood congeals into disciplined adult femininity, is not yet too self-conscious about her embodiment as female. This is followed by a recollection of the movement into adolescence: "Now you are fourteen. Your body has changed in certain decisive ways. Men look at you differently now, and as a result, the world is a fundamentally different place. . . . These breasts, hips, woman parts, which are apparently yours, are a presence. Are they in charge now?"

The still photos of the teenage girl give way to images and soundtrack from the famous 1960 teen movie, *Where the Boys Are*, about three college women finding romance on spring break in Fort Lauderdale, which provided a series of stock images for adolescent girls to memorize as poses or bodily postures, a way, in Braderman's words, "to begin your career as a woman." But the video returns shortly to the same still of Gardner, and this time a series of photos of adolescent black girls are laid down over it. Braderman identifies them as photos taken by her friend, the famed African American photographer Carrie Mae Weems. When Weems read Braderman's script, she exclaimed about her exclusion, "What you mean *you*? What you mean *we*? Check out this hair — does this look like a blonde, blue-eyed movie star?"

Although Braderman was careful to include her own, less than ideal body against the idealized body of the Hollywood star to exemplify what mass media does not represent, except as mother or demon, Weems makes apparent Braderman's definition of female identity as raced identity. The finished video's conceptualization of gendered identity as raced identity shows the way the work reaches out from autobiography to a community of women. It also provides another level of critique of mass-media institutions and their representations. The juxtaposition of the image of the adolescent black girl against the still of Gardner takes on new significance. Braderman states that MGM cast Gardner as Julie in *Showboat* instead of Lena Horne because they were afraid to cast a black woman in a tale of miscegenation. White stars are pitted against black, and studio and cultural politics collude to marginalize representations of African Americans even when issues of racial difference are central to the narratives.

The video moves on to explore how other Hollywood-produced images of femininity, such as those in teen films, film noir, and the star text of Vivien Leigh, excluded or demonized certain registers of identity. Split screen or inserts are used to juxtapose Leigh in her two most famous screen roles, Scarlett O'Hara and Blanche DuBois. Braderman's voice-over celebrates Leigh's demand for substantial roles, her ability to compete with her male actor contemporaries' bohemian lifestyle, the way her characters were so subversive that they were punished. But Leigh is also a pathetic figure for Braderman to the extent that she represents the lot of women who accept some of patriarchy's pathologization of the aging female body. The sadness of Blanche DuBois is matched by Leigh's self-destructive behavior, her manic-depression, her despair over aging, and her envy of Evita Peron, whom Leigh apparently said was lucky to die at age thirty-six. Although she has already exposed how Hollywood in part constructed Ava Gardner's star persona in a strategy to exclude raced feminine identity, Braderman ends the video with a meditation on Gardner. The star inspired the teenage Braderman looking for viable models of femininity as she inspires the forty-something Braderman now in how her defiant history is evident in the embodied self:

> Ava Gardner at thirty-seven appears as Moira—drunken, slutty, elegant, and cool, fun-loving and frustrated—in *On the Beach*, a film about the end of the world. The lines of her thirty-seven-year-old face and body are to me among the most excruciatingly beautiful on film. The close-ups move me to tears. Ava/Moira is a woman who has lived, and you can see her life on her face. This face is inspiring to some of us who've been

around lo these forty years, because her beauty is not about the innocence of youth, but about the experience of age. The basic beauty—the stuff that got her a contract at MGM—is still there, of course: the slant of her eyes, half-closed, the rich ovals of the face. They were put there by genetics or God. The spirit that animates it, though, is this woman herself, Ava Gardner, born in North Carolina, gorgeous and poor, as she appears through this lighting, this casting, this director, this narrative. This woman, Moira, in an impossible romance at the end of the world, as the hideous rays from the neutron bomb make their way across the planet to Australia, on location. I desired her, while desiring to be her. . . . On film she has a gift: world-weary and world-wise, her body and legs long and shapely, she has nonetheless the wrinkles and bulges which have now been criminalized by the TV figure fascists and aerobic storm troopers. Ava, neither young nor old, was considered just about over-the-hill at this time. Yes, over-the-hill. . . . Western culture's narratives need to just kill them or drive 'em nuts. . . . We know we have qualities of mind and spirit that we don't have to erase with under-eye concealer. . . . Ava at about forty spoke to me as a teen about the possibility for life after *Beach Blanket Bingo*. Okay, she was a movie star, an adventuress, not a rocket scientist. Sure, the movie made me cry because I'm caught in the melodrama reflex. Sure it turned me on, because "Waltzing Matilda" and the long, passionate kisses were underscored by the ultimate violence of the H-bomb—Hiroshima, mon amour. We know our jobs: consume, identify. But Ava did middle-age on her own, solo, in Spain, drinking and dancing with regular people, and on-camera with no apologies. I say, bravo.

The filmic image is conceptualized here in terms reminiscent of Andre Bazin's theories about film's fulfillment of humanity's need to preserve life, by arresting time, in art. Bazin argued that film, unlike other representational media, has an indexical relation to the object represented. The photochemical processes of film technology preserve the trace of the object photographed by the camera, giving it over to posterity. The "photo-effect" offers the represented object as once-present and attests to the cinema's ability to confer an aura on the film star even as it mass-produces her images. It gives us Ava Gardner, as she was once before the camera, "in this lighting . . . this narrative," the specificity of the moment attracting the auratic of the authentic. Bazin's belief in the mummifying powers of cinema will resonate in Barthes's belief that the photographic image attests to the death of the subject in its "having been there-ness."[67]

FIGURE 5.10 The close-ups of Ava Gardner in *On the Beach* (1959) bring Joan Braderman to tears. *Joan Sees Stars*, 1993.

Yet Braderman is not interested in essentializing or fetishizing the filmic image of Gardner as characterized by the pull a photograph of Barthes's dead mother had for him. She exposes its materiality and its historical value. This filmic image exists in videos that, as Braderman argued at the beginning of *Joan Sees Stars*, are owned by commercial media industries that create and feed the demands of the consumer spectator. Video has a flexibility; it is technologically a portable, low-end format for home consumers to create, record (or poach), or obsessively replay their own images and is commercially available to buy or rent at video stores, supermarkets, and libraries. This ubiquity and domesticity recall the metapsychological dimension of broadcast television, with its continual flow. It is, or can be, always there and replayed endlessly, and in this way video and television rival, if not supersede, film as a technology and delivery system cut to the measure of the subject's desire. For the critical video artist, an examination of this dimension can also demonstrate how the star, reappearing on video or television, is recontextualized as cultural memory available to feminist subjects for inspiration or reincorporation.

The video memories of Gardner retain, for Braderman, the power of film's photo-effect, and because of their consumer availability (unlike 35 or

16 mm film) they provide access to past cultural ideals of femininity, love, and loss, and past instances of resistance and defiance of some of those ideals. For Braderman, the poignancy of "love at the end of the world" represented in *On the Beach* is inextricable from the poignancy of Gardner's body at thirty-seven. This body, in the organic process of aging and decay, is fragile and vulnerable, but it is also a body embedded in social processes. In the late 1950s, when these images were filmed, narratives would sometimes demonize or kill the aging female body, but sometimes, as here, the aging female body was intelligible and desirable. Braderman believes that contemporary culture and mass media, with their aerobics police and obsession with youth, have denied this body intelligibility as a feminine ideal. As Patricia Mellencamp argues in *High Anxiety*, media typically participates in contemporary culture's dictum that women can now be older if they don't look it, what she calls "chronology disavowal."[68] Gardner is important to Braderman as evidence that patriarchal discourses of the female body don't exhaust all of that body's meanings nor erase evidence of a history lived in resistance to technologies of pain that pathologize femininity.

It is significant that Braderman places this final meditation on Gardner between a scene of her getting a tattoo after her illness has gone into remission and one in which she wipes off her makeup. Both of these technologies (marking the body with tattoos and makeup) are performances that construct the embodied self. In the voice-over accompanying the images at the tattoo parlor, Braderman says, "We all mark ourselves." In contrast to the unbidden and unpredictable pain of illness, she muses that by marking with tattoos, "you choose . . . you and the tattoo artist": "My illness marked the inside of my body. Like a cruel master, my immune system ate away at itself. When I went into remission, I marked the outside myself, with friends. These marks say we're alive. Our refusal is written in blood and paint and skin."

For Braderman, tattooing is a technology of pain that she can control, and in that controlling and feeling of the needle's smart, she can reclaim her body from its overpresence in severe illness *and* its disappearance in postmodern theoretical discourse and in the postindustrial flow of capital and labor. Making up one's face is a body technology that is performatively polyvalent, at once evidence of patriarchy's regulation of normative modes of femininity and, contrarily, a theatrical play with the belief that gender doesn't exist apart from or prior to its performances or enactment.

As she wipes off face paint and peels off eyelashes, Braderman sighs wearily, "You'll see, there is a human being under there." Does this line prompt the makeup striptease to be read as a conservative humanist claim on the body? As some feminist scholars of the embodied self remind us — perhaps most eloquently phrased by Vivian Sobchack — the body does give us "the material premises and, therefore, the logical grounds for the intelligibility of those moral categories that emerge from a bodily sense of gravity and finitude."[69] In other words, ethics comes from an embodied self. From this perspective, it *is* important that there is a human body under that makeup. Braderman's recognition of this as she reflects on and creates out of her own bodily pain allows her to empathize with and memorialize the gravity and finitude of her beloved friend Leland and her Hollywood muse, Ava Gardner.

CONCLUSION

Through their recycling of film stars from the past, experimental videos and films make big claims about media, history, memory, and subjectivity. The question of whether the images of Hollywood film stars have "corrupted" us or become "a part of" us is a point of departure for this experimental work. While Braderman et al. explore the place of past stars in our social imaginary through a self-conscious play with film form and film history informed by critical theory, I have argued throughout this book that star recycling has involved the complicity of audiences, producers, and acting labor in many different kinds of media, going all the way back to the years immediately following the emergence of the film star in the early twentieth century.

Which stars get recycled, what purposes their recycling serves, and which media recycles them are the result of many factors, including the iterative possibilities afforded by their originating media formats and institutions (which affects their availability as material objects to be reseen as well as the status of their legal ownership), the competition over them among media struggling for economic and social hegemony, and the historically situated valences and flexibility of the star's on- and off-screen personas. Although the last factor suggests the necessity for a star to meet certain social and psychological criteria to become a meaningful part of a culture's social imaginary, the possibility of a star enduring in that imaginary or resurfacing in a new social imaginary at a later time is dependent on those other material and intermedial conditions.

Many of the film players who emerged as stars in the 1910s and 1920s, such as Florence Lawrence and Mae Murray (who some consider to be the model for Norma Desmond), were unable to successfully resurface and have a place in a social imaginary of a later time. Their film companies might have folded, or their films might have been lost or no longer considered commercially viable within the exhibition conventions of a later time, or their star texts, as constructed out of press discourse and the kinds of characters they played, might have no longer captured the imagination of the public as the social realities changed. At most they could be remembered in some nonspecific, aggregate manner, mythologized into fictional types, such as the overly glamorous, commercially savvy Gloria Marlow of *Dreamboat* or the delusional, mad Norma Desmond of *Sunset Boulevard*. Unless, of course, the star from that era was the real actress Gloria Swanson, who resurfaced in the late 1940s and 1950s as a star on television and in film when she needed to freshly demonstrate her modernity by demonstrating a move forward into new media, and when those media needed the power of her particular association with the past to negotiate with audiences present industrial, social, and cultural transitions.

Many of the female stars developed by the vertically integrated studios during the silent era of the 1920s and the sound era of the 1930s, 1940s, and 1950s were more profitably recycled than the stars from the 1910s, whether in scandal magazines, programs produced for television, movies broadcast on television, or the videos and films of experimental filmmakers influenced by critical theory attentive to issues involving gender and sexuality. For the popular media of television and scandal magazines to profit from recycling stars from the past, there had to be a large, commercially viable audience that remembered enough about these stars to make sense of the recyclings; that is, to reincorporate the stars within the terms through which they experienced their contemporary social imaginary. New media in postwar America was economically and culturally successful when it negotiated audience attention and desire by appealing to familiarity as well as novelty. Their audience was made up of a generation of adults who were alive during these stars' first orbit and this generation's own children, many of whom are baby boomers. The baby boomers would have their first sighting of many of these stars on television, in programs such as *The Loretta Young Show* or *Twilight Zone*, or in their past films, which showed up on television in increasing numbers throughout the 1950s, 1960s, and 1970s. The experimental film- and video-makers discussed in this book, whose exploration of how stars from the past are a part of their generation's social imaginary, are baby boomers themselves. Although they experienced stars from their own generation in a variety of media, they shared with their parents' generation a cathected relation to stars from a prior Hollywood because both generations were addressed by the recyclings circulated by the same shared media: film, television, and print journalism.

Do recyclings of studio-era film stars have a prominent place in the social imaginary of today's culture? This is an audience whose experiences with media are characterized by an explosion in technologies and formats and a fragmented, narrow demographic address, understood not only by gender, race, and class but also by divisions in which a generational turnover seems to take place every three to five years. In the course of writing this book, *Time-Life* has published numerous glossy (and expensive) tribute magazines to commemorate the anniversaries of the deaths of Grace Kelly, Audrey Hepburn, Katharine Hepburn, and John Wayne, among the most successful stars from the studio era. New biographies of studio-era stars, whether claiming revelations based on newly archived documents or mere rehashes of known narratives, are published every year by the dozens by both trade and scholarly presses. (At the time of this writing, a new print biography of Gloria Swanson and a film biography of Grace Kelly, starring Nicole Kidman, were scheduled for release.) DVD box-sets sold as star collections (e.g., of Marlene Dietrich, Greta Garbo, Joan Crawford, Cary Grant) have had some success, at least before DVD sales in general declined at the end of the first decade of this century. Issues of popular magazines, such as *Vanity Fair* and *More*, feature photos of contemporary stars reenacting poses from old Hollywood films. In a 2008 issue of *New York* magazine, the twenty-something film and tabloid star Lindsay Lohan and the photographer Bert Stern re-created Marilyn Monroe's infamous last nude photo session before her death. Stern was the photographer at the Monroe session in 1962. Turner Classic Movies, which televises films from studio-era Hollywood (mostly, but not confined to, the Turner collection of Warner Bros., MGM, and RKO), is considered a premium channel by cable and satellite packages, but its narrower reception base is offset by its achievement of both a high cultural status (Martin Scorsese writes for its monthly magazine) and a franchise that includes a film festival, a film cruise, and a series of DVD collections. In 2013 TCM cosponsored a special event at the Hollywood Museum (located in the building that once housed the Max Factor cosmetics showroom for star makeovers) exhibiting the professional and personal belongings of Loretta Young in celebration of the centennial of her birth and of her contributions to film and television as an actress, producer, and fashion icon.

These examples suggest that Old Hollywood, especially via the image of the glamorous female star of that era, still *sells*. But to whom? With each passing year, there are fewer and fewer students in my film and television studies classes who know the names, films, or meanings of many film stars who emerged prior to the past five years, much less of those who first emerged before the 1950s. My observation about the relation of younger generations to past film stars does not come from melancholic nostalgia. The contemporary audience for popular culture is fragmented in terms of generation, among other demographics, and dispersed across multiple media technologies and multiple television channels—channels that number in the hundreds rather than the three to seven channels available in the era in which broadcast television emerged and gained hegemony as a mass medium. These realities mean that individual film stars from the past, and even many from the present, are unlikely to have as much significance for the social imaginary—if one can even speak of the social imaginary in the singular—as they once did.

Since new media and new practices of old media do not depend on addressing a mass audience, assumptions about widespread audience familiarity with film stars from the past is no longer operative in most contemporary cases of star recyclings. Nevertheless my students, like many people from a variety of generations, are still fascinated by and engage with film stars and other celebrities as they construct their own identity in terms of public and private, the body, aging, race, marriage and family, and sexuality. What is different now is that different generations do not share the same knowledge and meanings about or investment in the stars around whom such discussions coalesce. However, the explosion of new media technologies, formats, and venues has increased the amount, frequency, and possibilities for these star recyclings. Online venues, such as social networking sites (e.g., Facebook), blogs, wikis, video-sharing sites (such as YouTube), and even virtual auctions (such as eBay) are where many star recyclings take place. But it is important to make distinctions between online sites that generate images and texts about stars from the past and those that focus on the present because they vary in the ways they constrain potentials for star recyclings.

User-Generated, Socially Mediated Star Recyclings

Established media corporations, such as television networks and film studios, have a stake in the proliferation of new media outlets for their products and have partnered with various online sites, or copied aspects of them, to capture specific demographics or to recapture or maintain the sheer number of viewers needed to sustain the profitability of their products. The corporate-configured production, distribution, and exhibition practices of the film studios and television industry during the era of old media (i.e., the era of 35 mm theatrically released film and broadcast television programming) represented a top-down model for experiencing and controlling media images and texts. Between the late 1940s and the 1980s (when the proliferation of cable channels introduced narrowcasting) the competition between film and television for a mass audience meant that they had to produce a range of texts and images that could tap into cultural meanings shared by multiple generations and across taste categories. Online sites designed and maintained by contemporary film studios and television corporations typically control the social, legal, technological, and authorial terms by which their products and stars can be consumed there by users, and they conceptualize users within relatively narrow demographics. These sites, in other words, attract fans of stars and viewers of television or film texts so that they can be quantitatively and qualitatively measured as consumers for all the company's products. Media institutions exercise legal ownership of images and texts on the sites they control, as well as on user-generated sites (such as YouTube), to limit their appropriations by viewers and fans.

Online sites of user-generated content, such as Facebook, YouTube, and aggregated or individually generated blogs, on the other hand, provide locations and platforms that facilitate recyclings of stars from the past. Facebook users have created pages for favorite stars; at this writing, Loretta Young, Gloria Swanson, Maureen O'Hara, and Hazel Scott even have more than one. YouTube, which in the month of January 2009 alone was visited by 100 million viewers watching 6 billion videos, offers itself as a site for recyclings of old stars via user video uploads of feature films, of clips or complete episodes of television programs, and of user-created video mash-ups that juxtapose images and sounds from film clips, star publicity photos, home movies, and film trailers.[1] While corporate ownership of some media texts constrains their circulation on YouTube, many images and some of the texts in the public domain of silent and studio-era stars circulate there with relative accessibility and abundance. Hundreds of website blogs produced by fans and even relatives of film stars from the studio era incorporate images of personal belongings, press clippings, family snapshots, studio contracts, publicity materials, fashions, makeup tips, and even artwork of stars such as Carole Lombard, Jeanne Crain, Maureen O'Hara, Loretta Young, Marlene Dietrich, and Cary Grant. Many stars from the silent era, or stars known for their sense of style, are featured in blogs focused on particular historical eras in Hollywood history or on fashion.

The authorial origins of user-generated sites focused on film stars of the past represent fans from a variety of generations; some identify themselves as old enough to remember seeing the stars in films during the studio era or on early broadcasts of their films on television; others have created pages, written blogs, or uploaded videos because they are inspired to engage with stars as representatives of images and meanings of a past that they are too young to remember but long to embrace. Most user-generated sites facilitate networking, whereby others can add comments to a blogger's creation or video upload or can provide links to their own blog or video. Mash-up videos featuring film clips or still photos recontextualize star images to represent the perspectives and feelings of their fan authors. Such user-generated content constitutes "spreadable media," a term coined by Henry Jenkins, Sam Ford, and Joshua Green to describe media in which or by which users shape the context of images and texts.[2]

The typical video mash-up of star images on YouTube also contains many of the found footage or collage strategies employed by Barriga, Braderman, and Rappaport. These sites' reliance on user-generated content and collaborative participation and commentary does not mean that they represent a more authentic form of recycling stars than *Joan Sees Stars*, *Meeting Two Queens*, or *Dreamboat*. Although many popular and even some academic discourses celebrate the democratic, collaborative potentials of the collective intelligence characterizing the social media aspects of Web 2.0 culture, star recyclings via user-generated content online exemplify a range of motives, attitudes, functions, knowledges, and forms of participation. As a film and television historian, I am alternately impressed by and disappointed in the popular histories constructed by many blogs about stars from the past or by the contextual commentary and tagging that accompany videos uploaded on YouTube or descriptions of star-related materials listed on eBay; these range from in-depth and detailed contextualizations to inaccurate, incomplete, rumored, or absent information. Comments left by users are frequently disconnected from one another by months or years; they often provide intriguing traces of ideas from different historical moments but also expose the limitations of online dialogue. Some comments are disrespectful either of other users or of those represented in the videos or blogs. (This is truer of sites featuring images or stories about contemporary stars likely to appeal to younger audiences.)

Motivations behind the creation or performance of many blogs, social media pages, or uploaded video clips or mash-ups—or what can be discerned of these by textual effects if not explicit statement—include celebration of the featured stars, the need to organize and archive the vast amounts of virtual and material evidence about stars in cultural circulation, performance of the author's superior knowledge about stars and style (an aspect of many blogs devoted to star style and fashion), and the desire to create a forum for discussing social or moral issues that are relevant to aspects of a star's life. Online star recyclings exemplifying the last factor are especially interesting in regard to how female stars from studio-era Hollywood can still be the center of cultural discussions about gender and sexuality. For example, while several uploaded video mash-ups on YouTube celebrate Loretta Young's use of fashion in performing feminine glamour (typically these edit together different opening scenes of Young's program, in which she entered the set twirling her voluminous skirts), others focus on what is probably contemporary fans' central interest in Young and career: her brief affair with Clark Gable on the location shoot of *Call of the Wild*, which resulted in the birth of a daughter, whom she subsequently passed off as her adopted child. After the publication of Judy Lewis's memoir in 1994 and Young's posthumously published authorized biography, this one-time rumor was confirmed as fact, and it now animates a number of discussions, recyclings, and mash-up performances on YouTube. Uploaded images from *Call of the Wild* inevitably originate in or inspire a discussion of Young's pregnancy, the politics of morality clauses in studio contracts, the hypocrisy of how star or filmic sexuality was represented by Hollywood, the pressures sexually active working women faced in prefeminist eras, and men's cavalier sexual behavior. "Mernerwastaken," a YouTube content generator who has created and uploaded a video mash-up about the Young-Gable affair, juxtaposes the film's loves scenes with motion picture images of Judy Lewis as a child, possibly taken from home movie footage included in the DVD collections of Young's television programs. Mernerwastaken's participation in the accompanying comment thread suggests that her motivation in constructing the video was not to focus on the stars' romance (although the visuals from their film include only the love scenes) but to celebrate Young's moral choices, her "choosing life" (i.e., her refusal to get an abortion), while condemning Gable's treatment of the affair as a "another brief fling."

Christopher and Peter Lewis, Young's sons by her husband Tom Lewis (the one-time coproducer of her television show), have created and uploaded their own mash-up that also includes footage of *Call of the Wild* and home movies (as well as images from other sources), but they do so to create a posthumous tribute to the "full and accomplished life" of their half-sister Judy, who died in 2011. Like the children of Lucille Ball and Desi Arnaz, Young's sons have used new media forms to celebrate, question, and recontextualize aspects of their family history that remain personally or socially disturbing and have redefined the legacy of their famous parents. Also like the Arnaz children, the Lewis brothers administer their parents' estates. Christopher Lewis has created a website and uploaded a number of videos to YouTube to honor Young and to promote the release of more episodes of her television program on DVD. Judy Lewis's take on her mother's secret pregnancy, the way the event could have derailed Young's career, and her own ignorance of her parentage until adulthood, is accessible in a video clip of an interview she gave for a documentary on Clark Gable that premiered on the TNT and TCM channels in 1996.

All of these videos, with overlapping but different perspectives on Young's past, attempt to negotiate her private and professional lives in prefeminist social and industrial contexts. They also link to videos that recycle material documenting or alluding to Young's contemporary Joan Crawford and clips from television talk shows of the 1980s featuring her daughter Christina detailing the alleged abuse she suffered at the hands of her star mother. Comment threads accompanying these invariably include heated responses on whether Crawford actually abused her children and whether female stars and working women should attempt motherhood in the first place. These comment threads typically lack the critical vocabulary and political critiques evident in the experimental video work, but they are evidence that star figures from the past still animate discussions involving contemporary beliefs about women, work, sexuality, motherhood, and family.

Living in Time

While the digital turn may have, as one critic puts it, "enhanced our sense of rupture with . . . [the] past, magnifying our impression of inhabiting a privileged historical moment," the case studies I've discussed support the idea that the self is a historical project that makes use of the past.[3] The recyclings of stars in both old and new media attest that no identity comes from ground zero. The case of the "synthespian," or virtual actor, perhaps stretches limits of what is considered a historically produced self (or film star). The synthespian has emerged as an acting and star category during the period in which I have been writing this book. Synthespians, also known as "vactors" (virtual actors), combine the features of an animated character with the movements and expressions of a human actor that have been saved on a computer in motion or performance capture. This category is commonly employed in big-budget films to create photo-realistic, virtual bodies as extras in crowd scenes, to create supporting characters (such as Gollum in the *Lord of the Rings* trilogy), and to create animated versions of well-known stars (e.g., Tom Hanks in *The Polar Express*). However, it was once conceived as a way to recycle old stars. I want to conclude my musings on new media star recyclings with this moment in the film industry's interest in synthespians, a moment that brings us back to questions about the time and place of the star.

Starting in the 1990s there was a flurry of press releases and trade press articles touting the potentials of a synthespian that would combine motion-captured movements of a contemporary performer with the features of dead stars scanned from old movie footage. In fact Marlene Dietrich's estate sold the image rights of the late star to Virtual Celebrity Productions for this purpose. The company's proposed remake of *Casablanca*, starring the "synthespianized" Dietrich and the carbon-based, live son of the late Humphrey Bogart, has yet to happen.

The generational fragmentation in knowledge about past film stars begs a question about such synthespians: Why would new tech companies invest in the images of old, perhaps dead stars to digitize and reanimate them when there is a risk that only a small population will know or care about what they meant in the past? For *Sky Captain and the World of Tomorrow* film footage of the late Laurence Olivier was digitally altered for him to "play" a character in a brief scene. The film's poor box office suggested it needed some reanimation too. Would it matter to those audience members who do care about Dietrich, Olivier, and other dead stars whether, to paraphrase Braderman, there really is or was a person "in there"? Since this new technological operation is premised on denial of the star's mortality, it potentially could out-recycle any of the processes I've described in this book. Now the star might be able to transcend time. But what if one important function of the star is to remind us that we do, in fact, live *in* time?

NOTES

≝

Introduction

1. Richard Dyer, *Heavenly Bodies: Film Stars and Society* (New York: St. Martin's, 1966), 19; Brenda R. Silver, *Virginia Woolf Icon* (Chicago: University of Chicago Press, 1999), 28. Silver's work is an exemplary study of how (nonfilm) star signs change over long periods of time and through many different kinds of media. The phrase *transmutable star sign* comes from Ramona Curry, *Too Much of a Good Thing: Mae West as Cultural Icon* (Minneapolis: University of Minnesota Press, 1996), xix. For other diachronically ordered examinations of changes in a star's signs, see S. Paige Baty, *American Monroe: The Making of a Body Politic* (Berkeley: University of California Press, 1995); Gilbert B. Rodman, *Elvis after Elvis: The Posthumous Career of a Living Legend* (London: Routledge, 1996); Joanne Hershfield, *The Invention of Dolores del Rio* (Minneapolis: University of Minnesota Press, 2000); Michael DeAngelis, *Gay Fandom and Cross-Over Stardom: James Dean, Mel Gibson, and Keanu Reeves* (Durham, NC: Duke University Press, 2001); Adrienne L. McLean, *Being Rita Hayworth: Labor, Identity, and Hollywood Stardom* (New Brunswick, NJ: Rutgers University Press, 2004).

2. Karen Beckman, *Vanishing Women: Magic, Film, and Feminism* (Durham, NC: Duke University Press, 2003), 185. Many of Beckman's points about the ambivalence of star "presence," the metaphysical terms of the female star's vanishing and reappearances, are compatible with points I make in my own argument. However, in her study of disappearing women, Beckman looks at a variety of discursive and visual modes (imperial rhetoric, magic, spirit photography, film), and in two chapters she employs textual analysis of individual film texts as her prime methodology for investigating the phenomenon of the "vanishing woman" in cinema. While I examine general press discourses, star biographies and memoirs, trade publications, fan production, and multiple film, television, and video texts and genres, Beckman mainly discusses media industries and audiences as they are figured as visual and narrative elements *in* films rather than as active players in the recycling of female star images through their extratextual material practices and relations to multiple media.

3. Jennifer M. Bean, "Technologies of Early Stardom and the Extraordinary Body," in *A Feminist Reader in Early Cinema*, edited by Jennifer M. Bean and Diane Negra (Durham, NC: Duke University Press, 2002), 407.

4. See chapter 2 for a discussion of Hollywood films from the studio era on television in the 1950s. As Barbara Klinger notes, since the 1980s it has been movie channels such as AMC (American Movie Classics) and TCM (Turner Classic Movies) that are most responsible for the recycling of films from Hollywood's studio era. Although she provides a valuable in-depth look at the practices of recent media (movie cable channels, videos, DVDs, Internet websites) in relation to old films, Klinger only briefly references the phenomenon of Hollywood films' first emergence on broadcast television in the late 1940s. See Barbara Klinger, *Beyond the Multiplex: Cinema, New Technologies, and the Home* (Berkeley: University of California Press, 2006).

5. Kathryn H. Fuller, *At the Picture Show: Small-Town Audiences and the Creation of Movie Culture* (Washington, DC: Smithsonian Institution Press, 1996), 141.

6. In March 1910 Carl Laemmele devised an advertisement headlined "We Nail a Lie." It stated that "the blackest lie" planted by IMP's "enemies" was that Lawrence had been killed in a streetcar accident. Contrary to this lie, Lawrence was "in the best of health, will continue to appear in 'Imp' films." Quoted in Kelly R. Brown, *Florence Lawrence, the Biograph Girl: America's First Movie Star* (Jefferson, NC: McFarland, 1999), 51–52.

7. Janet Staiger, "Seeing Stars," in *Stardom: Industry of Desire*, edited by Christine Gledhill (London: Routledge, 1991), 6–11; Richard deCordova, *Picture Personalities: The Emergence of a Star System in America* (Urbana: University of Illinois Press, 1990), 50–92. For discussions of Lawrence's emergence as a star following the IMP stunt, see also Alexander Walker, *Stardom: The Hollywood Phenomenon* (London: Penguin Books, 1974); Brown, *Florence Lawrence*. Staiger, Brown, and deCordova all discuss how the events of the stunt have been analyzed or reported by other historians.

8. Sigmund Freud, *Beyond the Pleasure Principle* (New York: Norton, 1961), 8–11.

9. According to Rosi Braidotti, the social field is a "libidinal or affective landscape, as well as a normative — or disciplinary — framework." See "Becoming-Woman: Rethinking the Positivity of Difference," in *Feminist Consequences: Theory for the New Century*, edited by Elisabeth Bronfen and Misha Kavka (New York: Columbia University Press, 2001), 384.

10. Richard Dyer, *Stars* (London: BFI, 1979), 3.

11. Pamela Robertson, *Guilty Pleasures: Feminist Camp from Mae West to Madonna* (Durham, NC: Duke University Press, 1996), 142.

Chapter One. "The Elegance . . . Is Almost Overwhelming"

1. Jack Gould, "Program Reviews," *New York Times*, June 20, 1948.

2. According to Tino Balio, there were 742 actors under contract to the studios in 1947; by 1956 there were only 229. See Tino Balio, *The American Film Industry*, revised edition (Madison: University of Wisconsin Press, 1985), 402. For discussions of the changes in Hollywood that led to the decline in the number of actors and stars under long-term contract to the studios in the postwar period, see Joel

Finler, *The Hollywood Story* (London: Wallflower, 2003); Frank Rose, *The Agency: William Morris and the Hidden History of Show Business* (New York: HarperBusiness, 1995), 122–23; Richard Maltby, *Hollywood Cinema*, 2nd edition (Oxford: Blackwell, 2003).

3. The film was *Beyond the Forest*, and Davis was playing a part for which she realized she was too old. See the television documentary *Bette Davis: A Basically Benevolent Volcano* (1983), and James Spada, *More Than a Woman: An Intimate Biography of Bette Davis* (New York: Bantam, 1963), 257–60. In one of her memoirs, *The Lonely Life* (New York: Putnam, 1962), 275, Davis recalls, "I had to make a soundtrack for *Beyond the Forest*—the line 'I can't stand it here anymore,' these were the last words spoken by me on the Warner's lot. They certainly hit the nail on the head!"

4. See Barry King, "Stardom as an Occupation," in *The Hollywood Film Industry*, ed. Paul Kerr (London: Routledge and Kegan Paul, 1986), for a discussion of this concept.

5. Before divestment the five major studios owned about 70 percent of the key first-run theaters in the downtowns of the ninety-two largest American cities, according to Finler, *The Hollywood Story*, 19. Douglas Gomery, *Shared Pleasures: A History of Movie Presentation in the United States* (London: BFI, 1992), 83–93, pinpoints massive movement to the suburbs in the postwar era, about which he cites statistics and compares in scope to the migration of Europeans to the United States at the turn of the century, and the involvement of young adults in parenting in the baby boom as two of the major reasons for the downturn in movie attendance between the late 1940s and the start of the 1960s. Both demographic transitions kept "families away from the downtown location of the movie palaces." Richard Maltby, *Hollywood Cinema* (Oxford: Blackwell, 2003), 161–65, agrees with this assessment and adds that between 1947 and 1963, 48 percent of all four-wall theaters in the United States closed.

6. Jane Gaines, *Contested Culture: The Image, the Voice, and the Law* (Chapel Hill: University of North Carolina Press, 1991).

7. John Ellis, *Visible Fictions: Cinema, Television, Video* (London: Routledge and Kegan Paul, 1982), 97–105.

8. P. David Marshall, *Celebrity and Power: Fame in Contemporary Culture* (Minneapolis: University of Minnesota Press, 1997).

9. One television history that does make television stardom central to its focus is Susan Murray, *Hitch Your Antenna to the Stars: Early Television and Broadcast Stardom* (New York: Routledge, 2005). Murray states, quite rightly, that "television used its stars to define itself" (xiii). See also James Bennett, *Television Personalities: Stardom and the Small Screen* (London: Routledge, 2011). Bennett's findings about stardom in British television suggest that many of the discursive frameworks for constructing the ideal female star for early television in Britain were compatible with those I have identified as operative in press accounts of early television in the United States.

10. See Richard deCordova, *Picture Personalities: The Emergence of the Star System in America* (Urbana: University of Illinois Press, 1990).

11. See Jackie Stacey, *Star Gazing: Hollywood Cinema and Female Spectatorship* (London: Routledge, 1994), for a discussion of how fans negotiated the glamour of female film stars.

12. Popular histories (books, television movies and documentaries, magazine articles, etc.) of early television and television stardom have been skewed toward a focus on *network television stars*, most of whom had a background in *network radio* (following a career in vaudeville). Jack Benny, George Burns and Gracie Allen, Milton Berle, Sid Caesar, and Molly Goldberg have probably received the most attention. An exception to this trend is the popular and scholarly attention given to Lucille Ball, who, although she starred in network radio immediately prior to her move to television, was primarily identified as a film actress before her turn to television. See chapter 4.

For examples of scholarship focused on network radio or vaudeville stars who became television stars, see Patricia Mellencamp, "Situation Comedy, Feminism and Freud: Discourses of Gracie and Lucy," in *Studies in Entertainment: Critical Approaches to Mass Culture*, edited by Tania Modleski (Bloomington: Indiana University Press, 1986); Arthur Frank Wertheim, "The Rise and Fall of Milton Berle," in *American History/American Television*, edited by John E. O'Connor (New York: Ungar, 1987); Denise Mann, "The Spectacularization of Everyday Life: Recycling Hollywood Stars and Fans in Early Television Variety Shows," in *Private Screenings: Television and the Female Consumer*, edited by Lynne Spigel and Denise Mann (Minneapolis: University of Minnesota Press, 1992); Alexander Doty, "The Gay Straight Man," in *Making Things Perfectly Queer: Interpreting Mass Culture* (Minneapolis: University of Minnesota Press, 1993); Donald Weber, "Memory and Repression in Early Ethnic Television: The Example of Gertrude Berg and *The Goldbergs*," in *The Other Fifties: Interrogating Midcentury American Icons*, edited by Joel Foreman (Urbana: University of Illinois Press, 1997); Murray, *Hitch Your Antenna to the Stars*; Susan Murray, "Lessons from Uncle Miltie: Ethnic Masculinity and Early Television's Vaudeo Star," in *Small Screens, Big Ideas: Television in the 1950s*, edited by Janet Thumim (London: I. B. Tauris, 2002); Allison McCracken, "'Study of a Mad Housewife': Psychiatric Discourse, the Suburban Home, and the Case of Gracie Allen," in Thumim, *Small Screens, Big Ideas*. This scholarship is highly valuable in its interrogation of gender, sexual, and ethnic norms in the star texts of early television, as well as its discussion of early network television history, but in many cases it (implicitly or explicitly) defines the contours of television stardom too narrowly.

For scholarship that has given attention to nonnetwork stars or network television stars without a prior network radio or vaudeville stardom, see Mark Williams, "From 'Remote' Possibilities to Entertaining 'Difference': A Regional Study of the Rise of the Television Industry in Los Angeles, 1930–1952," PhD dissertation, University of Southern California, 1992; Victoria Johnson, "Citizen Welk: Bubbles, Blue Hair, and Middle America," in *The Revolution Wasn't Televised: Sixties Television and Social Conflict*, edited by Lynn Spigel and Michael Curtin (New York: Routledge, 1997); Madeleine Ritrosky-Winslow, "Hollywood Actresses

Negotiate Fifties TV: Designing a Series around a Female Star," paper presented at Console-ing Passions conference, Montreal, 1996; Mark Williams, "Considering Monty Margetts's *Cook's Corner*: Oral History and Television History," in *Television, History, and American Culture: Feminist Critical Essays*, edited by Mary Beth Haralovich and Lauren Rabinovitz (Durham, NC: Duke University Press, 2000); Donald Bogle, *Prime-Time Blues: African-Americans on Network Television* (New York: Farrar, Straus and Giroux, 2001); Mimi White and Marsha Cassidy, "Innovating Women's Television in Local and National Networks: Ruth Lyons and Arlene Francis," *Camera Obscura* 51 (2003): 31–69; Christine Becker, "'Glamor Girl Classed as TV Show Brain': The Body and Mind of Faye Emerson," *Journal of Popular Culture* 38.2 (2004): 242–60; Christine Becker, *It's the Pictures That Got Small: Hollywood Film Stars on 1950s Television* (Middletown, CT: Wesleyan University Press, 2008). Becker's work is among the minority of studies focused on the activities and presence of film stars in early television.

13. Carmel Myers, who played in a number of silent films, including MGM's 1925 version of *Ben-Hur*, had a talk show on television in 1951–52. She had mainly supporting roles in silent films rather than the kind of starring roles that Swanson's career clearly epitomized. Even though Myers's program was on the ABC network, it is easier to find press about Swanson's earlier program on the local independent station WPIX. I first saw a listing of Myers's show in Tim Brooks and Earle Marsh, *The Complete Directory to Prime-Time Network TV Shows, 1946–Present* (New York: Ballantine, 1992), during initial research for this book in the late 1990s. Since that time I've been fortunate to find a brief discussion of the program in Robert Dance's excellent overview of Myers's career, "Carmel Myers, Siren of the Silent Screen," *Classic Images*, December 2003, 70–77. Thanks to the author for sharing his work with me. See also a very short piece by Edyth T. M'Leod, "Silent Film Star Plans New Career," *Los Angeles Times*, September 3, 1951, and a somewhat longer one, Val Adams, "Format: A Ukulele and a Memory," *New York Times*, September 9, 1951, for what seem to be the only two mentions of the program in major newspapers (excluding local television schedule pages).

14. See Bogle, *Prime-Time Blues*. There are understandable reasons for why nonwhite performers have been so rarely examined, the most obvious being that they are very difficult to research. Periodical indexes and archive clipping files yield little information, not to mention the lack of kinescopes or tapes of the programs starring these figures. However, there are traces (mentions in the trade press, *Variety* reviews, and some attention in press addressed to specific raced or ethnic communities, such as *Ebony* magazine) of these performers and their programs that can be analyzed—enough material to make scholars question histories that neglect these figures. Notable exceptions to the lack of scholarship on nonwhite television performers in early television, in addition to Bogle, are Mark Williams, "Entertaining 'Difference': Strains of Orientalism in Early Los Angeles Television," in *Living Color: Race and Television in the United States*, edited by Sasha Torres (Durham, NC: Duke University Press, 1998), 12–34; Kristen A. McGee, *Some Liked It Hot: Jazz Women in Film and Television, 1928–1959* (Middletown, CT: Wesleyan

University Press, 2009). Shortly before this book went to press, Murray Forman's excellent *One Night on TV Is Worth Weeks at the Paramount: Popular Music on Early Television* (Durham, NC: Duke University Press, 2012) was published. His study includes information and analysis of some of the nonwhite performers discussed here.

15. The coaxial cable laid between sites of broadcasting (New York, Chicago, Los Angeles, etc.) is what made live, coast-to-coast transmission possible. The laying of coaxial cable was a long process that hooked up regions and broadcasting sites in steps, moving geographically east to west. By 1948 the major cities of the Eastern Seaboard were connected; by 1949 Chicago and parts of the Midwest were connected; but it wasn't until late 1951 to early 1952 that cable connections were made to the West Coast and even some of the southern states. Before the Midwest, South, and West were connected by cable and relay to the Eastern Seaboard the popular programs broadcast from New York, such as *The Texaco Star Theater* (Milton Berle's show), were not seen live in these other areas of the country. Instead they were shown on kinescope in a delayed broadcast. Because the quality of kinescopes was inferior to programs broadcast live, in some regions live, locally produced programs were more popular (and more attuned to regional stars, traditions, concerns, etc.) than the East Coast network programming. For more on the way local and regional programming responded to East Coast models of programming and stardom with their own production and industrial configurations, see *Quarterly Review of Film and Video* 16.3–4 (1999), a special issue on U.S. regional and nonnetwork television; Williams, "From 'Remote' Possibilities to Entertaining 'Difference.'"

16. Gloria Swanson, *Swanson on Swanson* (New York: Random House, 1980), 476. See also Sam Staggs, *Close-Up on Sunset Boulevard: Billy Wilder, Norma Desmond, and the Dark Hollywood Dream* (New York: St. Martin's, 2002), 52.

17. A helpful overview of Emerson's career is in Cary O'Dell, *Women Pioneers in Television: Biographies of Fifteen Industry Leaders* (Jefferson, NC: McFarland, 1997), 81–92.

18. Land, review of *World's Fair Beauty Contest*, *Variety*, June 28, 1939.

19. Hobe, review of *Tamara*, *Variety*, August 6, 1941.

20. For discussions of this mythology, see Teresa de Lauretis, *Alice Doesn't: Feminism, Semiotics, Cinema* (Bloomington: Indiana University Press, 1987); Elisabeth Bronfen, *Over Her Dead Body: Death, Femininity, and the Aesthetic* (New York: Routledge, 1992).

21. Carolyn Marvin, *When Old Technologies Were New: Thinking about Electric Communication in the Late Nineteenth Century* (New York: Oxford University Press, 1988), 109–51.

22. Jeffrey Sconce, *Haunted Media: Electronic Presence from Telegraphy to Television* (Durham, NC: Duke University Press, 2000), 44–49.

23. Marvin, *When Old Technologies Were New*, 138–39.

24. For a discussion of broadcasting's early appeals to the female consumer, see Robert Allen, *Speaking of Soap Operas* (Chapel Hill: University of North Caro-

lina Press, 1985); Michelle Hilmes, *Radio Voices: American Broadcasting, 1922–1952* (Minneapolis: University of Minnesota Press, 1997). For discussions of television's appeal to the female consumer in the 1950s, see Mary Beth Haralovich, "Sitcoms and Suburbs: Positioning the 1950s Homemaker," in Spigel and Mann, *Private Screenings*; Lynn Spigel, *Make Room for TV: Television and the Family Ideal in Postwar America* (Chicago: University of Chicago Press, 1992).

25. Anna McCarthy, *Ambient Television: Visual Culture and Public Space* (Durham, NC: Duke University Press, 2000), 66.

26. Donn., review of *What's New with Mademoiselle*, *Variety*, April 5, 1944.

27. Bril., review of *Fashions on Parade*, *Variety*, May 4, 1949.

28. Donn., review of *Fashions of the Times*, *Variety*, November 1944.

29. Mart., review of *Glamour Bazaar*, *Variety*, July 20, 1949.

30. Jose., review of *Fashions at the Waldorf*, *Variety*, November 2, 1949. For a discussion of the authority of women's voices in broadcast media, see Hilmes, *Radio Voices*; Mary Desjardins and Mark Williams, "Are You Lonesome Tonight? Gendered Discourse in *The Lonesome Gal* and *The Continental*," in *Communities of the Air: Radio Century, Radio Culture*, edited by Susan Squier (Durham, NC: Duke University Press, 2003), 251–74. For a general theoretical discussion of the issue of women's voices in relation to film, see Amy Lawrence, *Echo and Narcissus: Women's Voices in Classical Hollywood Cinema* (Berkeley: University of California Press, 1991).

31. Mart., review of *Telefashions*, *Variety*, March 23, 1949.

32. Mart., review of *Individually Yours*, *Variety*, March 9, 1949.

33. Andy., review of *Fashions in Your Living Room*, *Variety*, February 22, 1950.

34. Mann, "The Spectacularization of Everyday Life," 64.

35. "Is Hollywood Doomed?," *Modern Television and Radio*, January 1949, 28–30.

36. Harry Conover, "Glamour Is the Bunk," *Modern Television and Radio*, January 1949, 47–49.

37. "Glamor May Soon Out Dazzle Hollywood," *TV Guide*, April 10–16, 1953, 11, 12.

38. See Tino Balio, *Hollywood in the Age of Television* (Boston: Unwin Hyman, 1990); Michelle Hilmes, *Hollywood and Broadcasting: From Radio to Cable* (Urbana: University of Illinois Press, 1990); Timothy White, "Hollywood's Attempt to Appropriate Television: The Case of Paramount Pictures," PhD dissertation, University of Wisconsin–Madison, 1990; Williams, "From 'Remote' Possibilities to Entertaining 'Difference'"; Christopher Anderson, *Hollywood TV: The Studio System in the Fifties* (Austin: University of Texas Press, 1994).

39. Mary Desjardins, "'Marion Never Looked Lovelier': Hedda Hopper's Hollywood and the Re-negotiation of Hollywood Glamour in Post-war Los Angeles," *Quarterly Review of Film and Video* 16.3–4 (1999): 421–37. See also White and Cassidy, "Innovating Women's Television in Local and National Networks."

40. "TV Brings Hollywood Stars into Your Living Room!," *Radio Best*, June 1949, 28.

41. Jeanine Basinger, *Silent Stars* (New York: Knopf, 1999) provides an exceptionally vivid sense of the larger-than-life quality of so many stars of that era. She discusses Swanson in a manner that makes clear what audiences found so enchanting and intriguing about the star. See also Tricia Welsch, "From Pratfalls to Glamour:

Gloria Swanson Goes to Triangle," in *Not So Silent: Women in Cinema before Sound*, edited by Sofia Bull and Astrid Soderbergh Widding (Stockholm: Stockholm University, 2010); Mary Desjardins, "An Appetite for Living: Gloria Swanson, Colleen Moore, and Clara Bow," in *Idols of Modernity: Movie Stars of the 1920s*, edited by Patrice Petro (New Brunswick, NJ: Rutgers University Press, 2010).

42. Sumiko Higashi, *Cecil B. DeMille and American Culture: The Silent Era* (Berkeley: University of California Press, 1994), 166, 144.

43. "Gloria Swanson Starts," *Phillips Television World*, March 22, 1948, 3.

44. See "WPIX Set for Complete Coverage on Tele Newscasts," *Television World*, April 26, 1948, 5; "News on the Hour," *New York Daily News*, June 14, 1948, TV supplement, 24; Louis Fehr, "Program Promise: 'First and Finest,'" *New York Daily News*, June 14, 1948, TV supplement, 3. WPIX was the first station in the nation to have a full-scale local news broadcast. See Craig Allen, "Tackling the TV Titans in Their Own Backyard: WABC-TV, New York City," in *Television in America: Local Station History from Across the Nation*, edited by Michael D. Murray and Donald G. Godfrey (Ames: Iowa State University Press, 1997), 9.

45. "PIX Means Pictures," *Radio Mirror*, June 1948, 52–53.

46. "WPIX, New York TV Film Station, Brings Best Movies Right into Your Living Room," *Radio Best*, October 1949, 7; "Top Korda Films for WPIX Fans," *New York Daily News*, June 14, 1948, Special TV Supplement, 18; Jack Gould, "Television Station WPIX Has Premiere," *New York Times*, June 20, 1948.

47. Sam Reeback, "WPIX Debuts Tomorrow in Star-Spangled Setting," *New York Daily News*, June 14, 1948, Special TV Supplement, 3.

48. Gould, "Television Station WPIX Has Premiere."

49. Gloria Swanson, "Return Engagement," *Modern Television and Radio*, March 1949, 57.

50. "It's a New Kind of Screen for La Swanson," *Cue*, July 10, 1948, 17.

51. Odec., review of *The Gloria Swanson Hour*, *Variety*, June 23, 1948.

52. Jack Gould, "Programs in Review," *New York Times*, October 17, 1948.

53. Jack Gould, "Programs in Review," *New York Times*, June 20, 1948. According to Craig Allen, "Tackling the TV Titans," New York's WABC also tried programming oriented around news reporters. In 1949 they telecast a show, *I Cover Times Square*, in which actors re-created the daily activities of Broadway news columnists.

54. Jose., review of *Faye Emerson*, *Variety*, October 26, 1949.

55. Bril., review of *Faye Emerson*, *Variety*, April 26, 1950.

56. Val Adams, "Glamor Girl of the Television Screen," *New York Times*, February 19, 1950.

57. Pete Martin, "The Blonde Bombshell of TV," *Saturday Evening Post*, June 30, 1951, 129.

58. "Not Too Heavy," *Time*, April 24, 1950, 57.

59. "Faye's Décolleté Makes TV Melee," *Life*, April 10, 1950, 87–90.

60. Quoted in Martin, "The Blond Bombshell of TV," 126. This is one of the strangest pieces of star promotion I have encountered. Much of the article concerns Emerson's alleged tendency, due to her childhood "outsider" status as a tomboy, to have

violent reactions to other people's lack of respect (for her, for President Roose-velt, etc.). The article recounts two exemplifying incidents in detail: one in which Emerson allegedly threatened to sock a drunk female fan for her rudeness, an-other in which she shattered a glass door at a party where guests were being dis-respectful toward President Roosevelt.

61. For discussion of regulation of women's décolleté on television, see Henry F. and Katharine Pringle, "Congress vs. the Plunging Neckline," *Saturday Evening Post*, December 27, 1952, 25, 49–50.

62. Hal Humphrey, "'Look' Should Look Again," *Los Angeles Mirror*, January 5, 1951. Humphrey takes the "Kaffeeklatsch" line from an issue of *Look*, which was cur-rently on newsstands, giving Emerson and Godfrey their first annual television awards for "most appealing personality."

63. Karal Ann Marling, *As Seen on TV: The Visual Culture of Everyday Life in the 1950s* (Cambridge, MA: Harvard University Press, 1994), 17, emphasis added.

64. Marling, *As Seen on TV*, 22. Christine Becker argues persuasively that critics of Emerson sought to obscure or dismiss her intelligence and strong political opin-ions through a continual focus on her beauty and sexual allure ("'Glamor Girl,'" 254–55; *It's the Pictures That Got Small*, 102–4). While I don't deny these attempts (or that they might have succeeded), I am arguing that within understood con-texts of feminine culture there was room for multiple, indeed even positive evalua-tions of sexually attractive women expressing their intelligence in public settings. Another point of view on the topic of sexual difference, glamour, and television comes from James Bennett in his study of female announcers on early British tele-vision. He discusses how the BBC attempted to reconcile feminine glamour with "respectability" and with the organization's ideal of civic and class improvement. He uses Beverly Skeggs's argument that a certain kind of glamour—one that has the marks of education or wealth, for example—can hold together sexuality and respectability (*Television Personalities*, 66–87). This idea is, I believe, compatible with my own. Emerson (and to some extent Swanson) performed a sexually attrac-tive glamour marked by expertise, poise, and authority, and it was this marking that made these stars television successes, despite attempts by some critics to ob-scure their achievements by calling attention to their physical attributes.

65. "Television: Negro Performers Win Better Roles in TV Than in Any Other Enter-tainment Medium," *Ebony*, June 1950, 23. See also "Bull Moose Jackson," *Ebony*, January 1950, 27–29; "Television Marriage," *Ebony*, October 1950, 42–43; "Can TV Crack America's Color Line?," *Ebony*, May 1951, 56–65; "Is it True What They Say about Models," *Ebony*, November 1951, 60–64; "What Makes a Star," *Ebony*, November 1957, 142–47. Of course, in considering *Ebony*'s conceptions of glam-our, it is important to remember it was a magazine geared toward middle-class African Americans and would later be accused of promoting ideas of beauty ap-proximating "white" standards. See also Donald Bogle, *Bright Boulevards, Bold Dreams: The Story of Black Hollywood* (New York: Ballantine Books, 2005), for a discussion of the Hollywood social and industrial environments in which African Americans worked in a variety of employments.

66. Ethel Waters was not only the first African American but also one of the first women to appear on a major television broadcast. A variety show starring Waters, in which she performed in both musical and dramatic personae, was broadcast as a one-time event by NBC in their experimental broadcasts at the New York World's Fair in 1939. See "Television Reviews: Ethel Waters," *Variety*, June 28, 1939; Bogle, *Prime-Time Blues*, 9–10. Waters also was one of three actresses to play Beulah on the *Beulah* television show, which started in 1950. As with all of her film roles playing domestic characters, Waters's playing of Beulah suggests a distinctive individual not defined by the stereotype of the black maid. Her interpretation of the role makes for an interesting comparison with the interpretations by Hattie McDaniel and especially Louise Beavers, who plays the character as rather dim-witted.

67. "Society Pianists," *Ebony*, November 1950, 41.

68. See Bogle, *Prime-Time Blues*; review of the local New York CBS show *The Bob Howard Show*, *Variety*, August 4, 1948; review of the local New York WOR show on *The Bob Howard Show*, *Variety*, February 21, 1951; "Television: Negro Performers Win Better Roles." See also Forman, *One Night on TV*, 254–58, which was published too late for me to incorporate his arguments into my manuscript.

69. "Hadda Brooks: Singer Has New Hit Television Program on West Coast," *Ebony*, April 1951, 101–2. One obituary of Brooks briefly mentions her television work, stating that "in 1951 she became the first black woman in the country to host her own television variety show." "Hadda Brooks, 86, Performer Known as the Queen of the Boogie," *New York Times*, November 24, 2002. In "From 'Remote' Possibilities to Entertaining 'Difference,'" Williams mentions that Bobby Short, a nightclub and café society singer-pianist, had a local Los Angeles television program on KLAC in 1950. Discussions of these shows, even in publications geared toward African Americans, are hard to find; I was unable to find references to the Short program in *Ebony* or in either of Short's two memoirs, and searches in the *Los Angeles Times* of the period yielded no information about the program except its listings in the weekly television schedule. However, Short's live performances at local nightclubs are often mentioned in the paper's gossip columns at this time.

70. Josh Sides, *L.A. City Limits: African-American Los Angeles from the Great Depression to the Present* (Berkeley: University of California Press, 2003), 38. For discussions of the local African American music scene in Los Angeles from the 1940s to the 1960s, see Clora Bryant et al., eds., *Central Avenue Sounds: Jazz in Los Angeles* (Berkeley: University of California Press, 1998); Johnny Otis, *Upside Your Head! Rhythm and Blues on Central Avenue* (Hanover, NH: Wesleyan University Press and University Press of New England, 1993).

71. Bogle, *Prime-Time Blues*, 16. See also, Bril., review of *Hazel Scott Show*, *Variety*, April 19, 1950.

72. Bril., review of *Hazel Scott Show*.

73. Dwayne Mack, "Hazel Scott: A Career Curtailed," *Journal of African American History* 91.2 (2006): 153–70. See also David W. Stowe, "The Politics of Café Society," *Journal of American History* 84.4 (1998): 1384–406. Stowe argues that Bernard

Josephson created an atmosphere and working conditions in his club Café Society in direct contrast to the New York nightclubs catering to a mostly bourgeois, white clientele. He unionized all his employees, had special fund-raising shows for leftist causes, and, like the music producer and manager John Hammond (a patron of the club), coached black singers to disregard performing styles geared toward fulfilling the expectations of white, middle-class audiences. He apparently guided Lena Horne to adopt a performing style free from the genteel and regal mannerisms associated with her middle-class background so that she could sing the blues with "authenticity." While this might suggest an essentialist notion of blackness, Josephson also encouraged Horne to look at her white and mixed-race audiences directly in the eye when she sang, as their equal rather than subordinate (1391–93). This is confirmed by Horne's daughter in Gail Lumet Buckley, *The Hornes: An American Family* (New York: New American Library 1986), 140–45. Buckley also describes how Billie Holiday (whose famous performance of "Strange Fruit" was at Josephson's club) reassured and coached Horne in relation to Josephson's advice. This evidence suggests that aspects of the glamour of the black female nightclub singer or musician was forged as both a reaction against and in imitation of the signifiers of the white female film star, who was given some enunciative power through her glamour but was constructed to appeal to the white middle-class audience. There is not enough evidence to argue how much, if any, Hazel Scott's performing style was influenced by Josephson during her time in his employ at Café Society. However, it was under his management that she insisted on studio contracts that stipulated no maid roles in films. For a comparison of the personas of Scott and Horne, see Thomas Bogle, *Toms, Coons, Mulattoes, Mammies, and Bucks: An Interpretive History of Blacks in American Film*, 3rd edition (New York: Continuum, 1994), 122–27.

74. See "Hazel Scott Denies Any Red Sympathies," *New York Times*, September 16, 1950; "Hazel Scott Makes Denials at Inquiry," *New York Times*, September 23, 1950.

75. See Kathy Peiss, *Hope in a Jar: The Making of America's Beauty Culture* (New York: Henry Holt, 1998), for a discussion of these issues.

76. For excellent discussions of how racially inflected "exoticism" circulated as a beauty value in 1930s Hollywood, see Sarah Berry, *Screen Style: Fashion and Femininity in 1930s Hollywood* (Minneapolis: University of Minnesota Press, 2000); Joanne Hershfield, *The Invention of Dolores del Rio* (Minneapolis: University of Minnesota Press, 2000).

77. McGee, *Some Liked It Hot*, 225, 130–31.

78. Staggs, *Close-Up on Sunset Boulevard*, 52–54.

79. Gloria Swanson, letter to Robert L. Coe, January 4, 1949, Gloria Swanson Collection, File 154, Harry Ransom Center, University of Texas at Austin (hereafter HRC).

80. Gloria Swanson, letter to Harvey Marlow, July 30, 1948, Gloria Swanson Collection, File 154, HRC.

81. Gloria Swanson, letter to Robert L. Coe, November 24, 1948, Gloria Swanson Collection, File 154, HRC.

82. Gloria Swanson, in interview on *Hedda Hopper's Hollywood*, coproduced by Los Angeles independent television station KTLA for syndication. The program was filmed in late December 1959 but broadcast on NBC January 10, 1960. See Desjardins, "'Marion Never Looked Lovelier,'" for discussion of this television special.

83. Staggs, *Close-Up on Sunset Boulevard*, 309–10.

84. For analyses of *Sunset Boulevard*, see Brandon French, *On the Verge of Revolt: Women in American Films of the Fifties* (New York: Ungar, 1978); Janey Place, "Women in Film Noir," in *Women in Film Noir*, edited by E. Ann Kaplan (London: BFI, 1980); Lucy Fischer, "*Sunset Boulevard*: Fading Stars," in *Women and Film*, edited by Janet Todd (New York: Holmes and Meier, 1988); Lawrence, *Echo and Narcissus*; Lois Banner, *In Full Flower: Aging Women, Power, and Sexuality* (New York: Knopf, 1992); Virginia Wright-Wexman, *Creating the Couple: Love, Marriage, and Hollywood Performance* (Princeton: Princeton University Press, 1993); Jodi Brooks, "Performing Age / Performing Crisis (for Norma Desmond, Baby Jane, Margo Channing, Sister George—and Myrtle)," in *Figuring Age: Women, Bodies, Generations*, edited by Kathleen Woodward (Bloomington: Indiana University Press, 1999). Brooks uses Benjamin's theory of the return of the commodity fetish in ways similar to my own use in chapter 2.

85. It is debatable whether Swanson was the first big star to make a film in Europe or have a child, but the point is that these facts were part of what constituted her star mythology.

86. "Gloria Noted Actress, Inventor, Too," *Des Moines Tribune*, July 20, 1950, press scrapbook on *Sunset Boulevard*, Gloria Swanson Collection, HRC.

87. "Swanson Made Many Pictures, Not Only Glamour Gal but Real Actress," *Omaha Sunday World-Herald*, 1950, Gloria Swanson Collection, HRC.

88. "After Fifty Years, Gloria Still Glitters, Recognized though Years Off Screen," *St. Louis Star-Times*, June 5, 1950, Gloria Swanson Collection, HRC.

89. "Gloria Noted Actress."

90. "After Fifty Years."

91. "No Comeback, Says Gloria of New Film," *St. Louis Post-Dispatch*, June 4, 1950, Gloria Swanson Collection, HRC.

92. "After Fifty Years."

93. A two-part article in the *Saturday Evening Post* at this same time, the summer of 1950, might have given Paramount and Swanson pause, as it assumes an even more ambivalent—although ultimately positive—tone than the newspapers covering Swanson's junket. For instance, the headline to part 2 declares unequivocally that she "was a has-been." But it also was the one press report to provide extensive information about Swanson's patent development company and how she and her ex-husband Henri de la Falaise de la Coudraye "smuggled" the company's scientists, who were mostly Austrian Jews, out of Hitler-occupied Austria. An image of Swanson emerges as quite heroic even though the author pictures the star in Paris at the time of the "scientist smuggling" lamenting that crowds of adoring fans were no longer aroused at her appearance. Stanley Frank, "Grandma Gloria Swanson Comes Back," *Saturday Evening Post*, July 22 and July 29, 1950.

94. "'A Parade Roar' Comments on Actress," *Kansas City Star*, 1950, Gloria Swanson Collection, HRC.

95. "No Comeback."

96. "Special Teen Screening," *Des Moines Register*, July 22, 1950, Gloria Swanson Collection, HRC.

97. Swanson, *Swanson on Swanson*, 488.

98. In the mid-1950s Swanson was also involved in producing a musical version of *Sunset Boulevard* to be mounted on Broadway. She commissioned a score and libretto, which she and a cast recorded. She even sang one of the songs on an episode of *The Steve Allen Show* in 1957. Swanson had interested von Stroheim in reprising the role of the butler Max. But after stringing her along for a few years, Paramount never granted her the rights to the film. It was a bitter disappointment. Sam Staggs, in *Close-Up on Sunset Boulevard*, provides extensive coverage of this venture. In Swanson's private papers I found the song lyrics to the proposed musical. One song suggests she and the composers Dickson Hughes and Richard Stapley imagined Norma Desmond's comeback attempts in the context of the arrival of television and the "new Hollywood" it represented. Taped copies of the recordings occasionally come up for auction on eBay.

99. Gloria Swanson Collection, Files 162.3, 162.11, HRC.

100. See Dana Polan, *Scenes of Instruction: The Beginnings of the U.S. Study of Film* (Berkeley: University of California Press, 2007), for a history of the academic study of film history.

101. Adams, "Format: A Ukulele and a Memory."

Chapter Two. Norma Desmond, Your Spell Is Everywhere

The title of this chapter is a takeoff on a hit song, "Love, Your Magic Spell is Everywhere," Gloria Swanson performed in one of her talking picture successes, *The Trespasser*.

1. For a discussion of the critical reception of anthology series, see William Boddy, *Fifties Television: The Industry and Its Critics* (Urbana: University of Illinois Press, 1990).

2. Christine Becker, *It's the Pictures That Got Small: Hollywood Film Stars on 1950s Television* (Middletown, CT: Wesleyan University Press, 2008), 115, highlights critics' reviews of *The Loretta Young Show* to argue that the dramatic anthologies hosted by women were often dismissed as merely women's fare that required "hankies."

3. For discussions of these realities for women in the 1950s, see Stephanie Coontz, *The Way We Never Were: American Families and the Nostalgia Trap* (New York: Basic Books, 1992); Brett Harvey, *The Fifties: A Women's Oral History* (New York: Harper Collins, 1993).

4. My idea of the New Woman has been heavily influenced by the work of Rita Felski, in particular *The Gender of Modernity* (Cambridge, MA: Harvard University Press, 1995).

5. See Michelle Hilmes, *Hollywood and Broadcasting: From Radio to Cable* (Urbana: University of Illinois Press, 1990), 145–50.

6. Gloria Swanson Collection, File 155.10, Harry Ransom Center, University of Texas at Austin (hereafter HRC).

7. "The Birth of a Telefilm: *Crown Theater* Starts Shooting with Crosby Cash and Swanson Class," TV *Guide*, May 22, 1952, 11. The contract with Bing Crosby Enterprises is found in Gloria Swanson Collection, File 155.3, HRC.

8. "The Birth of a Telefilm," 11–12.

9. In her collected papers I found evidence of some investment she had in "My Last Duchess": a copy of the short story with her annotations, marked passages she found especially interesting, where the short story was an improvement or the script adaptation, and more. Gloria Swanson Collection, File 156.14, HRC.

10. Although Twentieth Century-Fox had under contract two of the most successful female stars during the studio era, Shirley Temple in the 1930s and Betty Grable in the 1940s, unlike MGM and RKO, it did not have a reputation for developing female talent, and it wasn't until the late 1940s and early 1950s (when Susan Hayward was at the studio) that it invested much in the production of women's pictures. There are also rumors that Darryl Zanuck employed "the casting couch" extensively. Warner Bros. did produce women's films (in particular those starring Ruth Chatterton, Kay Francis, and Bette Davis) but specialized in gangster, crime, and "newspaper" films in which female characters were supporting rather than lead. The studio was also notorious for exploitive practices regarding acting labor, and James Cagney, Bette Davis, Kay Francis, and Olivia de Havilland had well-publicized battles with the studio over pay, number of pictures per year, quality of roles, and suspension practices. Young had been under contract to First National, which was purchased by Warner Bros. in 1929. When Twentieth Century (where she had gone after her contract with Warner Bros. expired) merged with Fox in 1934, she ended up there. George Eels, *Ginger, Loretta and Irene Who?* (New York: G. P. Putnam, 1976), questions whether Young was capable of picking quality roles once she had her freedom from studio contracts. He also suggests that the connection between Young's performances on-screen and off-screen is their inauthenticity.

11. Judy Lewis, *Uncommon Knowledge* (New York: Pocket Books, 1994). The authorized biography, written at the end of Young's life, when she finally admitted publicly that Judy was her own daughter by Gable, is Joan Wester Anderson, *Forever Young: The Life, Loves and Enduring Faith of a Hollywood Legend* (Allen, Texas: Thomas More, 2000).

12. See "Letters to Loretta: 'The Queen' Stakes Her Crown on Television," TV *Guide*, December 4, 1953; "No Shrieks, No Screams," *Newsweek*, December 8, 1958, 58. For an in-depth study of Young's transition to television, see Madeleine Ritrosky-Winslow, "Transforming Stardom: Loretta Young's Journey from Movies to Television," PhD dissertation, Indiana University, 1997.

13. Loretta Young, "Have Faith in Yourself," *Radio-TV Mirror*, May 1954, 45, 94. It is doubtful that Young wrote this article, at least on her own. Helen Ferguson, one of the most powerful independent publicists in Hollywood, often served as a ghostwriter for many pieces under Young's byline (see next citation). See also my

essay "'As Told to Helen Ferguson': Hollywood Publicity, Gender, and the Public Sphere," in *When Private Talk Goes Public: Gossip in United States History*, edited by Kathleen Feeley and Jennifer Frost (New York: Palgrave Macmillan, 2014).

14. Loretta Young as told to Helen Ferguson, *The Things I Had to Learn* (New York: Bobbs Merrill, 1961), 77.

15. Rosalind Russell, an underexamined film star within academic discourse, did shift her acting focus to the stage, but she returned to film at moments in the 1950s—for example, to reprise her hit stage role of Auntie Mame in the 1958 film adaptation. In her most memorable films from the 1950s and 1960s besides *Auntie Mame*, she is cast in supporting or costarring roles that were also adapted from the stage, such as those in *Picnic* (1955) and *Gypsy* (1962). In addition she starred in the CBS Television Special adaptation of *Wonderful Town* (1958), in which she reprised her role from the stage musical of the same name (which was an adaptation of earlier versions of the source material by Ruth McKenny, including the film *My Sister Eileen*, which Russell had starred in at the peak of her film career in 1943). Russell, then, was involved in a series of remediated starring or costarring roles across three media—film, television, and live theater—in the era after her peak film stardom in the 1930s and 1940s. Irene Dunne, whose film career was over by 1952, made occasional forays into television, including briefly serving as the host of *Schlitz Playhouse* that same year. Jean Arthur would have a short-lived television program in the early 1960s. For very helpful statistical charts about film actors and actresses entering television in the 1950s, see Becker, *It's the Pictures That Got Small*, 239–53.

16. *The Things I Had to Learn*, Young's autobiographical memoir as told to her public relations representative, Helen Ferguson, prominently features Young's attitudes toward fashion.

17. For a review of Young's reading of proverbs, see "Recruits from Hollywood," *Time*, October 5, 1953, 80–81.

18. See Young and Ferguson, *The Things I Had to Learn*; Joe Morella and Edward Z. Epstein, *Loretta Young: An Extraordinary Life* (New York: Delacorte, 1986).

19. Two essays that best articulate how television programming at this time often simultaneously raised and denied the realities of women in the 1950s are Horace Newcomb and Paul M. Hirsch, "Television as a Cultural Forum," in *Television: The Critical View*, edited by Horace Newcomb, 5th edition (New York: Oxford University Press, 1993), 503–15; and Patricia Mellencamp, "Situation Comedy, Feminism, and Freud: Discourses of Gracie and Lucy," in *Studies in Entertainment: Critical Approaches to Mass Culture*, edited by Tania Modleski (Bloomington: Indiana University Press, 1986), 80–95.

20. Tom Lewis's belief that Young valued her career over their marriage—or over his position as the dominant partner in the marriage—is mentioned in every biography of Young. Lewis sued Young and his company partner Robert Shewalter in 1956, claiming that they had asked him to resign from Lewislor. Explanations for Lewis's departure from the show, however, are conspicuously absent from Young's

1961 memoir, published at a time when Lewis was still alive and Young considered herself still married to him (per Catholicism), although they had been separated for several years. As Morella and Epstein remark in their 1986 biography of Young, her creation of a façade of a happy marriage despite every bit of evidence to the contrary is perhaps the "most intriguing" part of book she wrote with Ferguson only a few years after the struggle for control over her program (*Loretta Young*, 277).

21. "The War of Two Worlds: TV and Movie Stars Battle for Dramatic Parts," TV *Guide*, March 12, 1954, 5–7. See also "Recruits from Hollywood."

22. "A Taste of TV: Hollywood Stars Sample New Fare," TV *Guide*, June 12, 1953, 8–9; "What Keeps Them Off TV?," TV *Guide*, October 23, 1953, 5–6; "Double Your Money's Worth: 'Lux Video Theater' Expands to Hour, Seeks Brightest Stars," TV *Guide*, August 21, 1954, 8–9; "Miss Rogers Consents: Last of the Holdouts (Movie Queen Division) Finally Takes the TV Plunge," TV *Guide*, October 12, 1954, 5–7.

23. "Letters to Loretta," 15.

24. "Is TV a Haven for Hollywood Has-Beens?," TV *Guide*, August 14, 1954. Bogart defends his statement and his appearance in "The Petrified Forest" for NBC's *Producer's Showcase* in "Bogart's on Television—but Not for Long," TV *Guide*, May 28, 1955, 7–9. Bogart had appeared in the film *The Petrified Forest* in the 1930s; he was appearing in a version on television for "pure nostalgia" and because it was a "good role for Betty [wife Lauren Bacall]."

25. Hal Humphrey, "TV, the Great Rejuvenator," *Los Angeles Mirror*, September 9, 1954.

26. To my knowledge, the "Sunset Boulevard" episode of *Robert Montgomery Presents* is not available in its entirety. The first ten minutes of this live (and then kinescoped) program is posted on YouTube, but I have not been able to track down a complete version. From what I have seen from the excerpt online, Astor plays the Desmond part with more anger and sarcasm and less of the pathos and pathology projected by Swanson in the same role.

27. Mary Astor, *My Story: An Autobiography* (New York: Doubleday, 1959), 312. See also Mary Astor, *A Life on Film* (New York: Delacorte, 1971).

28. See Robert R. Kirsch, "The Book Report," *Los Angeles Times*, January 7, 1959; Lydia Lane, "No Tears Shed for Vanishing Youth," *Los Angeles Times*, February 17, 1957. The star memoir is an understudied discourse of and in film history. For a discussion of some of the issues around the study of the memoirs of female film figures, see Amelie Hastie, *Cupboards of Curiosity: Women, Recollection, and Film History* (Durham, NC: Duke University Press, 2007); Mary Desjardins, "Dietrich Dearest: Family Memoir and the Fantasy of Origins," in *Dietrich Icon*, edited by Gerd Gemunden and Mary R. Desjardins (Durham, NC: Duke University Press, 2007), 310–27.

29. For excellent discussions of Lupino's directing career in film and television, see Annette Kuhn, ed., *Queen of the "B"s: Ida Lupino Behind the Camera* (Westport, CT: Praeger, 1995); Amelie Hastie, *The Bigamist* (London: BFI / Palgrave Macmillan, 2009). For a discussion of Lupino's involvement in *Four Star Theater* and in her sit-

com, *Mr. Adams and Eve*, see William Donati, *Ida Lupino: A Biography* (Lexington: University Press of Kentucky, 1996); Becker, *It's the Pictures That Got Small*.

30. Mary Ann Doane, *The Desire to Desire: The Woman's Film of the 1940s* (Blooming-ton: Indiana University Press, 1987), 123–75.

31. Amy Lawrence, *Echo and Narcissus: Women's Voices in Classical Hollywood Cinema* (Berkeley: University of California Press, 1991), discusses Norma's narcissism in terms of the myth of Echo and Narcissus. Lawrence also uses Doane's terms about the female spectator to argue for Norma Desmond's overinvestment in the image, but not her argument about the gothic and paranoid cycle of woman's films.

32. Jeffrey Sconce, *Haunted Media: Electronic Presence from Telegraphy to Television* (Durham, NC: Duke University Press, 2000), 133.

33. These articles include Adela Rogers St. John, "The Return of Florence Lawrence," *Photoplay*, May 1921; Frederick James Smith, "Photoplay Finds Mary Fuller," *Photo-play*, August 1924; Frederick James Smith, "Unwept, Unhonored, and Unfilmed," *Photoplay*, July 1924; Beatrice Washburn, "Marguerite Clark—Today," *Photoplay*, April 1925. Press accounts from the 1920s and 1930s about Murray's "sequestra-tion" can be found in the clipping file on her at the Margaret Herrick Library, Academy of Motion Pictures Arts and Sciences, Beverly Hills, California (AMPAS). For more extended discussions of fan magazine articles and press accounts about these stars, see my two essays "A Method to This Madness? The Myth of the Mad Silent Star," in *Not So Silent: Women in Cinema before Sound*, edited by Sofia Bull and Astrid Soderbergh Widding (Stockholm: Stockholm University, 2010), 357–68, and "Fading Stars and the Ruined Commodity Form: Star Discourses of Loss in Early Fan Magazines," in *Researching Women in Silent Cinema: New Findings and Perspectives*, edited by Monica Dall'Asta, Victoria Duckett, and Lucia Tralli (Bolo-gna: University of Bologna and University of Melbourne, 2013), 150–62.

34. In judging Mason's interpretation of Norman Maine, I am in agreement with Amy Lawrence, who argues that his enactment of the character suggests a man aware of his own ambitions and failures. This self-awareness is what Norma Desmond and Barbara Jean Trenton lack, and it is what leads Maine to commit suicide as an unselfish act toward his wife (in the film's terms, not mine). In other words, his self-awareness ennobles him and keeps him from collapsing into a feminine sub-ject position. For Lawrence's take, see "A Star Is Born Bigger Than Life," in *Larger Than Life: Movies Stars of the 1950s*, edited by R. Barton Palmer (New Brunswick, NJ: Rutgers University Press, 2010), 86–106.

35. The wonderful skit "Aggravation Boulevard" on a 1955 episode of *Your Show of Shows* uses the tragic star familiar from *Sunset Boulevard* and *A Star Is Born*, but like *Dreamboat*, it is a comic rendering of the star's situation. Sid Caesar plays a Valentino-like silent star who cannot succeed in sound films because of his high-pitched voice. He becomes a pathetic has-been as his wife, the star Mona Mona (Nanette Fabray), rises in popularity. This skit typifies the richness of *Your Show of Shows* parodies—at once a parody of Valentino, a comic retelling of the myth about the silent film star John Gilbert's inability to succeed in sound films, a par-ody of *Singin' in the Rain* and *Sunset Boulevard*—it is funny because it makes a

character like Lina Lamont (of *Singin'*) and Desmond into a male figure and makes fun of the way that feminization of men is seen to be tragic. For a debunking of the Gilbert myth, see Donald Crafton, *The Talkies: American Cinema's Transition to Sound, 1926–1931* (Berkeley: University of California Press, 1997).

36. There are other 1950s films about stardom but not focused on the silent era: *All About Eve*, *The Clown* (a remake of *The Champ*, with Red Skelton as a has-been clown who makes a comeback on television), *Calloway Went That-Away* (a spoof of the popularity of cowboy stars on television), *The Bad and the Beautiful*, *The Barefoot Contessa*, *The Goddess* (a loose biography of Marilyn Monroe), *I'll Cry Tomorrow* (a biography of Lillian Roth), *The Star* (Bette Davis doing a "Norma Desmond" but with a "happy" ending in which she accepts her age and opts for family instead of a comeback), and the remake of *A Star Is Born*.

37. I made a decision while writing the first draft of this book to not analyze *Singin' in the Rain*. This was fortuitous, as by the time I revised the manuscript, Steven Cohan's definitive analysis of the film (in its relation to camp, recycling, and 1950s film musical production) was published. See Steven Cohan, *Incongruous Entertainment: Camp, Cultural Value, and the MGM Musical* (Durham, NC: Duke University Press, 2005), 200–245.

38. See Crafton, *The Talkies*, for an excellent discussion of the impact of sound on star careers.

39. "Hollywood's Biggest Comeback," *Photoplay*, November and December 1957, is about the revival of interest in old stars because of films appearing on television. Quote is from the November issue, 42.

40. Pat Weaver, quoted in David Pierce, "'Senile Celluloid': Independent Exhibitors, the Major Studios, and the Fight over Feature Films on Television, 1939–1956," *Film History* 10 (1998): 142. The original quote was in a *Variety* article.

41. The industry attitudes and the events that led to the televising of old films are complex, beyond the scope of this volume. In addition to Pierce, "'Senile Celluloid,'" two of the best analyses are found in Michelle Hilmes, "Television: The Vault of Hollywood," in *Hollywood and Broadcasting*, 140–70; Derek Kompare, "(R): Film on Early Television," in *Rerun Nation: How Repeats Invented American Broadcasting* (New York: Routledge, 2005), 39–68.

42. Articles on the revived memories of stars seen in old films released to television in the 1950s include "Found! The Stars of Old TV Movies," *TV Guide*, July 24, 1953; "Hollywood's Biggest Comeback."

43. Richard deCordova, *Picture Personalities: The Emergence of the Star System in America* (Urbana: University of Illinois Press, 1990), 140–44.

44. One exception to the bachelor roles for Webb was *Cheaper by the Dozen* (1950), in which he portrayed Frank Gilbreth, a (real-life) time-efficiency engineer and father of twelve children. There is little promotion of Webb as a star in the major fan magazines, such as *Photoplay* and *Modern Screen*, in the mid-1940s to late 1950s, when he was a film star. In his clipping file at AMPAS are mainly articles from general interest magazines and newspapers detailing his Broadway career in the 1920s and 1930s. All seem to focus on his acting, his sophistication, and his

relationship with his mother. See William J. Mann, *Behind the Screen: How Gays and Lesbians Shaped Hollywood, 1910–1969* (New York: Viking, 2001), 249–59, for an interesting biography and discussion of Webb's star persona.

45. Richard Dyer, "Don't Look Now: The Instabilities of the Male Pin-Up," in *Only Entertainment* (London: Routledge, 1992), 116.

46. *Sitting Pretty* (1948) had already had two sequels by the time of *Dreamboat*, *Mr. Belvedere Goes to College* (1949) and *Mr. Belvedere Rings the Bell* (1951), so audiences of the time would have enjoyed the joke of seeing Mr. Belvedere as a character of Sayre/Blair's rather than of Webb's. However, it is difficult to say how much of that audience might have read the joke as having a gay subtext.

Chapter Three. Maureen O'Hara's "Confidential" Life

1. R. E. McDonald, "It Was the Hottest Show in Town When Maureen O'Hara Cuddled in Row 35," *Confidential*, March 1957, 11.

2. See Anne Helen Peterson, "The Gossip Industry: Producing and Distributing Star Images, Celebrity Gossip, and Entertainment News 1910–2010," PhD dissertation, University of Texas–Austin, 2011, for a discussion of the relation of contemporary tabloid magazines to earlier forms of star publicity.

3. Michel Foucault, *The History of Sexuality*, vol. 1: *An Introduction* (New York: Vintage Books, 1980).

4. Richard Dyer, *Stars* (London: BFI, 1979); Richard Dyer, *Heavenly Bodies: Film Stars and Society* (New York: St. Martin's, 1986).

5. John Ellis, *Visible Fictions: Cinema, Television, Video* (London: Routledge and Kegan Paul, 1982); P. David Marshall, *Celebrity and Power: Fame in Contemporary Culture* (Minneapolis: University of Minnesota Press, 1997).

6. Denise Mann, "The Spectacularization of Everyday Life: Recycling Hollywood Stars and Fans in Early Television Variety Shows," in *Private Screenings: Television and the Female Consumer*, edited by Lynn Spigel and Denise Mann (Minneapolis: University of Minnesota Press, 1992), 41–64.

7. Gladys Hall, "Four Magic Words," *TV-Radio Mirror*, ca. 1954, 99.

8. Fredda Balling, "The World Is His Neighbor," *TV-Radio Mirror*, June 1959, 30.

9. Ralph Edwards, quoted in "Sermon on the Air," *Time*, February 16, 1953. The article uses the Roth episode for many of its examples. Although often referred to in articles about the program, this episode was not part of the package of programs rebroadcast on the American Movie Classics channel in the late 1980s and early 1990s. I have also not found it in archives and libraries that have tapes of other episodes.

10. Mimi White, *Tele-advising: Therapeutic Discourse in American Television* (Chapel Hill: University of North Carolina Press, 1992), 187.

11. "Sermon on the Air."

12. Marsha Cassidy, "Visible Storytellers: Women Narrators on 1950s Daytime Television," *Style* 35.2 (2001): 354–74.

13. Given the degree to which Edwards emphasized how the program helped troubled

subjects, it is not surprising that the Roth episode was the favored default episode, repeated when a new show had to be cancelled at the last minute when the subject prematurely learned of the surprise.

14. "'Why I Am Through with Big TV Shows,'" *Sponsor*, May 1955, 95. Denise Mann, in "The Spectacularization of Everyday Life," analyzes Hazel Bishop's decision to drop sponsorship of *The Martha Raye Show*.

15. See Mark Williams, "History in a Flash: Notes on the Myth of TV Liveness," in *Collecting Visible Evidence*, edited by Jane Gaines and Michael Renov (Minneapolis: University of Minnesota Press, 1999); Jane Feuer, "The Concept of Live Television: Ontology as Ideology," in *Regarding Television*, edited by E. Ann Kaplan (Frederick, MD: University Publications of America, 1983); Klaus Dieter-Rath, "Live Television and Its Audiences: Challenges of Media Reality," in *Remote Control: Television, Audiences, and Cultural Power*, edited by Ellen Seiter et al. (London: Routledge, 1989); Mary Ann Doane, "Information, Crisis, Catastrophe," in *Logics of Television*, edited by Patricia Mellencamp (Indianapolis: Indiana University Press, 1992); James Friedman, ed., *Reality Squared: Televisual Discourse on the Real* (New Brunswick, NJ: Rutgers University Press, 2002).

16. Rhona Berenstein, "Acting Live: TV Performance, Intimacy, and Immediacy (1945–1955)," in Friedman, *Reality Squared*, 25–49.

17. In fact the alternative sponsor to Hazel Bishop was Proctor and Gamble, a household product and cosmetic firm that found great profitability in underwriting soap operas, another live genre associated with both confession and therapy. The star's naturalization of product endorsement on *This Is Your Life* would seem to obviate what Mann argues was audience skepticism about stars' relations to consumer corporate sponsorship.

18. Thomas Doherty, "Frank Costello's Hands: Film, Television, and the Kefauver Crime Hearings," *Film History* 10 (1998): 369.

19. The history of many of these magazines can be found in Alan Betrock, *Unseen America: The Greatest Cult Exploitation Magazines 1950–1966* (New York: Shake Books, 1990), 3–9.

20. See, for instance, Rochelle Gurstein, *The Repeal of Reticence: America's Cultural and Legal Struggles over Free Speech, Obscenity, Sexual Liberation, and Modern Art* (New York: Hill and Wang, 1996); Robert C. Post, "The Social Foundations of Defamation Law: Reputation and the Constitution," *California Law Review* 74 (May 1986): 691–742. For a discussion of how legal theories about privacy became foundational for laws and theories concerning rights to publicity, see Jane Gaines, *Contested Culture: The Image, the Voice, and the Law* (Chapel Hill: University of North Carolina Press, 1991).

21. Irwin O. Spiegel, "Public Celebrity v. Scandal Magazine: The Celebrity's Right to Privacy," *Southern California Law Review* 30 (1957): 287.

22. Spiegel, "Public Celebrity v. Scandal Magazine," 285–87.

23. C. J. Biggs quoted in Edward J. Bloustein, "Privacy as an Aspect of Human Dignity: An Answer to Dean Prosser," *New York University Law Review* 39 (December 1964): 962.

24. Robert E. Mensel, "'Kodakers Lying in Wait': Amateur Photography and the Right of Privacy in New York, 1885–1915," *American Quarterly* 43 (March 1991): 27.

25. Spiegel, "Public Celebrity v. Scandal Magazine," 307–11.

26. John D'Emilio and Estelle Freedman, *Intimate Matters: A History of Sexuality in America* (New York: Harper and Row, 1991), 280. See also Jay A. Gertzman, *Bookleggers and Smuthounds: The Trade in Erotica 1920–1940* (Philadelphia: University of Pennsylvania Press, 1999).

27. Patricia Mellencamp, *High Anxiety: Catastrophe, Scandal, Age, and Comedy* (Bloomington: Indiana University Press, 1992), in discussing the reemergence of mass-mediated scandal in the 1980s and early 1990s, defines gossip as a form of communication whose content is always already "recycled" material.

28. Thomas K. Wolfe, "Public Lives: *Confidential* Magazine; Reflections in Tranquility by the Former Owner, Robert Harrison, Who Managed to Get Away with It," *Esquire* 61 (April 1964): 87–90, 152–57.

29. This definition is provided by William A. Cohen, *Sex Scandal: The Private Parts of Victorian Fiction* (Durham, NC: Duke University Press, 1996), 1–96.

30. There are many versions of how and why the Hudson story was suppressed by *Confidential*, and many of them are intertwined with stories that Hudson was pressured into marrying Phyllis Gates in 1955 by his agent or studio to disprove the scandal stories should *Confidential* or another magazine publish reports of his homosexual activity. There were narratives about monetary pay-offs to the magazine; about his agent Henry Willson hiring a gangster to rough up the article's author, the editor, or those who signed affidavits (it isn't clear from accounts which); about Universal Studios and Willson offering the story of Rory Calhoun instead. See Fred Otash, *Investigation Hollywood!* (Chicago: Henry Regnery, 1976), 31–38 (Otash doesn't use Hudson's name, but it is very easy to figure out whom he's talking about); Rock Hudson and Sara Davidson, *Rock Hudson: His Story* (New York: Avon Books, 1987), 95–97; Phyllis Gates and Bob Thomas, *My Husband, Rock Hudson* (New York: Jove Books, 1989), 207–8. The account concerning Calhoun is supported by Ezra Goodman, *The Fifty-Year Decline of Hollywood* (New York: Simon and Schuster, 1961), 52–53 (he doesn't use Hudson's name, but it is clear from context that Hudson is the figure in question); by an interview with the writer Maurice Zolotow in the 1988 British television documentary *Hollywood Confidential*, in which Zolotow claims that Calhoun told him that the story about him had been offered up to kill the story about Hudson; and rather unenthusiastically by David Ehrenstein, *Open Secret: Gay Hollywood 1928–1998* (New York: William Morrow, 1998), 99–100. Not only did the trade for the Calhoun story make sense in terms of *Confidential*'s mass production of scandal, but Calhoun was, like Hudson, contracted to Universal and a client of Henry Willson (who, from every account I have read of him, used his clients like pawns, even blackmailing them about the affairs they had with *him*), and the story came out in 1955, about the time the story about Hudson was supposedly killed. For an interesting account of Willson's relationships with his clients by a former client, see John Gilmore, *Laid Bare* (Los Angeles: Amok Books, 1997). The story about Calhoun was Howard

Rushmore, "Rory Calhoun: But for the Grace of God, Still a Convict," *Confidential* 3 (May 1955): 23–25, 51–52. An unsigned editorial in the magazine's September 1955 issue followed up the story with quotes of praise for *Confidential*'s treatment of Calhoun's story from the priest who had helped the star.

31. Ehrenstein, *Open Secret*, 99–100.

32. In fact when Calhoun was informed that the story was going to be published by *Confidential*, he worked with the gossip columnist Hedda Hopper to have his past crimes first revealed by her, a Hollywood insider with a syndicated column in the legitimate press. In the next few months and years numerous general interest magazines and fan magazines published stories about Calhoun's past, using an up-lift narrative similar to *Confidential*'s. See, for example, Rory Calhoun, "My Dark Past," *American Weekly*, August 21 and 28, 1955; Rory Calhoun, "Look, Kid, How Stupid Can You Be?," *Photoplay* 51 (February 1957).

33. Cohen, *Sex Scandal*, 8.

34. Telford Taylor, *Two Studies in Constitutional Interpretation: Search, Seizure, and Surveillance and Fair Trial and Free Press* (Columbus: Ohio State University Press, 1969), 80–81.

35. Robert Harrison, "*Confidential* vs. Hollywood," *Confidential* 5 (September 1957): 22–23.

36. Philip K. Scheuer, "Motherhood Is Women's Real Career, Star Says," *Los Angeles Times*, June 8, 1947.

37. Maureen O'Hara, "My Most Important Role," in *The Star's Own Stories*, edited by Ivy Crane, ca. 1947, reprinted as *Hollywood in the 1940s: The Star's Own Stories* (New York: Frederick Ungar, 1980), 20–24.

38. Sidney Skolsky, "Tintypes," syndicated column, June 17, 1942.

39. Diane Negra, *Off-White Hollywood: American Culture and Ethnic Female Stardom* (London: Routledge, 2001), 26. Negra's discussion of Hedy Lamarr's television appearances in game and variety shows of the 1950s and 1960s also focuses on the way European ethnicity was negotiated via film stars in a changing cultural and industrial landscape. See "Re-made for Television: Hedy Lamarr's Post-war Star Textuality," in *Small Screens, Big Ideas: Television in the 1950s*, edited by Janet Thumim (London: I. B. Tauris, 2002).

40. Scheuer, "Motherhood Is Women's Real Career."

41. Viola Moore, "Pride of the Irish," *Modern Screen*, September 1949, 38–39, 87–88.

42. Erskin Johnson, column, *Los Angeles Daily News*, October 21, 1950.

43. Earl Wilson, "The Sparks Fly," *Los Angeles Mirror-News*, February 19, 1955.

44. Gladys Hall, "She Knows Where She's Going!," *Photoplay*, December 1952, 76.

45. Jack Jones, "Witness Tells of Wild Pool Party," *Los Angeles Times*, August 21, 1957, 18.

46. This headline appeared in the *Los Angeles Mirror News* on June 21, 1955, and possibly in New York papers. Other Los Angeles headlines included "Ex-Mate Accuses Maureen O'Hara, Demands Custody of Daughter, 11," *Los Angeles Times*, June 21, 1955; "Maureen O'Hara Lashes Back in Custody Fight," *Los Angeles Times*, June 24, 1955. On the witness stand Ross also mentioned "Accuses Star of Consorting with Wealthy Latin" from an unnamed paper.

47. Robert Durant, "The Strange Case of Maureen O'Hara," *On the* QT 1 (March 1956): 10–11.

48. McDonald, "It Was the Hottest Show in Town," 46.

49. Florabel Muir, "The Truth about Dope," *Photoplay* 34 (December 1948): 32–33, 72.

50. Wade Nichols, "An Open Letter to Robert Mitchum: The Case for the People," *Modern Screen* 38 (February 1949): 27.

51. Florabel Muir, "What Now for Mitchum?," *Photoplay* 34 (April 1949): 31, 98–99.

52. See Adrienne L. McLean, "The Cinderella Princess and the Instrument of Evil: Surveying the Limits of Female Transgression in Two Postwar Hollywood Scandals," *Cinema Journal* 34 (Spring 1995): 36–56, revised and reprinted in Adrienne L. McLean and David A. Cook, *Headline Hollywood: A Century of Film Scandal* (New Brunswick, NJ: Rutgers University Press, 2001), 163–89.

53. Elsa Maxwell, "I Call It Scandalous!," *Photoplay* 37 (June 1950): 100–102.

54. Louella Parsons, "Hollywood's Most Tragic People," *Modern Screen* 44 (June 1952): 30–31, 95–96.

55. N.A., "Hollywood's Ten Best Citizens," *Modern Screen* 39 (February 1950): 46–47, 73–74.

56. Fred Sammis, "The Other Side of the Hollywood Story," *Photoplay* 39 (August 1950): 31–35.

57. "*Modern Screen* Special Report: Morals in Hollywood," *Modern Screen* 41 (September 1950): 25, 54–60.

58. In 1955 Robert Mitchum and Lizabeth Scott and the heiress Doris Duke filed libel suits against *Confidential*, and the star James Mason filed a libel suit against *Rave*. The magazines received attention in "The Press in the Sewer," *Time*, July 11, 1955, 90; "The Curious Craze for 'Confidential' Magazines," *Newsweek*, July 11, 1955, 50–52.

59. Ann Higginbotham, "Scandal in Hollywood," *Photoplay* 46 (July 1955): 29.

60. Ted Maddox, "Kim Novak: Stabbed by Scandal," *Photoplay* 49 (February 1956): 54–55, 86–87. See also Robin Sharry, "What They Forgot to Say about Kim Novak," *Confidential* 3 (January 1956): 31–34. The scandal magazines were mostly bimonthly publications and often came out almost two months before the dates listed on covers; for example, the July 1957 *Confidential* issue with a story about Liberace was already on newsstands when he testified before the Los Angeles grand jury in May 1957. Advance copies of the magazine were usually available (and often sent) to the celebrities about whom a story was written (or the celebrities' studio). Although this was often a ploy to pressure stars into trading a story for the one to be published, it could also give the fan magazines (via press agents and studios) time to quickly write articles in reply. Thus *Photoplay* was able to quickly respond to the story about Novak in its February issue.

61. Gaylyn Studlar, "The Perils of Pleasure? Fan Magazine Discourse as Women's Commodified Culture in the 1920s," *Wide Angle* 13 (January 1991): 11. Richard deCordova, *Picture Personalities: The Emergence of a Star System in America* (Urbana: University of Illinois Press, 1990) also discusses how the fan magazines both silenced and spoke about scandal.

62. For information on studio–fan magazines relations in the 1930s, which were characterized by the studios clamping down on control over what the magazines published by blacklisting and whitelisting certain writers and story themes, see "Publicity Heads Unite to Curb Fan Mags," *Hollywood Reporter*, August 10, 1934; "Fan Mags Promise to be Good," *Hollywood Reporter*, August 16, 1934; Goodman, *The Fifty-Year Decline and Fall of Hollywood*, 77.

63. There is also evidence that the studios complained mightily to the fan magazines for their increased coverage of star scandals in the late 1940s and early 1950s; certainly one motivation for the fan magazines' turn in the early 1950s toward stories about the upstanding morals of most stars was to demonstrate to the studios that they were on the studios' side. However, by the arrival of the scandal magazines, the more traditional fan magazines were caught between powerful studio displeasure and a very real confusion about what to publish about stars now that their readers were potentially exposed to the "revelation," or fantasy, of even more private star "truths" by *Confidential* et al. For evidence of disagreements between studios and fan magazines over star publicity in the late 1940s, see the Association of Motion Picture and Television Producers collection at the Margaret Herrick Library, Academy of Motion Picture Arts and Sciences, Beverly Hills, California (AMPAS).

64. The film is vague about what Sawyer's trouble is; Martin says only that his mother helped her out of a "jam." According to notes by the screenwriter, Jerome Weidman, Sawyer was raped by an older man when she was a teen and gave birth to his child; Martin's mother helped her in childbirth. When the child died and its father was murdered, Sawyer went into a mental institution. Weidman expresses displeasure in this backstory and makes notes to make Sawyer less victimized so that Manly can appeal to Martin on the basis of Sawyer's complicity in her own past "sins." However, none of these details is in the film or even later drafts of the screenplay. See MGM production file on *Slander*, July 23, 1956, USC Archive of Performing Arts; Production Code Administration file on *Slander*, Margaret Herrick Library, AMPAS.

65. Bob Thomas, *Liberace: The True Story* (New York: St. Martin's, 1987), 129. Thomas also makes this assertion in the 1988 British television documentary *Hollywood Confidential*, as do two other Hollywood columnists from the period. In the same documentary Pat Brown, who was California's attorney general in 1957, claims that Hollywood did not pressure him into bringing charges against *Confidential*.

66. Articles covering the committee hearings include "Scandal Magazine Curb Looms after Raid Probe," *Los Angeles Herald-Examiner*, February 18, 1957; James Denver, "Girl Reveals Tips to Scandal Mag," *Los Angeles Mirror News*, February 19, 1957; "Giesler May Be Called in Scandal Hearings," *Los Angeles Times*, February 21, 1957; Gladwin Hill, "Sinatra Version of Raid Disputed," *New York Times*, February 28, 1957; "Film Star Blackmail, File Thefts Charged," *Los Angeles Mirror News*, February 28, 1957; Gladwin Hill, "Detective Tells Inquiry He 'Checked Out' 150 'Scandal' Articles for *Confidential*," *New York Times*, March 1, 1957; Gladwin Hill, "Scandal Inquiry Finds No Answer," *New York Times*, March 2, 1957.

67. "Scandal Magazine Quiz by U.S. Urged," *Los Angeles Times*, March 5, 1957.

68. For discussions of moral crusades against obscenity, see D'Emilio and Freedman, *Intimate Matters*; Gurstein, *The Repeal of Reticence*; Walter Kendrick, *The Secret Museum: Pornography in Modern Culture* (Berkeley: University of California Press, 1996).

69. "Film Stars Move to Quash Scandal," *Hollywood Citizen News*, July 29, 1957, 1.

70. "Maureen O'Hara Denies She 'Cuddled in Row 35,'" *Los Angeles Herald-Examiner*, August 18, 1957.

71. Gladwyn Hill, "Film Colony Fidgets in Confidential Case," *New York Times*, August 18, 1957.

72. "Film Biz Giving Only 'Lip Service' in Fight against Smear Mags — Giesler," *Daily Variety*, April 19, 1957.

73. Kenneth Anger, *Hollywood Babylon* (San Francisco: Straight Arrow Books, 1975), 265. Typically Anger gives no citations for his information. See Matthew Tinkcom, "Scandalous! Kenneth Anger and the Prohibition of Hollywood History," in *Out Takes: Essays on Queer Theory and Film*, edited by Ellis Hanson (Durham, NC: Duke University Press, 1999), 271–87, for an interesting discussion of Anger's fascination with *Confidential*.

74. "Hearing on Publisher," *New York Times*, July 24, 1957. Clarence A. Linn, assistant attorney general of California, made these remarks in the context of an argument made to the state of New York to extradite *Confidential*'s editor-publisher Robert Harrison to California.

75. "Witness Tells of Wild Pool Party," 18.

76. This claim is attributed to DeStefano in "The *Confidential* Story," *Inside* 2 (December 1957): 60. *Inside* was a pseudo–scandal magazine published for a short time in the late 1950s that tried to capitalize on the scandal caused by the scandal magazines. The fan magazine articles in question were probably Louella Parsons, "How the Ladds Reconciled," and William Barbour, "How Long Can It Last?," both in *Modern Screen* 49 (May 1955). The *Confidential* article even plays with the title of the latter story, turning "It" into "Dick."

77. "Laxity of Studios Charged in Trial," *New York Times*, August 26, 1957.

78. "Witness Tells of Wild Pool Party," 18.

79. "Atty Calls *Confidential* Tales Funny," *Los Angeles Mirror News*, August 30, 1957. See also "*Confidential* Trial to Move over to Grauman's Theater," *Los Angeles Times*, August 31, 1957, for testimony about the humorousness of the magazine's articles.

80. "Witness Tells of Wild Pool Party," 18.

81. Jack Jones, "Maureen O'Hara Angrily Denies Magazine Story; Dorothy Dandridge Also Charges Article about Her in *Confidential* Was Falsehood," *Los Angeles Times*, August 4, 1947.

82. California Senate Judiciary Committee, *The Interception of Messages by the Use of Electronic and Other Devices* (Sacramento: Senate of the State of California, 1957); Fred H. Kraft, *Report of the Senate Interim Committee on Collection Agencies, Private Detectives, and Debt Liquidators* (Sacramento: Senate of the State of California, 1957).

83. The literature on this topic is too voluminous to cite individually, but especially helpful to me were Alexander Charms, *Cloak and Gavel: FBI Wiretaps, Bugs, Informers, and the Supreme Court* (Urbana: University of Illinois Press, 1992); John D'Emilio, *Sexual Politics, Sexual Communities: The Making of a Homosexual Minority in the United States, 1940–1970*, 2nd edition (Chicago: University of Chicago Press, 1998); Richard F. Hixson, *Privacy in a Public Society: Human Rights in Conflict* (New York: Oxford University Press, 1987); Carey McWilliams, *Witch Hunt: The Revival of Heresy* (Boston: Little, Brown, 1950); Alan Theoharis, *Spying on Americans: Political Surveillance from Hoover to the Huston Plan* (Philadelphia: Temple University Press, 1978). When revising this book I also became aware of David K. Johnson, *The Lavender Scare: The Cold War Persecution of Gays and Lesbians in the Federal Government* (Chicago: University of Chicago Press, 2004), which briefly mentions *Confidential*.

84. Kraft, *Report of the Senate Interim Committee*, 5–8; California Senate Judiciary Committee, *The Interception of Messages*, 12–16.

85. Post, "The Social Foundations of Defamation Law," 711.

86. Post, "The Social Foundations of Defamation Law," 712.

87. DeCordova, *Picture Personalities*, 143.

88. Foucault, *History of Sexuality*, 27.

89. See Karen Halttunen, *Confidence Men and Painted Women: A Study of Middle-Class Culture in America, 1830–1870* (New Haven: Yale University Press, 1982); Warren I. Susman, *Culture as History: The Transformation of American Society in the Twentieth Century* (New York: Pantheon Books, 1984); Roland Marchand, *Advertising the American Dream: Making Way for Modernity 1920–1940* (Berkeley: University of California Press, 1985).

90. Lynn Spigel, *Make Room for TV: Television and the Family Ideal in Postwar America* (Chicago: University of Chicago Press, 1992).

91. David Riesman et al., *The Lonely Crowd: A Study of the Changing American Character* (New York: Doubleday Anchor Books, 1953); Erving Goffman, *The Presentation of Self in Everyday Life* (New York: Doubleday Anchor Books, 1959).

92. Sandra Lee Bartky, "Foucault, Femininity, and the Modernization of Patriarchal Power," in *Feminism and Foucault: Reflections on Resistance*, edited by Irene Diamond and Lee Quinby (Boston: Northeastern University Press, 1988); Elaine Tyler May, *Homeward Bound: American Families in the Cold War Era* (New York: Basic Books, 1988); Wini Breines, *Young, White, and Miserable: Growing Up Female in the Fifties* (Boston: Beacon, 1992); Karal Ann Marling, *As Seen on TV: The Visual Culture of Everyday Life in the 1950s* (Cambridge, MA: Harvard University Press, 1994); Joan Jacobs Brumberg, *The Body Project: An Intimate History of American Girls* (New York: Random House, 1997).

93. *The Sid Caesar Collection*, Creative Light Entertainment, 2000 (DVD). Andrew Ross, *No Respect: Intellectuals and Popular Culture* (New York: Routledge, 1989), suggests the 1959 television show *Candid Camera* was the first show to reinforce the link between voyeurism and surveillance. As this spoof suggests, *This Is Your*

Life might be the first to expose to what degree viewers enjoyed watching people squirm as they were caught in the act.

94. Goffman, *The Presentation of Self in Everyday Life*, 216–17.

95. Howard's remarks can be heard in the "extra material" after the "This Is Your Story" sketch on *The Sid Caesar Collection* DVD.

96. Jack Gould, "TV's Misery Shows," *New York Times*, February 7, 1954.

97. Gilbert Seldes, "Controversy: Two Points of View on *This Is Your Life*," *TV Guide*, October 11, 1958, 26–27. The positive point of view was written by the actress Gale Storm.

98. See "How Ralph Edwards Traps the Stars," *TV Guide*, September 11, 1953; review of *This Is Your Life*, *TV Guide*, May 29, 1953; "Sermon on the Air."

99. Jerry Blaine, "When the Element of Surprise Blew Up in Edwards' Face," *TV Scandals* 1 (August 1957): 20.

100. Frances Farmer, *Will There Really Be a Morning?* (New York: Dell, 1972), 298. Farmer died before finishing her autobiography, and it was finished by Jean Ratcliffe, a friend who had been helping her write it.

101. Brown's on-camera interview is used in *Hollywood Confidential*. Although this documentary was produced in 1988, judging by the film stock quality, decor, and dress styles apparent in the Brown interview, it appears that this particular segment was filmed in the 1970s. Brown had a longtime commitment to civil rights, working to end racial discrimination in the workplace going back to the period when he was a district attorney and state attorney general in the 1940s and 1950s. For that reason his claim that his motivations regarding the *Confidential* indictment were based on outrage over the magazine's racism has some credibility. See Ethan Rarick, *California Rising: The Life and Times of Pat Brown* (Berkeley: University of California Press, 2005), for an examination of Brown's role in civil rights prior to and during his governorship. Rarick, however, does not discuss the *Confidential* trial or any of the events leading up to it that might have involved Brown.

102. James L. Boyd, "Only the Birds and the Bees Saw What Dorothy Dandridge Did in the Woods," *Confidential* 5 (May 1957). According to Donald Bogle, *Dorothy Dandridge* (New York: Amistad, 1997), 375, Dandridge had a copy of the issue by March 1957.

103. Horton Streete, "Why Liberace's Theme Song Should Be, 'Mad about the Boy!,'" *Confidential* 5 (July 1957), 16–21, 59–60. See Thomas, *Liberace*, for discussion of a famous 1959 libel trial in which Liberace defended his reputation against charges of homosexuality from a British columnist pen-named "Cassandra."

104. We might also consider what the British public believed about Liberace's sexuality after the 1956 publication of the "Cassandra"-authored column in the British *Daily Mirror*. This column used language to out Liberace that was so vicious that *Confidential*'s article almost seems pro-gay in comparison. See Thomas, *Liberace*, 121–24. Darden Asbury Pyron, *Liberace: An American Boy* (Chicago: Chicago University Press, 2000), has an illuminating discussion of Liberace's libel cases, his closeted life, and his attitudes toward his sexuality. When discussing the *Confi-*

dential case, Pyron continually refers to the magazine as *Hollywood Confidential*, which it was never called, though there was an irregularly published magazine of that title. That magazine did not have the publishing reach and muscle of Harrison's *Confidential* and would be an unlikely target for the state of California.

105. "Maureen O'Hara, Liberace Hit 'Lies,'" *Los Angeles Times*, May 15, 1957.

106. Gurstein, *The Repeal of Reticence*, might see the jury's indecision as representative of a society and its legal system that link privacy and obscenity too closely to individual rights and property. Since the state didn't prove that the stars written about by *Confidential* were hurt by the libelous obscenities in terms of property, the jury was indecisive about the magazine's harmfulness. Gurstein argues that protection of the privacy of individuals — including things about them that might be considered "indecent" — is good for the whole society.

Chapter Four. After the Laughter

1. This "statistic" is repeated frequently in biographical material about Ball as well as *I Love Lucy* lore, but it seems apocryphal. Lee Tannen, a fan, friend, and relative by marriage (nephew by marriage of the sister of Gary Morton, Ball's second husband), attributes the statistic to *Guinness Book of World Records*. See his book, *I Loved Lucy: My Friendship with Lucille Ball* (New York: St Martin's, 2001), 99. It is mentioned, without attribution, in the CBS news special broadcast on the night of Ball's death (discussed later in this chapter). Susan M. Carinni, "Love's Labors Almost Lost: Managing Crisis during the Reign of *I Love Lucy*," *Cinema Journal* 43.1 (2003): 44–62, attributes it to *TV Guide* via a citation in Steven D. Stark, *Glued to the Set: The Sixty Television Shows That Made Us Who We Are Today* (New York: Bantam Doubleday, 1997), 35. I thank Susan for making her paper available to me before its publication, when I was working on an earlier version of this work.

2. For example, the comic bits of Lucy doing a commercial for Vitameatavegimin and of Lucy and Ethel working at the candy factory are represented on many ceramic, cloth, and paper collectibles, in clips from the television program played on every special or documentary (except *Lucy and Desi: A Home Movie*) about *I Love Lucy* or Lucille Ball that I viewed while writing this (seven specials and documentaries), and are even reinterpreted in parodic skits on other shows. For example, the candy factory skit is redone as violent parody in an "Itchy and Scratchy" cartoon on Fox's *The Simpsons* and reinterpreted as criminal activity in Fox's *Mad TV*, in which two actresses play Lucy and Ethel packing illegal drugs instead of candy on a conveyor belt. Clips or still photos picturing Arnaz and Ball kissing as Ricky and Lucy and Arnaz as Ricky singing "I Love Lucy" or "We're Having a Baby" to Ball as Lucy are often presented more than once in many specials and documentaries about the couple or the series. One of the two U.S. postage stamps to feature Lucille Ball is an image of Ball being kissed by Arnaz. The Apple computer "Think Different" campaign of 1998 plastered on billboards and printed in magazines an image of Arnaz and Ball in profile puckering up to kiss.

3. Jean Laplanche and J.-B. Pontalis, "Fantasies and the Origins of Sexuality," *International Journal of Psycho-analysis* 49 (1968): 11.

4. For use of fantasy theory in film and literature, see Victor Burgin et al., eds., *Formations of Fantasy* (London: Methuen, 1986); Elizabeth Cowie, "Fantasia," *m/f* 9 (1984), reprinted in Elizabeth Cowie, *Representing the Woman: Cinema and Psychoanalysis* (Minneapolis: University of Minnesota Press, 1997); Michael DeAngelis, *Gay Fandom and Crossover Stardom: James Dean, Mel Gibson, and Keanu Reeves* (Durham, NC: Duke University Press, 2001); Mary Desjardins, "*Meeting Two Queens*: Feminist Filmmaking, Fan Culture, Identity Politics, and the Melodramatic Fantasy," *Film Quarterly* 48.3 (1995): 26–33, which is part of chapter 5 of this volume; Sandy Flitterman-Lewis, *To Desire Differently: Feminism and the French Cinema* (Urbana: University of Illinois Press, 1990); Constance Penley, *The Future of an Illusion: Film, Feminism, and Psychoanalysis* (Minneapolis: University of Minnesota Press, 1989); Linda Williams, "Film Bodies: Gender, Genre, and Excess," *Film Quarterly* 44.4 (1991): 2–13. On fantasy in television, see Mimi White, *Tele-advising: Therapeutic Discourse in American Television* (Chapel Hill: University of North Carolina Press, 1992).

5. Comments made by David Marc in "Commentary" on the *I Love Lucy* Criterion Collection laserdisc, 1992. For more of Marc's work on *I Love Lucy*, see his books *Demographic Vistas: Television in American Culture* (Philadelphia: University of Pennsylvania Press, 1984) and *Comic Visions: Television Comedy and American Culture* (Boston: Unwin Hyman, 1989).

6. Williams, "Film Bodies," 12.

7. Lori Landay, *Madcaps, Screwballs, Con Women: The Female Trickster in American Culture* (Philadelphia: University of Pennsylvania Press, 1998), 173.

8. Alexander Doty, "The Cabinet of Lucy Ricardo: Lucille Ball's Star Image," *Cinema Journal* 29.4 (1990): 10.

9. Patricia Mellencamp, "Situation Comedy, Feminism, and Freud," in *Studies in Entertainment: Critical Approaches to Mass Culture*, edited by Tania Modleski (Bloomington: Indiana University Press, 1986), 88.

10. Mellencamp, "Situation Comedy," 93.

11. Landay, *Madcaps, Screwballs*, 160.

12. Gustavo Perez-Firmat, *Life on the Hyphen: The Cuban-American Way* (Austin: University of Texas Press, 1994).

13. Perez-Firmat, *Life on the Hyphen*, 34.

14. The name of this section is a reference to Mimi White's "Crossing Wavelengths: The Diegetic and Referential Imaginary of American Commercial Television," *Cinema Journal* 25.2 (1986): 51–64, and Bart Andrews's *Lucy and Ricky and Fred and Ethel: The Story of* I Love Lucy (New York: E. P. Dutton, 1976), which is the ur-guide to the series (in this edition or its revised and updated edition, *The* I Love Lucy *Book* [New York: Doubleday, 1985]).

15. Among scholarly recyclings of Ball, Alexander Doty's work is exceptional in taking on an analysis of the relation between Ball's television persona as Lucy Ricardo

(and later as Lucy Carmichael and Lucy Carter) and her film persona. Although Ball often implies in interviews that she wasn't typecast often enough to have an identifiable film star persona, Doty suggests that her film persona was the witty, independent, and stylish showgirl. While this insight has been made by even popular biographers and journalists—when they do bother to talk about her film work at all—Doty's argument is unique in demonstrating to what extent that persona "erupts" in the television persona as embodied in Lucy Ricardo. He argues that its eruptions remind us what Ball had to repress of other feminine (maybe even more feminist) personas in order to make Lucy Ricardo possible and her own marriage with Arnaz viable (so he could work with her). See "The Cabinet of Lucy Ricardo." Carini, "Love's Labor Almost Lost," takes up Doty's point but counters that Ball's film persona was more varied and ambiguous than Doty's definition of it suggests.

16. Landay, *Madcaps, Screwballs*, 190.

17. White, "Crossing Wavelengths," 52, 62.

18. Images, listings, and discussions of many of these ancillary products can be found in Ric B. Wyman, *For the Love of Lucy: The Complete Guide for Collectors and Fans* (New York: Abbeville, 1995). *Time* magazine recounted Ball's career and her courtship and early marriage to Arnaz in "Sassafrassa, the Queen," in the May 26, 1952, issue. On January 19, 1953, the very date of the double birthday of Desi Jr. and Little Ricky Ricardo, *Newsweek* published an article on how the Arnaz family negotiated Lucille Ball's / Lucy Ricardo's pregnancy on the air in "Desilu Formula for Top TV: Brains, Beauty, Now a Baby." *Life* covered Desi Jr.'s birth on January 19 in its February 2, 1953, issue. The Arnaz family appeared on the cover of *Life* on April 6, 1953, with the caption "TV's First Family." The article, "Lucy's Boys," detailed Lucy's recovery from childbirth in January 1953 and the use of twin babies to play Little Ricky on *I Love Lucy*. Between April 1953 and December 1955 the Arnaz family and the *I Love Lucy* television program were the subject of several articles in *TV Guide*, including the very first issue of the magazine: "Lucy's $50,000,000 Baby" (April 3, 1953), "TV Guide Goes Backstage" (May 1, 1953), "That Funny Looking Lucy" (October 9, 1953), and "Still in the Driver's Seat" (December 10, 1955). See also "At Home with Desi and Lucy," *Los Angeles Examiner Southland Living Magazine*, April 26, 1953, which gives postwar readers a glimpse of the Arnazes' idyllic life in their San Fernando Valley ranch home. Eleanor Harris wrote *The Real Story of Lucille Ball* (New York: Ballantine Books, 1954), the first book-length biography of Ball, based on material originally published in *The Reader's Digest* earlier that year. For further citations of contemporary press reports concerning the importance of Ball and Arnaz to the consumer industries of the 1950s, see the incredibly helpful sourcebook *Lucy A to Z: An Encyclopedic Biography of Lucille Ball*, 2nd edition (Lincoln, NE: Writer's Showcase, 2002); Susan Murray, *Hitch Your Antenna to the Stars: Early Television and Broadcast Stardom* (New York: Routledge, 2005), chapter 6.

19. Richard Dyer, *Stars* (London: British Film Institute, 1979); Richard Dyer, *Heavenly Bodies: Film Stars and Society* (New York: St. Martin's, 1986), especially the chapter

on Judy Garland. See also John Ellis, *Visible Fictions: Cinema, Television, Video* (London: Routledge and Kegan Paul, 1982). Lynn Spigel, *Make Room for TV: Television and the Family Ideal in Post-war America* (Chicago: University of Chicago Press, 1992), also discusses the constructedness or artificiality of the Ricardo family, but not as centrally from the perspective of the distinctions and blurrings of the real (star) and reel (average) couple; she is mainly concerned with situation comedies that use vaudeville techniques to theatricalize home life (146–80).

20. Lucille Ball was not, contrary to television mythology, the first actress to act on television while her pregnancy was visible and publicly known. In 1948 Mary Kay Stearns was pregnant in the *The Mary Kay and Johnny Show*, also starring her real-life husband. But Ball's pregnancy took place at the right moment, when her show was the top-rated program and when television was reaching millions of homes rather than a few thousand.

21. *Life*, February 2, 1953, 29.

22. *Newsweek*, January 19, 1953, 56.

23. Jack Gould, "Why Millions Love Lucy," *New York Times Magazine*, March 1, 1953, 16.

24. Harris, *The Real Story of Lucille Ball*, 86, 119.

25. "Lucy's $50,000,000 Baby," 7.

26. "Lucy's Boys," 89–95.

27. This information, which has become part of the *I Love Lucy* mythology, appears in Andrews, *Lucy and Ricky and Fred and Ethel*; Desi Arnaz, *A Book* (New York: William Morrow, 1976).

28. Brad Shortell, "Does Desi Really Love Lucy?," *Confidential* 2.6 (1955). See also "The Night Desi Arnaz Wasn't Even Half Safe," *Whisper*, August 1956.

29. Robert Harrison, "*Confidential* vs. Hollywood," *Confidential*, September 1957.

30. Hope and Ball had made two movies together before this television appearance, *Sorrowful Jones* (Paramount, 1949) and *Fancy Pants* (Paramount, 1950). They later made *The Facts of Life* (United Artists, 1960) and *Critic's Choice* (Warner Bros., 1963). The liminal status of the Ricardo living room continues to feature in more recent parodies of the show. There is usually great attention given to accurate or close-to-accurate re-creations of the room's details. In the 1970s NBC's *Saturday Night Live* had guest host Desi Arnaz Sr. participate in a parody of *I Love Lucy* that featured Lucy (played by Gilda Radner) confronting gangsters from *The Untouchables* (a controversial Desilu television series) in the Ricardo living room. In the 1990s Fox's *Mad TV* featured a number of parodies of *I Love Lucy*, two of which transformed the middle-class respectability of the Ricardo marriage into scenarios of contemporary sexual liberation or anxiety. In one Lucy is crying and begging Ricky to let her join Fred and Ethel in the entertainment. A bit later Fred, Ethel, and Ricky emerge from the bedroom into the living room in S & M garb and it is clear that the "entertainment" Lucy wanted to be in on is not a public show but a private sexual threesome that the other characters have been engaging in. In another episode the Ricardo living room includes a personal computer from which Lucy has been, despite Ricky's warnings, obsessively surfing the web.

She becomes convinced that Little Ricky has been snared by an online porn ring. I have not discussed these skits at length or in the body of this chapter because I do not have access to tapes of them to review their details. I am writing here from memory. (See note 2 for discussion of another parody.) In a nonparodic context, PBS's *American Masters* documentary *Finding Lucy*, written and directed by Pam Mason Wagner, ends with an image of the Ricardo living room, which has been rendered in miniature as a dollhouse room. The effect is eerie and uncanny, reminiscent of Susan Stewart's argument in *On Longing: Narratives of the Miniature, the Gigantic, the Souvenir, the Collection* (Durham, NC: Duke University Press, 1993) that miniaturization is linked to death.

31. Mellencamp, "Situation Comedy," 90. As is well known, the networks originally did not want Arnaz for Ball's costar because of his Cuban ethnicity. In *Life on the Hyphen*, Perez-Firmat writes that Desi/Ricky used Spanish for his own masquerades—for example, to disguise his swearing.

32. Perez-Firmat, *Life on the Hyphen*, 187. Apparently, in the rough draft of his autobiography, Arnaz suspects Ball had an affair with Hope.

33. Spigel, *Make Room for TV*, 148, 151.

34. Vance was required to wear dumpy clothes, and according to some commentators, she was contractually held to maintain a weight heavier than Ball's in order to reinforce Ethel's lack of sexual appeal. See Andrews, *Lucy and Ricky and Fred and Ethel*.

35. Alexander Doty, *Making Things Perfectly Queer: Interpreting Mass Culture* (Minneapolis: University of Minnesota Press, 1993), 39–48.

36. This doesn't mean that gay men don't have an investment in fantasizing about loving or being loved by Arnaz. See Bob Smith, "We Love Lucy," *Out*, November 2001, in which the author says that "the everlasting appeal of Lucy Ricardo for some gay men is that she's never going to lose the love of her man" (42).

37. See Stephanie Coontz, *The Way We Never Were: American Families and the Nostalgia Trap* (New York: Basic Books, 1992), 33. See also Wini Breines, *Young, White and Miserable: Growing Up Female in the Fifties* (Boston: Beacon, 1992); Brett Harvey, *The Fifties: A Woman's Oral History* (New York: HarperCollins, 1995); Elaine Tyler May, *Homeward Bound: American Families in the Cold War Era* (New York: Basic Books, 1988).

38. Mary Beth Haralovich, "Too Much Guilt Is Never Enough for Working Mothers: Joan Crawford, *Mildred Pierce*, and *Mommie Dearest*," *Velvet Light Trap*, no. 29 (Spring 1992): 51.

39. Coontz, *The Way We Never Were*, 34.

40. These statistics are taken from J. Fred MacDonald, *One Nation under Television: The Rise and Decline of Network TV* (New York: Pantheon Books, 1990), 221–30.

41. For a discussion of the kinds of recycling practices on Nick at Nite and TV Land, see Derek Kompare, "I've Seen This One Before: The Construction of 'Classic TV' on Cable Television," in *Small Screens, Big Ideas: Television in the 1950s*, edited by Janet Thumim (London: I. B. Tauris, 2002); Megan Mullen, "Surfing through TV Land: Notes towards a Theory of 'Video Bites' and Their Function on Cable

TV," *Velvet Light Trap* 36 (1995): 60–68; Lynn Spigel, "From the Dark Ages to the Golden Age: Women's Memories and Television Reruns," *Screen* 36.1 (1995): 16–33.

42. Nick Browne, "The Political Economy of the Television (Super) Text," *Quarterly Review of Film Studies* 9.3 (1984): 174–82. Browne coined the term *super-text* in one of the key documents of television theory.

43. Beverle Houston, "Viewing Television: The Metapsychology of Endless Consumption," *Quarterly Review of Film Studies* 9.3 (1984): 184.

44. As of this writing, *I Love Lucy* is nationally rerun on cable network TV Land, as well as on many local broadcast stations, such as the Fox affiliate in Los Angeles, KTTV (which is available nationwide in some satellite packages). In the L.A. market *I Love Lucy* sometimes airs two or three times a day on that channel alone. With the cable airing by TV Land and superstations available on cable or satellite packages, *I Love Lucy* might be seen five or six times a day!

45. John Antczak, "'I Love Lucy' Fans Give Comedienne's Husband a Block-Long Sympathy Card," UCLA *Daily Bruin*, May 3, 1989, Lucille Ball clipping file, Margaret Herrick Library, Academy of Motion Picture Arts and Sciences (hereafter AMPAS).

46. "Remembering Lucille Ball," Letters Page, *Los Angeles Times*, May 6, 1989, AMPAS clipping file.

47. Karen Cusolito, "Tributes in L.A., across U.S. for Lucy," *Los Angeles Herald-Examiner*, May 9, 1989, AMPAS clipping file.

48. Thomas J. Cottle, "A Fan of Lucy's," *Television Quarterly* 24.2 (1989): 81–82.

49. Lori Landay, *I Love Lucy* (Detroit: Wayne State University Press, 2010), conceptualizes the influence of *I Love Lucy* on American culture and television as "Lucy TV." While this notion overlaps in some ways with my ideas about Ball's thereness, what I am getting at is much more about the interplay among industrial developments, Ball's career, and the intersubjective aspects of the televisual apparatus. The apparatus is both a material condition, practice, and object and a set of subject effects and experiences that positions and is positioned by the larger social imaginary.

50. The CBS special's elision of much of Ball's career and life after the end of *I Love Lucy* and the marriage to Arnaz mimes (probably unwittingly) the trajectory of Desi Arnaz's autobiography, *A Book*, published in 1976. Arnaz conflates the end of the series and the end of his marriage, as if, in the words of Perez-Firmat, "both his life and his career ended with the divorce" (*Life on the Hyphen*, 76).

51. Timothy Carlson, "Lucy Movie Was Planned as a Tribute — but Her Family Says It's Been a 'Nightmare,'" *TV Guide*, February 9–15, 1991, 5. See also Monica Collins, "'Lucy' Movie in Controversy at CBS," *TV Guide*, February 24, 1990, 46. Interestingly Collins attributes Lucie Arnaz's reluctance to endorse the CBS movie to the negative publicity she received for saying on *The Joan Rivers Show* that her mother was strict and a "control freak." For more on that appearance, see "We Remember Mama," *Ladies' Home Journal*, May 1990, 72. For the record, many, many co-workers and friends have since said something similar about Ball when inter-

viewed for television or any of the many biographies of Ball and histories of *I Love Lucy*. For articles on *Lucy and Desi: A Home Movie* that document how the film was promoted and received a couple years after the television movie aired, see "Lucy Desi's Private Photo Album," *TV Guide*, February 13–19, 1993, 16–19; Diane Holloway, "A Valentine for 'Lucy and Desi,'" *Austin-American Statesman*, February 14, 1993.

52. Laurie Schulze, "The Made-for-TV Movie: Industrial Practice, Cultural Form, Popular Reception," in *Hollywood in the Age of Television*, edited by Tino Balio (Boston: Unwin Hyman, 1990), 362.

53. George Custen, *Bio/Pics: How Hollywood Constructed Public History* (New Brunswick, NJ: Rutgers University Press, 1992).

54. Schulze, "The Made-for-TV Movie," 365.

55. Coontz, *The Way We Never Were*, 3.

56. Jane Feuer, *Seeing through the Eighties: Television and Reaganism* (Durham, NC: Duke University Press, 1995), 26, 14.

57. Elayne Rapping, *The Movie of the Week: Private Stories, Public Events* (Minneapolis: University of Minnesota Press, 1992), 64–87.

58. In her introduction to the home movie footage, Lucie Arnaz says, "I was often surprised by people's candor, and how much they were willing to tell me . . . almost as if they had bottled it up for so long and they were so glad somebody finally asked."

59. Older viewers of *Toast of the Town* with good memories or readers of Arnaz's autobiography might remember hearing about Arnaz cleaning bird cages to help support his family.

60. Coontz, *The Way We Never Were*.

61. Patricia Zimmermann, "Hollywood, Home Movies, and Common Sense: Amateur Film as Aesthetic Dissemination and Social Control, 1950–1962," *Cinema Journal* 27.4 (1988): 30.

62. Mimi White discusses the apparent paradox of the contemporary therapeutic discourse signifying both loss and recovery in *Tele-advising*, 21.

63. Leslie Irvine, *Codependent Forevermore: The Invention of Self in a Twelve Step Group* (Chicago: University of Chicago Press, 1999), 5.

64. Desi Arnaz Jr.'s love affairs and fast living were the subject of many articles in movie and television fan magazines (such as *Photoplay*, *TV Radio Mirror*, *TV Radio Life*, and *Modern Screen*) during the late 1960s and 1970s. See also Desi Arnaz Jr., "My 16-Year Battle with Drugs," *Good Housekeeping*, January 1985, 97, 162–63; "We Remember Mama," 72; "A Different Drummer: The Mambo Kings Enables Desi Arnaz, Jr. to Honor His Cubano Father," *People*, May 11, 1992, 87–91; Joe Rhodes, "TV's First Son," *TV Guide*, October 13, 2001, 36–41, 67.

65. White, *Tele-advising*, 21.

66. Lucille Ball and Betty Hannah Hoffman, *Love, Lucy* (New York: Boulevard Books, 1996).

67. The CD-ROM, produced by Education Through Entertainment, is available from 4everCD Memories. See David Laurell, "Lucy Would Have Loved This Scrap-

book," *Collecting Online*, http://www.collectingmagazine.com//coll1297/lucy.htm, accessed February 15, 2008.

68. Pamela Wilson, "Virtual Kinship in a Postmodern World: Computer-Mediated Genealogy Communities," in *On a Silver Platter: CD-Roms and the Promises of a New Technology*, edited by Greg M. Smith (New York: New York University Press, 1999).

69. Marianne Hirsch, *Family Frames: Photography, Narrative, and Postmemory* (Cambridge, MA: Harvard University Press, 1997), 107. I also found the following helpful in thinking about family photos and albums: Julia Hirsch, *Family Photographs: Content, Meaning, and Effect* (London: Oxford University Press, 1981); Leo Spitzer, "The Album and the Crossing," in *The Familial Gaze*, edited by Marianne Hirsch (Hanover, NH: University Press of New England, 1999); Nancy Martha West, *Kodak and the Lens of Nostalgia* (Charlottesville: University Press of Virginia, 2000); Annette Kuhn, *Family Secrets: Acts of Memory and Imagination* (London: Verso, 1995).

70. Kuhn, *Family Secrets*, 17.

71. Hirsch, *Family Frames*, 10.

72. For interesting studies on how college-age women remember or experience *I Love Lucy* today, especially in relation to a feminist consciousness, in addition to the scholarly works already cited, see Andrea Press, *Women Watching Television: Gender, Class, and Generation in the American Television Experience* (Philadelphia: University of Pennsylvania Press, 1991); Spigel, "From the Dark Ages to the Golden Age."

Chapter Five. Star Bodies, Star Bios

1. Mary Rhiel and David Suchoff, "Introduction: The Seductions of Biography," in *The Seductions of Biography*, edited by Mary Rhiel and David Suchoff (New York: Routledge, 1996), 3.

2. Anne Balsamo, *Technologies of the Gendered Body: Reading Cyborg Women* (Durham, NC: Duke University Press, 1996), 3.

3. The concept of "stylized repetition of acts" comes from Judith Butler, *Gender Trouble: Feminism and the Subversion of Identity* (New York: Routledge, 1990).

4. Butler, *Gender Trouble*, 145.

5. William H. Epstein, *Recognizing Biography* (Philadelphia: University of Pennsylvania Press, 1987), 147.

6. Epstein, *Recognizing Biography*, 42.

7. Janet Malcolm, *The Silent Woman: Sylvia Plath and Ted Hughes* (New York: Vintage Books, 1994), 10–11.

8. Mark Rappaport, "Notes on *Rock Hudson's Home Movies*," *Film Quarterly* (Summer 1996): 22.

9. *Superstar* had already been shown extensively on the film festival circuit and had even been transferred to video for rental and purchase at the time A&M and the

Carpenters stopped it from legally circulating any further. However, because it had circulated for about a year and a half, the film was still available in some video rental stores and there are now many copies circulating as dubbed copies. I first saw the film from a rented copy before it was illegal to distribute it.

10. B. Ruby Rich, "New Queer Cinema," *Sight and Sound* 2.5 (1992): 30–34.

11. For excellent explorations of these tensions in identity politics, see Diana Fuss, "Inside/Out," in *Inside/Out: Lesbian Theories, Gay Theories*, edited by Diana Fuss (New York: Routledge, 1991); Alexander Doty, *Making Things Perfectly Queer: Interpreting Mass Culture* (Minneapolis: Minnesota University Press, 1993).

12. For theoretical discussions of the pleasure of Garbo's image, see Roland Barthes, "The Face of Garbo," and Kenneth Tynan, "Garbo," both in *Film Theory and Criticism*, edited by Gerald Mast and Marshall Cohen, 2nd edition (New York: Oxford University Press, 1979); Peter Matthews, "Garbo and Phallic Motherhood: A 'Homosexual' Visual Economy," *Screen* 29.3 (1988): 14–42. Dietrich's image has been discussed in two of the founding arguments of feminist film theory as exemplary of the kind of visual pleasure available to the male spectator of the Classical Hollywood film. See Laura Mulvey, "Visual Pleasure and Narrative Cinema," *Screen* 16.3 (1975): 6–18; Clair Johnston, "Women's Cinema as Counter-Cinema," in *Movies and Methods*, edited by Bill Nicholas (Berkeley: University of California Press, 1976). Dietrich has also been used as an example by theorists countering Mulvey's theory of visual pleasure and spectatorship. See Gail Seneca and Lucie Arbuthnot, "Pre-text and Text in *Gentlemen Prefer Blondes*," in *Issues in Feminist Film Criticism*, edited by Patricia Erens (Bloomington: Indiana University Press, 1990); Gaylyn Studlar, *In the Realm of Pleasure: Von Sternberg, Dietrich, and the Masochistic Aesthetic* (Urbana: University of Illinois Press, 1988); Gaylyn Studlar, "Masochism, Masquerade, and the Erotic Metamorphoses of Marlene Dietrich," in *Fabrications: Costume and the Female Body*, edited by Jane Gaines and Charlotte Herzog (New York: Routledge, 1990); Patricia White, "Hitchcock, Hommosexuality, and the Power of Interpretation," paper given at Society for Cinema Studies conference, Pittsburgh, 1992.

13. Michel de Certeau, *The Practice of Everyday Life* (Berkeley: University of California Press, 1984). See also Henry Jenkins, *Textual Poachers: Television Fans and Participatory Culture* (London: Routledge, 1992).

14. Lawrence Grossberg, "Is There a Fan in the House? The Affective Sensibility of Fandom," in *The Adoring Audience: Fan Culture and Popular Media*, edited by Lisa Lewis (London: Routledge, 1992), 57.

15. Patricia Meyer Spacks, *Gossip* (New York: Knopf, 1985), 46.

16. Andrea Weiss, "'I Get a Queer Feeling When I Look at You': Hollywood Stars and Lesbian Spectatorship of the 1930s," in *Stardom: Industry of Desire*, edited by Christine Gledhill (London: Routledge, 1991), 287.

17. Weiss, "'I Get a Queer Feeling,'" 288.

18. Sue-Ellen Case, "Towards a Butch-Femme Aesthetic," *Discourse* 11.1 (1988–89): 55–73.

19. Lucretia Knapp, "The Queer Voice in *Marnie*," *Cinema Journal* 32.4 (1993): 15.

20. See Patricia White, *Uninvited: Classical Hollywood Cinema and Lesbian Representability* (Bloomington: Indiana University Press, 1999), 37–58, on more about the films poached by Barriga for *Meeting Two Queens*.

21. See Patricia White, "Black and White: Mercedes de Acosta's Glorious Enthusiasms," *Camera Obscura* 45 (2001): 227–65, for a wonderful essay on de Acosta's relationships with Garbo and Dietrich and de Acosta's own fan relationship to their images.

22. See *Confidential* magazine, July 1955; Mercedes de Acosta, *Here Lies the Heart* (New York: Reynal, 1960). For a discussion or examples of publicity and promotion, see Katherine Albert, "She Threatens Garbo's Throne," *Photoplay*, December 1930; Ruth Rankin, "They're All Queening It," *Photoplay*, December 1933; Peter Matthews in "Garbo and Phallic Motherhood" discusses a caption for a photo of Garbo in terms of how it suggests the star's potential to "smite" women with equal force as she does men. Andrea Weiss in "'I Get a Queer Feeling'" discusses a poster for *Morocco* that declares Dietrich is "the woman all women want to see" (286).

23. Matthews, "Garbo and Phallic Motherhood," 18.

24. See Elizabeth Cowie, "Fantasia," in *The Woman in Question*, edited by Parveen Adams and Elizabeth Cowie (Cambridge, MA: MIT Press, 1990); Steve Neale, "Melodrama and Tears," *Screen* 27.6 (1986): 6–23; Linda Williams, "Film Bodies: Gender, Genre, and Excess," *Film Quarterly* 44.4 (1991): 2–13. These theorists all agree on the fundamentally utopian nature of fantasy. For a somewhat different view, see Mary Ann Doane, *The Desire to Desire: The Woman's Film of the 1940s* (Bloomington: Indiana University Press, 1987), 70–95.

25. Williams, "Film Bodies," 10.

26. Mary Ann Doane, "Veiling over Desire: Close-Ups of the Woman," in *Feminism and Psychoanalysis*, edited by Richard Feldstein and Judith Roof (Ithaca, NY: Cornell University Press, 1989), 108.

27. Diana Fuss, "Fashion and the Homospectatorial Look," *Critical Inquiry* 18 (Summer 1992): 722.

28. Studlar, *In the Realm of Pleasure*.

29. Matthews, "Garbo and Phallic Motherhood," 25, 38, 24.

30. Mulvey, "Visual Pleasure and Narrative Cinema."

31. I am not suggesting that proponents of outing are necessarily constructing a dichotomy. One of the theoretical conundrums about the implications of outing is whether it enforces a gay-straight binary (by saying "This person is gay, not straight") or blurs the binary by exposing sexuality's or gender's performativity (by saying "See, this person you thought was straight is gay"). For histories of the debates on outing, see Larry Gross, *Contested Closets: The Politics and Ethics of Outing* (Minneapolis: University of Minnesota Press, 1993); Michelangelo Signorile, *Queer in America: Sex, the Media, and the Closets of Power* (New York: Anchor Books, 1994). Gross's book is especially helpful since it reprints many of the mainstream and alternative press articles debating outing.

32. Rappaport, "Notes on *Rock Hudson's Home Movies*," 20.

33. Richard Meyer, "Rock Hudson's Body," in Fuss, *Inside/Out*, 275.

NOTES TO CHAPTER FIVE

289

34. Richard Dyer, "Rock: The Last Guy You'd Have Figured?," in *The Culture of Queers*, edited by Richard Dyer (London: Routledge, 2002), 162–63.

35. Rappaport, "Notes on *Rock Hudson's Home Movies*," 21.

36. As already stated, Rappaport felt prodded by the urgency of AIDS, as well as the emergence of homosexuality and gender as issues on the cultural agenda, to make this video. He suggests later in this same essay that the film was his own way of responding to the long period in which he would watch films and be bothered by "derogatory and degrading image[s] on the screen and accepted it or, worse yet, didn't respond to it or even notice it" ("Notes on *Rock Hudson's Home Movies*," 21). For the concept of a star's authorial agency as "witness" to film history, see Amelie Hastie, "Louise Brooks, Star Witness," *Cinema Journal* 36.3 (1997): 3–24.

37. Matthew Tinkcom, *Working Like a Homosexual: Camp, Capital, Cinema* (Durham, NC: Duke University Press, 2002), 46.

38. Steven Cohan, *Masked Men: Masculinity and the Movies in the Fifties* (Bloomington: Indiana University Press, 1997), 264–303. Michael DeAngelis's *Gay Fandom and Crossover Stars: James Dean, Mel Gibson, and Keanu Reeves* (Durham, NC: Duke University Press, 2001) is another nuanced reading of male star images in historical context. See Brett Farmer, *Spectacular Passions: Cinema, Fantasy, Gay Male Spectatorships* (Durham, NC: Duke University Press, 2000), for a discussion of Montgomery Clift as a gay icon.

39. Rappaport, in his next video, *From the Journals of Jean Seberg* (1996), examines the sexist treatment of a female star. In this video Rappaport uses a strategy similar to that of *Rock Hudson*: an actor (Mary Beth Hurt) plays Seberg and acts as a voice-over guide through the film clip juxtapositions. Rappaport continues his fascination with both stardom and film theory, exploring how editing strategies visually positioned politically left female stars like Seberg, Jane Fonda, and Vanessa Redgrave. Although it mostly garnered positive reviews, there was a heated exchange between Rappaport and two *Village Voice* film reviewers, Georgia Brown and Amy Taubin, over their scathing piece on the video, which stated that the work not only drained all the complexity out of the film clips used but was also sexist and mocking, scorning, and condescending toward Seberg, Fonda, and Redgrave. See Georgia Brown and Amy Taubin, "Seeing Seberg and Talking Back to the Screen," *Village Voice*, March 18, 1996; Mark Rappaport, "Rappaport in a Storm," letter, *Village Voice*, April 9, 1996.

40. Susan Littwin, "The Family's Memories vs. Hollywood's Version," *TV Guide*, December 31, 1988, 29.

41. None of the dolls used were actually the Barbie doll; according to Haynes, the doll used to portray Karen was a Tracy doll manufactured by Mattel to be Barbie's friend. A Ken doll does portray Richard (Ken was made by Mattel to be Barbie's boyfriend), but wigs were used on the doll for the film. See Sheryl Farber, "Getting to Bare Bones of Todd Haynes' *Superstar: The Karen Carpenter Story*," *Film Threat* 20 (1989): 19–20. My use of Barbie dolls in this essay to refer to the cast is meant to reflect the degree to which dolls portraying adult women are generically

referred to as "Barbie dolls," as are real adult women who seem to care only for a studied, overly feminine, fashion-model appearance.

42. Jean Luc Comolli, "Historical Fiction: A Body Too Much," *Screen* 19.2 (1978): 41–54.

43. George Custen, *Bio/Pics: How Hollywood Constructed Public History* (New Brunswick, NJ: Rutgers University Press, 1992), 175.

44. See Richard deCordova, *Picture Personalities: The Emergence of a Star System in America* (Urbana: University of Illinois Press, 1990), 117–51.

45. For more complete discussions of the issue of female audiences and made-for-television movies, see Laurie Schulze, "The Made-for-TV Movie: Industrial Practice, Cultural Form, Popular Reception," in *Hollywood in the Age of Television*, edited by Tino Balio (Boston: Unwin Hyman, 1990); Elayne Rapping, *The Movie of the Week: Private Stories, Public Events* (Minneapolis: University of Minnesota Press, 1992); Jane Feuer, *Seeing through the Eighties: Television and Reaganism* (Durham, NC: Duke University Press, 1995).

46. See Schulze, "The Made-for-TV Movie"; Rapping, *The Movie of the Week*; Feuer, *Seeing through the Eighties*.

47. Rapping, *The Movie of the Week*, 103.

48. Littwin, "The Family's Memories," 29.

49. Littwin, "The Family's Memories," 29.

50. For just a small sampling of the work done on this issue in feminist film studies, see Linda Williams, "Something Else Besides a Mother: Stella Dallas and the Maternal Melodrama," in *Home Is Where the Heart Is: Studies in Melodrama and the Woman's Film*, edited by Christine Gledhill (London: BFI, 1987); Suzanna Danuta Walters, *Lives Together, Worlds Apart: Mothers and Daughters in Popular Culture* (Berkeley: University of California Press, 1992).

51. Joan Jacobs Brumberg, *Fasting Girls: The History of Anorexia Nervosa*, revised edition (New York: Vintage Books, 2000), 31–32.

52. Despite the fact that his sister was slowly killing herself by self-starvation and he was addicted to sleeping pills, Richard complains that Hollywood always wants "conflict" when "there wasn't much at the time." See Littwin, "The Family's Memories," 29.

53. For discussions of this issue, see Kaja Silverman, *The Acoustic Mirror: The Female Voice in Psychoanalysis and Cinema* (Bloomington: Indiana University Press, 1988); Amy Lawrence, *Echo and Narcissus: Women's Voices in Classical Hollywood Cinema* (Berkeley: University of California Press, 1991).

54. Roland Barthes, "The Grain of the Voice," in *Image-Music-Text*, selected and translated by Stephen Heath (New York: Hill and Wang, 1977), 188.

55. If *Superstar* can be considered deliberately campy, *The Karen Carpenter Story* can be considered in some ways naïve camp. Susan Sontag argues that all "pure" camp is naïve, that is, unintentional. While I don't find labels such as "pure" productive, certainly there are instances in which it is possible to identify some texts as unintentionally campy and others as intentionally campy. Therefore, in this con-

text, the television movie's sincere rendering of Mrs. Carpenter's change of heart toward expressing love just at the moment when it is too late for Karen, the obvious foreshadowing of Karen's anorexia in showing her exercise mania throughout the film, her relation to food as a child, and so on can be read as stylistic and thematic features unintentionally excessive and artificial. In other words, it is unintentionally campy. See Susan Sontag, "Notes on Camp," in *Camp: Queer Aesthetics and the Performing Subject*, edited by Fabio Cleto (Ann Arbor: University of Michigan, 1999), 53–65. See Lucas Hilderbrand, "Grainy Days and Mondays: *Superstar* and Bootleg Aesthetics," *Camera Obscura* 57 (2004): 56–81, for a discussion of *Superstar*'s reception history and a complication of "camp" readings.

56. Farber, "Getting to Bare Bones," 18; original press kit for *Superstar*; Lisa Kennedy, "Doll Boy," *Village Voice*, November 24, 1987, 68; Edward Guthmann, "Barbie Doll Stars in Film on Karen Carpenter," *San Francisco Chronicle*, April 14, 1988; Justin Wyatt, "Cinematic/Sexual Transgression: An Interview with Todd Haynes," *Film Quarterly* 46 (1993): 4–5.

57. Susan Bordo, *Unbearable Weight: Feminism, Western Culture, and the Body* (Berkeley: University of California Press, 1993), 171. See also Sharlene Hesse-Biber, *Am I Thin Enough Yet? The Cult of Thinness and the Commercialization of Identity* (New York: Oxford University Press, 1996). Both Bordo and Hesse-Biber have extensive bibliographies on the topic of anorexia.

58. Jacqueline Urla and Alan C. Swedlund, "The Anthropometry of Barbie: Unsettling Ideals of the Feminine Body in Popular Culture," in *Deviant Bodies*, edited by Jennifer Terry and Jacqueline Urla (Bloomington: Indiana University Press, 1995), 285.

59. Lynn Spigel, *Welcome to the Dreamhouse: Popular Media and Postwar Suburbs* (Durham, NC: Duke University Press, 2001), 315.

60. See Farber, "Getting to Bare Bones"; Wyatt, "Cinematic/Sexual Transgression."

61. Susan Stewart, *On Longing: Narratives of the Miniature, the Gigantic, the Souvenir, the Collection* (Durham, NC: Duke University Press, 1993), 69, 44.

62. Maureen Turim, "Video Art: Theory for a Future," in *Regarding Television: Critical Approaches*, edited by E. Ann Kaplan (Frederick, MD: University Publications of America, 1983), 130.

63. Leigh Gilmore, *Autobiographics: A Feminist Theory of Women's Self-Representation* (Ithaca, NY: Cornell University Press, 1993).

64. Sidonie Smith, *Subjectivity, Identity, and the Body: Women's Autobiographical Practices in the Twentieth Century* (Bloomington: Indiana University Press, 1993), 3.

65. Ann Hunsaker Hawkins, *Reconstructing Illness: Studies in Pathography* (West Lafayette, IN: Purdue University Press, 1993), 17.

66. Beverle Houston, "Viewing Television: The Metapsychology of Endless Consumption," *Quarterly Review of Film Studies* 9.3 (1994): 184.

67. Andre Bazin, "The Ontology of the Photographic Image," in *What Is Cinema*, vol. 1 (Berkeley: University of California Press, 1971); Roland Barthes, *Camera Lucida: Reflections on Photography*, translated by Richard Howard (New York: Hill and Wang, 1981).

68. Patricia Mellencamp, *High Anxiety: Catastrophe, Scandal, Age, and Comedy* (Bloomington: Indiana University Press, 1992), 286.

69. Vivian Sobchack, "Beating the Meat / Surviving the Text, or How to Get Out of This Century Alive," in *The Visible Woman: Imaging Technologies, Gender, and Science*, edited by Paula Treichler et al. (New York: New York University Press, 1998), 316.

Conclusion

1. The statistics on YouTube are cited in William Uricchio, "The Future of a Medium Once Known as Television," in *The YouTube Reader*, edited by Pelle Snickers and Patrick Vonderau (Stockholm: National Library of Sweden, 2010), 27.

2. Henry Jenkins, Sam Ford, and Joshua Green, *Spreadable Media: Creating Value and Meaning in a Networked World* (New York: New York University Press, 2013).

3. Uricchio, "The Future of a Medium," 25.

SELECT BIBLIOGRAPHY

Anderson, Christopher. *Hollywood TV: The Studio System in the Fifties*. Austin: University of Texas Press, 1994.

Anderson, Joan Wester. *Forever Young: The Life, Loves, and Enduring Faith of a Hollywood Legend*. Allen, Texas: Thomas More, 2000.

Andrews, Bart. *Lucy and Ricky and Fred and Ethel: The Story of* I Love Lucy. New York: E. P. Dutton, 1976.

Anger, Kenneth. *Hollywood Babylon*. San Francisco: Straight Arrow Books, 1975.

Arnaz, Desi. *A Book*. New York: Harper Collins, 1976.

Astor, Mary. *A Life on Film*. New York: Delacorte, 1971.

———. *My Story: An Autobiography*. New York: Doubleday, 1959.

Balio, Tino. *The American Film Industry*. Revised edition. Madison: University of Wisconsin Press, 1985.

Ball, Lucille, and Betty Hannah Hoffman. *Love, Lucy*. New York: Boulevard Books, 1996.

Bartky, Sandra Lee. "Foucault, Femininity, and the Modernization of Patriarchal Power." In *Feminism and Foucault: Reflections on Resistance*, edited by Irene Diamond and Lee Quinby, 61–86. Boston: Northeastern University Press, 1988.

Basinger, Jeanine. *Silent Stars*. New York: Knopf, 1999.

Baty, S. Paige. *American Monroe: The Making of a Body Politic*. Berkeley: University of California Press, 1995.

Bean, Jennifer. "Technologies of Early Stardom and the Extraordinary Body." In *A Feminist Reader in Early Cinema*, edited by Jennifer M. Bean and Diane Negra, 404–43. Durham, NC: Duke University Press, 2002.

Becker, Christine. *It's the Pictures That Got Small: Hollywood Film Stars on 1950s Television*. Middletown, CT: Wesleyan University Press, 2008.

Beckman, Karen. *Vanishing Women: Magic, Film, and Feminism*. Durham, NC: Duke University Press, 2003.

Bennett, James. *Television Personalities: Stardom and the Small Screen*. London: Routledge, 2011.

Berenstein, Rhona. "Acting Live: TV Performance, Intimacy, and Immediacy (1945–1955)." In *Reality Squared: Televisual Discourse on the Real*, edited by James Friedman, 25–49. New Brunswick, NJ: Rutgers University Press, 2002.

Bloustein, Edward J. "Privacy as an Aspect of Human Dignity: An Answer to Dean Prosser." *New York University Law Review* 39 (December 1964): 962–1007.

Boddy, William. *Fifties Television: The Industry and Its Critics*. Urbana: University of Illinois Press, 1990.

Bogle, Donald. *Bright Boulevards, Bold Dreams: The Story of Black Hollywood*. New York: Ballantine Books, 2005.

——. *Prime-Time Blues: African-Americans on Network Television*. New York: Farrar, Straus and Giroux, 2001.

Bordo, Susan. *Unbearable Weight: Feminism, Western Culture, and the Body*. Berkeley: University of California Press, 1993.

Braidotti, Rosi. "Becoming-Woman: Rethinking the Positivity of Difference." In *Feminist Consequences: Theory for the New Century*, edited by Elisabeth Bronfen and Misha Kavka, 381–413. New York: Columbia University Press, 2001.

Brooks, Jodi. "Performing Age / Performing Crisis (for Norma Desmond, Baby Jane, Margo Channing, Sister George—and Myrtle)." In *Figuring Age: Women, Bodies, Generations*, edited by Kathleen Woodward, 232–47. Bloomington: Indiana University Press, 1999.

Brown, Kelly R. *Florence Lawrence, the Biograph Girl: America's First Movie Star*. Jefferson, NC: McFarland, 1999.

Browne, Nick. "The Political Economy of the Television (Super) Text." *Quarterly Review of Film Studies* 9.3 (1984): 174–82.

Brumberg, Joan Jacobs. *Fasting Girls: The History of Anorexia Nervosa*. Revised edition. New York: Vintage Books, 2000.

Buckley, Gail Lumet. *The Hornes: An American Family*. New York: New American Library, 1986.

Carinni, Susan M. "Love's Labors Almost Lost: Managing Crisis during the Reign of *I Love Lucy*." *Cinema Journal* 43.1 (2003): 44–62.

Case, Sue-Ellen. "Towards a Butch-Femme Aesthetic." *Discourse* 11.1 (1988–89): 55–73.

Cassidy, Marsha. "Visible Storytellers: Women Narrators on 1950s Daytime Television." *Style* 35.2 (2001): 354–74.

Clark, Danae. *Negotiating Hollywood: The Cultural Politics of Actors' Labor*. Minneapolis: University of Minnesota Press, 1995.

Cohan, Steven. *Incongruous Entertainment: Camp, Cultural Value, and the MGM Musical*. Durham, NC: Duke University Press, 2005.

——. *Masked Men: Masculinity and the Movies in the Fifties*. Bloomington: Indiana University Press, 1997.

Cohen, William A. *Sex Scandal: The Private Parts of Victorian Fiction*. Durham, NC: Duke University Press, 1996.

Comolli, Jean-Luc. "Historical Fiction: A Body Too Much." *Screen* 19.2 (1978): 41–54.

Coontz, Stephanie. *The Way We Never Were: American Families and the Nostalgia Trap*. New York: Basic Books, 1992.

Cowie, Elizabeth. "Fantasia." In *The Woman in Question*, edited by Parveen Adams and Elizabeth Cowie, 149–96. Cambridge, MA: MIT Press, 1990.

Crafton, Donald. *The Talkies: American Cinema's Transition to Sound, 1926–1931*. Berkeley: University of California Press, 1997.

Curry, Ramona. *Too Much of a Good Thing: Mae West as Cultural Icon*. Minneapolis: University of Minnesota Press, 1996.

Custen, George. *Bio/Pics: How Hollywood Constructed Public History*. New Brunswick, NJ: Rutgers University Press, 1992.

Davis, Bette. *The Lonely Life*. New York: Bantam, 1962.

DeAngelis, Michael. *Gay Fandom and Crossover Stardom: James Dean, Mel Gibson, and Keanu Reeves*. Durham, NC: Duke University Press, 2001.

deCordova, Richard. *Picture Personalities: The Emergence of a Star System in America*. Urbana: University of Illinois Press, 1990.

D'Emilio, John. *Sexual Politics, Sexual Communities: The Making of a Homosexual Minority in the United States, 1940–1970*. 2nd edition. Chicago: University of Chicago Press, 1998.

D'Emilio, John, and Estelle Freedman. *Intimate Matters: A History of Sexuality in America*. New York: Harper and Row, 1991.

Desjardins, Mary. "An Appetite for Living: Gloria Swanson, Colleen Moore, and Clara Bow." In *Idols of Modernity: Movie Stars of the 1920s*, edited by Patrice Petro, 108–36. New Brunswick, NJ: Rutgers University Press, 2010.

———. "Dietrich Dearest: Family Memoir and the Fantasy of Origins." In *Dietrich Icon*, edited by Gerd Gemunden and Mary R. Desjardins, 310–27. Durham, NC: Duke University Press, 2007.

———. "Fading Stars and the Ruined Commodity Form: Star Discourses of Loss in Early Fan Magazines." In *Researching Women in Silent Cinema: New Findings and Perspectives*, edited by Monica Dall'Asta, Victoria Duckett, and Lucia Tralli, 150–62. Bologna: University of Bologna and University of Melbourne, 2013.

———. "'Marion Never Looked Lovelier': Hedda Hopper's Hollywood and the Renegotiation of Hollywood Glamour in Post-war Los Angeles." *Quarterly Review of Film and Video* 16.3–4 (1999): 421–37.

———. "A Method to This Madness? The Myth of the Mad Silent Film Star." In *Not So Silent: Women in Cinema before Sound*, edited by Sofia Bull and Astrid Soderbergh, 357–68. Stockholm: Stockholm University, 2010.

Doane, Mary Ann. *The Desire to Desire: The Woman's Film of the 1940s*. Bloomington: Indiana University Press, 1987.

———. "Veiling over Desire: Close-Ups of the Woman." In *Feminism and Psychoanalysis*, edited by Richard Feldstein and Judith Roof, 105–41. Ithaca, NY: Cornell University Press, 1989.

Doherty, Thomas. "Frank Costello's Hands: Film, Television, and the Kefauver Crime Hearings." *Film History* 10 (1998): 359–74.

Donati, William. *Ida Lupino: A Biography*. Lexington: University Press of Kentucky, 1996.

Doty, Alexander. "The Cabinet of Lucy Ricardo: Lucille Ball's Star Image." *Cinema Journal* 29.4 (1990): 3–34.

———. *Making Things Perfectly Queer: Interpreting Mass Culture*. Minneapolis: University of Minnesota Press, 1993.

Dyer, Richard. *The Culture of Queers*. London: Routledge, 2002.

———. *Heavenly Bodies: Film Stars and Society*. New York: St. Martin's, 1986.

———. *Only Entertainment*. London: Routledge, 1992.

———. *Stars*. London: BFI, 1979.

Eels, George. *Ginger, Loretta, and Irene Who?* New York: G. P. Putnam, 1976.

Ehrenstein, David. *Open Secret: Gay Hollywood 1928–1998*. New York: William Morrow, 1998.

Ellis, John. *Visible Fictions: Cinema, Television, Video*. London: Routledge and Kegan Paul, 1982.

Epstein, William H. *Recognizing Biography*. Philadelphia: University of Pennsylvania Press, 1987.

Farmer, Brett. *Spectacular Passions: Cinema, Fantasy, Gay Male Spectatorships*. Durham, NC: Duke University Press, 2000.

Felski, Rita. *The Gender of Modernity*. Cambridge, MA: Harvard University Press, 1995.

Feuer, Jane. *Seeing through the Eighties: Television and Reaganism*. Durham, NC: Duke University Press, 1995.

Forman, Murray. *One Night on TV Is Worth Weeks at the Paramount: Popular Music on Early Television*. Durham, NC: Duke University Press, 2012.

Freud, Sigmund. *Beyond the Pleasure Principle*. New York: Norton, 1961.

Fuller, Kathryn H. *At the Picture Show: Small-Town Audiences and the Creation of Movie Culture*. Washington, DC: Smithsonian Institution Press, 1996.

Gaines, Jane. *Contested Culture: The Image, the Voice, and the Law*. Chapel Hill: University of North Carolina Press, 1991.

Gates, Phyllis, and Bob Thomas. *My Husband, Rock Hudson*. New York: Jove Books, 1989.

Gilmore, Leigh. *Autobiographies: A Feminist Theory of Women's Self-Representation*. Ithaca, NY: Cornell University Press, 1993.

Goffman, Erving. *The Presentation of Self in Everyday Life*. New York: Doubleday Anchor Books, 1959.

Gomery, Douglas. *Shared Pleasures: A History of Movie Presentation in the United States*. London: BFI, 1992.

Goodman, Ezra. *The Fifty-Year Decline of Hollywood*. New York: Simon and Schuster, 1961.

Gross, Larry. *Contested Closets: The Politics and Ethics of Outing*. Minneapolis: University of Minnesota Press, 1993.

Gurstein, Rochelle. *The Repeal of Reticence: America's Cultural and Legal Struggles over Free Speech, Obscenity, Sexual Liberation, and Modern Art*. New York: Hill and Wang, 1996.

Haralovich, Mary Beth. "Too Much Guilt Is Never Enough for Working Mothers: Joan Crawford, *Mildred Pierce*, and *Mommie Dearest*." *Velvet Light Trap* 29 (Spring 1992): 43–52.

Harris, Eleanor. *The Real Story of Lucille Ball*. New York: Ballantine, 1954.

Hastie, Amelie. *The Bigamist*. London: BFI / Palgrave Macmillan, 2009.

———. *Cupboards of Curiosity: Women, Recollection, and Film History*. Durham, NC: Duke University Press, 2007.

Hawkins, Ann Hunsaker. *Reconstructing Illness: Studies in Pathography*. West Lafayette, IN: Purdue University Press, 1993.

Hershfield, Joanne. *The Invention of Dolores del Rio*. Minneapolis: University of Minnesota Press, 2000.

Higashi, Sumiko. *Cecil B. DeMille and American Culture: The Silent Era*. Berkeley: University of California Press, 1994.

Hilderbrand, Lucas. "Grainy Days and Mondays: Superstar and Bootleg Aesthetics." *Camera Obscura* 57 (2004): 56–81.

Hilmes, Michele. *Hollywood and Broadcasting: From Radio to Cable*. Urbana: University of Illinois Press, 1990.

Hirsch, Marianne. *Family Frames: Photography, Narrative, and Postmemory*. Cambridge, MA: Harvard University Press, 1997.

Houston, Beverle. "The Metapsychology of Endless Consumption." *Quarterly Review of Film Studies* 9.3 (1984): 183–95.

Hudson, Rock, and Sara Davidson. *Rock Hudson: His Story*. New York: Avon Books, 1987.

Jenkins, Henry, et al. *Spreadable Media: Creating Value and Meaning in a Networked World*. New York: New York University Press, 2010.

Kendrick, Walter. *The Secret Museum: Pornography in Modern Culture*. Berkeley: University of California Press, 1996.

King, Barry. "Stardom as an Occupation." In *The Hollywood Film Industry*, edited by Paul Kerr, 154–83. London: Routledge and Kegan Paul, 1986.

Klinger, Barbara. *Beyond the Multiplex: Cinema, New Technologies, and the Home*. Berkeley: University of California Press, 2006.

Kompare, Derek. *Rerun Nation: How Repeats Invented American Broadcasting*. New York: Routledge, 2005.

Kuhn, Annette. *Family Secrets: Acts of Memory and Imagination*. London: Verso, 1995.

———. *Queen of the "B"s: Ida Lupino Behind the Camera*. Westport, CT: Praeger, 1995.

Landay, Lori. *I Love Lucy*. Detroit: Wayne State University Press, 2010.

———. *Madcaps, Screwballs, Con Women: The Female Trickster in American Culture*. Philadelphia: University of Pennsylvania Press, 1998.

Laplanche, Jean, and J.-B. Pontalis. "Fantasies and the Origins of Sexuality." *International Journal of Psychoanalysis* 49 (1968): 1–18.

Lawrence, Amy. *Echo and Narcissus: Women's Voices in Classical Hollywood Cinema*. Berkeley: University of California Press, 1991.

———. "James Mason: A Star Is Born Bigger Than Life." In *Larger Than Life: Movie Stars of the 1950s*, edited by R. Barton Palmer, 86–106. New Brunswick, NJ: Rutgers University Press, 2010.

———. *The Passion of Montgomery Clift*. Berkeley: University of California Press, 2010.

Lewis, Judy. *Uncommon Knowledge*. New York: Pocket Books, 1994.

Mack, Dwayne. "Hazel Scott: A Career Curtailed." *Journal of African-American History* 91.2 (2006): 153–70.

Malcolm, Janet. *The Silent Woman: Sylvia Plath and Ted Hughes*. New York: Vintage Books, 1994.

Mann, Denise. "The Spectacularization of Everyday Life: Recycling Hollywood Stars and Fans in Early Television Variety Shows." In *Private Screenings: Television and the Female Consumer*, edited by Lynn Spigel and Denise Mann, 41–64. Minneapolis: University of Minnesota Press, 1992.

Mann, William J. *Behind the Screen: How Gays and Lesbians Shaped Hollywood, 1910–1969.* New York: Viking, 2001.

Marc, David. *Comic Visions: Television Comedy and American Culture.* Boston: Unwin Hyman, 1989.

Marling, Karal Ann. *As Seen on TV: The Visual Culture of Everyday Life in the 1950s.* Cambridge, MA: Harvard University Press, 1994.

Marshall, P. David. *Celebrity and Power: Fame in Contemporary Culture.* Minneapolis: University of Minnesota Press, 1997.

Marvin, Carolyn. *When Old Technologies Were New: Thinking about Electric Communication in the Late Nineteenth Century.* New York: Oxford University Press, 1988.

Matthews, Peter. "Garbo and Phallic Motherhood: A 'Homosexual' Visual Economy." *Screen* 29.3 (1988): 14–42.

May, Elaine Tyler. *Homeward Bound: American Families in the Cold War Era.* New York: Basic Books, 1988.

McCarthy, Anna. *Ambient Television: Visual Culture and Public Space.* Durham, NC: Duke University Press, 2000.

McDonald, J. Fred. *One Nation under Television: The Rise and Decline of Network TV.* New York: Pantheon Books, 1990.

McGee, Kristen A. *Some Liked It Hot: Jazz Women in Film and Television, 1928–1959.* Middletown, CT: Wesleyan University Press, 2009.

McLean, Adrienne. *Being Rita Hayworth: Labor, Identity, and Hollywood Stardom.* New Brunswick, NJ: Rutgers University Press, 2004.

————. "The Cinderella Princess and the Instrument of Evil: Surveying the Limits of Female Transgression in Two Postwar Hollywood Scandals." *Cinema Journal* 34 (Spring 1995): 36–56.

McLean, Adrienne, and David Cook, eds. *Headline Hollywood: A Century of Film Scandal.* New Brunswick, NJ: Rutgers University Press, 2001.

Mellencamp, Patricia. *High Anxiety: Catastrophe, Scandal, Age, and Comedy.* Bloomington: Indiana University Press, 1992.

————. "Situation Comedy, Feminism, and Freud: Discourses of Gracie and Lucy." In *Studies in Entertainment: Critical Approaches to Mass Culture*, edited by Tania Modleski, 80–95. Bloomington: Indiana University Press, 1986.

Mensel, Robert E. "'Kodakers Lying in Wait': Amateur Photography and the Right of Privacy in New York, 1885–1915." *American Quarterly* 43 (March 1991): 24–45.

Meyer, Richard. "Rock Hudson's Body." In *Inside/Out: Lesbian Theories, Gay Theories*, edited by Diana Fuss, 259–88. New York: Routledge, 1991.

Morella, Joe, and Edward Z. Epstein. *Loretta Young: An Extraordinary Life.* New York: Delacorte, 1986.

Mullen, Megan. "Surfing through TV Land: Notes towards a Theory of 'Video Bites' and Their Function on Cable TV." *Velvet Light Trap* 36 (1995): 60–68.

Murray, Susan. *Hitch Your Antenna to the Stars: Early Television and Broadcast Stardom.* New York: Routledge, 2005.

Neale, Steve. "Melodrama and Tears." *Screen* 27.6 (1986): 6–23.

Negra, Diane. *Off-White Hollywood: American Culture and Ethnic Female Stardom.* London: Routledge, 2001.

Newcomb, Horace, and Paul M. Hirsch. "Television as Cultural Forum." In *Television: The Critical View,* 5th edition, edited by Horace Newcomb, 503–15. New York: Oxford University Press, 1993.

Perez-Firmat, Gustavo. *Life on the Hyphen: The Cuban-American Way.* Austin: University of Texas Press, 1994.

Pierce, David. "'Senile Celluloid': Independent Exhibitors, the Major Studios, and the Fight over Feature Films on Television, 1939–1956." *Film History* 10 (1998): 141–64.

Polan, Dana. *Scenes of Instruction: The Beginnings of the U.S. Study of Film.* Berkeley: University of California Press, 2007.

Post, Robert C. "The Social Foundations of Defamation Law: Reputation and Constitution." *California Law Review* 74 (May 1986): 691–742.

Press, Andrea. *Women Watching Television: Gender, Class, and Generation in the American Television Experience.* Philadelphia: University of Pennsylvania Press, 1991.

Rappaport, Mark. "Notes on *Rock Hudson's Home Movies.*" *Film Quarterly* 49.4 (1996): 16–22.

Rapping, Elyane. *The Movie of the Week: Private Stories, Public Events.* Minneapolis: University of Minnesota Press, 1992.

Rhiel, Mary, and David Suchoff. *The Seductions of Biography.* New York: Routledge, 1996.

Riesman, David, et al. *The Lonely Crowd: A Study of the Changing American Character.* New York: Doubleday Anchor Books, 1953.

Robertson, Pamela. *Guilty Pleasures: Feminist Camp from Mae West to Madonna.* Durham, NC: Duke University Press, 1996.

Rodman, Gilbert. *Elvis after Elvis: The Posthumous Career of a Living Legend.* London: Routledge, 1996.

Schulze, Laurie. "The Made-for-TV Movie: Industrial Practice, Cultural Form, Popular Reception." In *Hollywood in the Age of Television,* edited by Tino Balio, 351–76. Boston: Unwin Hyman, 1990.

Sconce, Jeffrey. *Haunted Media: Electronic Presence from Telegraphy to Television.* Durham, NC: Duke University Press, 2000.

Sides, Josh. *L.A. City Limits: African-American Los Angeles from the Great Depression to the Present.* Berkeley: University of California Press, 2003.

Silver, Brenda. *Virginia Woolf Icon.* Chicago: University of Chicago Press, 1999.

Smith, Sidonie. *Subjectivity, Identity, and the Body: Women's Autobiographical Practices in the Twentieth Century.* Bloomington: Indiana University Press, 1993.

Sobchack, Vivian. "Beating the Meat / Surviving the Text, or How to Get Out of This Century Alive." In *The Visible Woman: Imaging Technologies, Gender, and Science,* edited by Paula Treichler, Lisa Cartwright, and Constance Penley, 310–20. New York: New York University Press, 1998.

Spacks, Patricia Meyer. *Gossip*. New York: Knopf, 1985.

Spiegel, Irwin O. "Public Celebrity v. Scandal Magazine: The Celebrity's Right to Privacy." *Southern California Law Review* 30 (1957): 280–312.

Spigel, Lynn. *Make Room for TV: Television and the Family Ideal in Postwar America*. Chicago: University of Chicago Press, 1992.

———. *Welcome to the Doll House: Popular Media and Postwar Suburbs*. Durham, NC: Duke University Press, 2001.

Stacey, Jackie. *Star Gazing: Hollywood Cinema and Female Spectatorship*. London: Routledge, 1994.

Staggs, Sam. *Close-Up on Sunset Boulevard: Billy Wilder, Norma Desmond, and the Dark Hollywood Dream*. New York: St. Martin's, 2002.

Staiger, Janet. "Seeing Stars." In *Stardom: Industry of Desire*, edited by Christine Gledhill, 6–11. London: Routledge, 1991.

Stewart, Susan. *On Longing: Narratives of the Miniature, the Gigantic, the Souvenir, the Collection*. Durham, NC: Duke University Press, 1993.

Stowe, David W. "The Politics of Café Society." *Journal of American History* 84.4 (1998): 1384–406.

Studlar, Gaylyn. *In the Realm of Pleasure: Von Sternberg, Dietrich, and the Masochistic Aesthetic*. Urbana: University of Illinois Press, 1988.

———. "The Perils of Pleasure? Fan Magazine Discourse as Women's Commodified Culture of the 1920s." *Wide Angle* 13 (January 1991): 6–33.

Swanson, Gloria. *Swanson on Swanson*. New York: Random House, 1980.

Thomas, Bob. *Liberace: The True Story*. New York: St. Martin's, 1987.

Tinkcom, Matthew. "Scandalous! Kenneth Anger and the Prohibition of Hollywood History." In *Out Takes: Essays on Queer Theory and Film*, edited by Ellis Hanson, 271–87. Durham, NC: Duke University Press, 1999.

———. *Working Like a Homosexual: Camp, Capital, Cinema*. Durham, NC: Duke University Press, 2002.

Uricchio, William. "The Future of a Medium Once Known as Television." In *The YouTube Reader*, edited by Pelle Snickers and Patrick Vonderau, 24–39. Stockholm: National Library of Sweden, 2010.

Urla, Jacqueline, and Alan C. Swedlund. "The Anthropometry of Barbie: Unsettling Ideas of the Feminine Body in Popular Culture." In *Deviant Bodies*, edited by Jennifer Terry and Jacqueline Urla, 277–313. Bloomington: Indiana University Press, 1995.

Walker, Alexander. *Stardom: The Hollywood Phenomenon*. London: Penguin Books, 1974.

Weiss, Andrea. "'I Get a Queer Feeling When I Look at You': Hollywood Stars and Lesbian Spectatorship of the 1930s." In *Stardom: Industry of Desire*, edited by Christine Gledhill, 283–99. London: Routledge, 1991.

White, Mimi. "Crossing Wavelengths: The Diegetic and Referential Imaginary of American Commercial Television." *Cinema Journal* 25.2 (1986): 51–64.

———. *Tele-advising: Therapeutic Discourse in American Television*. Chapel Hill: University of North Carolina Press, 1992.

White, Mimi, and Marsha Cassidy. "Innovating Women's Television in Local and National Networks: Ruth Lyons and Arlene Francis." *Camera Obscura* 51 (2003): 31–69.

White, Patricia. *The Uninvited: Classical Hollywood Cinema and Lesbian Representability.*
Bloomington: Indiana University Press, 1999.

Williams, Linda. "Film Bodies: Gender, Genre, and Excess." *Film Quarterly* 44.4 (1991):
2–13.

Williams, Mark. "Entertaining 'Difference': Strains of Orientalism in Early Los Angeles
Television." In *Living Color: Race and Television in the United States*, edited by Sasha
Torres, 12–34. Durham, NC: Duke University Press, 1998.

———. "From 'Remote' Possibilities to Entertaining 'Difference': A Regional Study of
the Rise of the Television Industry in Los Angeles, 1930–1952." PhD dissertation,
University of Southern California, 1992.

Wilson, Pamela. "Virtual Kinship in a Postmodern World: Computer Mediated Genealogy Communities." In *On a Silver Platter: CD-Roms and the Promises of a New Technology*, edited by Gregory Smith, 184–210. New York: New York University Press,
1999.

Young, Loretta, as told to Helen Ferguson. *The Things I Had to Learn.* New York: Bobbs
Merrill, 1961.

Zimmerman, Patricia. "Hollywood, Home Movies, and Common Sense: Amateur
Film as Aesthetic Dissemination and Social Control, 1950–62." *Cinema Journal* 27.4
(1988): 23–44.